Greatest Ever FOOTBALLERS

THE DEFINITIVE LIST OF THE VERY BEST TEAMS AND PLAYERS OF ALL TIME

headline

**First published in 2007
by HEADLINE PUBLISHING GROUP**

1

Cataloguing in Publication Data is available from the British Library

ISBN 978 0 7553 15949

Typeset in Avenir, Bombardier and Industra
by Designsection at Butler and Tanner Printers Limited, Frome, Somerset

Printed and bound in Great Britain
by Mackays of Chatham Limited, Chatham, Kent

Headline's policy is to use papers that are natural, renewable and recyclable
products and made from wood grown in sustainable forests. The logging
and manufacturing processes are expected to conform to the environmental
regulations of the country of origin.

HEADLINE PUBLISHING GROUP
An Hachette Livre UK Company
338 Euston Road
London NW1 3BH

www.headline.co.uk

CONTENTS

SECTION 2

DOMESTIC

Greatest Ever would like to thank the Association of Football Statisticians for their invaluable support in producing this book. In particular Mark Baber, Trevor Bugg, Nick Taylor and Terry O'Neill.

Greatest Ever would also like to pay special thanks to the late Ron Hockings, to whom we are deeply indebted. The whole concept for the project sprang from Ron's collection of data for international fixtures and his belief that everyone who played international football should have their name and statistics recorded.

Paul Nicholson
Greatest Ever UK Ltd
October 2007

INTRODUCTION

A recent survey by UEFA 2008 sponsor Castrol revealed that more than a quarter of fanatical British football fans felt they received more respect from their peers for their 'football knowledge' as opposed to having a good job. Fanatics were defined as those who said football was their main passion. 'Knowledge is power' is a phrase often quoted in business circles and it certainly applies to football discussions.

For the football fanatic, the 'greatest ever' debate is a familiar one up and down the country. You're standing in the pub, trying to pick your all-time best club team, England team, British, or World IX. You can't get anyone to agree with you. Was Pele better than Maradona; Beckenbauer better than Cryuff; Best better than Cantona; Adams better than Moore; Le Tissier better than Bowles?

You know they are wrong, they know you are wrong, you both know you are right. But how do you solve these major issues? This book provides a statistical framework to compare and contrast, remember and debate and, most importantly, provide answers to who the players are who make up these greatest ever teams.

Greatest Ever Footballers is compiled from a number of databases that are the work of the Association of Football Statisticians (AFS). For more than 25 years the AFS has compiled comprehensive databases including information on every player to have played international football (over 750,000 caps), or to have won major honours, since records began in the late 1800s. This, along with Greatest Ever's extensive experience in developing sports rankings, has enabled the creation of accurate and credible ranking systems.

To determine the greatest ever footballers, we have created a flexible statistical algorithm, measuring players in terms of international games, international honours and domestic honours.

HOW THE RANKINGS ARE CALCULATED
International Caps
For each player the calculation takes into account all 'A' international appearances.

Each appearance is awarded points that are weighted by the following factors:

◆ **Team played for** – For example, appearances for a less successful nation in football terms, such as Trinidad and Tobago, would not score as highly as the same number of appearances for a nation like Argentina. The Argentinian player would also be more likely to earn points for being in a team that progressed further in international competition. Points are also awarded for the match result, whether it is a win, draw or loss, with a win obviously generating more points.

◆ **Level of match** – More points are awarded for competitive matches rather than friendlies. For example, Scotland against Brazil in the World Cup finals will earn a player more ranking points (as this fixture collects ranking points for the competition and the stage of the competition at which the match is played) than a friendly against the Faroe Islands.

◆ **Captaincy** – This will also earn a player increased ranking points, especially if the player leads the team through a particularly successful period. Didier Deschamps is an example of this for France and David Beckham for England. Deschamps led a very successful team to major World and European honours, while Beckham captained England on numerous occasions and at all the major competitions.

◆ **Substitution** – Appearance as a substitute scores ranking points but not as many as a player who started the match.

◆ **Goals and clean sheets** – Players who score goals or goalkeepers and defenders who keep clean sheets are also rewarded with extra points.

Team Honours

Players pick up ranking points when the team (domestic or international) for whom they play achieves honours – which vary from winning the World Cup to the English League Cup. All major honours won by all domestic and international teams are included.

Individual Honours

Over 500 different honours have been weighted and included in the system. Each has been weighted according to its status. So for example, FIFA World Player of the Year will gain more points than the English Football Writers' Association Player of the Year.

If we take Bobby Moore as a simple example of how a ranking is calculated. He earned 1800 points for honours won as below:

Player	Honour	Year	Points
Bobby Moore	Football Writers' Association Player of the Year	1964	300
	FA Cup	1964	100
	European-Cup Winners' Cup	1965	400
	World Cup	1966	1000

His 108 caps for England earned him another 3832 points and two international goals earned him a further 126 points, making an overall total of 5758 points.

The rankings within this book are calculated up to the end of the 2006–07 season.

The teams that have been picked are comprised of the highest-ranking players and are generally selected in a 4-4-2 formation. For certain teams other formations apply for earlier decades. For example, English teams in the 1960s generally played a 4-3-3 formation, while in the 1930s and 1940s they played a 2-3-5 formation. In these cases, the formation that was most played at the time has been selected for the team.

You might not agree that these players would necessarily be in your greatest ever teams or lists. But the statistics are the statistics – they make the difference between perception and reality.

STRUCTURE

This book is broken up into two sections: International and Domestic.

Section One kicks off with the Top 100 Greatest Ever Players. For its 100th anniversary in 2004 FIFA asked Pele to select the hundred best players the world has ever seen. It was an eclectic list and in the end numbered 125. Our Top 100 is based on ranking points only, calculated for club and international performances. We also include Top 20 lists by playing position.

Following the individual lists, we calculate what is the greatest World XI of all time, and by decade, from all countries. For the decade XIs, the calculations are based on points accumulated in that ten-year period only.

Attention is then turned to the home nations, the Republic of Ireland and all the World Cup-winning countries. For England, Northern Ireland, the Republic of Ireland, Scotland and Wales, we produce their greatest XI of all time, and by decade, together with lists of the Top 10 best players by position. And to really get the fur flying, we've added the combined best XI of all time from these countries.

For the countries that have won the World Cup, we have calculated the greatest XI of all time.

Section Two includes data for all the clubs that have appeared in the Premiership and Scottish Premier League, listing their most successful teams in each decade. The criteria for this ranking is based on the team's league performance over a season, rather than individual performance. We have also calculated their greatest ever XIs of each club, based on club and international points.

In magazines, on television, in pubs and in supporters' clubs around the world, fans vote for their all-time favourite players and teams. Such polls rarely match what the statisticians tell us. George Best in a World XI? Quite possibly in the public vote, but based on his international career, he won't make the cut in the statistical ranking.

So which system is correct? There is no simple answer.

Let the debate begin.

SECTION 1:
INTERNATIONAL

INTRODUCTION

The Top 100 players in this section have accumulated ranking points for every appearance they have made for club and country. The points have been accrued throughout their careers, and indeed some are still building their points totals (players marked with an '*' are still actively playing) and are likely to climb the table over the coming years. Most notable of these players is Ronaldinho who has many years of international and club football ahead of him. You can expect him to challenge for a top 20 position over the coming World Cup and European club campaigns. His new club-mate Thierry Henry can also be expected to gather points rapidly as Barcelona challenge for domestic and European honours, and France looks for success from a new generation of players.

Within this ranking there are a number of players of the most recent and great French footballing generation who have either retired or are near the end of their careers. They illustrate an important factor within this ranking of players. The French World Cup-winning team of 1998 was a team that had the bulk of its players competing in leagues outside France, in most cases leagues that were stronger than the French league.

The players were experiencing international success, but were also winning domestic trophies and challenging for European honours with their club sides. Hence they have gathered ranking points more quickly than players who may have stayed with a single club for a long period of time, or not been at title-winning clubs. A good example of this is Alan Shearer, who had a terrific goalscoring record for England and in club football, but who actually only won one domestic honour during his career, the championship with Blackburn in 1995.

Some players who are considered greats, like Eric Cantona, do not make it into the Top 100. This is primarily because they did not have international careers of great note. Few would doubt that they had the ability, but they didn't have long runs of international success that most of the other entrants have. Conversely there will be players on the list that it will be argued were not 'great' players. But these players have accumulated the ranking points, usually by being in the right place at the right time. The appearance of the Neville brothers and Sylvain Wiltord, for example, will doubtless raise eyebrows, but these players have gathered large numbers of club and international points by being almost ever-present. It must be remembered that these ranking points cover a whole career and not just one exquisite match or moment.

STRUCTURE OF THE INTERNATIONAL SECTION

The list of the Top 100 players of all time, from all countries, comes first, based on the Greatest Ever points ranking system. A biography of each player follows which helps to explain the reasons for their inclusion. Following this are the top 20 goalkeepers, defenders, midfielders and forwards of all time, again, based on their Greatest Ever ranking. Next we have the greatest World XI, from all countries, of all time, followed by the greatest per decade, beginning with the 1930s.

Assessing individual players by decade provides some interesting observations. In the teams of the earlier decades there is a dominance of players from European nations, particularly Italy, and from Argentina. In those early years of international football, many of football's current powerhouse nations either didn't enter the World Cup (for example, England first played in the World Cup in 1950) or failed to qualify, which meant that players had fewer opportunities to earn ranking points. This was also an era when players rarely moved between clubs. So if a great player played at a club that did not win many honours they would not have collected many ranking points.

The best combined international team of the 1970s should, many will argue, have a strong contingent from the wonderful Brazilian 1970 World Cup-winning team. Not so according to the Greatest Ever ranking system. The only member of the team that beat Italy 4-1 in the final to make the 1970s World XI is Rivelino. This is because many of the team did not play in the more competitive (and therefore higher weighted) club competitions of Europe in the way top players from Brazil do today and, indeed, did later in the 1970s. In addition, there was no unified league competition in Brazil until 1971 so ranking points were scarce too at club level. For these reasons, there are only a handful of players from that team in the Top 100 itself.

The great Pele does not even make the 1970s World XI, largely because he did not extend his international career far into the decade after the World Cup.

Another anomaly occurs when a player's career spread across two decades. A player may not feature in the World XI of either decade but still sit high up in the Top 100. For example, at number 25 Kenny Dalglish is higher up the general ranking than Johan Neeskens who just creeps in at number 100. But in the ranking for the 1970s Neeskens leaves Dalglish behind. This is simply because Dalglish gathered his ranking points in the 1970s and the 1980s, while Neeskens gathered almost all his points during the 1970s.

Having looked at world players, we turn the focus on the four home nations, the Republic of Ireland and the countries which have won the World Cup. Based once again on points accumulated over each player's entire career for club and country, we have calculated the greatest XI of all time for Ireland and each of the home countries. In addition, we have provided the greatest XIs for retired players and also for currently registered players in order for you to compare the real teams that take to the pitch over the coming season.

Following this we have broken down each of the five countries into the best XI of each decade, where possible – for instance, we do not have a team from the 1930s for the Republic because in that decade Ireland were not competing regularly on an international basis. We also include lists of the greatest ever players by position for each of these countries.

The combined Great Britain and Ireland XI is of all time (not by decade) and is based on points accumulated by the players throughout their entire careers.

Finally, the Greatest Ever XIs from all the countries which have won the World Cup concludes this first section. England's Greatest Ever IX is featured in the England section itself.

Rank	Player	Country	Points
1	Pele	Brazil	16799.44
2	Ronaldo*	Brazil	16793.14
3	Romario	Brazil	13444.86
4	Luis Figo*	Portugal	12951.16
5	Zinedine Zidane	France	12892.13
6	Diego Maradona	Argentina	12503.85
7	Lothar Matthaus	Germany	12416.36
8	Gerd Muller	Germany	12175.23
9	Franz Beckenbauer	Germany	12057.33
10	Cafu*	Brazil	12054.30
11	Roberto Carlos*	Brazil	11785.98
12	Marco van Basten	Holland	11681.92
13	Michel Platini	France	11477.91
14	Rivaldo*	Brazil	11176.64
15	Paolo Maldini*	Italy	10818.74
16	Zico	Brazil	10734.48
17	Raul*	Spain	10689.60
18	Ruud Gullit	Holland	10306.85
19	Eusebio	Portugal	10289.84
20	Ferenc Puskas	Hungary/Spain	10074.55
21	Johan Cruyff	Holland	10060.14
22	Alfredo di Stefano	Argentina/Spain	9973.13
23	Bobby Charlton	England	9860.07
24	Jurgen Klinsmann	Germany	9840.02
25	Kenny Dalglish	Scotland	9806.45
26	Ali Daei	Iran	9704.11
27	Karl-Heinz Rummenigge	Germany	9259.39
28	Gabriel Batistuta	Argentina	9165.79
29	Michael Laudrup	Denmark	9119.21
30	Hristo Stoichkov	Bulgaria	9039.16
31	Dennis Bergkamp	Holland	9031.85
32	Frank Rijkaard	Holland	9023.08
33	Thierry Henry*	France	8972.91
34	Pavel Nedved*	Czech Republic	8876.48
35	Gheorghe Hagi	Romania	8659.23
36	Peter Schmeichel	Denmark	8658.03
37	Andriy Shevchenko*	Ukraine	8627.59
38	Sepp Maier	Germany	8489.67
39	Didier Deschamps	France	8378.33
40	Lilian Thuram*	France	8315.78
41	Enzo Francescoli	Uruguay	8295.38
42	Hakan Sukur*	Turkey	8118.29
43	Paolo Rossi	Italy	7974.35
44	David Beckham*	England	7967.26
45	Jean-Pierre Papin	France	7910.48
46	Kevin Keegan	England	7902.42
47	Marcel Desailly	France	7895.00
48	Oliver Kahn*	Germany	7870.11
49	Alessandro Costacurta	Italy	7857.02
50	Clarence Seedorf*	Holland	7642.02

Rank	Player	Country	Points
51	Dino Zoff	Italy	7616.16
52	Patrick Kluivert*	Holland	7583.17
53	Jari Litmanen*	Finland	7538.97
54	Daniel Passarella	Argentina	7394.15
55	Bixente Lizarazu	France	7371.81
56	Gary Lineker	England	7367.97
57	Ronaldinho*	Brazil	7297.77
58	Sylvain Wiltord*	France	7267.08
59	Bebeto	Brazil	7265.08
60	Alessandro Del Piero*	Italy	7227.02
61	Davor Suker	Croatia	7226.80
62	Ryan Giggs*	Wales	7136.91
63	David Trezeguet*	France	7104.82
64	Demetrio Albertini	Italy	7087.52
65	Patrick Vieira*	France	7082.41
66	Jurgen Kohler	Germany	7073.08
67	Laurent Blanc	France	7063.44
68	Michael Owen*	England	6950.34
69	Youri Djorkaeff	France	6949.32
70	Frank De Boer	Holland	6924.14
71	Emilio Butragueno	Spain	6904.51
72	Hugo Sanchez	Mexico	6852.43
73	Rudi Voller	Germany	6811.31
74	Djalma Santos	Brazil	6788.03
75	Giacinto Facchetti	Italy	6778.02
76	Kanu*	Nigeria	6769.20
77	Franco Baresi	Italy	6759.64
78	Gianni Rivera	Italy	6725.64
79	Roberto Baggio	Italy	6706.91
80	Oscar Ruggeri	Argentina	6703.04
81	Gheorghe Popescu	Romania	6688.26
82	Jon Dahl Tomasson*	Denmark	6613.38
83	Raymond Kopa	France	6576.79
84	Carlos Valderrama	Colombia	6563.53
85	Rui Costa*	Portugal	6549.53
86	Gary Neville*	England	6544.10
87	Edgar Davids*	Holland	6538.15
88	Claudio Taffarel	Brazil	6536.65
89	Paul Scholes*	England	6524.14
90	Diego Simeone	Argentina	6516.07
91	Bryan Robson	England	6508.92
92	Roy Keane	Republic of Ireland	6502.90
93	Brian Laudrup	Denmark	6485.81
94	Henrik Larsson*	Sweden	6462.68
95	Fabien Barthez	France	6422.05
96	Michael Ballack*	Germany	6399.08
97	Jan Koller*	Czech Republic	6344.37
98	Edwin van der Sar*	Holland	6289.49
99	Robert Pires*	France	6281.11
100	Johan Neeskens	Holland	6274.88

13

1 Pele

Edson Arantes do Nascimento

Born
Tres Coracoes 23 October 1940
Country
Brazil
Position
Forward
Clubs
Santos New York Cosmos
International

Caps	Goals
92	77

Pele began playing for Santos at just 15, his national team at 16, and won his first World Cup at 17. Despite numerous offers from European clubs, he stayed loyal to Santos, remaining with them for two decades until his semi-retirement in 1975. Pele played as an inside forward and what later became known as the playmaker position. His technique and natural athleticism were unparalleled. He was renowned for his unstoppable dribbling and visionary passing as well as his pace, powerful shot, and exceptional heading ability, but above all he was a prolific goalscorer. Since retiring in 1977 Pele has undertaken various ambassadorial roles.

HONOURS WON

With Brazil

♛ World Cup 1958, 1962, 1970

With Santos

♛ Campeao Paulista 1958, 1960, 1961, 1962, 1964, 1965, 1967, 1968, 1969, 1973

♛ Torneio Rio–Sao Paulo 1959, 1963

♛ Copa do Brasil 1961, 1962, 1963, 1964, 1965

♛ Intercontinental Cup 1962, 1963

♛ Copa Libertadores 1962, 1963

♛ Torneio Roberto Gomes Pedrosa 1968

With New York Cosmos

♛ North American Soccer League 1977

Other Awards

★ Copa America Best Player 1959

★ *El Mundo*'s South American Player of the Year 1973

★ North American Soccer League's Most Valuable Player 1976

★ Voted Athlete of the Century by the International Olympic Committee (IOC) 1999

★ FIFA Order of Merit 1984

★ International Peace Award 1978

★ Honorary British knighthood 1997

2

Ronaldo

Luiz Nazario de Lima

Born	
Bento Ribeiro	
22 September 1976	

Country
Brazil

Position
Forward

Clubs
Social Ramos
Sao Cristovao
Cruzeiro
PSV Eindhoven
Barcelona
Inter Milan
Real Madrid
AC Milan

International	
Caps	Goals
89	56

A born match-winner, Ronaldo was first spotted, aged 14, by Brazilian legend Jairzinho. His club career in Brazil was short and he was soon in Europe with PSV Eindhoven where he scored 42 goals in 46 games. His prolific scoring ability comes from a near perfect alliance of speed, balance and strength, though in the later part of his career injury and weight problems have drawn criticism, especially from Brazil where the expectation on him to perform has been intense. He has scored more World Cup final tournament goals (15) than any other player, and has played in three World Cup finals, winning twice. The loss of the 1998 final to France is often attributed to his 'seizure' the night before the match. He made up for this in 2002, scoring in every game, except the quarter-final against England, and twice in the final against Germany. His club career with Barcelona, Inter Milan and Real Madrid has been nothing short of spectacular and his scoring rate has rarely dipped. He has been FIFA World Player of the Year a record three times (matched only by Zinedine Zidane).

HONOURS WON

With Brazil
🏆 World Cup 1994 (squad player), 2002
🏆 Copa America 1997, 1999
🏆 Confederations Cup 1997
With PSV Eindhoven
🏆 KNVB Beker (Dutch FA Cup) 1996
With Barcelona
🏆 European Cup-Winners' Cup 1997
🏆 Copa del Rey 1997
With Inter Milan
🏆 UEFA Cup 1998
With Real Madrid
🏆 Intercontinental Cup 2002
🏆 Primera Liga 2003
🏆 Spanish Supercopa 2003

Other Awards
★ FIFA World Player of the Year 1996, 1997, 2002
★ *World Soccer's* World Player of the Year 1996, 1997, 2002
★ European Footballer of the Year ('Ballon d'Or') 1997, 2002
★ UEFA Awards for Best Forward and Most Valuable Player 1998
★ World Cup 'Golden Ball' 1998
★ World Cup 'Silver Ball' 2002
★ Top scorer World Cup finals 2002

3

Romario

Romario de Souza Faria

Born
Rio de Janeiro
29 January 1966
Country
Brazil
Position
Forward
Clubs
Olaria
Vasco da Gama
PSV Eindhoven
Barcelona
Flamengo
Valencia
Fluminense
Al Saad
International

Caps	Goals
70	55

Romario's first silverware came when he was playing for Vasco da Gama who won the Carioca (Rio state championship) twice. He moved to Europe in 1989 and joined PSV Eindhoven where he won the Dutch league three times. In his first season at Barcelona the club won the Spanish league and he top-scored with 30 goals in 33 matches. He was named FIFA World Player of the Year in 1994. In 1995 he returned to Brazil to play for Flamengo. The highlight of his international career came in the USA in 1994 when Brazil won the World Cup. He scored 55 goals in 70 international matches, and is the second highest goalscorer in Brazil's history behind Pele. In May 2007 he claimed his 1000th goal with a penalty for Vasco da Gama. FIFA congratulated him on this milestone but stated that according to their records he was still on 929 goals. But whatever his total, there is no doubt that in the penalty box there has never been a striker like him.

HONOURS WON

With Brazil
🏆 Copa America 1989, 1997
🏆 World Cup 1994
🏆 Confederations Cup 1997

With Vasco da Gama
🏆 Campeao Carioca 1987, 1988
🏆 Copa Mercosur 2000

With PSV Eindhoven
🏆 Eredivisie 1989, 1991, 1992
🏆 KNVB Beker (Dutch FA Cup) 1989, 1990, 1991

With Barcelona
🏆 Primera Liga 1994

With Flamengo
🏆 Campeao Carioca 1996, 1999
🏆 Copa Mercosur 1999

With Fluminense
🏆 Campeonato Brasileiro 2000

Other Awards
★ Netherlands Player of the Year 1989
★ FIFA World Player of the Year 1994
★ World Cup 'Golden Ball' 1994
★ Confederations Cup 'Golden Ball' 1997
★ Campeonato Brasileiro Best Player ('Bola de Ouro') 2000
★ *El Pais*' South American Footballer of the Year 2000

4

Luis Figo

Luis Filipe Madeira Caeiro Figo

Born
Lisbon
4 November 1972

Country
Portugal

Position
Midfielder

Clubs
Sporting Lisbon
Barcelona
Real Madrid
Inter Milan

International	
Caps	**Goals**
124	32

Luis Figo has been the outstanding player in Portugal's rise as an international football force since the early 1990s. He can play on either wing and is renowned for his close control and dribbling skills. He won his first senior international cap in 1991 and went on to play at Euro 96, Euro 2000, and the 2002 and 2006 World Cups. He announced his retirement from international soccer after Portugal lost to Greece in the final of the 2004 European Championships in Lisbon, having won 117 caps and scored 31 goals. However, in June 2005 he reversed his decision and returned for the successful 2006 World Cup qualifying tournament. He captained the squad in Germany, leading them to the semi-finals, where they were beaten 1–0 by France. This was the furthest Portugal had reached in the tournament since 1966.

In 1995 he joined Barcelona, winning the Cup-Winners' Cup in 1997 and successive Primera Liga titles, playing 172 times and scoring 30 goals. In 2000 he moved to arch-rivals Real Madrid for a then world-record transfer fee of £38.7 million. Playing the best attacking football in Europe, Real, with Figo at the core, swept the board for the next three years including victory in the Champions League in 2002. In 2005 he moved to Inter Milan.

HONOURS WON

With Sporting Lisbon
♛ Taca de Portugal 1995
With Barcelona
♛ European Cup-Winners' Cup 1997
♛ Copa del Rey 1997, 1998
♛ Primera Liga 1998, 1999
With Real Madrid
♛ Primera Liga 2001, 2003
♛ Champions League 2002
♛ Intercontinental Cup 2002
♛ European Super Cup 2002
With Inter Milan
♛ Supercoppa Italiana 2005

Other Awards
★ *Record*'s Portuguese Player of the Year 1995
★ Associaçao de Jornalistas de Desporto's Portuguese Footballer of the Year 1995, 1996, 1997, 1998, 1999, 2000
★ *World Soccer*'s World Player of the Year 2000
★ European Footballer of the Year ('Ballon d'Or') 2000
★ FIFA World Player of the Year 2001

5 Zinedine Zidane

Born
Marseille
23 June 1972
Country
France
Position
Midfielder
Clubs
AS Cannes
Girondins de Bordeaux
Juventus
Real Madrid

International	
Caps	Goals
98	28

Of Algerian extraction, the popularly nicknamed 'Zizou' is an icon of the French national team having been the country's key player and playmaker during three World Cups and three European Championships. In the 1998 World Cup final he cemented his place in world football history with two headed goals during France's 3–0 victory over Brazil. It is ironic that his last act on the World Cup stage was his dismissal during extra-time in the 2006 final for headbutting Italian defender Marco Materazzi. His club career saw him in control of the midfield at four European clubs, most successfully at Juventus and Real Madrid where he won domestic championships and the Champions League. Zidane was elected FIFA World Player of the Year a record-equalling three times (1998, 2000, 2003), and finished in the top three an additional three times (1997, 2002, 2006). He was also named European Footballer of the Year in 1998. The world-record fee of €66 million (US$87 million, £47 million) for his transfer to Real Madrid in 2001 is the most ever paid for a player.

HONOURS WON

With France
- World Cup 1998
- European Championships 2000

With Juventus
- Intercontinental Cup 1996
- European Super Cup 1996
- Serie A 1997, 1998
- Supercoppa Italiana 1997

With Real Madrid
- Spanish Supercopa 2001, 2003
- Champions League 2002
- Intercontinental Cup 2002
- European Super Cup 2002
- Primera Liga 2003

Other Awards
- ★ FIFA World Player of the Year 1998, 2000, 2003
- ★ European Footballer of the Year ('Ballon d'Or') 1998
- ★ Chevalier of the Legion d'Honneur 1998

Diego Maradona

Diego Armando Maradona

Born
Villa Fiorito, Buenos Aires 30 October 1960

Country
Argentina

Position
Forward

Clubs
Argentinos Juniors Boca Juniors Barcelona Napoli Sevilla Newell's Old Boys

International	
Caps	**Goals**
91	34

Seldom have a country's hopes and expectations rested so firmly on one player as Argentina's did on Diego Maradona. In 1979, aged 18, he joined Boca Juniors in Buenos Aires. In 1982 he moved to Barcelona for a world-record transfer fee of £5 million. That year the World Cup was held in Spain and Maradona made his tournament debut on his new home ground, the Estadio Nou Camp. Two years later he was transferred to Napoli who he led to the first league title in the club's history in 1987. The 1986 World Cup will forever be synonymous with Maradona. He scored five goals in the tournament. Two came in the quarter-final against England. The first was the infamous 'Hand of God', the second one of the greatest goals ever seen at the World Cup. Napoli won the UEFA Cup in 1989 and another league title the following year. In 1990 the World Cup was held in Italy and Maradona captained Argentina to yet another final, but this time they lost to West Germany. Despite several comebacks he was never the same force again. He helped Argentina qualify for the 1994 World Cup in USA, but a failed drug test following a match against Nigeria effectively ended his career.

HONOURS WON

With Argentina
�troph World Cup 1986

With Barcelona
�troph Copa del Rey 1983

With Napoli
�troph Serie A 1987, 1990
�troph Coppa Italia 1987
�troph UEFA Cup 1989
�troph Supercoppa Italiana 1990

Other Awards
★ *El Mundo*'s South American Player of the Year 1979, 1980, 1986, 1989, 1990, 1992

★ Argentinian Player of the Year ('Olimpia de Plata') 1979, 1986
★ Argentinian Sportsman of the Year ('Olimpia de Oro') 1979, 1986
★ Argentinian Player of the Year ('Olimpia de Plata') 1980, 1981
★ Italy's Player of the Year 1985
★ World Cup 'Golden Ball' 1986
★ *World Soccer*'s Player of the Year 1986
★ World Cup 'Bronze Ball' 1990

INTERNATIONAL

7 Lothar Matthaus

Born	
Erlangen	
21 March 1961	

Country	
West Germany	
Germany	

Position	
Midfielder	

Clubs	
FC Herzogenaurach	
B. Monchengladbach	
Bayern Munich	
Inter Milan	
New Jersey MetroStars	

International	
Caps	Goals
150	23

Lothar Matthaus is one of the most successful players in world football. As an 18-year-old in 1979 he joined Borussia Monchengladbach, one of the strongest clubs in Europe at that time. By 1980 he was in the West German squad that won the European Championships and in 1982 he made his World Cup debut against Chile, coming on as a substitute in a game they won 4–1. West Germany reached the final but Matthaus only took part in one other game. In 1986 he had a good World Cup and played all the way through to the final, which Germany lost to Argentina. In 1984 Matthaus moved to Bayern Munich enjoying a spell in which they won three league titles before moving to Inter Milan and helping them to a league title in 1989. The 1990 World Cup in Italy was his best. Scoring four times from midfield, he propelled the Germans to the final in which they secured revenge over Argentina, a feat that also saw him voted European Player of the Year. More club honours and a return to Bayern Munich followed. He switched to the sweeper role for the 1994 World Cup where the Germans were knocked out in the quarter-finals. Although out of the German set-up, he was brought back for the 1998 World Cup in France and also played at Euro 2000, but retired subsequently, aged 39.

HONOURS WON

With Germany
🏆 European Championships 1980
🏆 World Cup 1990
With Inter Milan
🏆 Serie A 1989
🏆 UEFA Cup 1991
With Bayern Munich
🏆 Bundesliga 1985, 1986, 1987, 1994, 1997, 1999
🏆 DFB Pokal (German FA Cup) 1986, 1998
🏆 UEFA Cup 1996

Other Awards
★ World Soccer's World Player of the Year 1990
★ European Footballer of the Year ('Ballon d'Or') 1990
★ World Cup 'Silver Ball' 1990
★ German Player of the Year 1990, 1999
★ FIFA World Player of the Year 1991
★ Holds the record of 25 appearances in 5 World Cups

Gerd Muller

Gerhard Muller

Born	
Zinzen	
3 November 1945	
Country	
West Germany	
Position	
Forward	
Clubs	
TSV Nordlingen	
Bayern Munich	
Fort Lauderdale	
Strikers	
Smith Brothers' Lounge	

International	
Caps	**Goals**
62	68

Gerd Muller was the most prolific goal-poacher of his generation and until Ronaldo took his record in 2006, the World Cup's all-time top scorer. Nicknamed 'der Bomber', Muller banged in 68 goals in 62 appearances for his country and 365 in 427 Bundesliga games, being the league's top scorer for seven seasons. His peak was the World Cup in 1970 where he scored successive hat-tricks against Bulgaria and Peru, and two more goals in the semi-final which the Germans lost 4–3 to Italy in extra time. Nearly all Muller's goals came from inside the penalty area where his ability to turn and twist away from defenders created enough space for him to score. At club level he was part of the Bayern Munich team that won three successive European Cups between 1974 and 1976.

HONOURS WON

With West Germany

🏆 European Championships 1972

🏆 World Cup 1974

With Bayern Munich

🏆 DFB Pokal (German FA Cup) 1966, 1967, 1969, 1971

🏆 European Cup-Winners' Cup 1967

🏆 Bundesliga 1969, 1972, 1973, 1974

🏆 European Cup 1974, 1975, 1976

🏆 Intercontinental Cup 1976

Other Awards

★ Germany's Player of the Year 1967, 1969

★ European Footballer of the Year ('Ballon d'Or') 1970

★ All-time top scorer in the Bundesliga with 365 goals

★ FIFA Order of Merit 1998

9

Franz Beckenbauer

Born
Munich
11 September 1945
Country
West Germany
Position
Midfielder
Clubs
Bayern Munich
New York Cosmos
Hamburger SV
International

Caps	Goals
103	14

Franz Beckenbauer, nicknamed 'der Kaiser', dominated every football club he represented whether as a player, coach, manager, or more latterly, as an administrator. He was a versatile player, who started out as a midfielder but adapted to different roles on the pitch, and is best known internationally for inventing the modern role of sweeper or *libero*. He was twice elected the European Footballer of the Year, he appeared 103 times for West Germany and played in three World Cup tournaments. He lifted the World Cup trophy as captain in 1974, and repeated the feat as a manager in 1990. During an incredibly successful club career at Bayern Munich, he won four league titles, four cups, the European Cup-Winners' Cup and three consecutive European Cups from 1974 to 1976. He led Germany's successful bid to host the 2006 World Cup and chaired the organising committee.

HONOURS WON

With West Germany
🏆 European Championships 1972
🏆 World Cup 1974

With Bayern Munich
🏆 DFB Pokal (German FA Cup) 1966,
   1967, 1969, 1971
🏆 European Cup-Winners' Cup 1967
🏆 Bundesliga 1969, 1972, 1973, 1974
🏆 European Cup 1974, 1975, 1976
🏆 Intercontinental Cup 1976

With New York Cosmos
🏆 North American Soccer League
   1977, 1978

Other Awards
★ Germany's Player of the Year 1966,
   1968, 1974, 1976
★ European Footballer of the Year
   ('Ballon d'Or') 1972, 1976
★ North American Soccer League's
   'Most Valuable Player' 1977
★ FIFA Order of Merit 1984

10 Cafu

Marcos Evangelista de Moraes

Born
Sao Paulo
19 June 1970

Country
Brazil

Position
Defender

Clubs
Sao Paulo
Real Zaragoza
Palmeiras
AS Roma
AC Milan

International	
Caps	Goals
142	5

Cafu is the most-capped Brazilian player of all time for the most successful nation of all time. He has played 142 times for Brazil, including a record 21 World Cup final tournament appearances. He has played in four World Cups and three consecutive World Cup finals, winning twice in 1994 and 2002. He captained the side in 2002 and again in 2006. As a junior Cafu played at Sao Paulo where he was persuaded to switch from midfield to wing back. He soon made the first team which won the Copa Libertadores in 1992 and 1993, and was named South American Footballer of the Year in 1994. The following year he moved to Real Zaragoza in Spain, winning the Cup-Winners' Cup. After a brief spell back in Brazil with Palmeiras in 1996, Cafu returned to Europe with Roma, winning Serie A in 2001. Despite making the Coppa Italia final in 2003 with Roma, he moved to AC Milan where he won his second career Serie A title in 2004. He appeared in his first Champions League final against Liverpool in 2005, a match in which the Italian club sensationally let a 3–0 lead slip and were beaten on penalties, but had to sit it out in 2007 through injury when a rematch saw the Italians take revenge in a 2–1 win. He has just signed a contract extension with Milan which will keep him at the San Siro until 2008.

HONOURS WON

With Brazil
- 🏆 World Cup 1994, 2002
- 🏆 Confederations Cup 1997
- 🏆 Copa America 1997, 1999

With Sao Paulo
- 🏆 Campeao Paulista 1989, 1991, 1992
- 🏆 Campeonato Brasileiro 1991
- 🏆 Copa Libertadores 1992, 1993
- 🏆 Intercontinental Cup 1992, 1993
- 🏆 Recopa Sud-Americana 1992, 1993
- 🏆 Supercopa Libertadores 1993

With Real Zaragoza
- 🏆 European Cup-Winners' Cup 1995

With Palmeiras
- 🏆 Campeao Paulista 1996

With AS Roma
- 🏆 Serie A 2001

With AC Milan
- 🏆 Serie A 2004

Other Awards
- ★ South American Player of the Year 1994

11

Roberto Carlos

Roberto Carlos da Silva

Born
Garca, Sao Paulo
10 April 1973
Country
Brazil
Position
Defender
Clubs
Palmeiras
Inter Milan
Real Madrid
Fenerbahce
International

Caps	Goals
125	19

Roberto Carlos built a reputation on his cannoning left-foot shot and his speed at turning defence into attack on the left side. Carlos played in three World Cups, playing on the losing side in the final in France in 1998 and on the winning side in Japan four years later. He scored 19 goals in 125 appearances in the national team – a good record for a left back. He retired from international football following Brazil's 1–0 quarter-final defeat to eventual finalists France at the 2006 World Cup in Germany. His club career began at Palmeiras, before moving to Inter Milan, at the age of 22. In 1996 he settled with Real Madrid, playing at the Bernabeu for eleven years, making him the Spanish club's longest serving foreign player. He is one of only five players to have played more than 100 matches in the Champions League. In the summer of 2007 he left Real following his fourth title and moved to Turkey to play for Fenerbahce.

HONOURS WON

With Brazil

🏆 Confederations Cup 1997

🏆 Copa America 1997, 1999

🏆 World Cup 2002

With Palmeiras

🏆 Campeonato Brasileiro 1993, 1994

🏆 Campeao Paulista 1993, 1994

With Real Madrid

🏆 Primera Liga 1997, 2001, 2003, 2007

🏆 Champions League 1998, 2000, 2002

🏆 Intercontinental Cup 1998, 2002

🏆 European Super Cup 2002

Other Awards

★ UEFA Award for Best Defender 2002, 2003

12 Marco van Basten

Born
Utrecht
31 October 1964

Country
Holland

Position
Forward

Clubs
Ajax
AC Milan

International	
Caps	Goals
58	24

Marco van Basten was the most celebrated goalscorer of his generation. He was graceful, yet still had power. He was good with both feet and had excellent close control, all this allied with lightning speed on the turn and an outstanding ability in the air. Van Basten began his club career at Ajax. By 1986 he was the top marksman in Europe, winning the European Golden Boot award. With van Basten leading their attack, Ajax lifted three Dutch Championships, three Dutch Cups and the European Cup-Winners' Cup to which he contributed 128 goals in just 143 games. He then moved to AC Milan where he won a further three domestic championships and two European Cups in a team which also featured fellow countrymen Ruud Gullit and Frank Rijkaard. As a striker in the tough Italian league he took more than his fair share of knocks and injuries, but still scored another 90 goals in 147 Serie A games. Internationally he will mostly be remembered for his performances during the 1988 European Championships. Having sunk England in the group match, he sealed victory for his team in the 54th minute of the final against the Soviet Union when from an impossible angle he struck a blistering volley into the roof of the net. He retired in 1995 when he failed to overcome a persistent ankle injury. In 2004 he became coach of the Dutch national team.

HONOURS WON

With Holland
🏆 European Championships 1988

With Ajax
🏆 Eredivisie 1982, 1983, 1985
🏆 KNVB Beker (Dutch FA Cup) 1983, 1986, 1987
🏆 European Cup-Winners' Cup 1987

With AC Milan
🏆 Serie A 1988, 1992, 1993
🏆 Supercoppa Italiana 1988, 1992, 1993
🏆 European Cup 1989, 1990

🏆 European Super Cup 1989, 1990
🏆 Intercontinental Cup 1989, 1990

Other Awards
★ Dutch Player of the Year 1985
★ European 'Golden Boot' ('Soulier d'Or') Award 1986
★ European Footballer of the Year ('Ballon d'Or') 1988, 1989, 1992
★ *World Soccer*'s Player of the Year 1988, 1992
★ FIFA World Player of the Year 1992

INTERNATIONAL

13 Michel Platini

Born	
Joeuf	
21 May 1955	
Country	
France	
Position	
Midfielder	
Clubs	
AS Nancy	
AS Saint-Etienne	
Juventus	
International	
Caps	**Goals**
72	41

Michel Platini is one of the greatest midfield playmakers in the history of the game. Always graceful, his passing ability, skilful free kicks and his knack of arriving unmarked in the box to score placed him at the heart of every team for which he played, both at club and international level. His ability to read the game enabled him to execute passes that opened up even the tightest defences. He began his career at Nancy before moving to Saint-Etienne with whom he won his first domestic league title. In 1982 he left France for Italy, signing for Juventus in Turin. During a sparkling four seasons he led Juve to a host of trophies. He was Serie A's top scorer three times and was voted European Player of the Year three times. At international level he inspired a previously weak French team to fantastic performances at the 1982 and 1986 World Cups in which they twice lost to Germany in the semi-finals. But the highlight of his career was undoubtedly the European Championships in France in 1984. He dominated the tournament, scoring nine goals in five games, including the first in a 2–0 win in the final against Spain to enable France to secure its first major title. He retired aged 32 after playing 680 games and scoring 368 goals in a glittering career. In January 2007 he replaced Lennart Johansson as President of UEFA.

HONOURS WON

With France
🏆 European Championships 1984

With AS Nancy-Lorraine
🏆 Coupe de France 1978

With AS Saint-Etienne
🏆 Championnat 1981

With Juventus
🏆 Coppa Italia 1983
🏆 European Cup-Winners' Cup 1984
🏆 European Super Cup 1984
🏆 Serie A 1984, 1986
🏆 European Cup 1985
🏆 Intercontinental Cup 1985

Other Awards
★ France Football's French Player of the Year 1976, 1977
★ European Footballer of the Year ('Ballon d'Or') 1983, 1984, 1985
★ Italy's Player of the Year 1984
★ World Soccer's Player of the Year 1984, 1985
★ Chevalier of the Legion d'Honneur 1985
★ Ordre National du Merite 1994
★ Officier of the Legion d'Honneur 1998

14

Rivaldo

Vitor Borba Ferreira

Born	
Recife	
19 April 1972	
Country	
Brazil	
Position	
Midfielder	
Clubs	
Paulista	
Santa Cruz	
Mogi Mirim	
Corinthians	
Palmeiras	
Deportivo La Coruna	
Barcelona	
AC Milan	
Cruzeiro	
Olympiakos	
AEK Athens	

International	
Caps	**Goals**
74	34

Vitor Borba Ferreira, known worldwide as Rivaldo, played 74 times for Brazil, scoring 34 goals, and was a key member of the 2002 World Cup-winning team in Japan. Rivaldo is an attacking midfielder and became famous for a series of spectacular bicycle kicks. His best years as a club player were spent at Barcelona with whom he won the 1998 and 1999 league championships. In his first season at the Nou Camp he scored 19 goals in 34 matches as Barcelona won the league and cup Double. The following year, 1999, was a special one for him as he was named both FIFA World Player of the Year and European Footballer of the Year. That summer Rivaldo top scored with five goals as Brazil won the Copa America. His strikes included the equaliser from a trademark free-kick in a 2–1 win over Argentina in the quarter-final, and two in the 3–0 victory over Uruguay in the final. He was named Most Valuable Player of the tournament. After a disappointing spell at AC Milan he moved again, first back to Brazil and then to Greece. He is currently playing for AEK Athens in the Greek Super League.

27

HONOURS WON

With Brazil
- 🏆 Confederations Cup 1997
- 🏆 Copa America 1999
- 🏆 World Cup 2002

With Palmeiras
- 🏆 Campeonato Brasileiro 1994
- 🏆 Campeao Paulista 1996

With Barcelona
- 🏆 Primera Liga 1998, 1999
- 🏆 Copa del Rey 1998

With AC Milan
- 🏆 European Super Cup 2003
- 🏆 Coppa Italia 2003

With Olympiakos
- 🏆 Greek Championship 2005
- 🏆 Greek Cup 2005

Other Awards
- ★ Copa America Best Player 1999
- ★ FIFA World Player of the Year 1999
- ★ European Footballer of the Year ('Ballon d'Or') 1999

INTERNATIONAL

15 Paolo Maldini

Born	
Milan	
26 June 1968	
Country	
Italy	
Position	
Defender	
Clubs	
AC Milan	
International	
Caps	**Goals**
126	7

Paolo Maldini is Italy's most-capped player with 126 appearances. On the domestic front Maldini has played in eight Champions League finals (six in its current format), all with AC Milan where he has spent his entire career. He currently holds the most appearances for the club (as well as any player in Serie A) after passing Franco Baresi's record of 512. He made his 600th appearance in May 2007. He now plays at centre back although it was at left back where he really made his mark. At almost 40 years of age, he is still playing at the very highest level. This is confirmed by his inclusion in the FIFPro World XI in 2005, his nomination in the UEFA Champions League 2005 Most Valuable Defender shortlist, second place in Golden Foot nominations in 2005, a top-10 finish in the voting for the 2005 FIFA World Player of the Year and a Champions League winner's medal in 2007. He captained the national team for more than half his international career but never managed to win a trophy with Italy despite playing in the 1994 World Cup final and the 2000 European Championships final. Maldini also played in the 1990 and 1998 World Cups (coached by his father Cesare), Euro 88, and Euro 96.

HONOURS WON

With AC Milan

🏆 Serie A 1988, 1992, 1993, 1994, 1996, 1999, 2004

🏆 European Cup/Champions League 1989, 1990, 1994, 2003, 2007

🏆 Intercontinental Cup 1989, 1990

🏆 European Super Cup 1989, 1990, 1994, 2003

🏆 Supercoppa Italiana 1992, 1993, 1994

🏆 Coppa Italia 2003

Other Awards

★ *World Soccer*'s World Player of the Year 1994

16 Zico

Artur Antunes Coimbra

Born	
Rio de Janeiro 3 March 1953	
Country	
Brazil	
Position	
Midfielder	
Clubs	
Flamengo Udinese Kashima Antlers	
International	
Caps	Goals
72	52

Zico scored over 100 goals in his first two seasons of senior football. He made his league debut for Flamengo in 1973 and his international debut in 1976, against Uruguay, scoring with a free-kick, something for which he became world famous. He played in three World Cups, his best being in 1982 where Brazil's attacking style suited Zico's change of pace, body-swerves and dynamic shooting. In 1983 after 650 goals and three Brazilian championship medals, he made a £2.5 million move to Udinese in Italy, returning to Flamengo two years later. In all Zico played 1047 senior games, including 71 for Brazil, before retiring in 1990 and being appointed his country's sports minister. Three years later he returned to the field in Japan, joining the Kashima Antlers for the first season of the professional J.League.

HONOURS WON

With Flamengo

🏆 Campeao Carioca 1972, 1974, 1978, 1979, 1979 (Special), 1981, 1986

🏆 Campeonato Brasileiro 1980, 1982, 1983

🏆 Copa Libertadores 1981

🏆 Intercontinental Cup 1981

Other Awards

★ Campeonato Brasileiro Best Player ('Bola de Ouro') 1974, 1982

★ *El Mundo*'s South American Player of the Year 1977, 1981, 1982

★ *World Soccer*'s Player of the Year 1983

★ Awarded FIFA Order of Merit 1996

17 Raul

Raul Gonzalez Blanco

Born
Madrid
27 June 1977

Country
Spain

Position
Forward

Clubs
Real Madrid

International	
Caps	Goals
102	44

Raul has played more than 100 games for Spain and is the country's all-time leading goalscorer with 44 goals. He represented Spain in the 1998 World Cup, Euro 2000, the 2002 World Cup, Euro 2004 and the 2006 World Cup. Although initially signing for Atletico Madrid in his home city, he soon moved to Real. In 1994 he became the youngest player to play for the club at just 17 years and four months. He scored nine times in his first season in 28 appearances, including one in his second game against Atletico, and won the Spanish La Liga championship the following spring. Raul was a key player in Real Madrid's Galacticos. With him leading the line Real won three Champions League trophies in 1998, 2000 and 2002; he scored the clinching goal in the 2000 final against Valencia and the first in the 2002 final against Bayer Leverkusen. He is the all-time top scorer in the competition with 56 goals. On the domestic scene, he won five Spanish La Liga championships, in 1995, 1997, 2001, 2003 and 2007. He is currently the 12th highest goalscorer in the history of Spain's top flight, with 194 goals in 449 games. All of these goals were for Real Madrid, making him the club's third highest goalscorer of all time. He wears the number 7 shirt for both club and country, a number that not even the power of the David Beckham marketing machine could take off him.

HONOURS WON

With Real Madrid

🏆 Primera Liga 1995, 1997, 2001, 2003, 2007

🏆 Spanish Supercopa 1997, 2001, 2003

🏆 Champions League 1998, 2000, 2002

🏆 Intercontinental Cup 1998, 2002

🏆 European Super Cup 2002

Other Awards

★ Spanish Footballer of the Year 1997, 1999, 2000, 2001, 2002

★ UEFA Award for Best Forward 2000, 2001, 2003

★ Spanish Royal Order's Gold Medal for Sports Merit 2006

18 Ruud Gullit

Born	
Amsterdam 10 January 1962	
Country	
Holland	
Position	
Midfielder	
Clubs	
Haarlem Feyenoord PSV Eindhoven AC Milan Sampdoria Chelsea	

International	
Caps	**Goals**
66	17

Ruud Gullit was a versatile player who played in a number of different positions in his career. He made his debut for Holland against Switzerland in 1981 on his 19th birthday. He was one of the key players during the second wave of Total Footballers in Holland and helped his country win the European Championships in Germany in 1988. He also played in the 1990 World Cup. But the early 1990s saw unrest in the Dutch team and before the 1994 tournament, Gullit walked out of the training camp and retired from international football. His club career began in 1978, when he signed professional forms for second division Haarlem near Amsterdam. Gullit's influence – he made 91 league appearances and scored 32 goals – took them to the first division where they managed a fourth place finish. The next five years saw him ply his trade at Feyenoord and PSV Eindhoven. But it was his next move, to AC Milan in 1987, that proved most successful. From 1988 to 1992, Milan captured three Serie A titles and two European Cups (1989 and 1990). He won the European Footballer of the Year award in 1987 and dedicated it to Nelson Mandela. He ended his playing career at Chelsea where he was player-manager and became the first non-British manager to win the FA Cup when Chelsea beat Middlesbrough in 1997.

HONOURS WON

With Holland
🏆 European Championships 1988
With AC Milan
🏆 Serie A 1988, 1992, 1993
🏆 Supercoppa Italiana 1988, 1992, 1993
🏆 European Cup 1989, 1990
🏆 European Super Cup 1989, 1990
🏆 Intercontinental Cup 1989, 1990
With Sampdoria
🏆 Coppa Italia 1994

Other Awards
★ Netherlands Player of the Year 1984, 1986
★ European Footballer of the Year ('Ballon d'Or') 1987
★ *World Soccer's* Player of the Year 1987, 1989

19 | Eusebio

Eusebio da Silva Ferreira

Born
Lourenco Marques (today Maputo), Mozambique 25 January 1942

Country
Portugal

Position
Forward

Clubs
Sporting Lourenco M Benfica Rhode Island Oceaners Boston Minutemen Monterrey Toronto Metros-Croatia Beira Mar Las Vegas Quicksilver Uniao de Tomar New Jersey Americans

International	
Caps	Goals
64	46

Eusebio, nicknamed the 'Black Pearl', was born in Mozambique but brought to Portugal in 1961 by Benfica. In one of his first games for the club, he scored a hat-trick against Pele's Santos. The Black Pearl continued to impress, scoring twice against Real Madrid in the European Cup final of 1962. Speedy, skilful and powerful, Eusebio was effective whatever the strength of the midfield behind him. He was unstoppable in the Portuguese league where he scored more than a goal per game – 319 in 313 appearances. He helped Benfica win 10 Portuguese league championships and five domestic cup titles. He was six times top scorer in the Portuguese league and twice Golden Boot winner as top scorer in European football – 1968 and 1973 – and in 1965 he was voted European Player of the Year. Eusebio played for Portugal in just one World Cup, in England in 1966, a tournament in which he won the hearts of the crowds with his sportsmanship and further enhanced his reputation as a fearsome striker with nine goals. Not always properly rewarded for his talents, he played the twilight of his career in North America.

HONOURS WON

With Benfica

🏆 Campeonato da Primeira Divisao 1960, 1963, 1964, 1965, 1967, 1968, 1969, 1971, 1972, 1973

🏆 European Cup 1962

🏆 Taca de Portugal (Portuguese FA Cup) 1962, 1964, 1969, 1970, 1972

With Monterrey

🏆 Primera Division 1976

With Toronto Metros-Croatia

🏆 North American Soccer League 1976

Other Awards

★ European Footballer of the Year ('Ballon d'Or') 1965

★ World Cup 'Golden Boot' 1966

★ European 'Golden Boot' ('Soulier d'Or') Award 1968, 1973

★ *Diario Popular*'s Portuguese Footballer of the Year 1970

★ Associaco de Jornalistas de Desporto's Portuguese Footballer of the Year 1973

★ FIFA Order of Merit in 1994

20 Ferenc Puskas

Born	
Budapest 2 April 1927	
Country	
Hungary/Spain	
Position	
Midfielder	
Clubs	
Kispest-Honved Real Madrid	
International	
Caps	Goals
84 (Hun) 4 (Spa)	83 (Hun)

Ferenc Puskas was a Hungarian goal machine scoring 83 goals in 84 internationals, and 511 goals in 533 matches in the Hungarian and Spanish leagues. His deadly accurate left foot was his weapon of choice. During the 1950s he was both a prominent member and captain of the legendary Hungarian national team known as the Mighty Magyars. The team went on a run of 32 matches unbeaten, still an international record. He was top scorer in the Hungarian league on four occasions, and in 1948 he was the top goalscorer in Europe. He played in the 1954 World Cup final against West Germany and scored a late equaliser that was controversially ruled out. In 1958 he joined Real Madrid at the age of 31 and embarked on the second phase of his career. He scored 20 or more goals in each of his first six seasons in the Spanish league, and helped Real win the title five times in a row between 1961 and 1965. Puskas played 39 games for Real in the European Cup, scoring 35 goals. In the 1959 tournament he scored in the first leg and in the decisive replay of the semi-final against Atletico Madrid, but missed the final due to injury. However, the following season he would make up for it. Real beat Eintracht Frankfurt 7–3 at Hampden Park in one of the greatest ever European matches with Puskas scoring four goals and di Stefano scoring three. He was awarded Spanish citizenship in 1962 and was rewarded with a place in the Spain World Cup squad. In 1965 he scored five goals over two games against Feyenoord as he helped a new generation of Real Madrid players win the 1966 European Cup.

HONOURS WON

With Hungary

🏆 Olympic Football Tournament (gold medal) 1952

With Kispest-Honved

🏆 Nemzeti Bajnoksag (Hungarian League) 1950, 1952, 1954, 1955

With Real Madrid

🏆 European Cup 1959, 1960, 1966
🏆 Intercontinental Cup 1960
🏆 Primera Liga 1961, 1962, 1963, 1964, 1965
🏆 Copa del Generalisimo 1962

Other Awards

★ FIFA Order of Merit 1994

INTERNATIONAL

21 Johan Cruyff

Born
Amsterdam 25 April 1947
Country
Holland
Position
Forward
Clubs
Ajax Barcelona LA Aztecs Washington Diplomats Levante Feyenoord

International	
Caps	Goals
47	33

34

Johan Cruyff was the embodiment of the Total Football philosophy. The Dutch master was noted for his technical ability, speed and acceleration, but his greatest quality was his vision, which enabled him to read the game and his team-mates' movement as an attack unfolded. Positionally, Cruyff was a centre forward, but he would often drop deep or move to wide positions to confuse defences. Cruyff's talent saw him voted European Footballer of the Year three times in a career that began at Ajax and continued at Barcelona before moving to the US for one season. But it was internationally that Cruyff was most recognised. He was the shining light of a Dutch side that excited the world with its 'possession' football. At the 1974 World Cup the Dutch reached the final, beating Argentina and Brazil amongst others before losing to West Germany. In the first round match against Sweden, he thrilled millions of television viewers with the 'Cruyff turn', a move so dazzling it left a defender sitting on his bottom. Cruyff is a man of principle; he refused to play in the 1978 World Cup in Argentina because the country had just been taken over in a military coup. He also told Catalan fans he chose Barcelona ahead of Real Madrid because he would not play for a club associated with Franco. He scored 33 international goals in 47 matches. As a manager he was in charge of Ajax and Barcelona and is still closely linked with the Spanish club.

HONOURS WON

With Ajax
- 🏆 Eredivisie 1966, 1967, 1968, 1970, 1972, 1973, 1982, 1983
- 🏆 KNVB Beker (Dutch FA Cup) 1967, 1970, 1971, 1972, 1983
- 🏆 European Cup 1971, 1972, 1973
- 🏆 Intercontinental Cup 1972
- 🏆 European Super Cup 1972, 1973

With Barcelona
- 🏆 Primera Liga 1974
- 🏆 Copa del Rey 1978

Other Awards
- ★ European Footballer of the Year ('Ballon d'Or') 1971, 1973, 1974
- ★ Spain's Foreign Footballer of the Year 1977, 1978
- ★ North American Soccer League's Most Valuable Player 1979

22 Alfredo di Stefano

Born	
Buenos Aires 4 July 1926	

Country
Argentina/Spain

Position
Forward

Clubs
River Plate Huracan Millonarios Real Madrid Espanyol

International	
Caps	**Goals**
7 (Arg)	7 (Arg)
31 (Spa)	23 (Spa)

Alfredo di Stefano began his career in his native Argentina, signing for River Plate in 1943 at the age of 17. But he is best known for his time at Real Madrid where he was an integral part of one of the most successful club teams of all time. He scored a club record 216 league goals in 262 games for the Spanish giants, striking up a fearsome partnership with team-mate Ferenc Puskas. The two players were instrumental in the club's domination of the European Cup – they won the trophy every year between 1956 and 1960, the first five years of its existence. Di Stefano's 49 goals in 58 matches was the all-time highest tally in the competition, only surpassed in 2005 by Real Madrid's Raul. Di Stefano played with three different national teams during his career: Argentina, Colombia (who were not recognised by FIFA at the time) and Spain, but never in the World Cup finals. He acquired Spanish citizenship in 1956, and played four World Cup qualifying matches for his new country in 1957, but the team failed to qualify for the 1958 finals. Di Stefano finally helped Spain qualify for the World Cup of 1962 but a muscle injury just before the tournament prevented him from playing. He moved to Espanyol in 1964 where he played until hanging up his boots at the age of 40.

HONOURS WON

With Argentina
🏆 Copa America 1947
With River Plate
🏆 Campeonato Argentino 1945, 1947
With Millonarios
🏆 Division Mayor 1949, 1951, 1952
With Real Madrid
🏆 Primera Liga 1954, 1955, 1957, 1958, 1961, 1962, 1963, 1964
🏆 Latin Cup 1955, 1957
🏆 European Cup 1956, 1957, 1958, 1959, 1960

🏆 Intercontinental Cup 1960
🏆 Copa del Generalisimo 1962
Other Awards
★ European Footballer of the Year ('Ballon d'Or') 1957, 1959
★ Best European Footballer of All Time ('Super Ballon d'Or') 1989
★ FIFA Order of Merit 1994
★ Named Honorary President of Real Madrid 2000

INTERNATIONAL

23 | Bobby Charlton

Born	
Ashington, Northumberland 11 October 1937	
Country	
England	
Position	
Forward	
Clubs	
Manchester United Preston North End	
International	
Caps	**Goals**
106	49

Bobby Charlton was still a schoolboy when he joined Manchester United in 1953. He made his debut three years later, scoring twice in a 4–2 win at home to Charlton. Having survived the horror of the Munich air disaster in which eight of his team-mates died, Bobby Charlton proceeded to become one of football's greatest exponents. As one of the famed 'Busby Babes' he was tipped for a place at the top, but few could have envisaged just how big a star the Ashington-born player would become. Charlton possessed most of the vital assets needed in the make-up of a top player and they were blended into one of the finest attacking midfielders the British Isles has ever produced. Respected around the globe for his gentlemanly approach to the game, he collected virtually every major honour available including the World Cup in 1966. He joined the board of directors at Old Trafford after his playing days were over, but he will probably be best remembered for the thunderous long-range shooting that had goalkeepers quaking in their boots the world over.

HONOURS WON

With England
🏆 World Cup 1966

With Manchester United
🏆 Football League 1957, 1965, 1967
🏆 FA Cup 1963
🏆 European Cup 1968

Other Awards
★ European Footballer of the Year ('Ballon d'Or') 1966
★ Football Writers' Association Player of the Year 1966
★ OBE 1969
★ CBE 1974
★ FIFA Order of Merit 1984
★ PFA Merit Award 1974
★ Football Writers' Association Tribute Award 1989
★ Received a Knighthood 1994

24 Jurgen Klinsmann

Born	
Goppingen 30 July 1964	
Country	
West Germany Germany	
Position	
Forward	
Clubs	
Stuttgart Kickers VfB Stuttgart Inter Milan AS Monaco Tottenham Hotspur Bayern Munich Sampdoria Orange City Blue Stars	
International	
Caps	**Goals**
108	47

Jurgen Klinsmann started his career in Germany with second division Stuttgart Kickers in 1981, before joining the big club in the city, VfB, after three seasons. In 1988 he was top scorer in the Bundesliga and was voted German Player of the Year. In the summer of 1989 he joined Inter Milan with fellow countrymen Lothar Matthaus and Andreas Brehme in a team that mopped up the Serie A title in their first season. Klinsmann was a player who could easily adapt to new cultures. During a distinguished club career he played top-level football in England, Italy, Germany and France. And France was to be his next destination as he signed for Monaco in 1992. He won a World Cup winner's medal in Italy in 1990, playing five of the games on his home ground in Milan. The ageing German team were unable to continue their World Cup success in the USA in 1994 but Klinsmann was still outstanding during the tournament scoring five goals. He joined Spurs and was voted FWA Player of the Year in 1995. A year later he won the European Championships with Germany at Wembley. In all Klinsmann won 108 caps and scored nearly 50 international goals. He was hailed a national hero for coaxing good results out of a poor German national side at the World Cup in Germany in 2006.

HONOURS WON

With Germany
🏆 World Cup 1990
🏆 European Championship 1996
With Inter Milan
🏆 UEFA Cup 1991
With Bayern Munich
🏆 UEFA Cup 1996
🏆 Bundesliga 1997

Other Awards
★ Germany's Player of the Year 1988, 1994
★ Football Writers' Association Player of the Year 1995

INTERNATIONAL

25 Kenny Dalglish

Born
Dalmarnock, Glasgow 4 March 1951

Country
Scotland

Position
Forward

Clubs
Celtic
Liverpool

International	
Caps	**Goals**
102	30

Kenny Dalglish was a protestant Glaswegian who started his career at catholic Celtic. At the time Celtic were not only the best team in Scotland but had become the first British team to win the European Cup, beating the mighty Inter Milan in 1967. He made his debut in a benefit match in which Celtic beat Kilmarnock 7–2 – he scored six. In 1972–73 Dalglish, now playing up front having started at right midfield, was Celtic's leading marksman with 41 goals in all competitions. His trademark was his skill at holding on to the ball with his back to goal. Dalglish had a fantastic run at Celtic winning four Scottish Championships, four Scottish Cups and one Scottish League Cup, scoring 167 goals along the way. He moved to Liverpool in 1977 to take over from Kevin Keegan. In his first season he scored 30 goals as Liverpool retained the European Cup. Later in his career he developed from goalscorer to goalmaker and proved equally devastating at opening up opposing defences for others. The years up to 1985 were a golden period for Liverpool with Dalglish central to their relentless pursuit of trophies. Internationally Dalglish did not have as much success, but he still played in two World Cups. After hanging up his shooting boots he managed Liverpool to more trophies before winning the Premiership with Blackburn in 1995. He later also had a spell in the hot-seat at Newcastle. In all Kenny Dalglish holds the distinction of having won 13 championships as a player and manager in England and Scotland.

HONOURS WON

With Celtic
♛ Scottish League 1972, 1973, 1974, 1977
♛ Scottish FA Cup 1972, 1974, 1975, 1977
♛ Scottish League Cup 1975
With Liverpool
♛ European Super Cup 1977
♛ European Cup 1978, 1981, 1984

♛ Football League 1979, 1980, 1984, 1986
♛ League Cup 1983, 1984
♛ FA Cup 1986
Other Awards
★ Football Writers' Association Player of the Year 1979, 1983
★ PFA Player of the Year 1983
★ Football Writers' Association Tribute Award 1987

26 Ali Daei

Born
Ardabil
21 March 1969
Country
Iran
Position
Striker
Clubs
Esteghlal Ardabil
Taxirani
Bank Tejarat
Persepolis
Al-Sadd
Arminia Bielefeld
Bayern Munich
Hertha Berlin
Al-Shabab
Saba Battery
Saipa

International	
Caps	**Goals**
149	109

Ali Daei is the world's all-time leading goalscorer in international matches. The Iranian has hit the back of the net 109 times in 149 matches – the first player to reach three figures. Although never playing in the World Cup finals, he top scored in the Asian qualifiers in 1998 and 2006. Iran finished third in both the 1996 and 2004 Asian Cup tournaments, reaching the quarter-finals in 2000. At club level Daei came to prominence with the Tehran team Persepolis. Following his impressive performance in the Asian Cup in 1996, he signed for Arminia Bielefeld and joined the Bundesliga. A year later he moved to Bayern Munich in a record transfer fee for an Asian player. He also became the first Asian player to feature in the Champions League but due to limited opportunities he moved on again, this time to Hertha Berlin. In 2000 he played in the Champions League, top scoring with three goals in a poor campaign. In 2001, aged 34, he returned to the Middle East to play in the UAE league. He rejoined his old team Persepolis in 2003, then moved to Saba Battery, scoring 23 goals, winning the Hazfi Cup and playing in the Asian Champions League for the next two years. He was part of the Iran squad which qualified for the 2006 World Cup in Germany. In the summer of 2006 he joined Saipa FC where a coaching vacancy suddenly came up, and he announced that he would retire from playing and take the job. The following year he earned his first trophy as coach as they won the Persian Gulf Cup in 2007.

HONOURS WON

With Bayern Munich
♛ Bundesliga 1999

With Saba Battery
♛ Jaam Hazfi (Iranian FA Cup) 2005

27 | Karl-Heinz Rummenigge

Born	
Lippstadt	
25 September 1955	
Country	
West Germany	
Position	
Forward	
Clubs	
Borussia Lippstadt	
Bayern Munich	
Inter Milan	
Servette	
International	
Caps	**Goals**
95	45

Karl-Heinz Rummenigge followed in the West Germany tradition of world-class forwards. A Bayern Munich prodigy, he was a member of the 1976 European Cup-winning team and soon earned a place in the national squad. Coach Helmut Schon picked him for the World Cup in Argentina in 1978. By the 1982 World Cup in Spain he was one of the superstars of the world game. He led his team to the final where they lost 3–1 to Italy. He did win a European Championships winner's medal in 1980 when West Germany beat Belgium in the final and he was twice voted European Player of the Year. After 10 years with Bayern (162 goals in 314 appearances) he moved to Inter Milan. The World Cup in 1986 ended his international career.

Despite carrying injuries he played in every game of the tournament, scoring in the final that Germany lost 3–2 to Argentina. The final was his 52nd match as captain and his 95th and last international. He became the first captain to lose two World Cup finals. Having retired from playing, he remains an important part of the management structure at Bayern Munich.

HONOURS WON

With West Germany
♛ European Championships 1980

With Bayern Munich
♛ European Cup 1975, 1976
♛ Intercontinental Cup 1976
♛ Bundesliga 1980, 1981
♛ DFB Pokal (German FA Cup) 1982, 1984

Other Awards
★ Germany's Player of the Year 1980
★ European Footballer of the Year ('Ballon d'Or') 1980, 1981
★ World Cup 'Bronze Ball' 1982

28 Gabriel Batistuta

Born
Avellaneda, Santa Fe 1 February 1969

Country
Argentina

Position
Forward

Clubs
Newell's Old Boys River Plate Boca Juniors Fiorentina AS Roma Inter Milan Al-Arabi

International	
Caps	**Goals**
78	56

Gabriel Batistuta is the all-time highest scorer for Argentina with 56 goals in 78 matches. He represented his country at three World Cups and was the first player to score a hat-trick in two different tournaments. He played most of his club football at Fiorentina in Italy, and is the eighth highest scorer of all time in Serie A, having scored 184 goals in 318 matches between 1991 and 2003. He never won the championship with Fiorentina, but he moved to AS Roma in 2000 and in his first season at the Stadio Olimpico his new club won their first Scudetto in 19 years. He played his last season in Qatar with Al-Arabi before he retired in 2005. He currently works as a TV pundit for Argentinian television.

HONOURS WON

With Argentina
- 🏆 Copa America winner 1991, 1993
- 🏆 Confederations Cup 1992

With River Plate
- 🏆 Campeonato Argentino 1990

With Fiorentina
- 🏆 Coppa Italia 1996
- 🏆 Supercoppa Italiana 1996

With AS Roma
- 🏆 Serie A 2001
- 🏆 Supercoppa Italiana 2001

Other Awards
- ★ *El Mundo*'s South American Footballer of the Year 1991
- ★ Confederations Cup 'Golden Ball' winner 1992
- ★ Argentine Player of the Year ('Olimpia de Plata') 1998

29 Michael Laudrup

Born
Copenhagen 15 June 1964
Country
Denmark
Position
Midfielder/Forward
Clubs
KB Kobenhavn Brondby Lazio Juventus Barcelona Real Madrid Vissel Kobe Ajax
International

Caps	Goals
104	37

Michael Laudrup was a playmaking midfielder, known as one of the most effective passers, as well as one of the most skilful and elegant players in the game. His greatest success came with Spanish club Barcelona, with whom he won four straight championships as well as the 1992 European Cup. In 1994 he controversially moved across Spain to play for Barca's arch-rivals Real Madrid with whom he won his fifth La Liga title in a row. He scored 37 goals in a total of 104 appearances for his country but, unlike his brother Brian, he did not take part in their greatest triumph, the 1992 European Championships in Sweden, following differences with the coach. His father, Finn, also played for Denmark and both his sons are in the national junior sides.

HONOURS WON

With Denmark
🏆 Confederations Cup 1995
With Juventus
🏆 Serie A 1986
With Brondby
🏆 Danmarksturneringen (Danish League) 1987, 1988
With Barcelona
🏆 Primera Liga 1991, 1992, 1993, 1994
🏆 European Cup 1992
🏆 European Super Cup 1992

With Real Madrid
🏆 Primera Liga 1995
With Ajax
🏆 Eredivisie 1998
🏆 KNVB Beker (Dutch FA Cup) 1998
Other Awards
★ Spain's Foreign Footballer of the Year 1992

30 | Hristo Stoichkov

Born
Plovdiv
2 August 1966

Country
Bulgaria

Position
Forward

Clubs
CSKA Sofia/
CFKA Sredets Sofia
Barcelona
Parma
Al Ansar
Kashiwa Reysol
Chicago Fire
DC United

International	
Caps	Goals
83	37

Hristo Stoichkov was known for his explosive acceleration and speed dribbling, and for taking unpredictable shots on goal. He also established a reputation early in his career for his aggressive behaviour on the pitch. He began playing for his hometown club, moving to CSKA Sofia in 1985. There he was involved in a fight during the Bulgarian Cup final, which resulted in his suspension. However, two seasons later he won the European Golden Boot with CSKA by scoring 38 goals in 30 games. He then moved to Barcelona and was part of the club's most successful era, winning La Liga four years in a row between 1991 and 1994 and the European Cup in 1992. In his first season with the club Stoichkov was suspended for two months for stamping on a referee's foot, but he still netted 14 league goals and six more in the European Cup-Winners' Cup. In 1997 he helped Barcelona win the European Super Cup, the Copa del Rey and the Cup-Winners' Cup. In 1994 he was named European Footballer of the Year after leading his national side to the 1994 World Cup semi-finals – he was tournament top scorer. He retired from international football in 1999 with 37 goals in 83 appearances. He later took up coaching in the USA.

HONOURS WON

With CSKA Sofia/CFKA Sredets Sofia

🏆 Bulgarian Cup 1985, 1987, 1988, 1989
🏆 Premier League 1987, 1989, 1990

With Barcelona

🏆 Primera Liga 1991, 1992, 1993, 1994
🏆 European Cup 1992
🏆 European Super Cup 1992, 1997
🏆 Spanish Supercopa 1991, 1992, 1994
🏆 European Cup-Winners' Cup 1997
🏆 Copa del Rey 1997

Other Awards

★ Bulgarian Football Player of the Year 1989, 1990, 1991, 1992, 1994
★ European 'Golden Boot' ('Soulier d'Or') Award 1989
★ Spanish Foreign Footballer of the Year 1994
★ European Footballer of the Year ('Ballon d'Or') 1994
★ World Cup 'Bronze Ball' 1994
★ Bulgarian Athlete of the Year 1994

INTERNATIONAL

31 | Dennis Bergkamp

Born
Amsterdam
10 May 1969
Country
Holland
Position
Forward
Clubs
Ajax
Inter Milan
Arsenal

International	
Caps	**Goals**
79	37

Dennis Bergkamp was a major force in the Dutch international side after he made his debut in 1990. He impressed at Euro 92 when the Dutch were semi-finalists and in the 1994 World Cup. His winner in the last minute of the 1998 World Cup quarter-final against Argentina is regarded as one of the best goals ever. He retired after Holland were losing semi-finalists at Euro 2000, ending his international career as the country's leading goalscorer with 37 goals in 79 games (a record since surpassed by Patrick Kluivert). As a forward Bergkamp was at his best just behind the strikers, where his tactical awareness and clever passes were most effective. His club career began at Ajax where he was given his professional debut by coach Johan Cruyff in 1986. Bergkamp became a regular for Ajax, winning the Dutch league in 1990. From 1991 to 1993 he was top scorer in the Eredivisie, eventually scoring 122 goals in 239 games for his hometown club. In 1993, Bergkamp signed for Inter Milan but found it hard to adapt to the Italian defensive style of play, scoring just 11 times in 50 appearances. Two years later, he joined Arsenal and became a major contributor to the club's success. He hit his best form in 1998, top scoring with 22 goals as the Gunners won the Double. He retired in 2006 having scored 120 goals in 423 appearances.

HONOURS WON

With Ajax
- 🏆 European Cup-Winners' Cup 1987
- 🏆 KNVB Beker (Dutch FA Cup) 1987, 1993
- 🏆 Eredivisie 1990
- 🏆 UEFA Cup 1992

With Inter Milan
- 🏆 UEFA Cup 1994

With Arsenal
- 🏆 Premiership 1998, 2002, 2004
- 🏆 FA Cup 1998, 2002, 2003, 2005

Other Awards
- ★ Dutch Player of the Year 1991, 1992
- ★ PFA Footballer of the Year 1998
- ★ Football Writers' Association Player of the Year 1998

32 Frank Rijkaard

Born
Amsterdam
30 September 1962

Country
Holland

Position
Midfielder/Defender

Clubs
DWS Amsterdam
Ajax
Sporting Lisbon
Real Zaragoza
AC Milan

International	
Caps	Goals
73	10

Frank Rijkaard made his debut for Ajax in 1980 aged 17 and played a big part in the club's dominance of Dutch domestic football during the next eight years. After a season with Real Zaragoza in 1988 he moved to AC Milan where he transferred from being a central defender to a holding midfielder. A glittering four years at the San Siro saw him winning the European Cup and Serie A twice among other silverware. He returned to Ajax in 1993 to win two further Dutch Championships and the Champions League. He played for Holland 73 times, scoring 10 goals, teaming up many times with Ruud Gullit and Marco van Basten, and playing a key role in Holland's triumph in the 1988 European Championships. He also played in two World Cups and will be remembered by many for his spat with Rudi Voller. Since 2003 he has been the manager of FC Barcelona.

HONOURS WON

With Holland
♆ European Championships 1988

With Ajax
♆ Eredivisie 1982, 1983, 1985, 1994, 1995
♆ KNVB Beker (Dutch FA Cup) 1983, 1986, 1987
♆ European Cup-Winners' Cup 1987
♆ European Super Cup 1995
♆ Intercontinental Cup 1995
♆ Champions League 1995

With AC Milan
♆ European Cup 1989, 1990
♆ European Super Cup 1989, 1990
♆ Intercontinental Cup 1989, 1990
♆ Supercoppa Italiana 1992, 1993
♆ Serie A 1992, 1993

Other Awards
★ Italy's Player of the Year 1992

45

INTERNATIONAL

33 Thierry Henry

Born	
Les Ulis, Paris	
17 August 1977	
Country	
France	
Position	
Forward	
Clubs	
AS Monaco	
Juventus	
Arsenal	
Barcelona	
International	
Caps	**Goals**
92	40

Thierry Henry is a striker blessed with extreme pace and the ability to take the ball past players and find the opposition net with regularity. He signed with AS Monaco in 1990 and made his debut four years later. His good club form for the Principality earned him an international call-up and a big money move to Italian giants Juventus in 1998. But after a disappointing season playing on the wing in Turin, Arsenal's French manager Arsene Wenger persuaded him to move to London and play as a striker. Initially, he struggled in England, but gradually emerged as one of the finest players the Premiership has ever seen. Arsenal's top goalscorer in almost every season he is the club's all-time leading scorer with 226 goals. With Arsenal, Henry won two league titles and three FA Cups. He was also twice nominated for the FIFA World Player of the Year. Henry spent his final two seasons with Arsenal as club captain, leading them to the Champions League final in 2006. After eight years in an Arsenal shirt, he moved to Barcelona in the summer of 2007 for a fee of £16.1 million. With the French team Henry won the 1998 World Cup and Euro 2000. After disappointing at the World Cup in 2002 and Euro 2004, Henry bounced back as part of the French team that lost to Italy in the 2006 World Cup final in Germany.

HONOURS WON

With France
🏆 World Cup 1998
🏆 European Championships 2000
🏆 Confederations Cup 2001, 2003
With AS Monaco
🏆 Championnat 1997
With Arsenal
🏆 Premiership 2002, 2004
🏆 FA Cup 2002, 2003, 2005

Other Awards
★ Chevalier of the Legion d'Honneur 1998
★ France's Footballer of the Year 2000, 2003
★ Football Writers' Association Player of the Year 2003, 2004
★ PFA Player of the Year 2003, 2004

34 Pavel Nedved

Born
Cheb
30 August 1972

Country
Czech Republic

Position
Midfielder

Clubs
Dukla Prague
Sparta Prague
Lazio
Juventus

International	
Caps	Goals
91	18

Pavel Nedved began his club career with Dukla Prague before moving across town to Sparta Prague in 1992. Following his performances at Euro 96, he signed for Italian club Lazio in 1996 with whom he had considerable success, winning the Coppa Italia in 1998, the last European Cup-Winners' Cup in 1999 and Serie A in 2000. The following year he moved to Juventus as a replacement for Zinedine Zidane. His tremendous work rate and his ability to play the ball equally well off either foot were an integral part in Juventus' Serie A-winning teams of 2002, 2003, 2005 and 2006 (though they were stripped of two of the titles following a match-fixing scandal in 2006). He also helped them into the Champions League final in 2003 against AC Milan, but was forced to sit out the match because of suspension. At the end of the year he was voted European Footballer of the Year. Nedved scored 18 goals in 91 games for the Czechs and played for his country at Euro 96, Euro 2000, and Euro 2004. He came out of international retirement to play in the 2006 World Cup qualifiers which saw the Czech Republic win through to the finals. The 2006 World Cup was their first appearance since the partition of Czechoslovakia. Nedved retired from international football at the end of the tournament.

HONOURS WON

With Sparta Prague
🏆 1.liga 1993
🏆 1.liga CR 1994, 1995
🏆 Pohar CMFS (Czech Republic FA Cup) 1996

With Lazio
🏆 Coppa Italia 1998, 2000
🏆 Supercoppa Italiana 1998, 2000
🏆 European Cup-Winners' Cup 1999

🏆 European Super Cup 1999
🏆 Serie A 2000

With Juventus
🏆 Serie A 2002, 2003, 2005**, 2006**

Other Awards
★ European Footballer of the Year ('Ballon d'Or') 2003

** *Juventus were stripped of these titles following allegations of match-fixing*

35 Gheorghe Hagi

Born
Saucele
5 February 1965
Country
Romania
Position
Midfielder
Clubs
FC Constanta
Sportul Studentesc
Steaua Bucharest
Real Madrid
Brescia
Barcelona
Galatasaray

International	
Caps	**Goals**
125	35

Gheorghe Hagi played for Romania in three World Cups, 1990, 1994 and 1998, and three European Championships, 1984, 1996 and 2000. He won 125 caps and scored 35 goals in a superb international career. Hagi first came to international recognition playing for Steaua Bucharest, turning out 97 times and scoring 76 goals while winning the league and cup Double three years in succession in the late 1980s. After the 1990 World Cup, he signed for Real Madrid before being sold to Brescia in Italy. After a short spell he returned to Spain to play for Barcelona but was largely unsuccessful during his time there. However, in 1996 he moved to Galatasaray where he was both successful and highly popular among the Turkish supporters as the club won four league titles, two domestic cups, the UEFA Cup, and the European Super Cup in four seasons. But the crowning moment of his career came on the international stage when Hagi led the Romanian team to its best ever performance at the 1994 World Cup when they reached the quarter-finals, eventually losing to Sweden on penalties. He has since taken up a career as a coach in Turkey and Romania.

HONOURS WON

With Steaua Bucharest
- 🏆 Divizia A 1987, 1988, 1989
- 🏆 Romanian Cup 1987, 1988, 1989

With Galatasaray
- 🏆 Birinci Lig (Turkish league) 1997, 1998, 1999, 2000
- 🏆 Turkish Cup 1999, 2000
- 🏆 European Super Cup 2000
- 🏆 UEFA Cup 2000

Other Awards
- ★ Romanian Player of the Year 1985, 1987, 1993, 1994, 1997, 1999, 2000

36 Peter Schmeichel

Born
Gladsaxe
18 November 1963

Country
Denmark

Position
Goalkeeper

Clubs
Hvidovre
Brondby
Manchester United
Sporting Lisbon
Aston Villa
Manchester City

International	
Caps	Goals
129	1

Peter Schmeichel was widely regarded as the best goalkeeper in the world. At 6 ft 4 in and in an XXL shirt, Schmeichel was an immense physical presence in goal, making the space between the posts seem small to the onrushing striker. His most successful years were spent at Manchester United, with whom he collected a host of silverware including the league, cup and Champions League treble in 1999. In his second season at Old Trafford, 1992–93, he kept 22 clean sheets to help United win the championship for the first time in 26 years and kick-start a new golden era for the club. He holds the record for the greatest games-to-clean sheets ratio in the Premiership, with 42 per cent of the games he started ending without his team conceding. Schmeichel also scored 11 goals during his career, a tremendous record for a goalkeeper. He is Denmark's most capped player, with 129 games and one goal to his name between 1987 and 2001. Apart from Euro 92, where he was a key part of the defensive strategy that enabled the Danes to win the championship in neighbouring Sweden, he also played in the 1998 World Cup and three additional European Championships tournaments. He captained the national team in 30 matches.

HONOURS WON

With Denmark
🏆 European Championships 1992

With Brondby
🏆 Danmarksturneringen (Danish League) 1987, 1988, 1990, 1991
🏆 Landspokalturneringen (Danish FA Cup) 1989

With Manchester United
🏆 League Cup 1992
🏆 Premiership 1993, 1994, 1996, 1997, 1999

🏆 FA Cup 1994, 1996, 1999
🏆 Champions League 1999
🏆 Intercontinental Cup 1999

With Sporting Lisbon
🏆 Campeonato da Primeira Divisao 2000

Other Awards
★ Denmark's Player of the Year 1990
★ UEFA Goalkeeper of the Year 1998
★ MBE 2000

37 Andriy Shevchenko

Born	
Kiev	
29 September 1976	
Country	
Ukraine	
Position	
Forward	
Clubs	
Dynamo Kiev	
AC Milan	
Chelsea	
International	
Caps	Goals
73	33

Andriy Shevchenko began his career at Dynamo Kiev with whom he won five consecutive domestic league titles between 1995 and 1999. He then joined AC Milan for whom he scored 127 goals in 208 appearances – making him the club's second highest all-time goalscorer – in seven years. This was a period in which the Rossoneri were one of the most successful teams in Europe, his goals making the difference between Milan and their rivals. He played in three Champions League finals with Milan, winning the tournament in 2003, and won the Scudetto the following year. In 2006 he moved to London and joined Chelsea. He won the 2004 European Footballer of the Year award, was named a starting striker on the 2005 FIFPro World XI team, and is the second-highest goalscorer of all time in European club competitions with 59 goals, second only to Gerd Muller. Shevchenko has won 73 caps and scored 33 international goals, and has played at one World Cup finals tournament, in Germany in 2006.

HONOURS WON

With Dynamo Kiev

🏆 Ukrainian Championship 1995, 1996, 1997, 1998, 1999

🏆 Ukrainian Cup 1996, 1998, 1999, 2000

With AC Milan

🏆 Champions League 2003

🏆 European Super Cup 2003

🏆 Coppa Italia 2003

🏆 Serie A 2004

With Chelsea

🏆 FA Cup 2007

Other Awards

★ Ukrainian Player of the Year 1997, 1999, 2000, 2001

★ UEFA Award for Best Forward 1999

★ European Footballer of the Year ('Ballon d'Or') 2004

38 Josef 'Sepp' Maier

Born	
Metten	
28 February 1944	
Country	
West Germany	
Position	
Goalkeeper	
Clubs	
TSV Haar	
Bayern Munich	
International	
Caps	**Goals**
95	0

Josef-Dieter 'Sepp' Maier was the rock between the posts of the Bayern Munich goal for 19 seasons, making almost 400 consecutive appearances between 1966 and 1977. Wearing his trademark long black shorts he was a crowd favourite, often making impossible saves. Although only a substitute in the 1966 World Cup, he had established himself as Germany's Number 1 by 1970 when West Germany reached the semi-finals. Two years later he was in the team that won the European Championships in Belgium. The summer of 1974 was the highlight of his career. West Germany hosted and won the World Cup, beating Holland in a tight final in which he was outstanding. He kept a clean sheet in four of his country's seven matches en route to the final. It was a period of dominance for West German football at club level too as Bayern Munich won the European Cup three times and the Intercontinental Cup against Brazilian club Cruzeiro in 1976. A car accident in 1979 ended his career at the age of 35, having won almost a century of caps for his country and 15 major trophies for club and country.

HONOURS WON

With West Germany
- 🏆 European Championships 1972
- 🏆 World Cup 1974

With Bayern Munich
- 🏆 DFB Pokal (German FA Cup) 1966, 1967, 1969, 1971
- 🏆 European Cup-Winners' Cup 1967
- 🏆 Bundesliga 1969, 1972, 1973, 1974
- 🏆 European Cup 1974, 1975, 1976
- 🏆 Intercontinental Cup 1976

Other Awards
- ★ Germany's Player of the Year 1975, 1977, 1978

39 Didier Deschamps

Born
Bayonne
15 October 1968
Country
France
Position
Midfielder
Clubs

FC Nantes Atlantique
Olympique Marseille
Girondins de Bordeaux
Juventus
Chelsea
Valencia

International	
Caps	**Goals**
102	4

Didier Deschamps captained France to victory in both the 1998 World Cup and Euro 2000, playing his part in what has become known as the 'Golden Generation' in France. He first captained France in 1996 in a friendly against Germany during the warm-up for Euro 96. During the tournament, held in England, he led them all the way to the semi-finals, their best finish in an international tournament since the 1986 World Cup. If not the most spectacular of players, he was a master at controlling the match from deep midfield. He was a well-travelled club player, winning the Champions League with Marseille in 1993 (though they were later stripped of the title following allegations of match-fixing) before winning three Serie A titles, and the Champions League in 1996 with Juventus. He spent one season with Chelsea before finishing his playing career with Valencia, winning La Liga in 2001. After retiring from playing he has had success as a coach with both Monaco and Juventus.

HONOURS WON

With France
🏆 World Cup 1998
🏆 European Championships 2000
With Olympique Marseille
🏆 Championnat 1990, 1992, 1993**
🏆 Champions League 1993**
With Juventus
🏆 Coppa Italia 1995
🏆 Supercoppa Italiana 1995, 1997
🏆 Serie A 1995, 1997, 1998
🏆 Champions League 1996
🏆 European Super Cup 1996
🏆 Intercontinental Cup 1996

With Chelsea
🏆 FA Cup 2000
With Valencia
🏆 Primera Liga 2001
Other Awards
★ *France Football*'s French Player of the Year 1996
★ Chevalier of the Legion d'Honneur 1998

*** Marseille were stripped of these titles following allegations of match-fixing*

40 | Lilian Thuram

Born
Pointe-a-Pitre Guadaloupe 1 January 1972
Country
France
Position
Defender
Clubs
AS Monaco Parma Juventus Barcelona

International	
Caps	**Goals**
132	2

Lilian Thuram began his career in 1990 with AS Monaco, and by 1994 was an important member of the French national team as an attacking right back. His first major tournament was Euro 96 during which a talented French team reached the semi-finals. This experience served them well as they went on to win the World Cup in France two years later and the European Championships in 2000. He played at the 2002 World Cup and Euro 2004 before hanging up his international boots. However, together with Zinedine Zidane and Claude Makelele, Thuram came out of retirement to help France qualify for the 2006 World Cup, a tournament in which they lost in the final. A consummate full back, fast, tough tackling and good in the air, he has played more than 130 times for his country, making him the most capped French player. In 1996 Thuram left Monaco for Parma, and moved on to Juventus in 2001. He won a host of honours with the Turin team, including four league titles in five years. Following the Juventus match-fixing scandal, which stripped the club of its two most recent titles, he moved to Barcelona in 2006. He has been very active throughout his career in the campaign against racism and has been employed by the French government to help overcome racial unrest in the Paris suburbs in recent years.

HONOURS WON

With France
🏆 World Cup 1998
🏆 European Championships 2000
🏆 Confederations Cup 2003

With Parma
🏆 UEFA Cup 1999
🏆 Coppa Italia 1999

With Juventus
🏆 Serie A 2002, 2003, 2005**, 2006**
🏆 Supercoppa Italiana 2002, 2003

With Barcelona
🏆 Spanish Supercopa 2007

Other Awards
★ French Player of the Year 1997
★ Chevalier of the Legion d'Honneur 1998

** Juventus were stripped of these titles following allegations of match-fixing

41 Enzo Francescoli

Enzo Francescoli Uriarte

Born	
Montevideo 12 November 1962	
Country	
Uruguay	
Position	
Midfielder	
Clubs	
Wanderers River Plate Racing Club de Paris Olympique Marseille Cagliari Torino	
International	
Caps	Goals
73	17

Enzo Francescoli was a graceful Uruguay midfielder whose dynamic approach and goalscoring abilities drove Uruguay to victories in the Copa America in 1983, 1987 and 1995. Nicknamed 'The Prince' he played in the 1986 and 1990 World Cups for Uruguay. In 1984 he was voted South American player of the Year. He made his club debut with Wanderers from Montevideo before playing for several years with River Plate in Argentina. He top scored in the Argentine league in 1985, 1986, 1994 and 1996. In between those years he played in Europe with French clubs Racing Club de Paris, Olympique Marseille, and with Cagliari and Torino in Italy.

HONOURS WON

With Uruguay
🏆 Copa America 1983, 1987, 1995
With River Plate
🏆 Intercontinental Cup 1986
🏆 Copa Libertadores 1986, 1997
🏆 Apertura (championship) 1995, 1997, 1998
🏆 Clausura (championship) 1997
With Olympique Marseille
🏆 Championnat 1990

Other Awards
★ Best Player of Copa America 1983, 1995
★ *El Mundo*'s South American Player of the Year 1984
★ Argentinian Player of the Year ('Olimpia de Plata') 1985, 1995
★ *El Pais*' South American Player of the Year 1995

42 Hakan Sukur

Born
Adapazari 1 September 1971

Country
Turkey

Position
Forward

Clubs
Sakarya Bursaspor Galatasaray Torino Inter Milan Parma Blackburn Rovers

International	
Caps	**Goals**
109	51

Born in Turkey to Albanian parents, Hakan Sukur is so famous and loved in Turkey that his wedding was televised live. A member of the UEFA Cup-winning Galatasaray side of 2000, he is most fondly remembered by supporters for his spectacular goals in European competition that year – he top scored with six goals on the way to the final against Arsenal. He spent eight years with Galatasaray in the 1990s. In 2000, he moved to Inter Milan then played briefly at Parma and Blackburn Rovers before rejoining Galatasaray in 2003. He has scored more goals in Turkish top-flight football than any other player. In the 2002 World Cup, Turkey went all the way to the semi-finals. In the third place play-off against South Korea, he scored the fastest goal ever in a World Cup finals match after only 10.8 seconds. He was capped for the 100th time in a 2006 World Cup qualifier against Ukraine, becoming the third Turkish player to reach this landmark.

55

HONOURS WON

With Galatasaray

🏆 Turkish League 1993, 1994, 1997, 1998, 1999, 2000, 2006

🏆 Turkish Cup 1993, 1996, 1999, 2000

🏆 President's Cup 1993, 1997

🏆 UEFA Cup 2000

🏆 European Super Cup 2000

INTERNATIONAL

43 Paolo Rossi

Born	
Prato, nr Florence 23 September 1956	
Country	
Italy	
Position	
Forward	
Clubs	
Como Vicenza Perugia Juventus AC Milan Hellas Verona	
International	
Caps	**Goals**
48	20

Paolo Rossi's finest moment came in 1982 when his goals propelled Italy to World Cup victory, scoring six times in the tournament and also winning the Golden Boot and the Golden Ball. He remains the only player to have won all three honours at a single tournament. Rossi scored a hat-trick against the imperious Brazilians to see Italy through to the semi-finals. In all he scored 20 goals in 48 appearances for Italy. His career had been shrouded in controversy, having served a two-year ban for a betting scandal while on loan to Perugia in 1980, though he has always maintained his innocence. At club level he was most successful at Juventus with whom he won the Scudetto twice, the Cup-Winners' Cup in 1984 and the European Cup the following year. He retired in 1985 after a season with Hellas Verona.

HONOURS WON

With Italy
🏆 World Cup 1982

With Juventus
🏆 Serie A 1982, 1984
🏆 Coppa Italia 1983
🏆 European Cup-Winners' Cup 1984
🏆 European Super Cup 1984
🏆 European Cup 1985

Other Awards
★ World Cup 'Silver Ball' 1978
★ World Cup 'Golden Ball' 1982
★ World Cup 'Golden Boot' 1982
★ European Footballer of the Year ('Ballon d'Or') 1982
★ *World Soccer*'s Player of the Year 1982

44 David Beckham

Born
Leytonstone, London 2 May 1975
Country
England
Position
Midfielder
Clubs
Manchester United Preston North End Real Madrid LA Galaxy
International

Caps	Goals
96	17

David Beckham's club career began with Manchester United, making his first-team debut in 1992 aged 17. During his time at Old Trafford, United won the Premiership title six times, the FA Cup twice, and the Champions League in 1999 as part of a league and two-cup treble. He left Manchester United in 2003 to sign for Real Madrid, where he remained for four seasons winning La Liga in his last year. He has subsequently moved to LA Galaxy. Beckham has had an international career of fantastic highs and lows; from his sending-off against Argentina in 1998, to his last-minute 2002 World Cup qualifying goal from a free kick against Greece, he has always been at the centre of intense emotions and moments. Noted for his whipped-in dead ball kicks and crosses, he has always had a habit of coming up with the perfect playing response in all kinds of adversity. He captained England for 58 of his 96 appearances, resigning the captaincy at the end of the 2006 World Cup finals.

HONOURS WON

With Manchester United
- 🏆 Premiership 1996, 1997, 1999, 2000, 2001, 2003
- 🏆 FA Cup 1996, 1999
- 🏆 European Champions Cup 1999
- 🏆 Intercontinental Cup 1999

With Real Madrid
- 🏆 Primera Liga 2007

Other Awards
- ★ UEFA Best Midfielder 1999
- ★ UEFA Most Valuable Player 1999
- ★ OBE 2003

45 Jean-Pierre Papin

Born
Boulogne-sur-Mer 5 November 1963

Country
France

Position
Forward

Clubs
Valenciennes INF Vichy Club Bruges Olympique Marseille AC Milan Bayern Munich Girondins de Bordeaux Guingamp

International	
Caps	Goals
54	30

Jean-Pierre Papin was France's top striker during a time when they were serious underachievers. He scored 30 goals in 54 appearances for the national team with their biggest achievement at the World Cup in Mexico in 1986, when they finished third. At club level he was successful at Marseille, with whom he won the championship four times, also winning the Ballon d'Or in 1991 – becoming the only player to win it while playing in the French league. During his five years at Marseille he scored 157 goals in 254 matches. In 1993, as one of Europe's hottest properties, he moved to AC Milan with whom he won two championships and a European Cup winner's medal. His final silverware came at Bayern Munich with whom he won the UEFA Cup in 1996. Since his retirement Papin has pursued a career in management and in 2007 he guided Strasbourg back to Ligue 1 with a third-placed finish.

HONOURS WON

With France

🏆 Kirin Cup 1994

With Club Bruges

🏆 Belgian Cup 1986

With Olympique Marseille

🏆 Championnat 1989, 1990, 1991, 1992

🏆 Coupe de France 1989

With AC Milan

🏆 Supercoppa Italiana 1992, 1993, 1994

🏆 Serie A 1993, 1994

🏆 European Cup 1994

🏆 European Super Cup 1994

With Bayern Munich

🏆 UEFA Cup 1996

Other Awards

★ *France Football*'s French Player of the Year 1989, 1991

★ European Footballer of the Year ('Ballon d'Or') 1991

★ *World Soccer*'s Player of the Year 1991

46 Kevin Keegan

Born	
Armthorpe 14 February 1951	
Country	
England	
Position	
Forward	
Clubs	
Scunthorpe United Liverpool Hamburg Southampton Newcastle United	
International	
Caps	**Goals**
63	21

Kevin Keegan won his first domestic honours in 1973 when he and John Toshack formed a prolific goalscoring partnership that helped Liverpool win their first league championship in seven years as well as the UEFA Cup. After 323 appearances, a collection of domestic and international trophies, and exactly 100 goals, Keegan left Liverpool for Hamburg in 1977. His last game for the Merseyside club was the 3–1 European Cup final win against Borussia Monchengladbach. Two seasons later Hamburg won the Bundesliga title for the first time in its history with Keegan's unflinching commitment proving decisive. He was named European Footballer of the Year in 1978 and 1979, and played for Hamburg in the 1980 European Cup final, losing to Nottingham Forest. In 1980 Keegan was persuaded to return to England, joining Southampton for two seasons before going north to Newcastle and becoming a fans' favourite on Tyneside. He won 63 England caps, 31 as captain including during the 1980 European Championships, and scored 21 goals. He finally reached a World Cup when England got to the 1982 finals in Spain, but a back injury restricted him to just one appearance as a substitute. As a manager Keegan created one of the most exciting teams ever to grace the Premiership at Newcastle who finished second in 1996. He later managed Fulham, England and Manchester City.

HONOURS WON

With Liverpool

- 🏆 UEFA Cup 1973, 1976
- 🏆 Football League 1973, 1976, 1977
- 🏆 FA Cup 1974
- 🏆 European Cup 1977
- 🏆 European Super Cup 1977

With Hamburg

- 🏆 Bundesliga 1979
- 🏆 DFB Pokal (German FA Cup) 1979

Other Awards

- ★ Football Writers' Association Player of the Year 1976
- ★ European Footballer of the Year ('Ballon d'Or') 1978, 1979
- ★ OBE 1982

47 Marcel Desailly

Born
Accra, Ghana
7 September 1968

Country
France

Position
Defender/Midfielder

Clubs
FC Nantes-Atlantique
Olympique Marseille
AC Milan
Chelsea
Al-Gharafa
Qatar SC

International	
Caps	Goals
116	3

Solid central defender Marcel Desailly was another vital member of the French team that won the 1998 World Cup and Euro 2000. In 2001 Desailly was handed the captaincy of the national team and led France to victory in that summer's Confederations Cup. His club career began at Nantes, where he turned professional in 1986. In 1992 he moved to Olympique Marseille, and won the Champions League the following year beating Milan in the final (though the club was later stripped of the title). The next season he moved to Milan and won the Champions League again, making him the first player to win the tournament in consecutive seasons with different clubs. He was hugely successful at Milan, earning praise for his consistency and skilful but fair tackling, adding two Italian league titles, in 1994 and 1996, to his European success. Desailly's next move was to Chelsea in 1998, where he played centre-back until the end of the 2003–04 season. After Euro 2004, he retired from international football having played 116 times for France, a record subsequently passed by his team-mate Lilian Thuram. He then moved to Qatar to play out the last two seasons of his illustrious career.

HONOURS WON

With France
🏆 World Cup 1998
🏆 European Championships 2000
🏆 Confederations Cup 2001, 2003
With Olympique Marseille
🏆 Champions League 1993**
With AC Milan
🏆 Champions League 1994
🏆 Serie A 1994, 1996

With Chelsea
🏆 FA Cup 2000
With Al-Gharafa
🏆 Qatar League 2005
Other Awards
★ Chevalier of the Legion d'Honneur 1998

*** Marseille were stripped of this title following allegations of match-fixing*

48 Oliver Kahn

Born
Karlsruhe
15 June 1969
Country
Germany
Position
Goalkeeper
Clubs
Karlsruher SC
Bayern Munich
International

Caps	Goals
85	0

Big, volatile, headline grabbing, and when on-form, one of the finest goalkeepers in the world, Oliver Kahn was Germany's regular number 1 from 1995 to 2006. He joined Bayern Munich from Karlsruher in 1994 and played a huge part in their success, collecting seven Bundesliga titles and five German Cups in 13 years. He captained the team that made it to the Champions League final in 1999 only to be beaten by two injury-time goals by Manchester United. He was named Man of the Match two years later when Bayern won the competition, making several crucial saves in the penalty shootout against Valencia. He is the all-time clean-sheet record holder in the history of the Bundesliga with 185, and made his 500th Bundesliga appearance in April 2007. Kahn was the reserve keeper as Germany were victorious in Euro 96 in England. He also spent the 1998 World Cup on the bench, but made up for it in 2002 where his shot-stopping prowess and leadership carried the team to a surprise appearance in the final, letting in only three goals in the course of the competition. Kahn retired from international football after the World Cup in 2006 having played 85 times for Germany, 49 as captain.

HONOURS WON

With Bayern Munich

🏆 UEFA Cup 1996

🏆 Bundesliga 1997, 1999, 2000, 2001, 2003, 2005, 2006

🏆 DFB Pokal (German FA Cup) 1998, 2000, 2003, 2005, 2006

🏆 Champions League 2001

🏆 Intercontinental Cup 2001

Other Awards

★ UEFA Award for Best Goalkeeper 1999, 2000, 2001, 2002

★ Germany's Player of the Year 2000, 2001

★ World Cup 'Lev Yashin' Award 2002

★ World Cup 'Golden Ball' 2002

49 | Alessandro Costacurta

Born
Orago, Varese 24 April 1966

Country
Italy

Position
Defender

Clubs
AC Milan Monza (loan)

International	
Caps	Goals
59	2

Solid and dependable defender Alessandro Costacurta was a mainstay in the Italian national team throughout the 1990s. He played in the 1994 and 1998 World Cups, as well as Euro 96. He retired from international duty in 1998 with 59 caps. In 1994, he missed both the World Cup final (lost by Italy) and the Champions League final (won by Milan) through suspension. His club career was spent almost entirely at Milan (1985–2007) winning the Scudetto seven times, and the European Cup/Champions League five times. At the end of a long career – he played 458 times for his club – he became the oldest player ever to appear in the Champions League aged 41 years and 211 days. He has now taken on a coaching role as Carlo Ancelotti's assistant at AC Milan.

HONOURS WON

With AC Milan
♔ Serie A 1988, 1992, 1993, 1994, 1996, 1999, 2004
♔ European Cup/Champions League 1989, 1990, 1994, 2003, 2007

50 Clarence Seedorf

Born
Paramaribo, Surinam 1 April 1976

Country
Holland

Position
Midfielder

Clubs
Ajax Sampdoria Real Madrid Inter Milan AC Milan

International	
Caps	Goals
81	11

Clarence Seedorf was the first, and to date the only person to have won the European Cup/Champions League with three different clubs: Ajax in 1995, Real Madrid in 1998, and AC Milan in 2003 and 2007. He has also won four league championships, two with Ajax, one with Real Madrid and one with AC Milan. An industrious midfielder who scores the occasional spectacular goal, he has also played for other top European clubs in Sampdoria and Inter Milan. He has won 81 caps, competing at Euro 96, the 1998 World Cup, Euro 2000 and Euro 2004. He was not selected for the 2006 World Cup but was recalled to the Dutch team for two of the Euro 2008 qualifiers.

HONOURS WON

With Ajax

🏆 KNVB Beker (Dutch FA Cup) 1993
🏆 Nationale Supercup 1993, 1994
🏆 Eredivisie 1994, 1995
🏆 European Cup 1995

With Real Madrid

🏆 Primera Liga 1997
🏆 Supercopa 1997
🏆 European Cup 1998
🏆 Intercontinental Cup 1998

With AC Milan

🏆 Champions League 2003, 2007
🏆 Coppa Italia 2003
🏆 Serie A 2004
🏆 Supercoppa Italiana 2005

51 Dino Zoff

Born
Mariano del Friuli 28 February 1942
Country
Italy
Position
Goalkeeper
Clubs
Udinese Mantova Napoli Juventus

International	
Caps	**Goals**
112	0

Italy's legendary goalkeeper, Dino Zoff is the oldest player to have won the World Cup, aged 40, in 1982. He also holds the tournament's clean-sheet record, not conceding a goal from September 1972 to June 1974 (1142 minutes), finally conceding a goal in the first group match against Haiti in the 1974 tournament in Germany. Zoff played most of his club career at Napoli and Juventus, though his greatest success came in Turin where he won six league championships and the UEFA Cup in 1977. On the international stage, he earned a winner's medal at the 1968 European Championships in Italy, but was dropped for the Mexico World Cup two years later. He was back for the 1978 tournament for which Italy were among the favourites. Despite beating hosts and eventual winners Argentina in the group stage, they were eventually knocked out by Holland. But 1982 was to be Zoff's year. A brilliant campaign saw them beat Argentina and Brazil in the second round to set up a final against West Germany. A 3–1 victory gave Italy their third World Cup triumph. Zoff eventually retired in 1983 with 112 caps to his name. He has since pursued a successful career as a coach for several top clubs and the national team.

HONOURS WON

With Italy
🏆 European Championships 1968
🏆 World Cup 1982
With Juventus
🏆 Serie A 1973, 1975, 1977, 1978, 1981, 1982
🏆 UEFA Cup 1977
🏆 Coppa Italia 1979, 1983

Other Awards
★ FIFA Order of Merit 1984

52 Patrick Kluivert

Born
Amsterdam
1 July 1976

Country
Holland

Position
Forward

Clubs
Ajax
AC Milan
Barcelona
Newcastle United
Valencia
PSV Eindhoven
Lille

International	
Caps	Goals
79	40

A deadly striker, Patrick Kluivert scored on his professional debut for Ajax at the age of 18 in the 1994 Dutch Supercup against arch-rivals Feyenoord. Later that same season he came off the bench to score an 85th-minute winner in the 1995 Champions League final against AC Milan. Ajax had a new superstar, but not for long. After two years he moved to Milan in 1997, and then to Barcelona in 1998 where he immediately got a league championship winner's medal under his belt. He left the Nou Camp in 2004 and has since played at Newcastle, Valencia and PSV Eindhoven. At international level, Kluivert earned 79 caps, playing in the 1998 World Cup and Euro 2000, and remains Holland's all-time leading scorer with 40 goals. He currently plays in France with Lille.

HONOURS WON

With Ajax
♛ Nationale Supercup 1994, 1995
♛ Champions League 1995
♛ European Super Cup 1995
♛ Eredivisie 1995, 1996
♛ Intercontinental Cup 1995

With AC Milan
♛ European Super Cup 1998
With Barcelona
♛ Primera Liga 1999
♛ Copa del Rey 1999

53 | Jari Litmanen

Born
Lahti
20 February 1971

Country
Finland

Position
Midfielder

Clubs
HJK Helsinki
MyPa
Ajax
Barcelona
Liverpool
FC Lahti
Hansa Rostock
Malmo FF

International	
Caps	Goals
108	28

Jari Litmanen is Finland's greatest ever footballer. He has captained his country since 1996, playing more than 100 times and scoring 28 goals, making him the most-capped player and top scorer. At club level, he left Finland in 1992 and joined Ajax. He came to prominence two years later as top scorer with 26 goals as Ajax won the Dutch league title. He was one of the star players of Louis van Gaal's side that dominated Dutch football in the 1990s and reached the Champions League final two years in a row. They won the cup in 1995 and in 1996 Litmanen was the competition's top scorer with nine goals, including the equaliser in the final against Juventus, which Ajax lost 4–2 on penalties. He won four Dutch championships and three Dutch Cups at Ajax and remains the club's top scorer in European competition with 24 goals in 44 matches. In 1999 Litmanen joined Barcelona before moving to Liverpool in 2001, but injuries limited his appearances at both clubs. He is now playing in Sweden with Malmo FF, but in his native Finland he is regarded as a national institution.

HONOURS WON

With MyPa
🏆 Finnish Cup 1992

With Ajax
🏆 Eredivisie 1994, 1995, 1996, 1998
🏆 KNVB Beker (Dutch FA Cup) 1993, 1998, 1999
🏆 Nationale Supercup 1993, 1994, 1995
🏆 Champions League 1995
🏆 European Super Cup 1995
🏆 Intercontinental Cup 1995

With Liverpool
🏆 UEFA Cup 2001
🏆 European Super Cup 2001

Other Awards
★ Finnish Player of the Year 1990, 1992, 1993, 1994, 1995, 1996, 1997, 1998, 2000
★ Dutch Player of the Year 1993

54 Daniel Passarella

Born
Chacabuco
25 May 1953
Country
Argentina
Position
Defender
Clubs
River Plate
Fiorentina
Inter Milan

International	
Caps	**Goals**
70	22

Daniel Passarella was one of the most commanding sweepers/defenders in World Cup history. He was the perfect leader for any team, passionate but always calm and well organised, and became captain for both club and country at an early age. He played most of his club career at River Plate in Buenos Aires where he won several league championships. But the highlight of his career was undoubtedly the World Cup finals of 1978 in Argentina where he captained the host nation to victory, at the age of 25. Despite being a defender he had an impressive scoring record with 99 goals in 298 games in the Argentinian league. In 1982 he moved to Italy to play for Fiorentina and Inter Milan and the goals kept coming: for a while he held the all-time record for a goalscoring defender netting 134 goals in 431 matches. He retired from international football in 1986 having made 70 appearances and scored 22 goals. He returned to River Plate for two more years before retiring. He soon took up management and led Argentina at the 1994 and 1998 World Cups also taking the hot seat for Uruguay and a host of top clubs.

HONOURS WON

With Argentina
🏆 World Cup winner 1978
With River Plate
🏆 Metropolitan League 1975, 1977, 1979, 1980
🏆 National League 1975, 1979, 1981

Other Awards
★ Argentinian Player of the Year ('Olimpia de Plata') 1976

INTERNATIONAL

55 Bixente Lizarazu

Born
Saint-Jean-De-Luz 9 December 1969
Country
France
Position
Defender
Clubs
Girondins de Bordeaux Athletic Bilbao Bayern Munich Olympique Marseille

International	
Caps	Goals
97	2

A skilful and resolute left back, but equally at home bombing down the wing, Bixente Lizarazu was capped 97 times for France, helping them to win the 1998 World Cup and Euro 2000. At club level, he was most successful at Bayern Munich, where in two spells he won six Bundesliga titles, as well as five German Cups, the Champions League and the Intercontinental Cup. Lizarazu also played for Girondins de Bordeaux, for whom he played in the 1996 UEFA Cup final against Bayern, and Athletic Bilbao, where he was the club's first non-Spanish player since the First World War. He also spent a short time at Olympique Marseille in 2004–05 before returning to Bayern. He retired from football in 2006.

HONOURS WON

With France

🏆 World Cup 1998

🏆 European Championships 2000

🏆 Confederations Cup 2001, 2003

With Bayern Munich

🏆 DFB Pokal (German FA Cup) 1998, 2000, 2003, 2005, 2006

🏆 Bundesliga 1999, 2000, 2001, 2003, 2005, 2006

🏆 Champions League 2001

🏆 Intercontinental Cup 2001

Other Awards

★ Chevalier of the Legion d'Honneur 1998

56   Gary Lineker

Born	
Leicester	
30 November 1960	
Country	
England	
Position	
Forward	
Clubs	
Leicester City	
Everton	
Barcelona	
Tottenham Hotspur	
Nagoya Grampus Eight	
International	
Caps	**Goals**
80	48

A born goalscorer in the Gerd Muller mould, Gary Lineker started his career at Leicester City, scoring nearly 100 goals in less than 200 appearances. In 1985, a year before the World Cup in Mexico, he moved to Everton and scored 40 goals in the season in which the Toffees ended up runners-up in both the league and the FA Cup behind local rivals Liverpool. At the 1986 World Cup Lineker top scored for the tournament despite England's exit in the quarter-finals. At the World Cup in 1990 England reached the semi-finals and Lineker scored another four goals. He finished his international career in 1992 with 48 goals from 80 matches. At club level Lineker had spells with Barcelona, with whom he won a Cup-Winners' Cup medal, and Tottenham, where he won the FA Cup. Since retirement Gary has been appointed Vice President of Leicester City and carved out a successful career as a sports broadcaster.

HONOURS WON

With Barcelona
🏆 European Cup-Winners' Cup 1989
🏆 Copa del Rey 1988
With Tottenham Hotspur
🏆 FA Cup 1992

Other Awards
★ English Football Writers' Association Player of the Year 1986, 1992
★ World Cup 'Golden Boot' 1986
★ Football Writers' Tribute Award 1990
★ FIFA Fair Play Award 1990

57 Ronaldinho

Ronaldo de Assis Moreira

Born
Porto Alegre
21 March 1980

Country
Brazil

Position
Midfielder

Clubs
Gremio
Paris Saint-Germain
Barcelona

International	
Caps	Goals
76	31

Ronaldinho is a ball control phenomenon and currently regarded as one of the best players in the world. He began his club career at Gremio in 1998 where his goalscoring soon attracted the interest of the Brazilian national team selectors in 1999. He has since played international football at every level. He was a key player in Brazil's World Cup triumph in 2002 and featured again in 2006. He was both top player and top scorer in the 1999 Confederations Cup, though Brazil lost to Mexico in the final, and was pivotal in Brazil's win again in 2005. In 2001, Ronaldinho joined PSG in France, but his desire to be at one of Europe's biggest clubs saw him move to Barcelona in 2003 for £21 million. With Barcelona he has won two league championships and the Champions League and is undoubtedly the star of the show at the Nou Camp. His speed of thought, superb skills and the accuracy and originality of his passing make him one of the world's most exciting footballers. He has signed for the club until 2010.

HONOURS WON

With Brazil
🏆 Copa America 1999
🏆 Confederations Cup 2005
🏆 World Cup 2002
With Gremio
🏆 Rio Grande do Sul (State championship) 1999
With Barcelona
🏆 Primera Liga 2005, 2006
🏆 Champions League 2006

Other Awards
★ Selected for FIFA All-Star squad 2002
★ FIFA World Player of the Year 2004, 2005
★ European Footballer of the Year ('Ballon d'Or') 2005

58 Sylvain Wiltord

Born
Neuilly sur Marne 10 May 1974

Country
France

Position
Forward

Clubs
Stade Rennais Girondins de Bordeaux Arsenal Olympique Lyonnais

International	
Caps	Goals
92	26

Although not the most celebrated of French forwards, Sylvain Wiltord, armed with pace and determination, has been effective enough to earn 92 caps for his country. He scored 26 goals in those games, the most important of which was his 94th-minute equaliser in the European Championships final against Italy in 2000. France went on to win the title with a golden goal by David Trezeguet. Wiltord also played for his country in the 2002 and 2006 World Cups and in Euro 2004. Starting his club career at Stade Rennais in 1992, he moved on in 1997 to Girondins de Bordeaux with whom he won the French league title. He became part of the French connection at Arsenal in 2000 playing his part in two title-winning Premiership campaigns at Highbury. Perhaps his most memorable moment was scoring the winner for the Gunners at Old Trafford that secured the title in 2002. He also won two FA Cup winner's medals. In 2004 he moved to Lyon, where he won three consecutive league titles. In 2007 his club career came full circle when he returned to Stade Rennais.

HONOURS WON

With France
🏆 European Championships 2000
🏆 Confederations Cup 2001, 2003
With Girondins de Bordeaux
🏆 Championnat 1999

With Arsenal
🏆 Premiership 2002, 2004
🏆 FA Cup 2002, 2003
With Olympique Lyonnais
🏆 Championnat 2005, 2006, 2007

59

Bebeto

Jose Roberto Gama de Oliveira

Born	
Salvador 16 February 1964	
Country	
Forward	
Position	
Brazil	
Clubs	
Vitoria Flamengo Vasco da Gama Botafogo Deportivo La Coruna Seville Cruzeiro Toros Neza Kashima Antlers Al Ittihad	
International	
Caps	**Goals**
76	42

The highlight of Bebeto's career was watched by millions of people around the world as he celebrated his goal against Holland in the 1994 World Cup quarter-final. His wife had given birth to a baby a few days before the match and he ran to the cameras putting out his arms as if to rock his newborn. Brazil went on to win the tournament after a penalty shootout against Italy. In all, Bebeto played in three World Cups – 1990, 1994, and 1998 – though he barely featured in 1998. In total he played 76 matches for his country, scoring 42 goals. A well-travelled club player he won the Brazilian national title with Vasco da Gama and was South American Footballer of the Year in 1989. He also played for Vitoria and Botafogo in Brazil, Deportivo La Coruna and Seville in Spain, Toros Neza in Mexico, Kashima Antlers in Japan, and Al Ittihad in Saudi Arabia before retiring in 2002.

HONOURS WON

With Brazil

🏆 World Cup 1994

🏆 Copa America 1989

🏆 Confederations Cup 1997

🏆 Pan-American Games 1987

With Flamengo

🏆 Campeao Carioca (State Championship) 1986

With Vasco da Gama

🏆 Campeonato Brasileiro 1989

With Deportivo La Coruña

🏆 Copa del Rey 1995

🏆 Spanish Supercopa 1995

With Vitoria

🏆 Campeonato Bahia 1997

With Botafogo

🏆 Torneio Rio–Sao Paulo 1998

Other Awards

★ *El Pais'* South American Footballer of the Year 1989

★ Primera Liga Top Scorer ('Trofeos Pichichi') 1993

★ Brazilian Bola de Prata (*Placar*) 1992

60 Alessandro Del Piero

Born	
Treviso	
9 November 1974	
Country	
Italy	
Position	
Forward	
Clubs	
Padova	
Juventus	
International	
Caps	Goals
85	27

Alessandro Del Piero started his professional career in 1991 with Padova in Serie B. In 1993 he moved to Juventus, and has been there ever since. With the Turin club he has won the Serie A championship seven times adding the Champions League and the Intercontinental Cup to his trophy cabinet in 1996. His best season was in 1997–98, when he scored 21 league goals and 10 goals in the Champions League. Although he started his career as a striker, his technical ability and passing skills have meant he has become more suited to the central playmaker role, just behind the strikers. He has made over 500 appearances for Juventus and scored over 200 goals. His first tournament for Italy was Euro 96 when they went home early. But four years later, at Euro 2000, they went all the way to the final, losing to the agony of a golden goal in extra time. In all he has played at three World Cups – 1998, 2002 and 2006 – and now has 85 caps to his name. In 2006 he scored in the semi-final and in the penalty shootout in the final as Italy were crowned World Champions for the fourth time in their history.

HONOURS WON

With Italy

🏆 World Cup 2006

With Juventus

🏆 Serie A 1995, 1997, 1998, 2002, 2003, 2005**, 2006**

🏆 Coppa Italia 1995

🏆 Supercoppa Italiana 1995, 1997, 2003

🏆 Champions League 1996

🏆 Intercontinental Cup 1996

🏆 European Super Cup 1996

** Juventus were stripped of these titles due to allegations of match-fixing

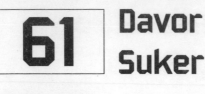

61 Davor Suker

Born
Osijek, Croatia
1 January 1968

Country
Yugoslavia/Croatia

Position
Forward

Clubs
Dinamo Zagreb
Seville
Real Madrid
Arsenal
West Ham United
TSV 1860 Munich

International	
Caps	Goals
2 (Yug)	1 (Yug)
69 (Cro)	45 (Cro)

74

Davor Suker's greatest moment was at the 1998 World Cup in France, where he became the top goalscorer for the tournament with six goals in seven matches, leading Croatia to a third-place finish in their first World Cup appearance. At club level Suker made his mark at Dinamo Zagreb where he played two seasons, scoring 34 goals in 60 league matches and earning selection for the Yugoslav national team. In 1991 he moved to Seville in Spain and then on to Real Madrid with whom he won a league title in 1997 and a Champions League winner's medal the following season. In all, he scored 114 goals in 239 appearances in the Spanish league. Although he had two seasons in England and two more in Germany, it was as Croatia's talismanic goalscorer that he will be remembered. In qualifying for their first international tournament, Euro 96, he scored 12 goals in 10 games, and a further three at the tournament. He also appeared briefly at the World Cup in 2002. His 46 goals in 71 international appearances remains one of the highest strike rates ever in international football.

HONOURS WON

With Real Madrid
🏆 Primera Liga 1997
🏆 Champions League 1998
🏆 Intercontinental Cup 1998

Other Awards
★ World Cup 'Golden Boot' 1998

62 Ryan Giggs

Born	
Cardiff	
29 November 1973	
Country	
Wales	
Position	
Forward	
Clubs	
Manchester United	
International	
Caps	**Goals**
64	13

Ryan Giggs is Manchester United's longest-serving current player, having made his first appearance for the club on 2 March 1991 against Everton. He is second to Bobby Charlton in all-time appearance makers for United with over 700 games to his name, and has won a club record 23 trophies since 1992 when he won a League Cup winner's medal. Once a flying winger, now more a left-footed attacking midfielder, Giggs' pace and technique have lit up the Premiership every season since it began in 1992–93. In a career full of highlights his extra-time winner in the 1999 FA Cup semi-final against Arsenal at Villa Park was unforgettable. Without doubt one of Wales' finest ever players, along with Billy Meredith and Mark Hughes, Giggs won 64 caps and scored 13 goals for his country between 1991 and 2007, but never played at the World Cup finals or a European Championships as Wales failed to qualify. He was appointed captain of Wales in 2004 but retired from international football in 2007 in order to extend his career at United.

HONOURS WON

With Manchester United
🏆 League Cup 1992, 2006
🏆 Premiership 1993, 1994, 1996, 1997, 1999, 2000, 2001, 2003, 2007
🏆 FA Cup 1994, 1996, 1999, 2004
🏆 Champions League 1999

Other Awards
★ Wales' Player of the Year 1996, 2006
★ OBE 2007

INTERNATIONAL

63 David Trezeguet

Born	
Rouen	
15 October 1977	
Country	
France	
Position	
Forward	
Clubs	
Platense	
AS Monaco	
Juventus	
International	
Caps	**Goals**
69	34

A consummate striker and goal poacher, David Trezeguet is not as celebrated as his international strike partner Thierry Henry, even though he has a higher strike rate. He was part of the French side that won the 1998 World Cup and the 2000 European Championships, in which Trezeguet scored the golden goal in the final against Italy to give his team the title. He also played for France in the 2002 and 2006 World Cups and Euro 2004. He has made 69 appearances for the French national side, scoring 34 goals. He played in the 2006 World Cup final against Italy and was the only person to miss a penalty in the shootout. At club level, Trezeguet made his professional debut for Platense in Argentina in 1993, before moving to Europe and signing for Monaco two years later. He found his best form with Italian giants Juventus for whom he signed in 2001, and with whom he has won the Serie A title four times (reduced to two as the club was stripped of the 2005 and 2006 titles due to allegations of match-fixing). He has scored more than 125 goals in 207 matches for Juventus.

HONOURS WON

With France
♛ World Cup 1998
♛ European Championships 2000
With AS Monaco
♛ Championnat 1997, 2000
With Juventus
♛ Serie A 2002, 2003, 2005**, 2006**
♛ Supercoppa Italiana 2003

Other Awards
★ Chevalier of the Legion d'Honneur 1998

*** Juventus were stripped of these titles due to allegations of match-fixing*

64 Demetrio Albertini

Born
Besana in Brianza, Milan
23 August 1971

Country
Italy

Position
Midfielder

Clubs
AC Milan
Padova
Atletico Madrid
Lazio
Atalanta
Barcelona

International	
Caps	Goals
79	3

A stylish player, armed with a strong tackle and an excellent range of passing, Demetrio Albertini was a product of the youth system at AC Milan. He spent 14 years at the club, making his debut as a 17-year-old in 1989. He won a host of honours in his 293 matches including five Italian league championships. He was part of the side that reached three consecutive Champions League finals between 1993 and 1995, winning the trophy in 1994. He won 79 caps for Italy, usually playing in a deeper role where he was more able to dictate the pace of the game, appearing at the 1994 and 1998 World Cups, Euro 96, and Euro 2000. He left Milan in 2002 and played for various clubs, ending up for his final season at Barcelona before retiring in 2005.

HONOURS WON

With AC Milan

🏆 Serie A 1992, 1993, 1994, 1996, 1999

🏆 Supercoppa Italiana 1992, 1993, 1994

🏆 Champions League 1994

🏆 UEFA Super Cup 1994

65 Patrick Vieira

Born
Dakar, Senegal 23 June 1976
Country
France
Position
Midfielder
Clubs
AS Cannes AC Milan Arsenal Juventus Inter Milan
International

Caps	Goals
101	6

Patrick Vieira began his club career with AS Cannes in France in 1993 and moved to AC Milan two years later. He joined Arsenal in 1996 after new manager Arsene Wenger had stipulated in his contract talks that the club buy the midfielder. At Arsenal Vieira won league and cup Doubles in 1998 and 2002. He was made captain the following season, leading his side to the FA Cup again in 2003. The following year was his finest as he led the Gunners through an entire season unbeaten – the record P38, W26, D12, L0 – the first time this had been achieved since 1889. The season that followed was a quiet one but Vieira still managed to score the decisive spot-kick in the 2005 FA Cup final against Manchester United. That was to be his Arsenal farewell as he returned to Italy to play for Juventus. A year later, following the match-fixing scandal where Juventus were stripped of the title, he was transferred to Inter Milan. He made his international debut in February 1997 against the Netherlands and came on as a substitute as the French defeated Brazil to win the 1998 World Cup final. He had become a fixture in the side by the time they won the 2000 European Championships. He also appeared at the World Cups of 2002 and 2006, only losing to Italy on penalties in the final in Germany.

HONOURS WON

With France
- ♛ World Cup winner 1998
- ♛ European Championships 2000
- ♛ Confederations Cup 2001

With Arsenal
- ♛ Premiership 1998, 2002, 2004
- ♛ FA Cup 1998, 2002, 2003, 2005

With Juventus
- ♛ Serie A 2006**

With Inter Milan
- ♛ Serie A 2007
- ♛ Supercoppa Italiana 2007

Other Awards
- ★ France's Player of the Year 2001
- ★ Chevalier of the Legion d'Honneur 1998

*** Juventus were stripped of this title due to allegations of match-fixing*

66 Jurgen Kohler

Born	
Lambsheim 6 October 1965	
Country	
Germany	
Position	
Defender	
Clubs	
SV Waldhof Mannheim FC Cologne Bayern Munich Juventus Borussia Dortmund	

International	
Caps	**Goals**
105	2

Rock solid defender Jurgen Kohler had a 20-year career that saw him play club football in the Bundesliga and Serie A. He also played 105 times for Germany during which time he earned winner's medals at the World Cup in 1990 and the European Championships in 1996. At his peak in 1990 he won the Bundesliga with Bayern Munich before going to Italy with the national squad. In 1991 he moved to Italy where he won the UEFA Cup in 1993 and Serie A in 1995. But he was most successful at club level with Borussia Dortmund for whom he played 191 times, winning the Bundesliga in 1996 and 2002 and the Champions League in 1997. He retired from playing in 2002 to take up a career in coaching. He has managed the German Under-21 team, been sports director of Bayer Leverkusen and coach at MSV Duisburg.

HONOURS WON

With Germany
🏆 World Cup 1990
🏆 European Championships 1996
Bayern Munich
🏆 Bundesliga 1990
With Juventus
🏆 UEFA Cup 1993
🏆 Serie A 1995

With Borussia Dortmund
🏆 Bundesliga 1996, 2002
🏆 Champions League 1997
🏆 Intercontinental Cup 1997

INTERNATIONAL

67 Laurent Blanc

Born	
Ales	
19 November 1965	

Country
France

Position
Defender

Clubs
Montpellier
Napoli
Nimes
AS Saint-Etienne
Auxerre
Barcelona
Olympique Marseille
Inter Milan
Manchester United

International	
Caps	Goals
97	16

Laurent Blanc's calm demeanour and superb sense of positioning served him well during his 20-year career at centre back. Another member of France's 'Golden Generation' who won the World Cup in 1998 and the European Championships two years later, he missed the final in 1998 through suspension having been sent off in the semi-final against Croatia. However, he has the distinction of having scored the first golden goal in World Cup history in the second round of that tournament against Paraguay. He also played in the European Championships in 1992 and 1996, making 97 appearances in all for his country. He began his professional career at Montpellier in 1983 where he stayed until 1991, making 251 appearances and scoring 77 times. He subsequently had spells at Napoli, Nimes, Saint-Etienne and Auxerre, before signing for Spanish giants Barcelona. He returned to France with Marseille, then had spells in Italy with Inter Milan and England with Manchester United, where he earned a Premiership winner's medal in 2003, before hanging up his boots. He was named manager of Girondins de Bordeaux in June 2007.

HONOURS WON

With France
🏆 World Cup 1998
🏆 European Championships 2000
With Montpellier
🏆 Coupe de France 1990
With Auxerre
🏆 Championnat 1996
🏆 Coupe de France 1996

With Barcelona
🏆 Spanish Supercopa 1996
🏆 European Cup-Winners' Cup 1997
With Manchester United
🏆 Premiership 2003
Other Awards
★ *France Football*'s French Player of the Year 1990
★ Chevalier of the Legion d'Honneur 1998

Michael Owen

Born
Chester
14 December 1979

Country
England

Position
Forward

Clubs
Liverpool
Real Madrid
Newcastle United

International	
Caps	Goals
82	37

Michael Owen made his debut for England against Chile in February 1998, the youngest player ever to represent England. He earned international recognition at the 1998 World Cup in France with a sensational goal against Argentina in a game that ended 2–2 but England lost on penalties. He has since played in Euro 2000, the 2002 World Cup and Euro 2004, scoring goals in all three tournaments – the only player ever to have scored in four major tournaments for England. He also played at the 2006 World Cup but was injured in the final group game. He has been capped 82 times for England and scored 37 goals. Owen signed for Liverpool as a junior and for eight years led the Liverpool line. His most successful season was in 2001 when the club won the League Cup, FA Cup and UEFA Cup, with Owen scoring two goals in the last few minutes against Arsenal in the FA Cup final to turn what had appeared to be a 1–0 defeat into a 2–1 victory. A transfer to star-studded Real Madrid saw him make 41 appearances, often as a substitute, scoring 16 goals, before he transferred back to England and Newcastle United where injuries have restricted him to just a handful of appearances so far.

HONOURS WON

With Liverpool

🏆 League Cup 2001, 2003
🏆 FA Cup 2001
🏆 UEFA Cup 2001
🏆 European Super Cup 2001

Other Awards

★ *World Soccer*'s World Player of the Year 2000
★ European Footballer of the Year ('Ballon d'Or') 2001

 **69** | **Youri Djorkaeff**

Born
Lyon
9 March 1968
Country
France
Position
Forward
Clubs
Grenoble
Strasbourg
AS Monaco
Paris Saint Germain
Inter Milan
FC Kaiserslautern
Bolton Wanderers
Blackburn Rovers
NY/NJ MetroStars

International	
Caps	**Goals**
82	28

Youri Djorkaeff was a significant contributor to France's 1998 World Cup and Euro 2000-winning teams. Whether deployed as a striker or an attacking midfielder his pace allied with excellent technique and dribbling was capable of unlocking any defence in the world. If he didn't score himself, he would create gilt-edged chances for his team-mates. He played 82 times for France, scoring 28 goals. He started his career in 1984 with lower-league Grenoble, before moving to Strasbourg in 1989, Monaco in 1990, and then PSG in 1995. In 1994, Djorkaeff was top scorer in the Championnat with 20 goals. In 1996, he signed with Italian giants Inter Milan, and in 1999 went to Germany with Kaiserslautern. He played out the twilight of his career in the English Premiership with Bolton Wanderers and Blackburn Rovers and ended it playing in New York in the MLS.

HONOURS WON

With France
🏆 World Cup 1998
🏆 European Championships 2000
🏆 Confederations Cup 2001
With Paris Saint Germain
🏆 European Cup-Winners' Cup 1996

With Inter Milan
🏆 UEFA Cup 1998
Other Awards
★ Chevalier of the Legion d'Honneur 1998

70 Frank De Boer

Born
Hoorn
15 May 1970

Country
Holland

Position
Defender

Clubs
Ajax
Barcelona
Galatasaray
Rangers
Al-Rayyan
Al-Shamal

International	
Caps	**Goals**
112	13

Frank de Boer is the younger twin brother of Ronald de Boer. He made his debut for Holland in 1990 against Italy, going on to play a record 112 times for his country, competing at the 1994 and 1998 World Cups, Euro 92, Euro 2000 and Euro 2004. He began his career at Ajax as a left-back, later switching to centre-back, and making up for a lack of speed with a clear reading of the game and sheer effort. After winning domestic honours and both the Champions League and UEFA Cup while at Ajax, he joined Barcelona. He made almost 150 appearances for the Spanish giants but in 2001 tested positive for the banned substance nandrolone. He briefly moved to Galatasaray in the summer of 2003 before joining Rangers in January 2004. He left Rangers after Euro 2004 along with twin brother Ronald (his team-mate at Ajax, Barcelona, and Rangers) to play the rest of his football career in Qatar with Al-Rayyan and then Al-Shamal. He is currently working as a coach at former club Ajax.

HONOURS WON

With Ajax
- 🏆 Eredivisie 1994, 1995, 1996, 1998
- 🏆 KNVB Beker (Dutch FA Cup) 1993, 1998
- 🏆 Champions League 1995
- 🏆 UEFA Cup 1992

With Barcelona
- 🏆 Primera Liga 1999

71

Emilio Butragueno

Emilio Butragueno Santos

Born	
Madrid	
22 July 1963	
Country	
Spain	
Position	
Forward	
Clubs	
Real Madrid	
Castilla	
Atletico Celaya	
International	
Caps	Goals
69	26

Nicknamed 'the Vulture' for his ability to pick up and devour chances in the box, Emilio Butragueno was one of the most lethal strikers in Europe in the 1980s. Born in Madrid, he started playing for Real, the club he served for most of his career, forming a deadly partnership with Mexican Hugo Sanchez, winning five consecutive league titles. Butragueno scored on his international debut for Spain against Wales in October 1984, just months after Spain finished second in the European Championships in France. He was a regular in the team by the 1986 World Cup in Mexico and became the first man since Eusebio in 1966 to score four goals in a World Cup match as Spain beat Denmark 5–1. A defeat to Belgium on penalties in the following round ended Spain's dream of a first World Cup victory. In Italy four years later he captained the team to the second round where they were beaten by Yugoslavia. He retired from international football in 1992 but went on to win more trophies with Real Madrid. In 1995 he left the club, playing out his last seasons at Castilla and then in Mexico with Atletico Celaya where he teamed up again with Hugo Sanchez.

HONOURS WON

With Real Madrid
🏆 UEFA Cup 1985, 1986
🏆 Primera Liga 1986, 1987, 1988, 1989, 1990, 1995
🏆 Copa del Rey 1989, 1993
🏆 Spanish Supercopa 1988, 1989, 1990, 1993

72 Hugo Sanchez

Born
Mexico City 11 July 1958

Country
Mexico

Position
Forward

Clubs
UNAM Pumas San Diego Sockers Atletico Madrid Real Madrid CF America Rayo Vallecano Atlante Linz Dallas Burn Atletico Celaya

International	
Caps	Goals
60	29

There are few people more closely associated with Mexican football than Hugo Sanchez. Generally regarded as the country's finest ever player, he appeared in three World Cups, earning 60 caps and scoring 29 goals, and is now the national team coach. He started his club career at Pumas where he had five successful years. A year-long loan to the United States gave him the taste for travel and in 1981 he signed for Atletico Madrid in Spain. By the 1984–85 season he was scoring regularly with a team that won the Copa del Rey, finished in second place in the Spanish league and won the Supercopa. That year he won his first Pichichi trophy as top scorer in the Spanish league. At the high point of his career, in 1985, he signed for Real Madrid. In seven magnificent seasons he won five consecutive league titles, the Copa del Rey in 1989, and the UEFA Cup in 1986. He also won four consecutive Pichichi trophies, scoring 207 goals in 283 games, including 27 or more in four consecutive seasons between 1986 and 1990. In all Sanchez played 12 seasons in the Spanish Primera Liga and is the second highest goalscorer in its history. His trademark was to perform a celebratory somersault after each goal he scored, honouring his sister, who was a gymnast and participated In the Montreal Olympics.

HONOURS WON

With UNAM Pumas
♛ Primera Division 1977, 1981
♛ CONCACAF Cup 1980
With Atletico Madrid
♛ Copa del Rey 1985
♛ Spanish Supercopa 1985

With Real Madrid
♛ UEFA Cup 1986
♛ Primera Liga 1986, 1987, 1988, 1989, 1990
♛ Spanish Supercopa 1988, 1989, 1990
♛ Copa del Rey 1989

 **73**

Rudi Voller

Born
Hanau
13 April 1960

Country
West Germany

Position
Forward

Clubs
TSV 1860 Hanau
Offenbacher FC Kickers
TSV 1860 Munich
Werder Bremen
AS Roma
Olympique Marseille
Bayer Leverkusen

International	
Caps	Goals
90	47

Rudi Voller has been closely involved in German football for over 20 years. A stocky striker, he was first capped in 1982 and played up front for Germany 90 times, scoring 47 goals, 8 in World Cup finals. He won the World Cup in 1990 as a player when West Germany defeated Argentina and coached the national team to second place at the 2002 World Cup when they lost to Brazil. Voller also played in Euro 84, the 1986 World Cup, Euro 88, Euro 92, and the 1994 World Cup. Voller began his Bundesliga career with Werder Bremen in 1982. In five years with the club he scored 97 goals in 137 games. In 1987 he was transferred to AS Roma, where he became a mainstay of the team and earned the nickname 'il Tedesco volante' (the flying German). He won the Italian Cup in 1991 and scored 45 times in 145 games. In 1992, Voller joined Olympique Marseille, winning the Champions League in 1993. He finished his playing career at Bayer Leverkusen in 1996. In 2000 he was surprisingly appointed coach of the national team despite not having the necessary coaching qualifications. He has since also been coach at AS Roma.

HONOURS WON

With West Germany
🏆 World Cup 1990
With AS Roma
🏆 Coppa Italia 1991
With Olympique Marseille
🏆 Championnat 1993
🏆 Champions League 1993**

Other Awards
★ German Player of the Year 1983

*** Marseille were later stripped of this title following allegations of match-fixing*

74 Djalma Santos

Born
Sao Paulo
27 February 1929
Country
Brazil
Position
Defender
Clubs
Portuguesa
Palmeiras
Atletico Paranaense

International	
Caps	**Goals**
98	3

Djalma Santos is one of the greatest defenders ever to have played for Brazil. Rock solid at right back, he appeared in four World Cups, winning two winner's medals – in Sweden in 1958 and in Chile in 1962. He played his last World Cup in 1966 aged 37. While primarily known for his defensive skills, he found time to raid down the right flank and was unrelenting in support of the attacking game. In the 1962 World Cup, he was at the height of his powers and formed a great understanding with Garrincha. In the final when Brazil beat Czechoslovakia 3–1 he helped create the third goal, scored by Vava, to seal Brazil's second tournament victory in a row.

HONOURS WON

With Brazil
🏆 World Cup 1958, 1962

With Portuguesa
🏆 Torneio Rio–Sao Paulo 1952, 1955

With Palmeiras
🏆 Campeao Paulista 1959, 1963, 1966
🏆 Torneio Rio–Sao Paulo 1965

With Atletico Paranaense
🏆 Campeonato Paranaense 1970

75 | Giacinto Facchetti

Born
Bergamo 18 July 1942
Country
Italy
Position
Defender
Clubs
Trevigliese Inter Milan

International	
Caps	**Goals**
94	3

Giacinto Facchetti began his football life as a forward before Inter Milan coach Helenio Herrera launched him into Serie A in 1961 as a full-back. The change of role was successful and he developed into one of the most effective defenders in Italian soccer, playing his part in the development of *catenaccio*, the water-tight defensive formation most associated with Italian football. He won four championships at Inter in a career lasting 17 years. Always encouraged to support the attack he scored 60 league goals for his club and also won two European Cups, in 1964 and 1965, the Italian Cup in 1978 and two Intercontinental Cups, also in 1964 and 1965.

Facchetti made his international debut in 1963 and was capped 94 times, 70 as captain. He played at the 1966, 1970 (where Italy were runners-up to Brazil losing 4–1 in the final), and 1974 World Cups. He was also part of the Italian squad that won the European Championships in 1968. He finally hung up his boots in 1978. Subsequently Inter retired the number 3 shirt in his honour.

HONOURS WON

With Italy
🏆 European Championships 1968
With Inter Milan
🏆 Serie A 1963, 1965, 1966, 1971
🏆 European Cup 1964, 1965
🏆 Intercontinental Cup 1964, 1965
🏆 Coppa Italia 1978

76 Kanu

Nwankwo Kanu

Born
Owerri
1 August 1976

Country
Nigeria

Position
Forward

Clubs
Federation Works
Iwuanyanwu Nationale
Ajax
Inter Milan
Arsenal
West Bromwich Albion
Portsmouth

International	
Caps	Goals
66	13

Nwankwo Kanu has won more trophies than any other African footballer with over 10 awards to boast of, including Champions League and UEFA Cup winner's medals and two African Player of the Year awards. He was spotted at the Under-17 World Championships and signed by Ajax in 1993, making his debut the following year. He played 54 times for the Dutch side, scoring 25 goals and appearing in their 1995 Champions League final win over AC Milan. In 1996, he moved to Inter Milan. That summer he captained the Nigerian team to gold at the Olympics in Atlanta and was also named African Footballer of the Year. A medical examination at Inter revealed a serious heart defect and he underwent surgery in November 1996. Many thought his career was finished but he returned to Inter in April 1997. Two years later he moved to Arsenal where he became known for scoring spectacular goals. He was part of the team that won the Double in 2002, the FA Cup in 2003 and the Premiership again in 2004. In five years with the Gunners he played 197 games, scoring 44 goals. Kanu has been a member of the Nigerian national team since 1994, making 66 appearances and scoring 13 goals. He played in the 1998 and 2002 World Cups. However, Nigeria failed to qualify for the tournament in 2006. He currently plays his football at Portsmouth.

HONOURS WON

With Nigeria

🏆 Olympic Football Tournament Gold Medal 1996

With Ajax

🏆 Champions League 1995

With Arsenal

🏆 Premiership 2002, 2004

🏆 FA Cup 2002, 2003

Other Awards

★ African Footballer of the Year 1996, 1999

77 | Franco Baresi

Born
Travagliato 8 May 1960

Country
Italy

Position
Defender

Clubs
AC Milan

International	
Caps	Goals
81	1

Franco Baresi spent his entire career at AC Milan and came to dominate and redefine the role of the modern sweeper during the 1980s and 1990s. Calm under pressure, his brilliant reading of the game and effortlessly timed tackling provided the defensive base for this dominant club side. But he was not just a defender and often moved forward with and without the ball to give his team extra options in an attack that already featured Ruud Gullit and Marco van Basten. He led Milan to four Serie A titles and two European Cups. His international career started in 1982 and reached its peak as he captained Italy at the World Cup in 1994. Injured during the tournament Baresi was fit enough to captain the side in the final against Brazil. In a painful irony Baresi, who had a brilliant match, shot over the bar in the penalty shootout to hand the advantage to eventual winners Brazil. When he retired in 1997 Milan also retired the number 6 shirt as a mark of respect.

HONOURS WON

With AC Milan

🏆 Serie A 1979, 1988, 1992, 1993, 1994, 1996

🏆 Supercoppa Italiana 1988, 1992, 1993, 1994

🏆 European Cup/Champions League 1989, 1990, 1994

🏆 Intercontinental Cup 1989, 1990

🏆 European Super Cup 1989, 1990, 1994

Other Awards

★ Italy's Player of the Year 1990

Gianni Rivera

Born
Valle San Bartolomeo, Alessandria 18 August 1943
Country
Italy
Position
Midfielder
Clubs
AC Milan

International	
Caps	**Goals**
60	14

Technically gifted, with tremendous passing skills and a powerful shot especially from distance, Gianni Rivera spent his entire career at the San Siro with AC Milan. He won his first championship in 1962, aged 18, and then went to Chile to play in the World Cup. He played in two further World Cups, including the final in 1970 when Italy were beaten by Brazil. He appeared 60 times for Italy, scoring 14 goals. He was a dominant player at Milan during a time when the club was hugely successful. They won the European Cup in 1963 with Rivera setting up both goals for Altafini in the final against Benfica. He was also influential as the Rossoneri won Serie A again in 1968 and the European Cup again the following year when he was also crowned European Player of the Year. In 19 years at the San Siro he played 501 matches and scored 160 goals. He retired in 1979 and became vice-president of his lifetime club. He is currently a Member of the European Parliament for the Uniti nell'Ulivo party.

HONOURS WON

With Italy
🏆 European Championships 1968
With AC Milan
🏆 Serie A 1962, 1968, 1979
🏆 European Cup 1963, 1969
🏆 Coppa Italia 1967, 1972, 1973, 1977
🏆 European Cup-Winners' Cup 1968, 1973
🏆 Intercontinental Cup 1969

Other Awards
★ European Footballer of the Year ('Ballon d'Or') 1969

79 Roberto Baggio

Born	
Caldogno	
18 February 1967	
Country	
Italy	
Position	
Midfielder	
Clubs	
Vicenza	
Fiorentina	
Juventus	
AC Milan	
Bologna	
Inter Milan	
Brescia	

International	
Caps	**Goals**
56	27

Roberto Baggio signed for Fiorentina in 1985 aged 18. Five seasons there saw him become one of Italian football's hottest properties and in 1990, a week after losing to Juventus in the UEFA Cup final, he left Fiorentina for the Turin giants. There was such an outcry among Fiorentina fans that the police had to be called in to quell the rioting. Another five seasons saw him win the UEFA Cup and Serie A, scoring 79 goals in 99 league games. He made his World Cup debut in 1990 and after being voted World Player of the Year in 1993 he was the focus of Italian hopes in the USA in 1994. The team were not playing well but *Il Divino Codino* ('the Divine Ponytail'), as he had become known because of his well-known Buddhism and his hairstyle, produced miracles. He scored a last-minute equaliser and an extra-time penalty winner against Nigeria in the second round, the deciding goal in the quarter-final against Spain and two goals against Bulgaria in the semi-final. His penalty miss in the final against Brazil was as agonising as it was unexpected. The following year he moved to AC Milan, helping the club win Serie A and becoming the first player to win the Scudetto in consecutive years with different teams. In 1997 he transferred to Bologna, scoring a personal best 22 goals that year. After the 1998 World Cup, Baggio signed with Inter Milan where he played for two seasons before moving to Brescia until his retirement in 2004.

HONOURS WON

With Juventus
🏆 UEFA Cup 1993
🏆 Serie A 1995
🏆 Coppa Italia 1995

With AC Milan
🏆 Serie A 1996

Other Awards
★ FIFA World Player of the Year 1993
★ *World Soccer's* World Player of the Year 1993
★ European Footballer of the Year ('Ballon d'Or') 1993
★ World Cup 'Silver Ball' 1994

Oscar Alfredo Ruggeri

Born
Corral de Bustos (Cordoba)
26 January 1962
Country
Argentina
Position
Defender
Clubs
Boca Juniors
River Plate
Logrones
Real Madrid
Velez Sarsfield
Ancona
CF America
San Lorenzo
Lanus

International	
Caps	Goals
97	7

Argentina's World Cup success in 1986 is often presented as Diego Maradona's personal triumph, but without the tough and uncompromising defending of Oscar Ruggeri Argentina would have been a lesser team. Argentina achieved an even better defensive record in 1990, despite a stunning opening game defeat by Cameroon and losing to West Germany in the final. But Ruggeri and his team-mates' cynical attitude, encouraged by Bilardo's win-at-all-costs philosophy, won them few friends. Ruggeri was back for the 1994 finals, but Argentina's campaign was overshadowed by Maradona's ejection from the tournament after a positive drugs test. In the second round, Romania tore the once-impenetrable Argentine defence apart, and Ruggeri's international career, after 97 caps, was over. Nicknamed El Cabezon, Ruggeri started his club career at Boca Juniors, playing with Maradona, with whom he won a league title in 1981. In 1985 he moved to rivals River Plate, where he won the Libertadores Cup, the Intercontinental Cup and another league title in 1986. In 1988 he left for Europe where he played for Spanish clubs Logrones and Real Madrid, where he won yet another league championship. He also played for Velez Sarsfield, Ancona in Italy, America in Mexico, San Lorenzo and Lanus, where he ended his career.

HONOURS WON

With Argentina
🏆 World Cup 1986
🏆 Copa America 1991, 1993
With Boca Juniors
🏆 Torneo Metropolitano 1981
With River Plate
🏆 Copa Libertadores 1986
🏆 Toyota European/South American Cup 1986
🏆 Argentine League 1986

With Real Madrid
🏆 Primera Liga 1989
With San Lorenzo
🏆 Torneo Clausura 1995
Other Awards
★ *El Pais*' South American Footballer of the Year 1991

81 Gheorghe Popescu

Born
Calafat
9 October 1967
Country
Romania
Position
Defender
Clubs
Universitatea Craiova
Steaua Bucharest
PSV Eindhoven
Tottenham Hotspur
Barcelona
Galatasaray
US Lecce
Dinamo Bucharest
Hannover 96

International	
Caps	**Goals**
115	16

Gheorghe Popescu was the foundation of the Romanian national team's defence in the 1990s and played in all the major championships during that decade. A formidable defender, his skills as sweeper were central to Romania's counter-attacking style of play. He is Romania's all-time highest appearance maker with 115 caps to his name. Well travelled at club level Popescu has won a host of honours at many of Europe's top clubs. His three most successful stops were in Holland with PSV Eindhoven, Spain with Barcelona and Turkey with Galatasaray with whom he won three consecutive league titles and the UEFA Cup. Between 1989 and 1996 he was Romanian Footballer of the Year six times. He retired from playing in 2003.

HONOURS WON

With Steaua Bucharest
♛ Romanian League 1988
With PSV Eindhoven
♛ Eredivisie 1991, 1992
♛ Nationale Supercup 1993
With Barcelona
♛ Copa del Rey 1997
♛ European Cup-Winners' Cup 1997

With Galatasaray
♛ Turkish League 1998, 1999, 2000
♛ UEFA Cup 2000
♛ European Super Cup 2000
Other Awards
★ Romanian Footballer of the Year
1989, 1990, 1991, 1992, 1995, 1996

82 Jon Dahl Tomasson

Born
Copenhagen
29 August 1976
Country
Denmark
Position
Forward
Clubs

Koge BK
Heerenveen
Newcastle United
Feyenoord
AC Milan
VfB Stuttgart
Villarreal

International	
Caps	**Goals**
90	46

A free-scoring striker with Heerenveen, Jon Dahl Tomasson moved to Newcastle for £2 million in 1997. The move was not successful and he returned to Holland in 1998 to join Feyenoord with whom he re-found his scoring form. Four years in Rotterdam saw him score 54 goals in 122 games, winning the league title in 1999 and the UEFA Cup in 2002. A fast and elusive striker with a high work-rate, Tomasson moved on to AC Milan in 2002 where he had further success, winning the Champions League in 2003 and Serie A in 2004. At international level he has scored 46 goals in 90 matches for Denmark, appearing at the 2002 World Cup and the 2004 European Championships, where three goals in four games saw him named in the UEFA Team of the Tournament. He left Milan in 2005, spent two years in the Bundesliga with Stuttgart and then joined Villarreal in Spain.

HONOURS WON

With Feyenoord
🏆 Eredivisie 1999
🏆 Dutch Supercup 1999
🏆 UEFA Cup 2002
With AC Milan
🏆 Coppa Italia 2003
🏆 Champions League 2003
🏆 Serie A 2004
🏆 Supercoppa Italiana 2004

Other Awards
★ Danish Player of the Year 2002, 2004

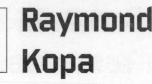

83 Raymond Kopa

Born
Nœux-les-Mines
13 October 1931
Country
France
Position
Forward
Clubs
Angers SCO
Stade de Reims
Real Madrid

International	
Caps	**Goals**
45	18

Raymond Kopa was France's first footballing superstar, winning the European Footballer of the Year award in 1958. A deep-lying centre forward, he was integral to the French national teams of the 1950s. Born in France, the son of Polish immigrants, he began his professional career at 17 with Angers SCO, and was transferred two years later to Stade de Reims. Then one of the dominant clubs in French football, Reims won the championship in 1953 and 1955. In 1956 they reached the final of the inaugural European Cup losing 4–3 to Real Madrid. Kopa impressed the Spanish giants enough to move to Spain the following season. In three fantastic years at the Bernabeu he won two championships and three successive European Cups. Kopa returned to France in 1959 to finish his career with Reims, where he won the Championnat in 1960 and 1962. In total, he scored 75 goals in 346 matches in Ligue 1. On the international stage he scored 18 goals in 45 games for France between 1952 and 1962. He played in the 1954 World Cup in Switzerland where he was voted Best Young Player of the Tournament. He was outstanding at the 1958 tournament in Sweden where the French team finished third and he was voted Best Player of the Tournament.

HONOURS WON

With Stade de Reims
🏆 Championnat 1953, 1955, 1960, 1962
With Real Madrid
🏆 Primera Liga 1957, 1958
🏆 European Cup 1957, 1958, 1959
🏆 Latin Cup 1957

Other Awards
★ European Footballer of the Year ('Ballon d'Or') 1958
★ Chevalier of the Legion d'Honneur 1970

84

Carlos Valderrama

Carlos Alberto Valderrama Palacio

Born
Santa Marta
2 September 1961

Country
Colombia

Position
Midfielder

Clubs
Union Magdelena
Millonarios
Deportivo Cali
Montpellier
Valladolid
Medellin
Atletico Junior
Tampa Bay Mutiny
Miami Fusion
Colorado Rapids

International	
Caps	Goals
111	11

Carlos Valderrama was one of the most instantly recognisable figures in world football with his mass of curly blonde hair and all his jewellery. The talented midfielder was regarded as one of the very best in his position in South America with his excellent passing and ability to control play. Generally regarded as his country's finest ever player Valderrama made his debut for Colombia in October 1985 and soon became captain, leading his country in three World Cups. At club level, he started his career at Union Magdelena, outside whose stadium there still stands a statue, in Colombia's first division. In 1998 he signed for French side Montpellier and also played in Spain for Valladolid. He returned home to his native Colombia to play for Atletico Junior where he won two league championships. He left again in 1996 to join Tampa Bay Mutiny in the MLS where he played at various clubs up to his retirement in 2004.

97

HONOURS WON

With Montpellier
🏆 Coupe de France 1990
With Atletico Junior
🏆 Division Mayor 1993, 1995

Other Awards
★ *El Mundo*'s South American Player of the Year 1987, 1993
★ Copa America Best Player 1987
★ Colombia's Player of the Year 1987, 1992 and 1993
★ *El Pais*' South American Player of the Year 1987 and 1993
★ Major League Soccer's Most Valuable Player 1996

INTERNATIONAL

85

Rui Costa

Rui Manuel Cesar Costa

Born
Lisbon
29 March 1972
Country
Portugal
Position
Midfielder
Clubs
AD Fafe
Benfica
Fiorentina
AC Milan

International	
Caps	Goals
94	26

Rui Costa is an attacking Portuguese midfielder with pinpoint accurate passing and a ferocious right-foot shot. The Portuguese Under-20 national team won two successive World Youth Championships in 1989 and 1991 with Rui Costa and Figo starring in 1991. At senior level they reached the semi-finals at Euro 2000, qualified for the 2002 World Cup and reached Portugal's first-ever major final at Euro 2004, losing to Greece. Despite being principally a creator of goals, Rui Costa has chipped in with an impressive 26 goals in 94 games for the national team. At club level he played for Benfica before moving to Italy where he played for seven seasons at Fiorentina winning the Italian Cup in 1996 and 2001. He moved to Milan in 2001 and enjoyed the finest moments of his career. He played for five seasons at the San Siro, and was irreplaceable for two seasons when Milan won the Champions League and Serie A. His first team chances became limited in 2005 with the arrival of Brazilian player Kaka and he returned to his first love, Benfica, where he has announced he will play out the rest of his distinguished career.

HONOURS WON

With Benfica
🏆 Portuguese Cup 1993
🏆 Portuguese League 1994
With Fiorentina
🏆 Coppa Italia 1996, 2001
🏆 Supercoppa Italiana 1996

With AC Milan
🏆 Coppa Italia 2003
🏆 Champions League 2003
🏆 European Super Cup 2003
🏆 Serie A 2004

86 Gary Neville

Born	
Bury	
18 February 1975	
Country	
England	
Position	
Defender	
Clubs	
Manchester United	
International	
Caps	**Goals**
85	0

Gary Neville is England's most-capped right-back, having played 85 times for his country. He was the youngest first-choice player in the England team during Euro 96, his first tournament, playing in each game until the semi-final, when he was suspended and England were subsequently knocked out by eventual winners, Germany. He also played in the 1998 World Cup and Euro 2000. A broken foot put paid to his hopes of playing in the 2002 World Cup, but he quickly returned to the side after regaining fitness, and was once again the first-choice right-back by the time of Euro 2004. Injury again restricted his appearances at the 2006 World Cup. He has spent his whole club career at Manchester United, appearing in over 500 matches and winning seven Premiership titles, three FA Cups, one League Cup and one Champions League trophy. He has played for much of his career with his brother Phil in the same club and national sides. He is the current captain of Manchester United.

99

HONOURS WON

With Manchester United

🏆 Premiership 1996, 1997, 1999, 2000, 2001, 2003, 2007

🏆 FA Cup 1996, 1999, 2004

🏆 Champions League 1999

🏆 Intercontinental Cup 1999

🏆 League Cup 2006

87 Edgar Davids

Born
Paramaribo, Surinam 13 March 1973

Country
Holland

Position
Midfielder

Clubs
Ajax AC Milan Juventus Barcelona Inter Milan Tottenham Hotspur

International	
Caps	Goals
74	6

Edgar Davids is a midfielder known for his strong work ethic and immediately recognisable with his dreadlocked hair and distinctive protective goggles (he suffers from glaucoma). He started his career at Ajax in 1991, where he was nicknamed 'the Pit Bull', helping the Amsterdam club to three domestic titles, as well as international success winning the UEFA Cup in 1992 and the Champions League in 1995. He moved to Italy in 1996 to play for AC Milan, but soon moved on again, this time to league rivals Juventus. He won several domestic titles with the Turin side but in 2001 he was suspended by FIFA after testing positive for nandrolone. Since returning from his ban he has played for Barcelona, Inter Milan and Tottenham Hotspur. He is currently back at Ajax. On the international stage he has played 74 times for Holland and been a key member of the team since his debut in 1994. At the 1998 World Cup he was named in the Team of the Tournament.

HONOURS WON

With Ajax
♛ UEFA Cup 1992
♛ KNVB Beker (Dutch FA Cup) 1993
♛ Eredivisie 1994, 1995, 1996
♛ Champions League 1995
♛ Intercontinental Cup 1995
♛ European Super Cup 1995

With Juventus
♛ Serie A 1998, 2002, 2003
♛ Coppa Italia 1998
♛ Supercoppa Italiana 2002, 2003
With Inter Milan
♛ Coppa Italia 2005

Claudio Taffarel

Claudio Andre Mergen Taffarel

Born
Santa Rosa
8 May 1966
Country
Brazil
Position
Goalkeeper
Clubs
Internacional
Parma
Reggiana
Atletico Mineiro
Galatasaray

International	
Caps	**Goals**
101	0

Claudio Taffarel was Brazil's goalkeeper when they won the 1994 World Cup in the USA. He let in just one goal in the first round, two in the knockout phase and two penalty kicks in the final. He was also between the posts four years later when Brazil lost in the final of the 1998 tournament to hosts France. In the semi-finals against Holland, he saved twice in the penalty shoot-out victory. At club level, Taffarel played for Internacional and Atletico Mineiro in Brazil, Parma and Reggiana in Italy, and Galatasaray in Turkey. He had a key role in Galatasaray's UEFA Cup triumph over Arsenal in 2000 and was named the man of the match. He also helped Galatasaray win the European Super Cup in 2000 and reach the quarter-finals of the Champions League in 2001. At international level Taffarel showed his safe handling and superb distribution in 101 matches, making him the most capped Brazilian goalkeeper ever. He also played in the 1990 World Cup and was Brazil's keeper during their Copa America successes in 1989 and 1997.

HONOURS WON

With Brazil

🏆 Copa America 1989, 1997

🏆 World Cup 1994

With Parma

🏆 Coppa Italia 1992

🏆 European Cup-Winners' Cup 1993

With Galatasaray

🏆 UEFA Cup 2000

🏆 European Super Cup 2000

Other Awards

Brazilian Player of the Year ('Bola de Ouro') 1988

89

Paul Scholes

Born	
Salford 16 November 1974	
Country	
England	
Position	
Midfielder	
Clubs	
Manchester United	
International	
Caps	**Goals**
66	14

Paul Scholes has spent his whole career at Manchester United. One of the best attacking midfielders of his generation, he is marked by his technical ability, his pinpoint one-touch passing and his excellent shooting. Never in the headlines, Scholes has gone quietly about the business of being part of most of United's club triumphs since the advent of the Premiership. He missed their Champions League win in 1999 because of suspension. On the international stage Scholes was an undisputed regular in an England shirt for five years, scoring some memorable goals including a hat-trick against Poland in 2000. He retired from international football in 2004 with 66 caps to his name in order to concentrate on his club career.

HONOURS WON

With Manchester United

🏆 Premiership 1996, 1997, 1999, 2000, 2001, 2003, 2007

🏆 FA Cup 1996, 1999, 2004

🏆 Champions League 1999

🏆 Intercontinental Cup 1999

🏆 League Cup 2006

90 Diego Simeone

Born
Buenos Aires
28 April 1970

Country
Argentina

Position
Midfielder

Clubs
Velez Sarsfield
Pisa
Seville
Atletico Madrid
Inter Milan
Lazio
Racing Club

International	
Caps	**Goals**
106	11

Diego Simeone has played 106 times for Argentina since his debut in 1988, and is the country's third most-capped player. A tough and uncompromising midfielder on the pitch, he is a true gentleman off it, claiming he was 'embarrassed' when he passed Diego Maradona's record as Argentina's record appearance maker. He was the player David Beckham kicked in the 1998 World Cup, resulting in Beckham's dismissal. He played in the 1994, 1998 and 2002 World Cups, won two Copa America winner's medals in 1991 and 1993 and was a member of the team that won the silver medal at the 1996 Olympics in Atlanta. Always considered a leader on the pitch, Simeone plied his trade at club level in Argentina, Italy and Spain. He won a Spanish league and cup Double with Atletico Madrid in 1996, the UEFA Cup with Inter Milan in 1998 and an Italian league championship with Lazio in 2000. He ended his playing career with Racing Club in Buenos Aires in 2006, immediately taking the post of coach at the same club. He is currently coach at Estudiantes.

HONOURS WON

With Argentina
🏆 Copa America 1991, 1993
With Atletico Madrid
🏆 Primera Liga 1996
🏆 Copa del Rey 1996
With Inter Milan
🏆 UEFA Cup 1998

With Lazio
🏆 European Super Cup 1999
🏆 Serie A 2000
🏆 Coppa Italia 2000
🏆 Supercoppa Italiana 2000

91

Bryan Robson

Born
Born Witton Gilbert, County Durham 11 January 1957
Country
England
Position
Midfielder
Clubs
West Bromwich Albion Manchester United Middlesbrough

International	
Caps	**Goals**
90	26

Bryan Robson made his debut for West Bromwich Albion in 1975. But it was at Manchester United, for whom he signed in 1981, that he built his reputation as a tough, wholly committed and skilful midfield general. Despite a career disrupted by injuries he played 461 games for United, winning league titles and FA Cups and scoring 99 goals. Robson was a regular player for England throughout the 1980s and continued his international career until 1991, during which time he played a prominent role in helping them reach the World Cup second round in 1982, the quarter-finals in 1986 and the semi-finals in 1990 where they lost to Germany on penalties. Nicknamed 'Captain Marvel' by England manager Bobby Robson, he was a leader from the front in all respects. At the close of his playing career he was player/manager at Middlesbrough in his native north-east, and has also managed West Bromwich Albion, where he started as a player, among other clubs. He is currently manager of Sheffield United.

HONOURS WON

With Manchester United
♔ European Cup-Winners' Cup 1991
♔ Premiership 1993, 1994
♔ FA Cup 1983, 1985, 1990

92 Roy Keane

Born
Cork
10 August 1971

Country
Republic of Ireland

Position
Midfielder

Clubs
Cobh Ramblers
Nottingham Forest
Manchester United
Celtic

International	
Caps	Goals
66	9

Roy Keane was a dominating and uncompromising central midfielder. A highly effective ball winner, a skilful passer and a player whose commitment to the cause was total, Roy Keane was hugely popular with the fans of whichever team he played for. In a highly successful 16-year club career, he played for Cobh Ramblers, Nottingham Forest and, most notably, Manchester United, before ending his career at Celtic. Keane captained Manchester United from 1997 until his departure in 2005, winning seven Premiership titles, four FA Cups and one Champions League title. He represented the Republic of Ireland for 14 years, most of which he spent as captain, playing 66 times and scoring 9 goals. He played in every game in the 1994 World Cup, although he was sent home from the 2002 tournament after an argument with manager Mick McCarthy. After leaving Manchester United he played for Celtic for a season winning a league and cup Double. He has now turned to management and during his first season as manager at Sunderland, he took the club from 23rd position in the Coca-Cola Championship to the top of the table and promotion.

105

HONOURS WON

With Manchester United
🏆 **Premiership** 1994, 1996, 1997, 1999, 2000, 2001, 2003
🏆 FA Cup 1994, 1996, 1999, 2004
🏆 Champions League 1999
🏆 Intercontinental Cup 1999
With Celtic
🏆 Scottish Premier League 2006
🏆 Scottish League Cup 2006

Other Awards
★ PFA Footballer of the Year 2000
★ Football Writers' Player of the Year 2000

INTERNATIONAL

Brian Laudrup

Born
Born Vienna, Austria 22 February 1969

Country
Denmark

Position
Forward

Clubs
Brondby
Bayer Uerdingen
Bayern Munich
Fiorentina
AC Milan
Rangers
Chelsea
FC Kobenhavn
Ajax

International	
Caps	**Goals**
82	21

A mazy dribbler and crowd pleaser Brian Laudrup's greatest moment was winning the 1992 European Championships with Denmark where his speed was used as the main strike point of a primarily defensive strategy. Brother of Michael, he started his club career in Denmark before moving to Germany. In 1992 he completed a lifelong ambition by signing for Fiorentina in Italy's Serie A, and moved to AC Milan the following year, but his time in Italy was unsuccessful. He signed for Rangers in Scotland in 1994 and really hit form. He helped the Glasgow club complete their nine-in-a-row sweep of Scottish league titles, from 1989 to 1997. After four years at Ibrox he had seasons at Chelsea, Copenhagen and Ajax before retiring in 2000. He played in just one World Cup, in 1998, alongside his brother Michael, reaching the quarter-finals – both were selected as part of the 16 players of the all-star Team of the Tournament. He was voted Danish player of the year four times, appearing 82 times for Denmark and scoring 21 goals.

HONOURS WON

With Denmark
- ♛ European Championship 1992
- ♛ Confederations Cup 1995

With Brondby
- ♛ Danmarksturneringen (Danish League) 1987, 1988

With AC Milan
- ♛ Champions League 1994
- ♛ European Super Cup 1994
- ♛ Serie A 1994
- ♛ Supercoppa Italiana 1994

With Rangers
- ♛ Scottish Premier League 1995, 1996, 1997
- ♛ Scottish FA Cup 1996
- ♛ Scottish League Cup 1997

Other Awards
- ★ Danish Player of the Year 1989, 1992, 1995, 1997
- ★ Confederations Cup 'Golden Ball' 1995
- ★ Scotland's Player of the Year 1995, 1997

94 | Henrik Larsson

Born
Helsingborg
20 September 1971
Country
Sweden
Position
Forward
Clubs
Hogaborgs BK
Helsingborgs IF
Feyenoord
Celtic
Barcelona
Helsingborgs IF
Manchester United

International	
Caps	**Goals**
93	36

A lightning fast striker Henrik Larsson began his career in Sweden but is best known for his exploits with Celtic, helping the club win four titles in seven years, playing 221 matches and scoring a remarkable 173 goals. He subsequently had a two-year spell at Barcelona, where he won two more titles and the Champions League. In the summer of 2006 he retired from international football and returned to his home town club of Helsingborgs IF; however, he was persuaded to join Manchester United on a brief loan spell between January and March 2007 and helped them win the Premiership. Larsson's international record is impressive with 36 goals in 93 games, many of which he played in midfield or as a winger. Larsson liked to make his mark on the big occasions and has scored at three World Cups – 1994, when Sweden came third, 2002 and 2006 – and two European Championships – 2000 and 2004.

HONOURS WON

With Feyenoord
🏆 KNVB Beker (Dutch FA Cup) 1994, 1995

With Celtic
🏆 Scottish Premier League 1998, 2001, 2002, 2004
🏆 Scottish League Cup 1998, 2001
🏆 Scottish Cup 2001, 2004

With Barcelona
🏆 Primera Liga 2005, 2006
🏆 Spanish Supercopa 2006
🏆 Champions League 2006

With Hensingborgs IF
🏆 Swedish Cup 2006

INTERNATIONAL

95 Fabien Barthez

Born
Lavelanet
28 June 1971
Country
France
Position
Goalkeeper
Clubs
Toulouse FC
Olympique Marseille
AS Monaco
Manchester United
Nantes

International	
Caps	**Goals**
87	0

Fabien Barthez was the French goalkeeper in the 1998 World Cup and Euro 2000 winning teams, and was again in goal when France reached the final of the 2006 World Cup. He is considered by many to be France's best ever keeper. He shares the record for most clean sheets in World Cup finals tournaments with Peter Shilton, at 10. Since his international debut in 1994 he appeared 87 times for his country. Barthez made his debut for Toulouse in 1991. He joined Olympique Marseille the following year and won both the championship and the European Cup in his first season. However, the club were later stripped of both titles due to allegations of match-fixing. In 1995, Barthez joined AS Monaco and won Ligue 1 titles in 1997 and 2000. His appearances in the 1998 World Cup and the European Championships in 2000 earned him a move to Manchester United who were still trying to replace Peter Schmeichel between the posts. His first season was a triumph as United won the Premiership title. The next season was mixed as Barthez developed a reputation for dropping expensive clangers. His form continued to stutter and despite winning the title again in 2003 Barthez was sold back to Marseille that summer.

HONOURS WON

With France

♟ World Cup 1998

♟ European Championships 2000

♟ Confederations Cup 2001, 2003

With Olympique Marseille

♟ Championnat 1993**

♟ European Cup 1993**

♟ Intertoto Cup 2005

With AS Monaco

♟ Championnat 1997, 2000

With Manchester United

♟ Premiership 2001, 2003

Other Awards

★ Chevalier of the Legion d'Honneur 1998

*** Marseille were stripped of these titles following allegations of match-fixing*

96 Michael Ballack

Born
Gorlitz
26 September 1976
Country
Germany
Position
Midfielder
Clubs
BSG Motor Karl-Marx-Stadt
Chemnitzer FC
1.FC Kaiserslautern
Bayer Leverkusen
Bayern Munich
Chelsea

International	
Caps	**Goals**
77	35

Michael Ballack is one of the most complete midfielders to have played for Germany. Although winning a Bundesliga title at Kaiserslautern in 1998, he really made his name with Bayer Leverkusen where he operated as the central midfielder, taking on both defensive and attacking responsibilities. He left Leverkusen after a memorable, if ultimately heartbreaking, 2001–02 season when they came second in the Bundesliga to Borussia Dortmund and were beaten in both the Champions League final by Real Madrid and in the German Cup final by Schalke. Ballack moved to Bayern Munich where he excelled in a deeper role, getting forward less often and instead concentrating on protecting the back four and distributing the ball. He won three titles at Bayern, playing 107 games and scoring 44 goals. His power and skills earned him a place in the German national team in 1999 where he has excelled in a box-to-box role. He can play off either foot, as well as being strong in the air. With 77 caps the experienced Ballack is now captain of his country. He played in the 2002 World Cup, but missed the final through suspension, and in 2006 when as hosts Germany reached the semi-finals and made many friends through their attractive attacking football. Ballack was transferred to Chelsea in 2006 where he has been in and out of the first team.

HONOURS WON

With 1.FC Kaiserslautern
🏆 Bundesliga 1998
With Bayern Munich
🏆 Bundesliga 2003, 2005, 2006
🏆 German Cup 2003, 2005, 2006
With Chelsea
🏆 League Cup 2007

Other Awards
★ German Player of the Year 2002, 2003, 2005
★ UEFA Award for Best Midfielder 2002

109

INTERNATIONAL

97 Jan Koller

Born
Smetanova Lhota
30 March 1973
Country
Czech Republic
Position
Forward
Clubs
Sparta Prague
KSC Lokeren
RSC Anderlecht
Borussia Dortmund
AS Monaco

International	
Caps	**Goals**
78	49

Jan Koller is one of the Czech Republic's outstanding players. The 6 ft 8 in colossus, affectionately known as 'Dino', is unbeatable in the air, rides challenges with ease, combining these attributes with excellent technical ability and a great touch for such a big man. He began his career with Sparta Prague at the age of 20 before moving to Lokeren in 1996. The next couple of seasons saw his emergence as a prolific finisher, leading the Belgian scoring charts in 1998–99 with 24 goals. Koller's form earned him a move to Anderlecht, where he collected two league titles. In 2001 he signed for Borussia Dortmund in Germany, winning the Bundesliga title in his very first season. Over the next couple of years Koller forged a reputation as one of the most feared strikers in the Bundesliga. He has made headlines in national colours too, opening his international account on his debut in a 1–1 draw with Belgium in 1999. A year later, he had carved out a regular berth in the national team, and travelled to the 2000 and 2004 European Championships. The aerial powerhouse passed a significant milestone in 2005 in qualifying for the 2006 World Cup Germany when the Czechs met Andorra in Liberec. Koller took his international total to 35 goals during the course of an 8–1 victory, thus overtaking previous leading scorer Antonin Puc. He currently plays his club football with AS Monaco in France.

HONOURS WON

With Sparta Prague
🏆 1.Liga 1995
🏆 Czech Republic Cup 1996
With Anderlecht
🏆 Jupiler League 2000, 2001
With Borussia Dortmund
🏆 Bundesliga 2002

Other Awards
★ Belgian Player of the Year 2000
★ Czech Republic Player of the Year 2001

98 Edwin van der Sar

Born
Voorhout
29 October 1970

Country
Holland

Position
Goalkeeper

Clubs
Ajax
Juventus
Fulham
Manchester United

International	
Caps	Goals
119	0

Edwin van der Sar progressed through the ranks of Ajax's youth system and enjoyed a long and successful career with the Amsterdam club, winning the UEFA Cup in 1992, four league titles and the Champions League in 1995. In total, he made 226 appearances for Ajax and was named Best European Goalkeeper in 1993 and 1995. He went on to play for Juventus in Italy before moving to Fulham in 2001 and Manchester United in 2005. Perhaps the greatest accolade that this dependable and commanding goalkeeper has ever had is that Sir Alex Ferguson finally feels that he has found a replacement for Peter Schmeichel. Van der Sar's performances played a big part in United's Premiership victory in 2007. Van der Sar is also captain of Holland and was in goal for Euro 96, the 1998 World Cup and Euro 2000 – from which Holland were eliminated in penalty shootouts. Prior to the 2006 World Cup group match against Ivory Coast, van der Sar had kept a clean sheet in 10 consecutive competitive matches, not conceding a goal for 1,013 minutes – a European record. He is also Holland's most capped player with 119 appearances.

HONOURS WON

With Ajax
- 🏆 UEFA Cup 1992
- 🏆 KNVB Pokal (Dutch FA Cup) 1993, 1998, 1999
- 🏆 Eredivisie 1994, 1995, 1996, 1998
- 🏆 Champions League 1995
- 🏆 European Super Cup 1995
- 🏆 Intercontinental Cup 1995

With Fulham
- 🏆 Intertoto Cup 2002

With Manchester United
- 🏆 League Cup 2006
- 🏆 Premiership 2007

99 | Robert Pires

Born
Reims
29 October 1973
Country
France
Position
Midfielder
Clubs
Metz
Olympique Marseille
Arsenal
Villarreal

International	
Caps	**Goals**
79	14

Robert Pires is a graduate of the FC Metz youth academy, making his senior debut in 1993 against Lyon. During his six seasons there, he scored 43 goals in 162 matches, and won the Coupe de la Ligue, before moving to Olympique Marseille in 1998. Two years later he moved to England and became part of the French revolution at Arsenal. Once he had adapted to the physicality of the English game he started to blossom, scoring 62 goals in 189 games. He played a major part in the Gunners' league and cup Double in 2001–02 when he was voted Player of the Year. He won another league championship in 2004 and two more FA Cup winner's medals, scoring the only goal of the final against Southampton in 2003.

A regular fixture in the French national team since 1996, he has played 79 times for his country and scored 14 goals. He played in the 1998 World Cup final and in the European Championships final in 2000, laying on the goal for David Trezeguet that won the match in extra time. He missed the 2002 World Cup through injury. In 2006 he left Arsenal and currently plays in Spain with Villarreal.

HONOURS WON

With France
- 🏆 World Cup 1998
- 🏆 European Championships 2000
- 🏆 Confederations Cup winner 2001, 2003

With Metz
- 🏆 French League Cup 1996
- 🏆 Championnat 1998

With Arsenal
- 🏆 Premiership 2002, 2004
- 🏆 FA Cup 2002, 2003

Other Awards
- ★ Chevalier of the Legion d'Honneur 1998
- ★ Football Writers' Association Player of the Year 2002

100 Johan Neeskens

Born	
Heemstede	
15 September 1951	
Country	
Holland	
Position	
Midfielder	
Clubs	
Ajax	
Barcelona	
New York Cosmos	
FC Groningen	
Fort Lauderdale Sun	
FC Baar	
FC Zug	

International	
Caps	**Goals**
49	17

Often overshadowed by his team-mate Johan Cruyff, Johan Neeskens was one of the greatest midfield players of the 1970s and a key exponent of the Dutch school of Total Football. Integral to the mighty Ajax side that won three consecutive European Cups in the early 1970s, he was also a vital part of the Dutch international team that reached the World Cup finals of 1974 and 1978. Armed with pace, skill and tremendous ball control he dominated the midfield at Ajax when the club swept all before them both domestically and in Europe. He followed Cruyff to Barcelona after the 1974 World Cup and spent five good years in Spain winning domestic and European honours. In 1979 he joined the trail of players to the NASL in the United States, playing with Carlos Alberto and Franz Beckenbauer among others. He wound down his career in America and at various smaller clubs in Europe before retiring in 1991. He is currently assistant coach at Barcelona.

HONOURS WON

With Ajax
🏆 Eredivisie 1970, 1972, 1973
🏆 European Cup 1971, 1972, 1973
🏆 Intercontinental Cup 1972
🏆 European Super Cup 1972, 1973
With Barcelona
🏆 Copa del Rey 1978
🏆 European Cup-Winners' Cup 1979

With New York Cosmos
🏆 North American Soccer League 1980, 1982
Other Awards
★ Spain's Foreign Footballer of the Year 1976

GREATEST EVER
PLAYERS OF ALL TIME BY POSITION

TOP 20 GOALKEEPERS

Rank	Player	Country	Points
1	Peter Schmeichel	Denmark	8658.03
2	Sepp Maier	Germany	8489.67
3	Oliver Kahn	Germany	7870.11
4	Dino Zoff	Italy	7616.16
5	Claudio Taffarel	Brazil	6536.65
6	Fabien Barthez	France	6422.05
7	Edwin van der Sar	Holland	6289.49
8	Ray Clemence	England	6172.88
9	Nelson Dida	Brazil	6092.15
10	Peter Shilton	England	5898.77
11	Jim Leighton	Scotland	5342.56
12	Gilmar	Brazil	5188.12
13	Andy Goram	Scotland	4926.21
14	Gianluigi Buffon	Italy	4560.38
15	David Seaman	England	4257.33
16	Pat Jennings	Northern Ireland	4254.26
17	Ubaldo Matildo Fillol	Argentina	4206.36
18	Iker Casillas	Spain	4189.28
19	Jorge Campos	Mexico	4185.37
20	Neville Southall	Wales	3891.94

TOP 20 DEFENDERS

Rank	Player	Country	Points
1	Franz Beckenbauer	Germany	12057.33
2	Cafu	Brazil	12054.30
3	Roberto Carlos	Brazil	11785.98
4	Paolo Maldini	Italy	10818.74
5	Lilian Thuram	France	8315.78
6	Marcel Desailly	France	7895.00
7	Alessandro Costacurta	Italy	7857.02
8	Daniel Passarella	Argentina	7394.15
9	Bixente Lizarazu	France	7371.81
10	Jurgen Kohler	Germany	7073.08
11	Laurent Blanc	France	7063.44
12	Frank De Boer	Holland	6924.14
13	Djalma Santos	Brazil	6788.03
14	Giacinto Facchetti	Italy	6778.02
15	Franco Baresi	Italy	6759.64
16	Oscar Alfredo Ruggeri	Argentina	6703.04
17	Gheorghe Popescu	Romania	6688.26
18	Gary Neville	England	6544.10
19	Claudio Suarez	Mexico	6190.92
20	Giuseppe Bergomi	Italy	5906.21

TOP 20 MIDFIELDERS

Rank	Player	Country	Points
1	Zinedine Zidane	France	12892.13
2	Diego Maradona	Argentina	12503.85
3	Lothar Matthaus	Germany	12416.36
4	Michel Platini	France	11477.91
5	Zico	Brazil	10734.48
6	Ruud Gullit	Holland	10306.85
7	Ferenc Puskas	Hungary/Spain	10074.55
8	Michael Laudrup	Denmark	9119.21
9	Frank Rijkaard	Holland	9023.08
10	Pavel Nedved	Czech Republic	8876.48
11	Gheorghe Hagi	Romania	8659.23
12	Didier Deschamps	France	8378.33
13	Enzo Francescoli	Uruguay	8295.38
14	David Beckham	England	7967.26
15	Clarence Seedorf	Holland	7642.02
16	Jari Litmanen	Finland	7538.97
17	Ronaldinho	Brazil	7297.77
18	Ryan Giggs	Wales	7136.91
19	Demetrio Albertini	Italy	7087.52
20	Patrick Vieira	France	7082.41

TOP 20 FORWARDS

Rank	Player	Country	Points
1	Pele	Brazil	16799.44
2	Ronaldo	Brazil	16793.14
3	Romario	Brazil	13444.86
4	Luis Figo	Portugal	12951.16
5	Gerd Muller	West Germany	12175.23
6	Marco van Basten	Holland	11681.92
7	Rivaldo	Brazil	11176.64
8	Raul	Spain	10689.60
9	Eusebio	Portugal	10289.84
10	Johan Cruyff	Holland	10060.14
11	Alfredo di Stefano	Argentina/Spain	9973.13
12	Bobby Charlton	England	9860.07
13	Jurgen Klinsmann	Germany	9840.02
14	Kenny Dalglish	Scotland	9806.45
15	Ali Daei	Iran	9704.11
16	Karl-Heinz Rummenigge	West Germany	9259.39
17	Gabriel Batistuta	Argentina	9165.79
18	Hristo Stoichkov	Bulgaria	9039.16
19	Dennis Bergkamp	Holland	9031.85
20	Thierry Henry	France	8972.91

INTERNATIONAL

GREATEST EVER
WORLD XI OF ALL TIME

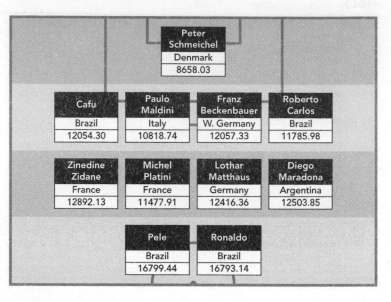

	Peter Schmeichel Denmark 8658.03		
Cafu Brazil 12054.30	Paulo Maldini Italy 10818.74	Franz Beckenbauer W. Germany 12057.33	Roberto Carlos Brazil 11785.98
Zinedine Zidane France 12892.13	Michel Platini France 11477.91	Lothar Matthaus Germany 12416.36	Diego Maradona Argentina 12503.85
	Pele Brazil 16799.44	Ronaldo Brazil 16793.14	

GREATEST EVER
WORLD XI BY DECADE

1930s

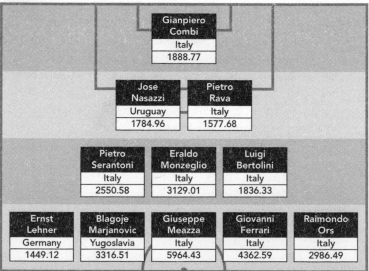

		Gianpiero Combi Italy 1888.77		
	Jose Nasazzi Uruguay 1784.96	Pietro Rava Italy 1577.68		
	Pietro Serantoni Italy 2550.58	Eraldo Monzeglio Italy 3129.01	Luigi Bertolini Italy 1836.33	
Ernst Lehner Germany 1449.12	Blagoje Marjanovic Yugoslavia 3316.51	Giuseppe Meazza Italy 5964.43	Giovanni Ferrari Italy 4362.59	Raimondo Ors Italy 2986.49

1940s

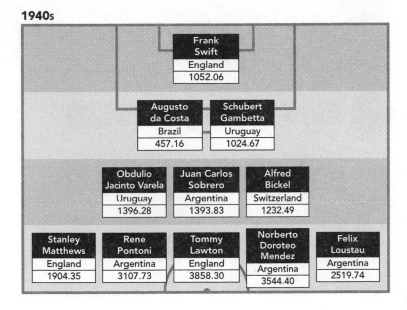

	Frank Swift	
	England	
	1052.06	

Augusto da Costa	Schubert Gambetta
Brazil	Uruguay
457.16	1024.67

Obdulio Jacinto Varela	Juan Carlos Sobrero	Alfred Bickel
Uruguay	Argentina	Switzerland
1396.28	1393.83	1232.49

Stanley Matthews	Rene Pontoni	Tommy Lawton	Norberto Doroteo Mendez	Felix Loustau
England	Argentina	England	Argentina	Argentina
1904.35	3107.73	3858.30	3544.40	2519.74

1950s

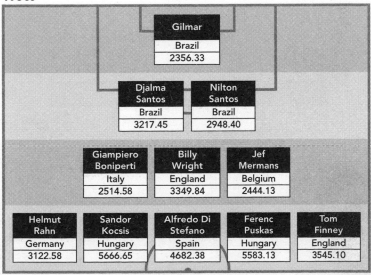

	Gilmar	
	Brazil	
	2356.33	

Djalma Santos	Nilton Santos
Brazil	Brazil
3217.45	2948.40

Giampiero Boniperti	Billy Wright	Jef Mermans
Italy	England	Belgium
2514.58	3349.84	2444.13

Helmut Rahn	Sandor Kocsis	Alfredo Di Stefano	Ferenc Puskas	Tom Finney
Germany	Hungary	Spain	Hungary	England
3122.58	5666.65	4682.38	5583.13	3545.10

1960s

	Gilmar Brazil 2705.69		

Djalma Santos Brazil 3120.57	**Giacinto Facchetti** Italy 4413.84	**Bobby Moore** England 4395.51	**Ray Wilson** England 3110.45
Garrincha Brazil 2832.70	**Gianni Rivera** Italy 3387.04	**Bobby Charlton** England 7943.04	**George Best** N. Ireland 2663.84

	Eusebio Portugal 6140.48	**Pele** Brazil 9194.03	

1970s

	Sepp Maier W. Germany 6940.45		

Berti Vogts W. Germany 3713.24	**Franz Beckenbauer** W. Germany 8685.68	**Emlyn Hughes** England 4079.12	**Paul Breitner** W. Germany 4965.92
Kevin Keegan England 5654.65	**Johan Neeskens** Holland 5316.12	**Johan Cruyff** Holland 8080.65	**Rivelino** Brazil 4769.81

	Kenny Dalglish Scotland 4845.62	**Gerd Muller** W. Germany 9173.61	

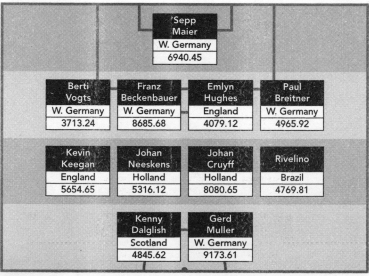

1980s

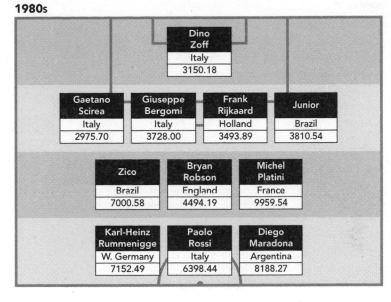

	Dino Zoff Italy 3150.18		
Gaetano Scirea Italy 2975.70	**Giuseppe Bergomi** Italy 3728.00	**Frank Rijkaard** Holland 3493.89	**Junior** Brazil 3810.54
	Zico Brazil 7000.58	**Bryan Robson** England 4494.19	**Michel Platini** France 9959.54
	Karl-Heinz Rummenigge W. Germany 7152.49	**Paolo Rossi** Italy 6398.44	**Diego Maradona** Argentina 8188.27

119

1990s

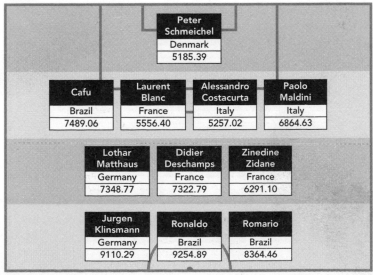

	Peter Schmeichel Denmark 5185.39		
Cafu Brazil 7489.06	**Laurent Blanc** France 5556.40	**Alessandro Costacurta** Italy 5257.02	**Paolo Maldini** Italy 6864.63
	Lothar Matthaus Germany 7348.77	**Didier Deschamps** France 7322.79	**Zinedine Zidane** France 6291.10
	Jurgen Klinsmann Germany 9110.29	**Ronaldo** Brazil 9254.89	**Romario** Brazil 8364.46

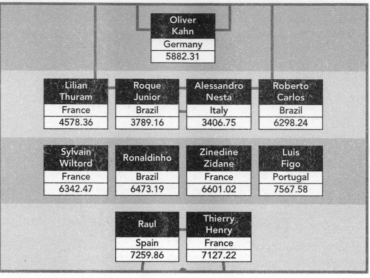

Oliver Kahn			
Germany			
5882.31			

Lilian Thuram	Roque Junior	Alessandro Nesta	Roberto Carlos
France	Brazil	Italy	Brazil
4578.36	3789.16	3406.75	6298.24

Sylvain Wiltord	Ronaldinho	Zinedine Zidane	Luis Figo
France	Brazil	France	Portugal
6342.47	6473.19	6601.02	7567.58

Raul	Thierry Henry
Spain	France
7259.86	7127.22

GREATEST EVER
ENGLAND XI OF ALL TIME

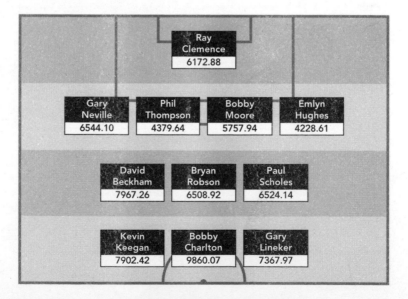

| Ray Clemence |
| 6172.88 |

| Gary Neville | Phil Thompson | Bobby Moore | Emlyn Hughes |
| 6544.10 | 4379.64 | 5757.94 | 4228.61 |

| David Beckham | Bryan Robson | Paul Scholes |
| 7967.26 | 6508.92 | 6524.14 |

| Kevin Keegan | Bobby Charlton | Gary Lineker |
| 7902.42 | 9860.07 | 7367.97 |

GREATEST EVER
ENGLAND XI OF REGISTERED PLAYERS

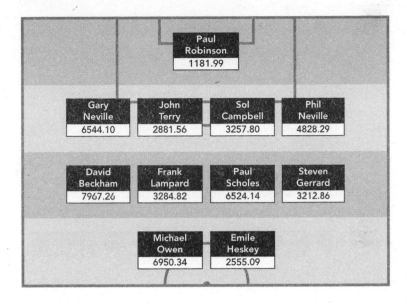

	Paul Robinson 1181.99		
Gary Neville 6544.10	John Terry 2881.56	Sol Campbell 3257.80	Phil Neville 4828.29
David Beckham 7967.26	Frank Lampard 3284.82	Paul Scholes 6524.14	Steven Gerrard 3212.86
	Michael Owen 6950.34	Emile Heskey 2555.09	

GREATEST EVER
ENGLAND XI OF RETIRED PLAYERS

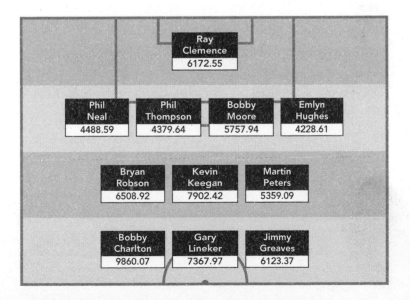

	Ray Clemence 6172.55		
Phil Neal 4488.59	Phil Thompson 4379.64	Bobby Moore 5757.94	Emlyn Hughes 4228.61
	Bryan Robson 6508.92	Kevin Keegan 7902.42	Martin Peters 5359.09
	Bobby Charlton 9860.07	Gary Lineker 7367.97	Jimmy Greaves 6123.37

GREATEST EVER
ENGLAND XI BY DECADE

1930s

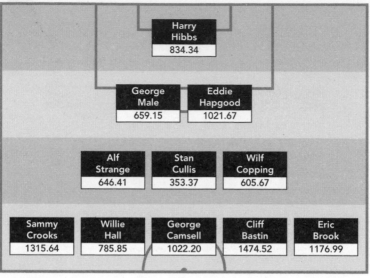

Harry Hibbs	
834.34	

George Male	Eddie Hapgood
659.15	1021.67

Alf Strange	Stan Cullis	Wilf Copping
646.41	353.37	605.67

Sammy Crooks	Willie Hall	George Camsell	Cliff Bastin	Eric Brook
1315.64	785.85	1022.20	1474.52	1176.99

1940s

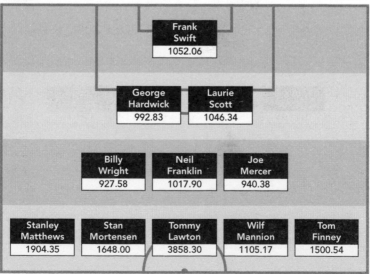

Frank Swift	
1052.06	

George Hardwick	Laurie Scott
992.83	1046.34

Billy Wright	Neil Franklin	Joe Mercer
927.58	1017.90	940.38

Stanley Matthews	Stan Mortensen	Tommy Lawton	Wilf Mannion	Tom Finney
1904.35	1648.00	3858.30	1105.17	1500.54

1950s

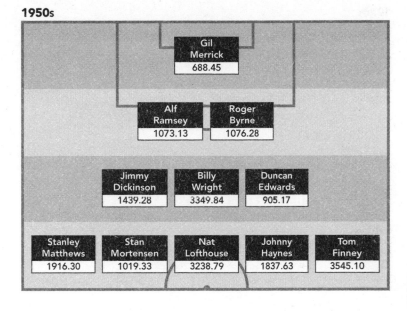

Gil Merrick	688.45

Alf Ramsey	1073.13	**Roger Byrne**	1076.28

Jimmy Dickinson	1439.28	**Billy Wright**	3349.84	**Duncan Edwards**	905.17

Stanley Matthews	**Stan Mortensen**	**Nat Lofthouse**	**Johnny Haynes**	**Tom Finney**
1916.30	1019.33	3238.79	1837.63	3545.10

123

1960s

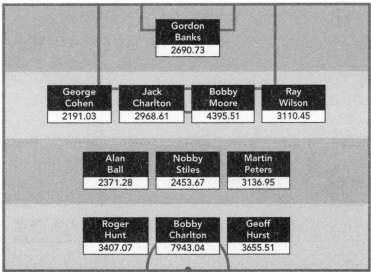

Gordon Banks	2690.73

George Cohen	**Jack Charlton**	**Bobby Moore**	**Ray Wilson**
2191.03	2968.61	4395.51	3110.45

Alan Ball	**Nobby Stiles**	**Martin Peters**
2371.28	2453.67	3136.95

Roger Hunt	**Bobby Charlton**	**Geoff Hurst**
3407.07	7943.04	3655.51

1970s

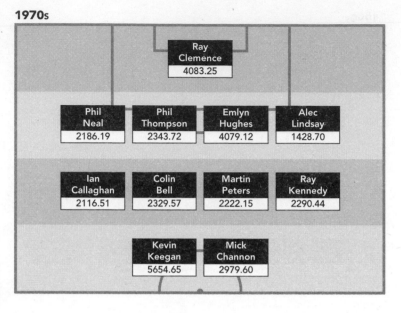

Player	Value
Ray Clemence	4083.25
Phil Neal	2186.19
Phil Thompson	2343.72
Emlyn Hughes	4079.12
Alec Lindsay	1428.70
Ian Callaghan	2116.51
Colin Bell	2329.57
Martin Peters	2222.15
Ray Kennedy	2290.44
Kevin Keegan	5654.65
Mick Channon	2979.60

1980s

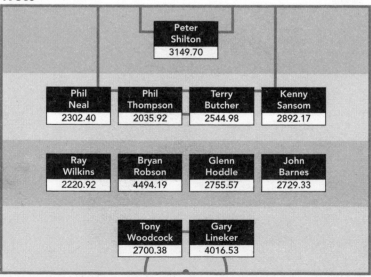

Player	Value
Peter Shilton	3149.70
Phil Neal	2302.40
Phil Thompson	2035.92
Terry Butcher	2544.98
Kenny Sansom	2892.17
Ray Wilkins	2220.92
Bryan Robson	4494.19
Glenn Hoddle	2755.57
John Barnes	2729.33
Tony Woodcock	2700.38
Gary Lineker	4016.53

1990s

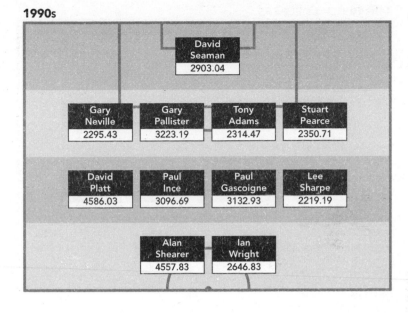

	David Seaman 2903.04		
Gary Neville 2295.43	**Gary Pallister** 3223.19	**Tony Adams** 2314.47	**Stuart Pearce** 2350.71
David Platt 4586.03	**Paul Ince** 3096.69	**Paul Gascoigne** 3132.93	**Lee Sharpe** 2219.19
	Alan Shearer 4557.83	**Ian Wright** 2646.83	

2000s

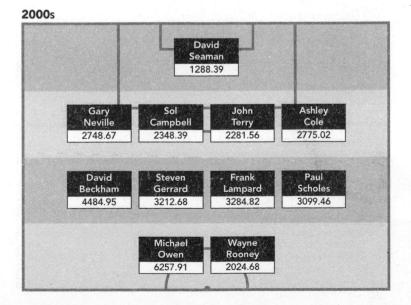

	David Seaman 1288.39		
Gary Neville 2748.67	**Sol Campbell** 2348.39	**John Terry** 2281.56	**Ashley Cole** 2775.02
David Beckham 4484.95	**Steven Gerrard** 3212.68	**Frank Lampard** 3284.82	**Paul Scholes** 3099.46
	Michael Owen 6257.91	**Wayne Rooney** 2024.68	

INTERNATIONAL

GREATEST EVER
ENGLAND INTERNATIONAL PLAYERS BY POSITION

TOP 10 GOALKEEPERS

Rank	Player	Points
1	Ray Clemence	6172.88
2	Peter Shilton	5898.77
3	David Seaman	4257.33
4	Gordon Banks	3718.90
5	Chris Woods	2439.95
6	Bert Williams	1309.90
7	Paul Robinson	1181.99
8	David James	1168.77
9	Ron Springett	1080.35
10	Frank Swift	1052.06

TOP 10 DEFENDERS

Rank	Player	Points
1	Gary Neville	6544.10
2	Bobby Moore	5757.94
3	Phil Neville	4828.29
4	Phil Neal	4488.59
5	Phil Thompson	4379.64
6	Emlyn Hughes	4228.61
7	Tony Adams	4007.14
8	Jack Charlton	3575.52
9	Martin Keown	3466.97
10	Sol Campbell	3257.80

TOP 10 MIDFIELDERS

Rank	Player	Points
1	David Beckham	7967.26
2	Paul Scholes	6524.14
3	Bryan Robson	6508.92
4	Martin Peters	5359.09
5	Nicky Butt	5041.82
6	David Platt	4586.03
7	Alan Ball	3851.05
8	Chris Waddle	3615.25
9	Terry McDermott	3555.41
10	Steve McManaman	3472.00

TOP 10 FORWARDS

Rank	Player	Points
1	Bobby Charlton	9860.07
2	Kevin Keegan	7902.42
3	Gary Lineker	7367.97
4	Michael Owen	6950.34
5	Jimmy Greaves	6123.37
6	Alan Shearer	5364.71
7	Stanley Matthews	5130.09
8	Tom Finney	5045.64
9	Teddy Sheringham	4856.53
10	Geoff Hurst	4650.15

GREATEST EVER
NORTHERN IRELAND XI OF ALL TIME

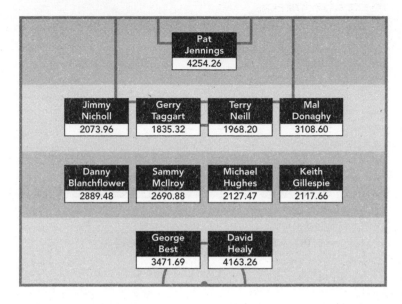

Player	Value
Pat Jennings	4254.26
Jimmy Nicholl	2073.96
Gerry Taggart	1835.32
Terry Neill	1968.20
Mal Donaghy	3108.60
Danny Blanchflower	2889.48
Sammy McIlroy	2690.88
Michael Hughes	2127.47
Keith Gillespie	2117.66
George Best	3471.69
David Healy	4163.26

GREATEST EVER
NORTHERN IRELAND XI OF REGISTERED PLAYERS

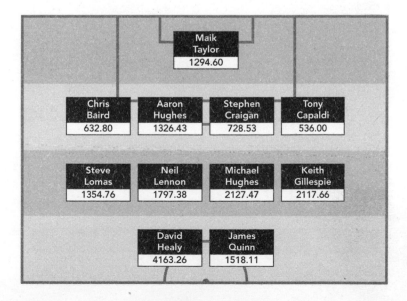

Player	Value
Maik Taylor	1294.60
Chris Baird	632.80
Aaron Hughes	1326.43
Stephen Craigan	728.53
Tony Capaldi	536.00
Steve Lomas	1354.76
Neil Lennon	1797.38
Michael Hughes	2127.47
Keith Gillespie	2117.66
David Healy	4163.26
James Quinn	1518.11

GREATEST EVER
NORTHERN IRELAND XI OF RETIRED PLAYERS

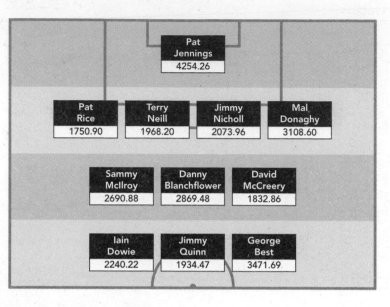

Pat Jennings — 4254.26

Pat Rice — 1750.90
Terry Neill — 1968.20
Jimmy Nicholl — 2073.96
Mal Donaghy — 3108.60

Sammy McIlroy — 2690.88
Danny Blanchflower — 2869.48
David McCreery — 1832.86

Iain Dowie — 2240.22
Jimmy Quinn — 1934.47
George Best — 3471.69

GREATEST EVER
NORTHERN IRELAND XI BY DECADE

1950s

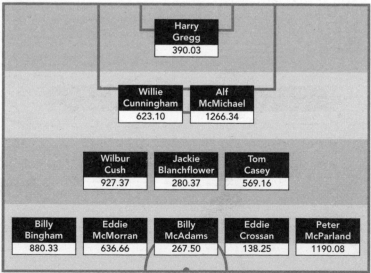

Harry Gregg — 390.03

Willie Cunningham — 623.10
Alf McMichael — 1266.34

Wilbur Cush — 927.37
Jackie Blanchflower — 280.37
Tom Casey — 569.16

Billy Bingham — 880.33
Eddie McMorran — 636.66
Billy McAdams — 267.50
Eddie Crossan — 138.25
Peter McParland — 1190.08

1960s

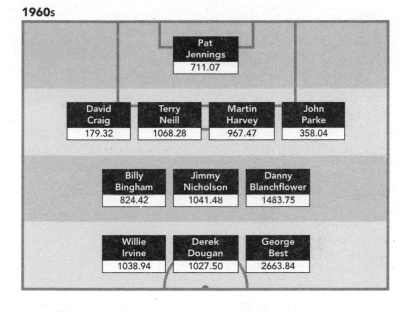

| Pat Jennings |
| 711.07 |

| David Craig | Terry Neill | Martin Harvey | John Parke |
| 179.32 | 1068.28 | 967.47 | 358.04 |

| Billy Bingham | Jimmy Nicholson | Danny Blanchflower |
| 824.42 | 1041.48 | 1483.75 |

| Willie Irvine | Derek Dougan | George Best |
| 1038.94 | 1027.50 | 2663.84 |

1970s

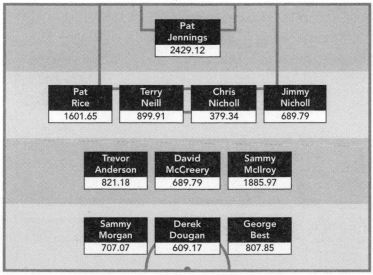

| Pat Jennings |
| 2429.12 |

| Pat Rice | Terry Neill | Chris Nicholl | Jimmy Nicholl |
| 1601.65 | 899.91 | 379.34 | 689.79 |

| Trevor Anderson | David McCreery | Sammy McIlroy |
| 821.18 | 689.79 | 1885.97 |

| Sammy Morgan | Derek Dougan | George Best |
| 707.07 | 609.17 | 807.85 |

1980s

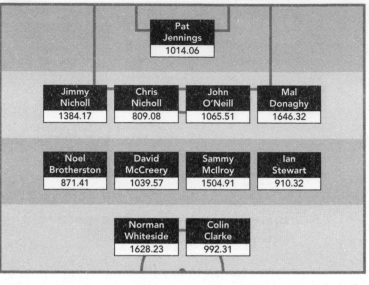

	Pat Jennings		
	1014.06		

Jimmy Nicholl	Chris Nicholl	John O'Neill	Mal Donaghy
1384.17	809.08	1065.51	1646.32

Noel Brotherston	David McCreery	Sammy McIlroy	Ian Stewart
871.41	1039.57	1504.91	910.32

Norman Whiteside	Colin Clarke
1628.23	992.31

1990s

	Tommy Wright		
	724.18		

Gary Fleming	Gerry Taggart	Steve Morrow	Keith Rowland
572.03	1629.41	1561.43	541.64

Neil Lennon	Steve Lomas	Jim Magilton	Nigel Worthington
861.38	898.67	1306.98	1097.32

Kevin Wilson	Iain Dowie
1123.84	2164.72

2000s

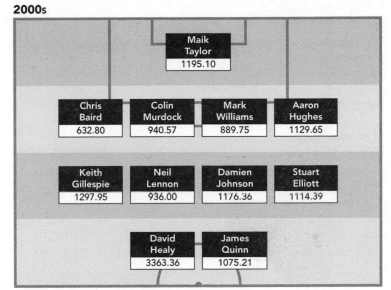

		Maik Taylor
		1195.10

Chris Baird	Colin Murdock	Mark Williams	Aaron Hughes
632.80	940.57	889.75	1129.65

Keith Gillespie	Neil Lennon	Damien Johnson	Stuart Elliott
1297.95	936.00	1176.36	1114.39

David Healy	James Quinn
3363.36	1075.21

GREATEST EVER
NORTHERN IRELAND INTERNATIONAL PLAYERS BY POSITION

TOP 10 GOALKEEPERS

Rank	Player	Points
1	Pat Jennings	4254.26
2	Maik Taylor	1294.60
3	Roy Carroll	832.65
4	Tommy Wright	800.34
5	Harry Gregg	719.17
6	Alan Fettis	635.21
7	Jim Platt	579.60
8	Allen McKnight	259.65
9	Norman Uprichard	178.00
10	Ted Hinton	176.70

TOP 10 DEFENDERS

Rank	Player	Points
1	Mal Donaghy	3108.60
2	Jimmy Nicholl	2073.96
3	Terry Neill	1968.20
4	Gerry Taggart	1835.32
5	Pat Rice	1750.90
6	Steve Morrow	1612.03
7	Chris Nicholl	1600.42
8	Alan McDonald	1538.38
9	Alf McMichael	1342.84
10	Aaron Hughes	1326.43

INTERNATIONAL

TOP 10 MIDFIELDERS

Rank	Player	Points
1	Danny Blanchflower	2889.48
2	Sammy McIlroy	2690.88
3	Michael Hughes	2127.47
4	Keith Gillespie	2117.66
5	David McCreery	1832.86
6	Neil Lennon	1797.38
7	Jim Magilton	1745.71
8	Nigel Worthington	1743.79
9	Jimmy Nicholson	1525.92
10	Bryan Hamilton	1513.75

TOP 10 FORWARDS

Rank	Player	Points
1	David Healy	4163.26
2	George Best	3471.69
3	Iain Dowie	2240.22
4	Jimmy Quinn	1934.47
5	Colin Clarke	1791.44
6	Norman Whiteside	1748.73
7	Derek Dougan	1662.83
8	James Quinn	1518.11
9	Kevin Wilson	1456.74
10	Billy Hamilton	1417.95

132

GREATEST EVER
REPUBLIC OF IRELAND XI OF ALL TIME

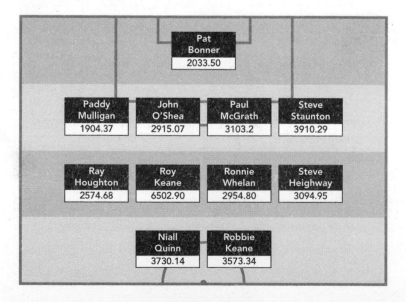

GREATEST EVER
REPUBLIC OF IRELAND XI OF REGISTERED PLAYERS

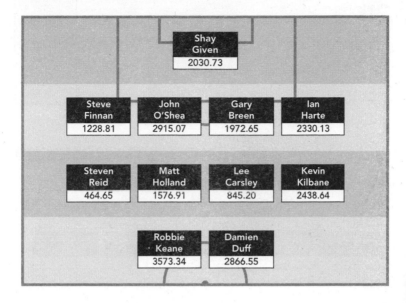

Shay Given
2030.73

Steve Finnan
1228.81

John O'Shea
2915.07

Gary Breen
1972.65

Ian Harte
2330.13

Steven Reid
464.65

Matt Holland
1576.91

Lee Carsley
845.20

Kevin Kilbane
2438.64

Robbie Keane
3573.34

Damien Duff
2866.55

GREATEST EVER
REPUBLIC OF IRELAND XI OF RETIRED PLAYERS

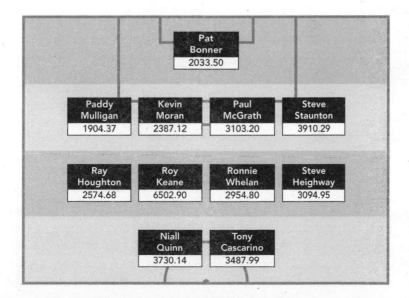

Pat Bonner
2033.50

Paddy Mulligan
1904.37

Kevin Moran
2387.12

Paul McGrath
3103.20

Steve Staunton
3910.29

Ray Houghton
2574.68

Roy Keane
6502.90

Ronnie Whelan
2954.80

Steve Heighway
3094.95

Niall Quinn
3730.14

Tony Cascarino
3487.99

INTERNATIONAL

GREATEST EVER
REPUBLIC OF IRELAND XI BY DECADE

1940s

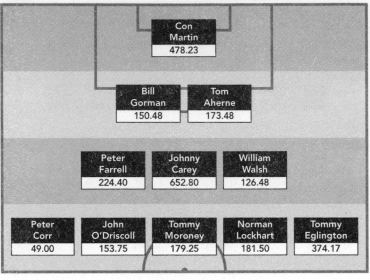

Con Martin	478.23

Bill Gorman	150.48	Tom Aherne	173.48

| Peter Farrell | 224.40 | Johnny Carey | 652.80 | William Walsh | 126.48 |

| Peter Corr | 49.00 | John O'Driscoll | 153.75 | Tommy Moroney | 179.25 | Norman Lockhart | 181.50 | Tommy Eglington | 374.17 |

134

1950s

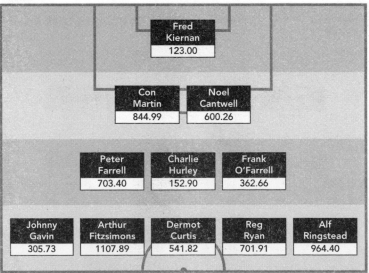

| Fred Kiernan | 123.00 |

| Con Martin | 844.99 | Noel Cantwell | 600.26 |

| Peter Farrell | 703.40 | Charlie Hurley | 152.90 | Frank O'Farrell | 362.66 |

| Johnny Gavin | 305.73 | Arthur Fitzsimons | 1107.89 | Dermot Curtis | 541.82 | Reg Ryan | 701.91 | Alf Ringstead | 964.40 |

1960s

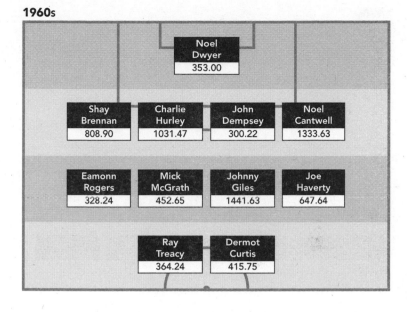

	Noel Dwyer 353.00		
Shay Brennan 808.90	Charlie Hurley 1031.47	John Dempsey 300.22	Noel Cantwell 1333.63
Eamonn Rogers 328.24	Mick McGrath 452.65	Johnny Giles 1441.63	Joe Haverty 647.64
	Ray Treacy 364.24	Dermot Curtis 415.75	

1970s

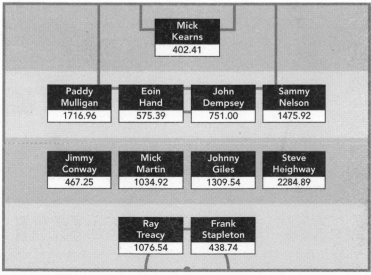

	Mick Kearns 402.41		
Paddy Mulligan 1716.96	Eoin Hand 575.39	John Dempsey 751.00	Sammy Nelson 1475.92
Jimmy Conway 467.25	Mick Martin 1034.92	Johnny Giles 1309.54	Steve Heighway 2284.89
	Ray Treacy 1076.54	Frank Stapleton 438.74	

INTERNATIONAL

1980s

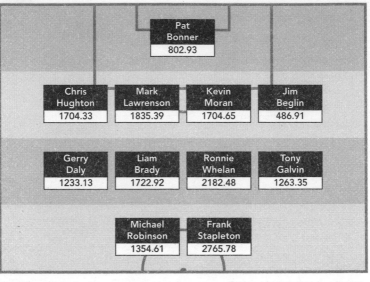

	Pat Bonner 802.93	

Chris Hughton 1704.33	Mark Lawrenson 1835.39	Kevin Moran 1704.65	Jim Beglin 486.91

Gerry Daly 1233.13	Liam Brady 1722.92	Ronnie Whelan 2182.48	Tony Galvin 1263.35

Michael Robinson 1354.61	Frank Stapleton 2765.78

1990s

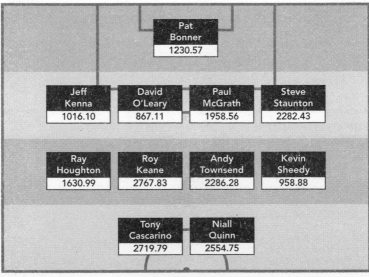

	Pat Bonner 1230.57	

Jeff Kenna 1016.10	David O'Leary 867.11	Paul McGrath 1958.56	Steve Staunton 2282.43

Ray Houghton 1630.99	Roy Keane 2767.83	Andy Townsend 2286.28	Kevin Sheedy 958.88

Tony Cascarino 2719.79	Niall Quinn 2554.75

2000s

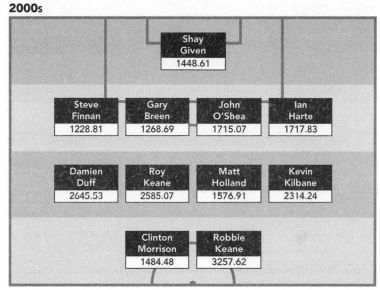

Shay Given 1448.61

Steve Finnan 1228.81 — Gary Breen 1268.69 — John O'Shea 1715.07 — Ian Harte 1717.83

Damien Duff 2645.53 — Roy Keane 2585.07 — Matt Holland 1576.91 — Kevin Kilbane 2314.24

Clinton Morrison 1484.48 — Robbie Keane 3257.62

GREATEST EVER
REPUBLIC OF IRELAND INTERNATIONAL PLAYERS BY POSITION

TOP 10 GOALKEEPERS

Rank	Player	Points
1	Pat Bonner	2033.50
2	Shay Given	2030.73
3	Con Martin	1323.22
4	Nick Colgan	921.00
5	Gerry Peyton	852.18
6	Mick Kearns	501.66
7	Noel Dwyer	353.00
8	Paddy Roche	273.72
9	Dean Kiely	196.50
10	Paddy Kenny	171.25

TOP 10 DEFENDERS

Rank	Player	Points
1	Steve Staunton	3910.29
2	Paul McGrath	3103.20
3	John O'Shea	2915.07
4	Kevin Moran	2387.12
5	Ian Harte	2330.13
6	David O'Leary	2151.77
7	Mark Lawrenson	2013.39
8	Gary Breen	1972.65
9	Noel Cantwell	1933.89
10	Paddy Mulligan	1904.37

TOP 10 MIDFIELDERS

Rank	Player	Points
1	Roy Keane	6502.90
2	Ronnie Whelan	2954.80
3	Liam Brady	2867.79
4	Kevin Sheedy	2866.73
5	Damien Duff	2866.50
6	Johnny Giles	2751.17
7	Ray Houghton	2574.68
8	Kevin Kilbane	2438.64
9	Andy Townsend	2389.76
10	Gerry Daly	2119.53

TOP 10 FORWARDS

Rank	Player	Points
1	Niall Quinn	3730.14
2	Robbie Keane	3573.34
3	Tony Cascarino	3487.99
4	Frank Stapleton	3473.52
5	John Aldridge	3102.30
6	Steve Heighway	3094.95
7	David Connolly	1901.51
8	Billy Bingham	1704.75
9	Clinton Morrison	1484.48
10	Ray Treacy	1465.78

GREATEST EVER
SCOTLAND XI OF ALL TIME

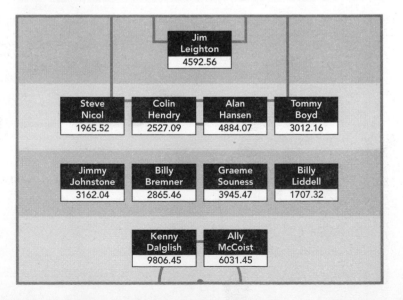

Jim Leighton 4592.56

Steve Nicol 1965.52 | Colin Hendry 2527.09 | Alan Hansen 4884.07 | Tommy Boyd 3012.16

Jimmy Johnstone 3162.04 | Billy Bremner 2865.46 | Graeme Souness 3945.47 | Billy Liddell 1707.32

Kenny Dalglish 9806.45 | Ally McCoist 6031.45

GREATEST EVER
SCOTLAND XI OF REGISTERED PLAYERS

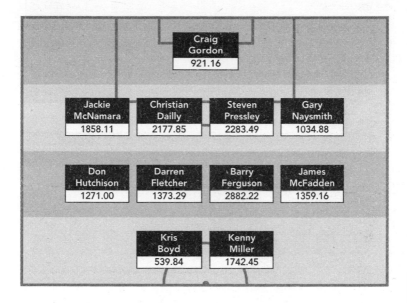

	Craig Gordon		
	921.16		

Jackie McNamara	Christian Dailly	Steven Pressley	Gary Naysmith
1858.11	2177.85	2283.49	1034.88

Don Hutchison	Darren Fletcher	Barry Ferguson	James McFadden
1271.00	1373.29	2882.22	1359.16

Kris Boyd	Kenny Miller
539.84	1742.45

GREATEST EVER
SCOTLAND XI OF RETIRED PLAYERS

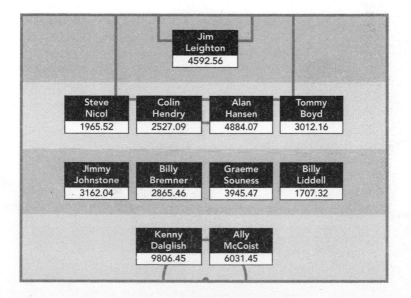

	Jim Leighton		
	4592.56		

Steve Nicol	Colin Hendry	Alan Hansen	Tommy Boyd
1965.52	2527.09	4884.07	3012.16

Jimmy Johnstone	Billy Bremner	Graeme Souness	Billy Liddell
3162.04	2865.46	3945.47	1707.32

Kenny Dalglish	Ally McCoist
9806.45	6031.45

INTERNATIONAL

GREATEST EVER
SCOTLAND XI BY DECADE

1930s

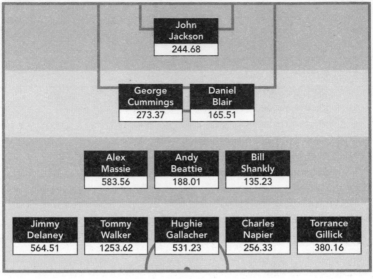

		John Jackson	244.68	
	George Cummings — 273.37	Daniel Blair — 165.51		
	Alex Massie — 583.56	Andy Beattie — 188.01	Bill Shankly — 135.23	
Jimmy Delaney — 564.51	Tommy Walker — 1253.62	Hughie Gallacher — 531.23	Charles Napier — 256.33	Torrance Gillick — 380.16

1940s

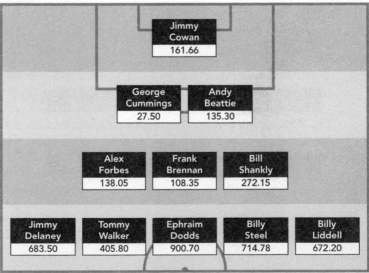

		Jimmy Cowan	161.66	
	George Cummings — 27.50	Andy Beattie — 135.30		
	Alex Forbes — 138.05	Frank Brennan — 108.35	Bill Shankly — 272.15	
Jimmy Delaney — 683.50	Tommy Walker — 405.80	Ephraim Dodds — 900.70	Billy Steel — 714.78	Billy Liddell — 672.20

1950s

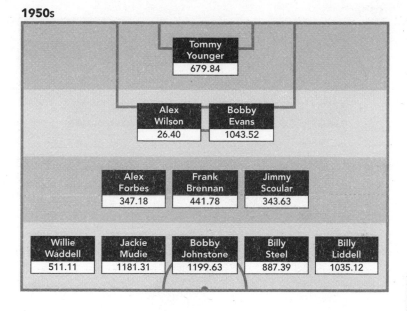

	Tommy Younger 679.84	
Alex Wilson 26.40	**Bobby Evans** 1043.52	
Alex Forbes 347.18	**Frank Brennan** 441.78	**Jimmy Scoular** 343.63
Willie Waddell 511.11	**Jackie Mudie** 1181.31	**Bobby Johnstone** 1199.63	**Billy Steel** 887.39	**Billy Liddell** 1035.12

1960s

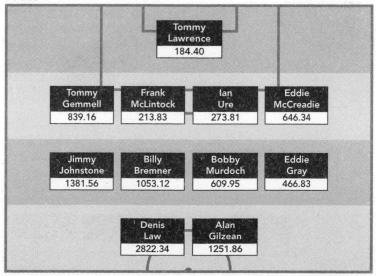

	Tommy Lawrence 184.40		
Tommy Gemmell 839.16	**Frank McLintock** 213.83	**Ian Ure** 273.81	**Eddie McCreadie** 646.34
Jimmy Johnstone 1381.56	**Billy Bremner** 1053.12	**Bobby Murdoch** 609.95	**Eddie Gray** 466.83
Denis Law 2822.34	**Alan Gilzean** 1251.86		

1970s

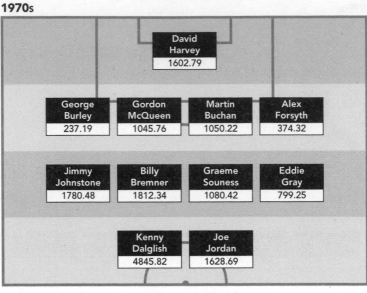

	David Harvey	
	1602.79	

George Burley	Gordon McQueen	Martin Buchan	Alex Forsyth
237.19	1045.76	1050.22	374.32

Jimmy Johnstone	Billy Bremner	Graeme Souness	Eddie Gray
1780.48	1812.34	1080.42	799.25

Kenny Dalglish	Joe Jordan
4845.82	1628.69

1980s

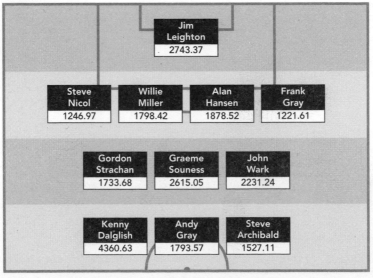

	Jim Leighton	
	2743.37	

Steve Nicol	Willie Miller	Alan Hansen	Frank Gray
1246.97	1798.42	1878.52	1221.61

Gordon Strachan	Graeme Souness	John Wark
1733.68	2615.05	2231.24

Kenny Dalglish	Andy Gray	Steve Archibald
4360.63	1793.57	1527.11

1990s

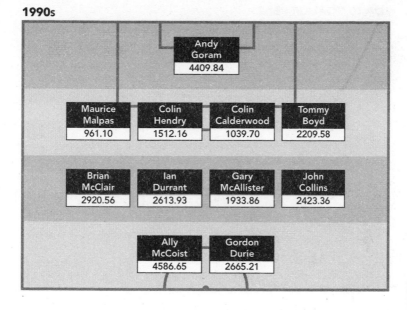

	Andy Goram 4409.84	

| Maurice Malpas 961.10 | Colin Hendry 1512.16 | Colin Calderwood 1039.70 | Tommy Boyd 2209.58 |

| Brian McClair 2920.56 | Ian Durrant 2613.93 | Gary McAllister 1933.86 | John Collins 2423.36 |

| Ally McCoist 4586.65 | Gordon Durie 2665.21 |

143

2000s

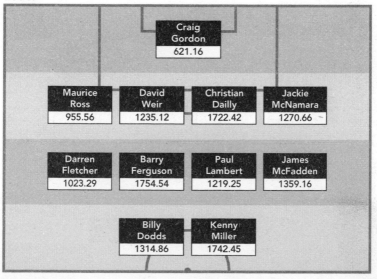

	Craig Gordon 621.16	

| Maurice Ross 955.56 | David Weir 1235.12 | Christian Dailly 1722.42 | Jackie McNamara 1270.66 |

| Darren Fletcher 1023.29 | Barry Ferguson 1754.54 | Paul Lambert 1219.25 | James McFadden 1359.16 |

| Billy Dodds 1314.86 | Kenny Miller 1742.45 |

GREATEST EVER
SCOTLAND INTERNATIONAL PLAYERS BY POSITION

TOP 10 GOALKEEPERS

Rank	Player	Points
1	Jim Leighton	5342.56
2	Andy Goram	4926.21
3	David Harvey	1952.79
4	Alan Rough	1685.00
5	Neil Sullivan	780.84
6	Tommy Younger	679.84
7	Craig Gordon	621.16
8	George Farm	379.55
9	Ronnie Simpson	338.49
10	John Jackson	244.68
10	Paul Gallacher	244.68

TOP 10 DEFENDERS

Rank	Player	Points
1	Alan Hansen	4884.07
2	Tommy Boyd	3012.06
3	Colin Hendry	2527.09
4	Richard Gough	2401.31
5	Steven Pressley	2283.49
6	Christian Dailly	2177.85
7	Maurice Malpas	2096.15
8	Steve Nicol	1965.52
9	Willie Miller	1912.55
10	Jackie McNamara	1858.11

TOP 10 MIDFIELDERS

Rank	Player	Points
1	Graeme Souness	3695.47
2	Brian McClair	3455.46
3	Jimmy Johnstone	3162.04
4	Barry Ferguson	2882.22
5	Billy Bremner	2865.46
6	Paul Lambert	2815.68
7	John Collins	2706.40
8	Gary McAllister	2583.86
9	John Wark	2546.43
10	Archie Gemmill	2496.22

TOP 10 FORWARDS

Rank	Player	Points
1	Kenny Dalglish	9806.45
2	Ally McCoist	6031.45
3	Denis Law	3475.24
4	Gordon Durie	3298.15
5	Kevin Gallacher	2345.99
6	Joe Jordan	2116.88
7	Billy Dodds	1823.94
8	Kenny Miller	1707.32
9	Billy Liddell	1659.42
10	Tommy Walker	1602.17

144

GREATEST EVER
WALES XI OF ALL TIME

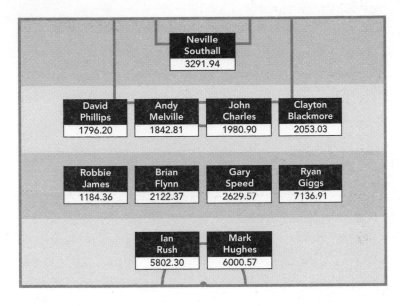

Neville Southall 3291.94

David Phillips 1796.20
Andy Melville 1842.81
John Charles 1980.90
Clayton Blackmore 2053.03

Robbie James 1184.36
Brian Flynn 2122.37
Gary Speed 2629.57
Ryan Giggs 7136.91

Ian Rush 5802.30
Mark Hughes 6000.57

GREATEST EVER
WALES XI OF REGISTERED PLAYERS

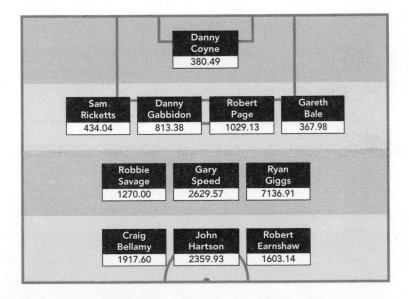

Danny Coyne 380.49

Sam Ricketts 434.04
Danny Gabbidon 813.38
Robert Page 1029.13
Gareth Bale 367.98

Robbie Savage 1270.00
Gary Speed 2629.57
Ryan Giggs 7136.91

Craig Bellamy 1917.60
John Hartson 2359.93
Robert Earnshaw 1603.14

GREATEST EVER
WALES XI OF RETIRED PLAYERS

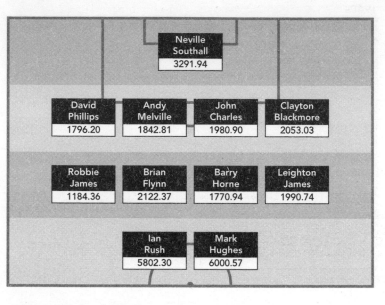

	Neville Southall		
	3291.94		
David Phillips	Andy Melville	John Charles	Clayton Blackmore
1796.20	1842.81	1980.90	2053.03
Robbie James	Brian Flynn	Barry Horne	Leighton James
1184.36	2122.37	1770.94	1990.74
	Ian Rush	Mark Hughes	
	5802.30	6000.57	

GREATEST EVER
WALES XI BY DECADE

1930s

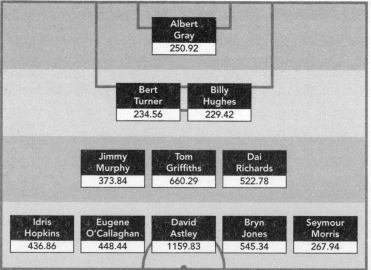

		Albert Gray		
		250.92		
	Bert Turner	Billy Hughes		
	234.56	229.42		
	Jimmy Murphy	Tom Griffiths	Dai Richards	
	373.84	660.29	522.78	
Idris Hopkins	Eugene O'Callaghan	David Astley	Bryn Jones	Seymour Morris
436.86	448.44	1159.83	545.34	267.94

1940s

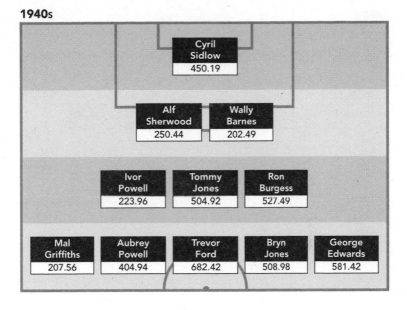

		Cyril Sidlow 450.19		
	Alf Sherwood 250.44	Wally Barnes 202.49		
	Ivor Powell 223.96	Tommy Jones 504.92	Ron Burgess 527.49	
Mal Griffiths 207.56	Aubrey Powell 404.94	Trevor Ford 682.42	Bryn Jones 508.98	George Edwards 581.42

147

1950s

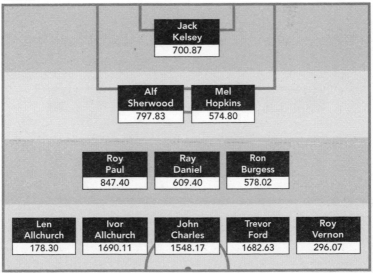

		Jack Kelsey 700.87		
	Alf Sherwood 797.83	Mel Hopkins 574.80		
	Roy Paul 847.40	Ray Daniel 609.40	Ron Burgess 578.02	
Len Allchurch 178.30	Ivor Allchurch 1690.11	John Charles 1548.17	Trevor Ford 1682.63	Roy Vernon 296.07

1960s

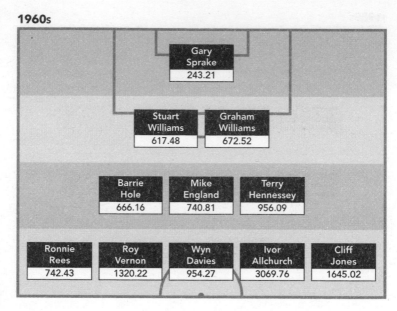

Gary Sprake	243.21

Stuart Williams	617.48	Graham Williams	672.52

Barrie Hole	666.16	
Mike England	740.81	
Terry Hennessey	956.09	

Ronnie Rees	742.43	Roy Vernon	1320.22	Wyn Davies	954.27	Ivor Allchurch	3069.76	Cliff Jones	1645.02

1970s

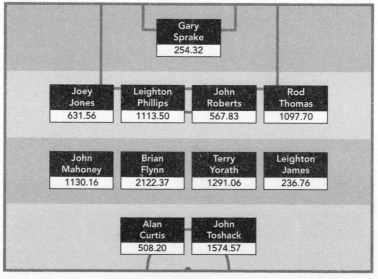

Gary Sprake	254.32

Joey Jones	631.56	Leighton Phillips	1113.50	John Roberts	567.83	Rod Thomas	1097.70

John Mahoney	1130.16	Brian Flynn	2122.37	Terry Yorath	1291.06	Leighton James	236.76

Alan Curtis	508.20	John Toshack	1574.57

1980s

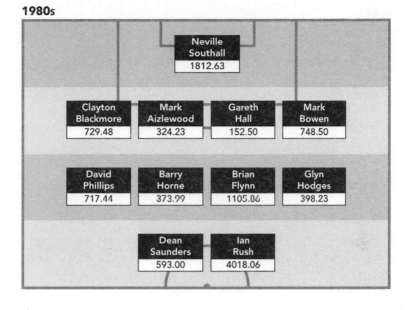

	Neville Southall		
	1812.63		

Clayton Blackmore	Mark Aizlewood	Gareth Hall	Mark Bowen
729.48	324.23	152.50	748.50

David Phillips	Barry Horne	Brian Flynn	Glyn Hodges
717.44	373.99	1105.06	398.23

Dean Saunders	Ian Rush
593.00	4018.06

1990s

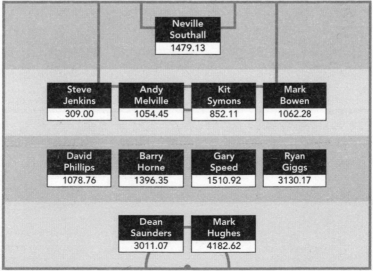

	Neville Southall		
	1479.13		

Steve Jenkins	Andy Melville	Kit Symons	Mark Bowen
309.00	1054.45	852.11	1062.28

David Phillips	Barry Horne	Gary Speed	Ryan Giggs
1078.76	1396.35	1510.92	3130.17

Dean Saunders	Mark Hughes
3011.07	4182.62

INTERNATIONAL

2000s

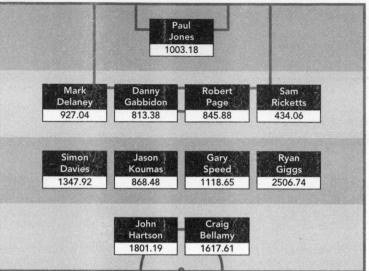

	Paul Jones
	1003.18

Mark Delaney	Danny Gabbidon	Robert Page	Sam Ricketts
927.04	813.38	845.88	434.06

Simon Davies	Jason Koumas	Gary Speed	Ryan Giggs
1347.92	868.48	1118.65	2506.74

John Hartson	Craig Bellamy
1801.19	1617.61

GREATEST EVER
WALES INTERNATIONAL PLAYERS BY POSITION

TOP 10 GOALKEEPERS

Rank	Player	Points
1	Neville Southall	3891.94
2	Paul Jones	1277.91
3	Jack Kelsey	1055.79
4	Gary Sprake	1043.82
5	Cyril Sidlow	450.19
6	Mark Crossley	397.25
7	Danny Coyne	380.49
8	Andy Marriott	176.25
9	Darren Ward	124.00
10	Tony Norman	121.34

TOP 10 DEFENDERS

Rank	Player	Points
1	Andy Melville	1842.81
2	Mark Bowen	1540.78
3	Mel Hopkins	1504.49
4	Alf Sherwood	1048.27
5	Robert Page	1029.13
6	Kit Symons	1008.02
7	Chris Coleman	993.27
8	Mark Aizlewood	979.17
9	Terry Hennessey	956.09
10	Mark Delaney	927.04

TOP 10 MIDFIELDERS

Rank	Player	Points
1	Ryan Giggs	7136.91
2	Gary Speed	2629.57
3	Brian Flynn	2122.37
4	Clayton Blackmore	2053.03
5	David Phillips	1796.20
6	Barry Horne	1770.94
7	Mark Pembridge	1734.90
8	Simon Davies	1372.92
9	Robbie Savage	1270.11
10	John Robinson	1122.35

TOP 10 FORWARDS

Rank	Player	Points
1	Mark Hughes	6000.57
2	Ian Rush	5802.30
3	Dean Saunders	3818.06
4	Ivor Allchurch	3069.76
5	Trevor Ford	2365.05
6	John Hartson	2359.93
7	John Charles	1980.90
8	Craig Bellamy	1917.60
9	Robbie James	1634.36
10	Robert Earnshaw	1603.14

GREATEST EVER
COMBINED BRITISH ISLES AND IRELAND XI OF ALL TIME

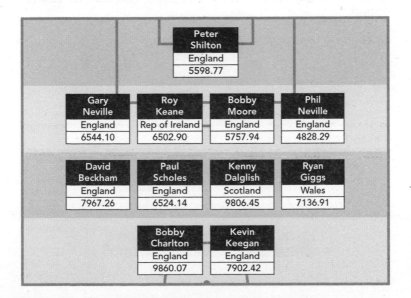

Peter Shilton — England — 5598.77

Gary Neville — England — 6544.10
Roy Keane — Rep of Ireland — 6502.90
Bobby Moore — England — 5757.94
Phil Neville — England — 4828.29

David Beckham — England — 7967.26
Paul Scholes — England — 6524.14
Kenny Dalglish — Scotland — 9806.45
Ryan Giggs — Wales — 7136.91

Bobby Charlton — England — 9860.07
Kevin Keegan — England — 7902.42

GREATEST EVER
XIs OF COUNTRIES THAT HAVE WON THE WORLD CUP

ARGENTINA

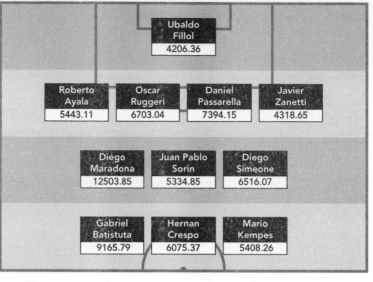

Ubaldo Fillol			
4206.36			

Roberto Ayala	Oscar Ruggeri	Daniel Passarella	Javier Zanetti
5443.11	6703.04	7394.15	4318.65

Diego Maradona	Juan Pablo Sorin	Diego Simeone
12503.85	5334.85	6516.07

Gabriel Batistuta	Hernan Crespo	Mario Kempes
9165.79	6075.37	5408.26

BRAZIL

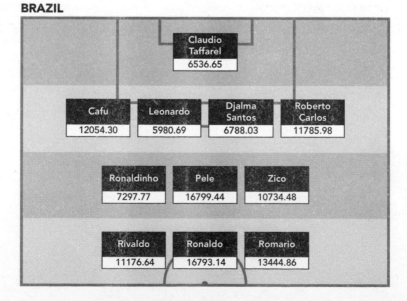

Claudio Taffarel			
6536.65			

Cafu	Leonardo	Djalma Santos	Roberto Carlos
12054.30	5980.69	6788.03	11785.98

Ronaldinho	Pele	Zico
7297.77	16799.44	10734.48

Rivaldo	Ronaldo	Romario
11176.64	16793.14	13444.86

FRANCE

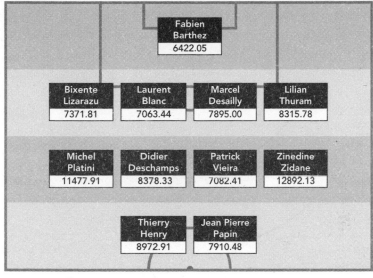

	Fabien Barthez 6422.05		
Bixente Lizarazu 7371.81	Laurent Blanc 7063.44	Marcel Desailly 7895.00	Lilian Thuram 8315.78
Michel Platini 11477.91	Didier Deschamps 8378.33	Patrick Vieira 7082.41	Zinédine Zidane 12892.13
	Thierry Henry 8972.91	Jean Pierre Papin 7910.48	

GERMANY (INCLUDING WEST GERMANY)

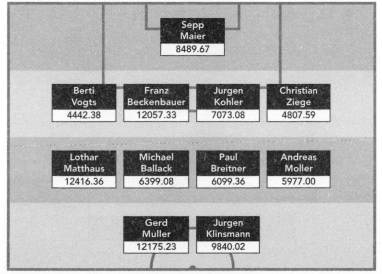

	Sepp Maier 8489.67		
Berti Vogts 4442.38	Franz Beckenbauer 12057.33	Jurgen Kohler 7073.08	Christian Ziege 4807.59
Lothar Matthaus 12416.36	Michael Ballack 6399.08	Paul Breitner 6099.36	Andreas Moller 5977.00
	Gerd Muller 12175.23	Jurgen Klinsmann 9840.02	

ITALY

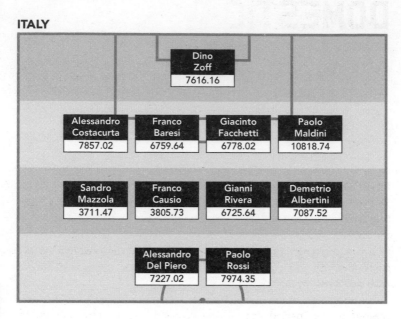

	Dino Zoff	
	7616.16	

Alessandro Costacurta	Franco Baresi	Giacinto Facchetti	Paolo Maldini
7857.02	6759.64	6778.02	10818.74

Sandro Mazzola	Franco Causio	Gianni Rivera	Demetrio Albertini
3711.47	3805.73	6725.64	7087.52

Alessandro Del Piero	Paolo Rossi
7227.02	7974.35

URUGUAY

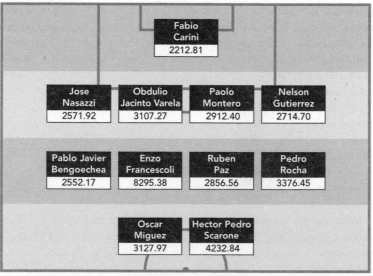

	Fabio Carini	
	2212.81	

Jose Nasazzi	Obdulio Jacinto Varela	Paolo Montero	Nelson Gutierrez
2571.92	3107.27	2912.40	2714.70

Pablo Javier Bengoechea	Enzo Francescoli	Ruben Paz	Pedro Rocha
2552.17	8295.38	2856.56	3376.45

Oscar Miguez	Hector Pedro Scarone
3127.97	4232.84

SECTION 2:
DOMESTIC

INTRODUCTION

This section lists the clubs that have featured at any time in the English and Scottish Premier Leagues, not merely those who play in the top divisions in the 2007–08 season. These lists are constructed in a different format to the International section. The aim here is to identify the most successful season (highlighted in bold in our tables), and therefore the most successful team for each club, listed by decade.

Our assessment of the greatest ever club teams in England and Scotland is based on their performance in their domestic league competition. After much consideration, we decided not to include cup competitions in our analysis for two main reasons. First, we believe it is accepted that it is the genuine opinion of professionals within the sport that league games are the most significant in any season. How a team performs in the league in which they play is the truest reflection of the quality of that team.

Secondly, it is extremely difficult to establish a trustworthy formula that would truly reflect the validity of a team's cup success. Whereas a league campaign has a solid base of uniformity (in so far as each team usually plays every other team on a home-and-away basis), there are many more variables in a cup competition.

For instance, the luck of the draw can see one team win a trophy in a given year having predominantly faced lower division or even non-league opposition at home while, the following year, another team could prevail having competed against a series of teams from the highest division at the opposition's grounds. In more recent years there is also the growing phenomenon of the top clubs fielding so-called weakened teams, which can skew the level of success, or lack of it, of that team and those that they meet along the way.

The basis of our conclusion is, therefore, predominantly focused on the team's highest average points per game during a league season. This need not necessarily be the most points they accumulated in a season due to variables such as the number of games played and points per win.

155

DOMESTIC

In England the number of teams in the top division has changed on a number of occasions. Moreover, two points were awarded for a win until the start of the 1981–82 season when it was increased to three. The breakdown of games played in the top division is as follows:

Period	Games per season
1946–47 to 1986–87	42
1987–88 only	40
1988–89 to 1990–91	38
1991–92 to 1994–95	42
1995–96 to 2006–07	38

It has been the same story in Scotland where the number of teams has varied more widely and the introduction of three points for a win happened at the start of the 1994–95 season. The breakdown of games played in the top division in Scotland is as follows:

Period	Games per season
1946–47 to 1954–55	30
1955–56 to 1974–75	34
1975–76 to 1985–86	36
1986–87 to 1987–88	44
1988–89 to 1990–91	36
1991–92 to 1993–94	44
1994–95 to 1999–00	36
2000–01 to 2006–07	38

Accordingly, the ranking is worked out through the average points won per game throughout the season as if all matches were played on a three points per win and one point per draw basis.

But that is not all. Weight is also given to the team's final league position and the league in which it was playing. Ending the season in the upper half of the top division for a newly promoted side is regarded as a greater success than the initial promotion from the lower league. Equally, a promotion season is worth more than a bottom third finish in the division above.

The structure of the English and Scottish leagues has also changed over the years, as follows:

ENGLAND
- up to 1991–92 : Division 1, Division 2, Division 3, Division 4
- 1992–93 to 2003–04 : Premier League, First Division ('L1' in the tables), Second Division ('L2'), Third Division ('L3')
- 2004–05 to 2006–07 : Premier League, Championship, League 1, League 2

SCOTLAND
- up to 1955–56 : Division A ('A' in the tables), Division B ('B')
- 1956–57 to 1974–75 : Division 1 ('1' in the tables), Division 2 ('2')
- 1975–76 to 1993–94 : Premier Division, Division 1, Division 2
- 1994–95 to 1997–98 : Premier Division, Division 1, Division 2, Division 3

◆ 1998–99 to 2006–07 : Scottish Premier League ('SPL' in the tables),
   Division 1, Division 2, Division 3

Teams are listed by squad (i.e. players who made at least one appearance) rather than just as an XI to ensure that all the players that contributed to the season are included.

For some clubs, such as Wigan Athletic and Gretna for example, we do not list earlier decades because such clubs had either not been formed or were not playing at a high enough league level to trigger significant data collection.

After the club listings the most successful team of the decade is given for both England and Scotland utilising the ranking system described above and comparing all clubs.

Reverting to the individual ranking system described in the International section for the clubs playing in the English Premiership in the 2007–08 season, we have analysed all the players that have ever played for those clubs and have compiled each club's greatest ever XI. These are based on the points the individual players have accumulated for their club and international performances. To qualify for inclusion in the greatest ever XI, the player must have played at least one full international game for their country while at the club. The points awarded for club performances are not just the games played for the individual club under consideration, but all clubs the player played for. Thus we have the greatest XI that have ever worn that team's colours.

For Scotland, equivalent reliable data is only available for Celtic and Rangers and their greatest ever XIs are listed in the Scottish section.

We then turn to the greatest ever combined teams. That is the greatest ever XIs selected from all teams who have ever played in the top flight of English football and, separately, in the top flight of Scottish football. Based on individual players' total points accumulated for club and country, we provide the greatest ever XI of all time, and then the greatest ever XI of all time by decade. The points awarded to players in the listings by decade are only those won by the player during that decade (where the player played for more than one top-flight club, the points are totalled for all those clubs and the clubs are listed).

Finally, the best ever players to have played in the English and Scottish leagues at any time, of any nationality, are listed by playing position. These lists are based on full career points won for both club and country.

GREATEST EVER
ENGLISH CLUBS BEST SEASONS AND SQUADS

ARSENAL

Season	League	League Position	P	W	D	L	F	A	Pts	3 Point Equivalent
1947–48	**Division 1**	**1**	**42**	**23**	**13**	**6**	**81**	**32**	**59**	**1.952381**
1952–53	Division 1	1	42	21	12	9	97	64	54	1.785714
1951–52	Division 1	3	42	21	11	10	80	61	53	1.761905
1958–59	Division 1	3	42	21	8	13	88	68	50	1.690476
1956–57	Division 1	5	42	21	8	13	85	69	50	1.690476
1949–50	Division 1	6	42	19	11	12	79	55	49	1.619048
1948–49	Division 1	5	42	18	13	11	74	44	49	1.595238
1950–51	Division 1	5	42	19	9	14	73	56	47	1.571429
1955–56	Division 1	5	42	18	10	14	60	61	46	1.523810
1954–55	Division 1	9	42	17	9	16	69	63	43	1.428571
1953–54	Division 1	12	42	15	13	14	75	73	43	1.380952
1946–47	Division 1	13	42	16	9	17	72	70	41	1.357143
1957–58	Division 1	12	42	16	7	19	73	85	39	1.309524

1940s & 50s

SQUAD 1947–48   CHAMPIONS OF DIVISION 1

Walley BARNES	Full back	Ian McPHERSON	Winger
Denis COMPTON	Outside left	Joe MERCER	Wing half
Les COMPTON	Centre half	Ronnie ROOKE	Centre forward
Alf FIELDS	Centre half	Don ROPER	Winger
Alex FORBES	Wing half	Laurie SCOTT	Full back
Bryn JONES	Inside forward	Paddy SLOAN	Wing half
Reg LEWIS	Centre forward	Lionel SMITH	Full back
Jimmy LOGIE	Inside forward	George SWINDIN	Goalkeeper
Archie MACAULAY	Inside forward/Wing half	Joe WADE	Full back
George MALE	Full back		

Season	League	League Position	P	W	D	L	F	A	Pts	3 Point Equivalent
1968–69	**Division 1**	**4**	**42**	**22**	**12**	**8**	**56**	**27**	**56**	**1.857143**
1962–63	Division 1	7	42	18	10	14	86	77	46	1.523810
1966–67	Division 1	7	42	16	14	12	58	47	46	1.476190
1963–64	Division 1	8	42	17	11	14	90	82	45	1.476190
1967–68	Division 1	9	42	17	10	15	60	56	44	1.452381
1961–62	Division 1	10	42	16	11	15	71	72	43	1.404762
1964–65	Division 1	13	42	17	7	18	69	75	41	1.380952
1960–61	Division 1	11	42	15	11	16	77	85	41	1.333333
1959–60	Division 1	13	42	15	9	18	68	80	39	1.285714
1965–66	Division 1	14	42	12	13	17	62	75	37	1.166667

1960s

SQUAD 1968–69   4TH IN DIVISION 1

George ARMSTRONG	Winger	Terry NEILL	Centre half
David COURT	Midfielder	John RADFORD	Forward
Bobby GOULD	Forward	Jimmy ROBERTSON	Winger
George GRAHAM	Forward/Midfielder	Jon SAMMELS	Midfielder
David JENKINS	Forward	Peter SIMPSON	Central defender
George JOHNSTON	Forward	Peter STOREY	Defender
Frank McLINTOCK	Central defender	Ian URE	Centre half
Bob McNAB	Left back	Bob WILSON	Goalkeeper

Season	League	League Position	P	W	D	L	F	A	Pts	3 Point Equivalent
1970–71	**Division 1**	**1**	**42**	**29**	**7**	**6**	**71**	**29**	**65**	**2.238095**
1972–73	Division 1	2	42	23	11	8	57	43	57	1.904762
1971–72	Division 1	5	42	22	8	12	58	40	52	1.761905
1977–78	Division 1	5	42	21	10	11	60	37	52	1.738095
1978–79	Division 1	7	42	17	14	11	61	48	48	1.547619
1976–77	Division 1	8	42	16	11	15	64	59	43	1.404762
1973–74	Division 1	10	42	14	14	14	49	51	42	1.333333
1969–70	Division 1	12	42	12	18	12	51	49	42	1.285714
1974–75	Division 1	16	42	13	11	18	47	49	37	1.190476
1975–76	Division 1	17	42	13	10	19	47	53	36	1.166667

_1970s_

SQUAD 1970–71   CHAMPIONS OF DIVISION 1

George ARMSTRONG	Winger	Sammy NELSON	Left back
Charlie GEORGE	Forward	John RADFORD	Forward
George GRAHAM	Forward/Midfielder	Pat RICE	Right back
Eddie KELLY	Midfielder	John ROBERTS	Central defender/Forward
Ray KENNEDY	Midfielder/Forward	Jon SAMMELS	Midfielder
Peter MARINELLO	Winger	Peter SIMPSON	Central defender
Frank McLINTOCK	Central defender	Peter STOREY	Defender
Bob McNAB	Left back	Bob WILSON	Goalkeeper

Season	League	League Position	P	W	D	L	F	A	Pts	3 Point Equivalent
1988–89	**Division 1**	**1**	**38**	**22**	**10**	**6**	**73**	**36**	**76**	**2.000000**
1980–81	Division 1	3	42	19	15	8	61	45	53	1.714286
1981–82	Division 1	5	42	20	11	11	48	37	71	1.690476
1979–80	Division 1	4	42	18	16	8	52	36	52	1.666667
1986–87	Division 1	4	42	20	10	12	58	35	70	1.666667
1987–88	Division 1	6	40	18	12	10	58	39	66	1.650000
1985–86	Division 1	7	42	20	9	13	49	47	69	1.642857
1984–85	Division 1	7	42	19	9	14	61	49	66	1.571429
1983–84	Division 1	6	42	18	9	15	74	60	63	1.500000
1982–83	Division 1	10	42	16	10	16	58	56	58	1.380952

_1980s_

SQUAD 1988–89   CHAMPIONS OF DIVISION 1

Tony ADAMS	Defender/Centre back	Paul MERSON	Midfielder
Steve BOULD	Centre back	David O'LEARY	Central defender
Gus CAESAR	Central defender	Niall QUINN	Forward
Paul DAVIS	Midfielder	Kevin RICHARDSON	Midfielder
Lee DIXON	Full back	David ROCASTLE	Winger/Midfielder
Perry GROVES	Forward	Alan SMITH	Forward
Martin HAYES	Midfielder	Michael THOMAS	Midfielder
John LUKIC	Goalkeeper	Nigel WINTERBURN	Defender/Left back
Brian MARWOOD	Winger		

ARSENAL

Season	League	League Position	P	W	D	L	F	A	Pts	3 Point Equivalent
1990–91	**Division 1**	**1**	**38**	**24**	**13**	**1**	**74**	**18**	**83**	**2.236842**
1997–98	Premier League	1	38	23	9	6	68	33	78	2.052632
1998–99	Premier League	2	38	22	12	4	59	17	78	2.052632
1996–97	Premier League	3	38	19	11	8	62	32	68	1.789474
1991–92	Division 1	4	42	19	15	8	81	46	72	1.714286
1993–94	Premier League	4	42	18	17	7	53	28	71	1.690476
1995–96	Premier League	5	38	17	12	9	49	32	63	1.657895
1989–90	Division 1	4	38	18	8	12	54	38	62	1.631579
1992–93	Premier League	10	42	15	11	16	40	38	56	1.333333
1994–95	Premier League	12	42	13	12	17	52	49	51	1.214286

SQUAD 1990–91 CHAMPIONS OF DIVISION 1

Tony ADAMS	Defender/Centre back	Andy LINIGHAN	Defender/Centre back
Steve BOULD	Centre back	Paul MERSON	Midfielder
Kevin CAMPBELL	Forward	David O'LEARY	Central defender
Andy COLE	Forward	Colin PATES	Central defender
Paul DAVIS	Midfielder	David ROCASTLE	Winger/Midfielder
Lee DIXON	Full back	David SEAMAN	Goalkeeper
Perry GROVES	Forward	Alan SMITH	Forward
David HILLIER	Midfielder	Michael THOMAS	Midfielder
Sigurdur JONSSON	Defender	Nigel WINTERBURN	Defender/Left back
Anders LIMPAR	Midfielder		

Season	League	League Position	P	W	D	L	F	A	Pts	3 Point Equivalent
2003–04	**Premier League**	**1**	**38**	**26**	**12**	**0**	**73**	**26**	**90**	**2.368421**
2001–02	Premier League	1	38	26	9	3	79	36	87	2.289474
2004–05	Premier League	2	38	25	8	5	87	36	83	2.184211
2002–03	Premier League	2	38	23	9	6	85	42	78	2.052632
1999–2000	Premier League	2	38	22	7	9	73	43	73	1.921053
2000–01	Premier League	2	38	20	10	8	63	38	70	1.842105
2006–07	Premier League	4	38	19	11	8	63	35	68	1.789474
2005–06	Premier League	4	38	20	7	11	68	31	67	1.763158

SQUAD 2003–04 CHAMPIONS OF THE PREMIER LEAGUE

Jeremie ALIADIERE	Forward	Martin KEOWN	Defender/Centre back
David BENTLEY	Midfielder	Bissan Etame-Mayer LAUREN	Defender
Dennis BERGKAMP	Forward	Jens LEHMANN	Goalkeeper
Sol CAMPBELL	Defender/Centre back	Freddie LJUNGBERG	Midfielder
Gael CLICHY	Defender	Ray PARLOUR	Midfielder
Ashley COLE	Defender/Left back	Robert PIRES	Midfielder
Pascal CYGAN	Defender/Centre back	Jose Antonio REYES	Forward
Cesar Gaspar EDU	Midfielder	Gilberto SILVA	Midfielder
Thierry HENRY	Forward	Kolo TOURE	Defender
Justin HOYTE	Defender	Patrick VIEIRA	Midfielder
Nwankwo KANU	Forward	Sylvain WILTORD	Forward

ASTON VILLA

Season	League	League Position	P	W	D	L	F	A	Pts	3 Point Equivalent
1954–55	**Division 1**	**6**	**42**	**20**	**7**	**15**	**72**	**73**	**47**	**1.595238**
1947–48	Division 1	6	42	19	9	14	65	57	47	1.571429
1951–52	Division 1	6	42	19	9	14	79	70	47	1.571429
1946–47	Division 1	8	42	18	9	15	67	53	45	1.500000
1948–49	Division 1	10	42	16	10	16	60	76	42	1.380952
1956–57	Division 1	10	42	14	15	13	65	55	43	1.357143
1953–54	Division 1	13	42	16	9	17	70	68	41	1.357143
1949–50	Division 1	12	42	15	12	15	61	61	42	1.357143
1952–53	Division 1	11	42	14	13	15	63	61	41	1.309524
1957–58	Division 1	14	42	16	7	19	73	86	39	1.309524
1950–51	Division 1	15	42	12	13	17	66	68	37	1.166667
1955–56	Division 1	20	42	11	13	18	52	69	35	1.095238
1958–59	Division 1	21	42	11	8	23	58	87	30	0.976190

1940s & 50s

SQUAD 1954–55 — 6TH IN DIVISION 1

Peter ALDIS	Full back	Con MARTIN	Centre half/Goalkeeper
Bill BAXTER	Wing half	Peter McPARLAND	Outside left
Trevor BIRCH	Wing half	Amos MOSS	Wing half
Danny BLANCHFLOWER	Midfielder	Frank MOSS	Centre half
Roy CHAPMAN	Inside forward	Derek PACE	Centre forward
Norman CLARKE	Wing half	Harry PARKES	Full back
Vic CROWE	Wing half	Dennis PARSONS	Goalkeeper
Johnny DIXON	Inside forward	Mike PINNER	Goalkeeper
Eddie FOLLAN	Inside forward	Arthur PROUDLER	Half back
Colin GIBSON	Outside right	Ken ROBERTS	Outside right
Ray HOGG	Full back	Tommy SOUTHREN	Winger
Keith JONES	Goalkeeper	Tommy THOMPSON	Inside forward
Norman LOCKHART	Outside left	Joe TYRELL	Inside forward
Stan LYNN	Full back	David WALSH	Centre forward

161

Season	League	League Position	P	W	D	L	F	A	Pts	3 Point Equivalent
1959–60	**Division 2**	**1**	**42**	**25**	**9**	**8**	**89**	**43**	**59**	**2.000000**
1961–62	Division 1	7	42	18	8	16	65	56	44	1.476190
1960–61	Division 1	9	42	17	9	16	78	77	43	1.428571
1962–63	Division 1	15	42	15	8	19	62	68	38	1.261905
1964–65	Division 1	16	42	16	5	21	57	82	37	1.261905
1967–68	Division 2	16	42	15	7	20	54	64	37	1.238095
1965–66	Division 1	16	42	15	6	21	69	80	36	1.214286
1968–69	Division 2	18	42	12	14	16	37	48	38	1.190476
1963–64	Division 1	19	42	11	12	19	62	71	34	1.071429
1966–67	Division 1	21	42	11	7	24	54	85	29	0.952381

1960s

SQUAD 1959–60 — CHAMPIONS OF DIVISION 2

Jimmy ADAM	Outside left	Jimmy MacEWAN	Outside right
Norman ASHE	Outside right	Peter McPARLAND	Outside left
Trevor BIRCH	Wing half	Terry MORRALL	Centre half
Harry BURROWS	Outside left	John NEAL	Full back
Vic CROWE	Wing half	Pat SAWARD	Wing half
Alan DEAKIN	Wing half	Jackie SEWELL	Inside forward
Johnny DIXON	Inside forward	Nigel SIMS	Goalkeeper
Jimmy DUGDALE	Centre half	Bobby THOMSON	Wing half/Inside forward
Brian HANDLEY	Centre forward	Mike TINDALL	Wing half
Gerry HITCHENS	Centre forward	Doug WINTON	Full back
Kevin KEELAN	Goalkeeper	Ron WYLIE	Inside forward/Wing half
Stan LYNN	Full back		

1970s

Season	League	League Position	P	W	D	L	F	A	Pts	3 Point Equivalent
1971–72	Division 3	1	46	32	6	8	85	32	70	2.217391
1974–75	Division 2	2	42	25	8	9	79	32	58	1.976190
1976–77	**Division 1**	**4**	**42**	**22**	**7**	**13**	**76**	**50**	**51**	**1.738095**
1972–73	Division 2	3	42	18	14	10	51	47	50	1.619048
1970–71	Division 3	4	46	19	15	12	54	46	53	1.565217
1977–78	Division 1	8	42	18	10	14	57	42	46	1.523810
1978–79	Division 1	8	42	15	16	11	59	49	46	1.452381
1973–74	Division 2	14	42	13	15	14	48	45	41	1.285714
1975–76	Division 1	16	42	11	17	14	51	59	39	1.190476
1969–70	Division 2	21	42	8	13	21	36	62	29	0.880952

SQUAD 1976–77 — 4TH IN DIVISION 1

John BURRIDGE	Goalkeeper		Steve HUNT	Winger
Mick BUTTRESS	Full back		Ivor LINTON	Midfielder
Frank CARRODUS	Winger		Brian LITTLE	Forward
Gordon COWANS	Forward		Keith MASEFIELD	Full back
Alex CROPLEY	Midfielder		Dennis MORTIMER	Midfielder
John DEEHAN	Forward		Chris NICHOLL	Central defender
Jake FINDLAY	Goalkeeper		Leighton PHILLIPS	Central defender/Midfielder
John GIDMAN	Right back		John ROBSON	Full back
Andy GRAY	Forward		Gordon SMITH	Full back
Ray GRAYDON	Winger		Charlie YOUNG	Central defender
David HUGHES	Midfielder			

1980s

Season	League	League Position	P	W	D	L	F	A	Pts	3 Point Equivalent
1980–81	**Division 1**	**1**	**42**	**26**	**8**	**8**	**72**	**40**	**60**	**2.047619**
1987–88	Division 2	2	44	22	12	10	68	41	78	1.772727
1982–83	Division 1	6	42	21	5	16	62	50	68	1.619048
1979–80	Division 1	7	42	16	14	12	51	50	46	1.476190
1983–84	Division 1	10	42	17	9	16	59	61	60	1.428571
1981–82	Division 1	11	42	15	12	15	55	53	57	1.357143
1984–85	Division 1	10	42	15	11	16	60	60	56	1.333333
1988–89	Division 1	17	38	9	13	16	45	56	40	1.052632
1985–86	Division 1	16	42	10	14	18	51	67	44	1.047619
1986–87	Division 1	22	42	8	12	22	45	79	36	0.857143

SQUAD 1980–81 — CHAMPIONS OF DIVISION 1

Des BREMNER	Midfielder		Tony MORLEY	Left winger
Gordon COWANS	Forward		Dennis MORTIMER	Midfielder
Eamonn DEACY	Full back		Jimmy RIMMER	Goalkeeper
Allan EVANS	Central defender		Gary SHAW	Forward
David GEDDIS	Forward		Kenny SWAIN	Right back
Colin GIBSON	Left back/Midfielder		Gary WILLIAMS	Full back
Ken McNAUGHT	Central defender		Peter WITHE	Forward

Season	League	League Position	P	W	D	L	F	A	Pts	3 Point Equivalent
1989–90	Division 1	2	38	21	7	10	57	38	70	1.842105
1992–93	**Premier League**	**2**	**42**	**21**	**11**	**10**	**57**	**40**	**74**	**1.761905**
1995–96	Premier League	4	38	18	9	11	52	35	63	1.657895
1996–97	Premier League	5	38	17	10	11	47	34	61	1.605263
1997–98	Premier League	7	38	17	6	15	49	48	57	1.500000
1998–99	Premier League	6	38	15	10	13	51	46	55	1.447368
1991–92	Division 1	7	42	17	9	16	48	44	60	1.428571
1993–94	Premier League	10	42	15	12	15	46	50	57	1.357143
1994–95	Premier League	18	42	11	15	16	51	56	48	1.142857
1990–91	Division 1	17	38	9	14	15	46	58	41	1.078947

1990s

SQUAD 1992–93   2ND IN THE PREMIER LEAGUE

Dalian ATKINSON	Forward
Earl BARRETT	Defender
Stefan BEINLICH	Midfielder
Chris BODEN	Defender
Mark BOSNICH	Goalkeeper
Matthias BREITKREUTZ	Midfielder
Martin CARRUTHERS	Forward
Neil COX	Defender
Tony CULLEN	Forward
Ugo EHIOGU	Defender/Centre back
Dave FARRELL	Midfielder
Steve FROGGATT	Midfielder
Ray HOUGHTON	Midfielder
Frank McAVENNIE	Forward
Paul McGRATH	Central defender/Midfielder
Garry PARKER	Midfielder
Cyrille REGIS	Forward
Kevin RICHARDSON	Midfielder
Dean SAUNDERS	Forward
Bryan SMALL	Defender/Left back
Nigel SPINK	Goalkeeper
Steve STAUNTON	Defender
Shaun TEALE	Defender/Centre back
Dwight YORKE	Forward

Season	League	League Position	P	W	D	L	F	A	Pts	3 Point Equivalent
1999–2000	**Premier League**	**6**	**38**	**15**	**13**	**10**	**46**	**35**	**58**	**1.526316**
2003–04	Premier League	6	38	15	11	12	48	44	56	1.473684
2000–01	Premier League	8	38	13	15	10	46	43	54	1.421053
2001–02	Premier League	8	38	12	14	12	46	47	50	1.315789
2006–07	Premier League	11	38	11	17	10	43	41	50	1.315789
2004–05	Premier League	10	38	12	11	15	45	52	47	1.236842
2002–03	Premier League	16	38	12	9	17	42	47	45	1.184211
2005–06	Premier League	16	38	10	12	16	42	55	42	1.105263

2000s

SQUAD 1999–2000   6TH IN THE PREMIER LEAGUE

Gareth BARRY	Defender/Midfielder
Jonathan BEWERS	Defender/Right back
George BOATENG	Midfielder
Colin CALDERWOOD	Defender/Centre back
Benito CARBONE	Forward
Neil CUTLER	Goalkeeper
Mark DELANEY	Defender/Right back
Mark DRAPER	Midfielder
Dion DUBLIN	Defender/Forward
Ugo EHIOGU	Defender/Centre back
Peter ENCKELMAN	Goalkeeper
Najwan GHRAYIB	Full back
Lee HENDRIE	Midfielder
David JAMES	Goalkeeper
Julian JOACHIM	Forward
Paul MERSON	Midfielder
JLloyd SAMUEL	Defender/Centre back
Gareth SOUTHGATE	Defender/Centre back
Steve STONE	Midfielder
Ian TAYLOR	Midfielder
Alan THOMPSON	Midfielder
Darius VASSELL	Forward
Richard WALKER	Forward
Steve WATSON	Defender
Alan WRIGHT	Defender/Left back

ASTON VILLA

BARNSLEY

Season	League	League Position	P	W	D	L	F	A	Pts	3 Point Equivalent
1954–55	**Division 3 North**	**1**	**46**	**30**	**5**	**11**	**86**	**46**	**65**	**2.065217**
1953–54	Division 3 North	2	46	24	10	12	77	57	58	1.782609
1946–47	Division 2	10	42	17	8	17	84	86	42	1.404762
1950–51	Division 2	15	42	15	10	17	74	68	40	1.309524
1947–48	Division 2	12	42	15	10	17	62	64	40	1.309524
1948–49	Division 2	9	42	14	12	16	62	61	40	1.285714
1957–58	Division 2	14	42	14	12	16	70	74	40	1.285714
1949–50	Division 2	13	42	13	13	16	64	67	39	1.238095
1951–52	Division 2	20	42	11	14	17	59	72	36	1.119048
1956–57	Division 2	19	42	12	10	20	59	89	34	1.095238
1955–56	Division 2	18	42	11	12	19	47	84	34	1.071429
1958–59	Division 2	22	42	10	7	25	55	91	27	0.880952
1952–53	Division 2	22	42	5	8	29	47	108	18	0.547619

SQUAD 1954–55   CHAMPIONS OF DIVISION 3 NORTH

Ron ARCHER	Wing half	Doug KELLY	Centre forward
Frank BARTLETT	Inside forward	Tommy LUMLEY	Inside forward
Barrie BETTS	Full back	Harry MAY	Full back
Bobby BROWN	Inside forward	Frank PATTISON	Winger
Lol CHAPPELL	Centre forward	Ron SMILLIE	Outside right
Malcolm GRAHAM	Inside forward	Norman SMITH	Wing half
Tom HOLMES	Inside forward	George SPRUCE	Centre half
Harry HOUGH	Goalkeeper	Joe THOMAS	Full back
Maurice JACKSON	Full back	Henry WALTERS	Wing half
John JARMAN	Wing half	Billy WARDLE	Outside left
Arthur KAYE	Outside right	Bobby WOOD	Wing half

Season	League	League Position	P	W	D	L	F	A	Pts	3 Point Equivalent
1967–68	Division 4	2	46	24	13	9	68	46	61	1.847826
1960–61	**Division 3**	**9**	**46**	**21**	**7**	**18**	**83**	**80**	**49**	**1.521739**
1968–69	Division 3	10	46	16	14	16	58	63	46	1.347826
1959–60	Division 3	17	46	15	14	17	65	66	44	1.282609
1962–63	Division 3	18	46	15	11	20	63	74	41	1.217391
1965–66	Division 4	16	46	15	10	21	74	78	40	1.195652
1966–67	Division 4	16	46	13	15	18	60	64	41	1.173913
1961–62	Division 3	20	46	13	12	21	71	95	38	1.108696
1963–64	Division 3	20	46	12	15	19	68	94	39	1.108696
1964–65	Division 3	24	46	9	11	26	54	90	29	0.826087

SQUAD 1960–61   9TH IN DIVISION 3

Dave BARBER	Wing half	Jack LUNN	Outside left
Frank BARTLETT	Inside forward	Ken OLIVER	Inside forward
Frank BEAUMONT	Inside forward	Roy SAWYER	Centre half
George BENNETT	Full back	Duncan SHARP	Centre half
Colin BROOKES	Outside left	Ron SMILLIE	Outside right
Eric BROOKES	Left back	John STAINSBY	Centre forward
Allan GREEN	Full back	Colin SWIFT	Right back
Alan HILL	Goalkeeper	Bert TINDILL	Inside forward
Ollie HOPKINS	Centre half	Peter WHYKE	Winger
Billy HOUGHTON	Defender	Clarrie WILLIAMS	Goalkeeper
George JAGGER	Winger	Barrie WOOD	Inside forward
Don LEESON	Goalkeeper	Bobby WOOD	Wing half

	Season	League	League Position	P	W	D	L	F	A	Pts	3 Point Equivalent
1970s	**1978–79**	**Division 4**	**4**	**46**	**24**	**13**	**9**	**73**	**42**	**61**	**1.847826**
	1976–77	Division 4	6	46	23	9	14	62	39	55	1.695652
	1969–70	Division 3	7	46	19	15	12	68	59	53	1.565217
	1977–78	Division 4	7	46	18	14	14	61	49	50	1.478261
	1970–71	Division 3	12	46	17	11	18	49	52	45	1.347826
	1973–74	Division 4	13	46	17	10	19	58	64	44	1.326087
	1975–76	Division 4	12	46	14	16	16	52	48	44	1.260870
	1972–73	Division 4	14	46	14	16	16	58	60	44	1.260870
	1974–75	Division 4	15	46	15	11	20	62	65	41	1.217391
	1971–72	Division 3	22	46	9	18	19	32	64	36	0.978261

SQUAD 1978–79 · 4TH IN DIVISION 4

Ian BANKS	Midfielder	Mick McCARTHY	Central defender
Derek BELL	Forward	Aly MILLAR	Midfielder
Phil CHAMBERS	Left back	John PEACHEY	Forward
Allan CLARKE	Forward	Mike PRENDERGAST	Forward
John COLLINS	Full back	Graham PUGH	Midfielder
Gary COPLEY	Goalkeeper	Graham REED	Right back
Tommy GRAHAM	Midfielder	Glyn RILEY	Forward
Brian JOICEY	Forward	John SAUNDERS	Central defender
Alan LITTLE	Midfielder	David SPEEDIE	Forward
Gary MALLENDER	Midfielder	Peter SPRINGETT	Goalkeeper

	Season	League	League Position	P	W	D	L	F	A	Pts	3 Point Equivalent
1980s	1980–81	Division 3	2	46	21	17	8	72	45	59	1.739130
	1988–89	Division 2	7	46	20	14	12	66	58	74	1.608696
	1981–82	**Division 2**	**6**	**42**	**19**	**10**	**13**	**59**	**41**	**67**	**1.595238**
	1984–85	Division 2	11	42	14	16	12	42	42	58	1.380952
	1982–83	Division 2	10	42	14	15	13	57	55	57	1.357143
	1979–80	Division 3	11	46	16	14	16	53	56	46	1.347826
	1985–86	Division 2	12	42	14	14	14	47	50	56	1.333333
	1986–87	Division 2	11	42	14	13	15	49	52	55	1.309524
	1987–88	Division 2	14	44	15	12	17	61	62	57	1.295455
	1983–84	Division 2	15	42	15	7	20	57	53	52	1.238095

SQUAD 1981–82 · 6TH IN DIVISION 2

Trevor AYLOTT	Forward	Joe JOYCE	Right back
Ian BANKS	Midfielder	Nicky LAW	Central defender
Stewart BARROWCLOUGH	Winger	Paul LONGDEN	Left back
Alan BIRCH	Winger	Jimmy MANN	Midfielder
Winston CAMPBELL	Winger	Mick McCARTHY	Central defender
Phil CHAMBERS	Left back	Ray McHALE	Midfielder
Neil COOPER	Central defender	Derrick PARKER	Forward
Ian EVANS	Central defender	Glyn RILEY	Forward
Ronnie GLAVIN	Midfielder	Colin WALKER	Forward
Bobby HORN	Goalkeeper	David WILKES	Midfielder

Season	League	League Position	P	W	D	L	F	A	Pts	3 Point Equivalent
1996–97	L1	2	46	22	10	14	76	55	80	1.652174
1994–95	L1	6	46	20	14	12	63	52	72	1.608696
1992–93	L1	13	46	17	20	9	56	60	60	1.543478
1993–94	L1	18	46	16	23	7	55	67	55	1.543478
1990–91	Division 2	8	46	19	12	15	63	48	69	1.500000
1991–92	Division 2	16	46	16	11	19	46	57	59	1.282609
1998–99	L1	13	46	14	15	17	59	56	59	1.239130
1995–96	L1	10	46	14	14	18	60	66	60	1.217391
1989–90	Division 2	19	46	13	15	18	49	71	54	1.173913
1997–98	Premier League	19	38	10	5	23	37	82	35	0.921053

SQUAD 1996–97   2ND IN FIRST DIVISION

Matty APPLEBY	Defender	Adie MOSES	Defender/Centre back
Jovo BOSANCIC	Midfielder	Neil REDFEARN	Midfielder
Martin BULLOCK	Midfielder	Dave REGIS	Forward
Steve DAVIS	Defender/Centre back	Darren SHERIDAN	Midfielder
Arjan DE ZEEUW	Defender/Centre back	Peter SHIRTLIFF	Defender/Centre back
Nicky EADEN	Defender/Right back	Laurens TEN-HEUVEL	Forward
John HENDRIE	Forward	Neil THOMPSON	Defender/Left back
Glynn HURST	Forward	Carel VAN DER VELDEN	Midfielder
Scott JONES	Defender/Left back	David WATSON	Goalkeeper
Andy LIDDELL	Forward	Paul WILKINSON	Forward
Clint MARCELLE	Forward		

Season	League	League Position	P	W	D	L	F	A	Pts	3 Point Equivalent
1999–2000	L1	4	46	24	12	10	88	67	82	1.826087
2005–06	League 1	5	46	18	18	10	62	44	72	1.565217
2000–01	L1	16	46	15	22	9	49	62	54	1.456522
2002–03	L2	19	46	13	20	13	51	64	52	1.282609
2003–04	L2	12	46	15	14	17	54	58	62	1.282609
2004–05	League 1	13	46	14	13	19	69	64	61	1.195652
2001–02	L1	23	46	11	20	15	59	86	48	1.152174
2006–07	Championship	20	46	15	5	26	53	85	50	1.086957

SQUAD 1999–2000   4TH IN FIRST DIVISION

Matty APPLEBY	Defender	Scott JONES	Defender/Left back
Kevin AUSTIN	Defender/Centre back	Sean McCLARE	Midfielder
Chris BARKER	Defender/Left back	Kevin MILLER	Goalkeeper
Darren BARNARD	Defender/Left back	Chris MORGAN	Defender/Centre back
Keith BROWN	Defender	Adie MOSES	Defender/Centre back
Tony BULLOCK	Goalkeeper	Kevin RICHARDSON	Midfielder
Martin BULLOCK	Midfielder	Mike SHERON	Forward
Steve CHETTLE	Defender/Centre back	Neil SHIPPERLEY	Forward
John CURTIS	Defender/Right back	Geoff THOMAS	Midfielder
Bruce DYER	Forward	Eric TINKLER	Midfielder
Nicky EADEN	Defender/Right back	Mike TURNER	Forward
Craig HIGNETT	Midfielder	Dave TUTTLE	Defender/Centre back
Georgi HRISTOV	Forward	Robin VAN DER LAAN	Midfielder
Mark JACKSON	Defender/Centre back		

BIRMINGHAM CITY

1940s & 50s

Season	League	League Position	P	W	D	L	F	A	Pts	3 Point Equivalent
1947–48	Division 2	1	42	22	15	5	55	24	59	1.928571
1946–47	Division 2	3	42	25	5	12	74	33	55	1.904762
1954–55	Division 2	1	42	22	10	10	92	47	54	1.809524
1951–52	Division 2	3	42	21	9	12	67	56	51	1.714286
1950–51	Division 2	4	42	20	9	13	64	53	49	1.642857
1952–53	Division 2	6	42	19	10	13	71	66	48	1.595238
1958–59	**Division 1**	**9**	**42**	**20**	**6**	**16**	**84**	**68**	**46**	**1.571429**
1953–54	Division 2	7	42	18	11	13	78	58	47	1.547619
1955–56	Division 1	6	42	18	9	15	75	57	45	1.500000
1956–57	Division 1	13	42	15	9	18	69	69	39	1.285714
1957–58	Division 1	13	42	14	11	17	76	89	39	1.261905
1948–49	Division 1	17	42	11	15	16	36	38	37	1.142857
1949–50	Division 1	22	42	7	14	21	31	67	28	0.833333

SQUAD 1958–59 — 9TH IN DIVISION 1

George ALLEN	Full back
Gordon ASTALL	Outside right
Eddie BROWN	Centre forward
Brian FARMER	Full back
Johnny GORDON	Inside forward
Ken GREEN	Full back
Jeff HALL	Full back
Mike HELLAWELL	Outside right
Harry HOOPER	Outside right
Brian HOUGHTON	Centre forward
Billy HUME	Inside forward
Alex JACKSON	Centre forward
David JONES	Inside forward
Bunny LARKIN	Wing half/Inside forward
Gil MERRICK	Goalkeeper
Peter MURPHY	Inside forward
Dick NEAL	Wing half
Bryan ORRITT	Inside forward
Johnny SCHOFIELD	Goalkeeper
Graham SISSONS	Defender
Trevor SMITH	Centre half
Robin STUBBS	Centre forward
Brian TAYLOR	Outside left
Johnny WATTS	Wing half

167

1960s

Season	League	League Position	P	W	D	L	F	A	Pts	3 Point Equivalent
1967–68	**Division 2**	**4**	**42**	**19**	**14**	**9**	**83**	**51**	**52**	**1.690476**
1968–69	Division 2	7	42	18	8	16	73	59	44	1.476190
1965–66	Division 2	10	42	16	9	17	70	75	41	1.357143
1966–67	Division 2	10	42	16	8	18	70	66	40	1.333333
1961–62	Division 1	17	42	14	10	18	65	81	38	1.238095
1959–60	Division 1	19	42	13	10	19	63	80	36	1.166667
1960–61	Division 1	19	42	14	6	22	62	84	34	1.142857
1962–63	Division 1	20	42	10	13	19	63	90	33	1.023810
1963–64	Division 1	20	42	11	7	24	54	92	29	0.952381
1964–65	Division 1	22	42	8	11	23	64	96	27	0.833333

SQUAD 1967–68 — 4TH IN DIVISION 2

Malcolm BEARD	Wing half
Barry BRIDGES	Centre forward
Micky DARRELL	Midfielder
Ronnie FENTON	Inside forward
Winston FOSTER	Centre half
Colin GREEN	Full back
Jim HERRIOT	Goalkeeper
Trevor HOCKEY	Midfielder
Graham LEGGAT	Winger
Ray MARTIN	Full back
Bert MURRAY	Outside right
Malcolm PAGE	Defender
Fred PICKERING	Centre forward
Brian SHARPLES	Centre half
John SLEEUWENHOEK	Centre half
Phil SUMMERILL	Forward
Bobby THOMSON	Wing half/Inside forward
Denis THWAITES	Outside left
Terry TWELL	Goalkeeper
Johnny VINCENT	Midfielder
Geoff VOWDEN	Forward
Ron WYLIE	Inside forward/Wing half

1970s

Season	League	League Position	P	W	D	L	F	A	Pts	3 Point Equivalent
1971–72	Division 2	2	42	19	18	5	60	31	56	1.785714
1970–71	Division 2	9	42	17	12	13	58	48	46	1.500000
1977–78	Division 1	11	42	16	9	17	55	60	41	1.357143
1972–73	**Division 1**	**10**	**42**	**15**	**12**	**15**	**53**	**54**	**42**	**1.357143**
1974–75	Division 1	17	42	14	9	19	53	61	37	1.214286
1976–77	Division 1	13	42	13	12	17	63	61	38	1.214286
1973–74	Division 1	19	42	12	13	17	52	64	37	1.166667
1975–76	Division 1	19	42	13	7	22	57	75	33	1.095238
1969–70	Division 2	18	42	11	11	20	51	78	33	1.047619
1978–79	Division 1	21	42	6	10	26	37	64	22	0.666667

SQUAD 1972–73   10TH IN DIVISION 1

Keith BOWKER	Forward	Mike KELLY	Goalkeeper
Kenny BURNS	Central defender	Dave LATCHFORD	Goalkeeper
Jimmy CALDERWOOD	Midfielder	Bob LATCHFORD	Forward
Alan CAMPBELL	Midfielder	Ray MARTIN	Full back
Tommy CARROLL	Right back	Malcolm PAGE	Defender
Paul COOPER	Goalkeeper	Garry PENDREY	Defender
Trevor FRANCIS	Forward	Steve PHILLIPS	Forward
Stan HARLAND	Wing half	John ROBERTS	Central defender/Forward
Bob HATTON	Forward	George SMITH	Midfielder
Paul HENDRIE	Midfielder	Phil SUMMERILL	Forward
Bobby HOPE	Midfielder	Gordon TAYLOR	Winger
Dave HOWITT	Full back	Tony WANT	Left back
Roger HYND	Central defender	Alan WHITEHEAD	Central defender

1980s

Season	League	League Position	P	W	D	L	F	A	Pts	3 Point Equivalent
1984–85	Division 2	2	42	25	7	10	59	33	82	1.952381
1979–80	Division 2	3	42	21	11	10	58	38	53	1.761905
1980–81	**Division 1**	**13**	**42**	**13**	**12**	**17**	**50**	**61**	**38**	**1.214286**
1982–83	Division 1	16	42	12	14	16	40	55	50	1.190476
1986–87	Division 2	19	42	11	17	14	47	59	50	1.190476
1983–84	Division 1	20	42	12	12	18	39	50	48	1.142857
1987–88	Division 2	19	44	11	15	18	41	66	48	1.090909
1981–82	Division 1	16	42	10	14	18	53	61	44	1.047619
1988–89	Division 2	23	46	8	11	27	31	76	35	0.760870
1985–86	Division 1	21	42	8	5	29	30	73	29	0.690476

SQUAD 1980–81   13TH IN DIVISION 1

Alan AINSCOW	Midfielder	Ian HANDYSIDES	Winger
Keith BERTSCHIN	Forward	Phil HAWKER	Defender/Midfielder
Kevan BROADHURST	Defender	Paul IVEY	Forward
Tony COTON	Goalkeeper	David LANGAN	Right back
Alan CURBISHLEY	Midfielder	Terry LEES	Full back
Mark DENNIS	Left back	Steve LYNEX	Winger
Kevin DILLON	Midfielder	Malcolm PAGE	Defender
Tony EVANS	Forward	Colin TODD	Central defender
Joe GALLAGHER	Central defender	Pat VAN DEN HAUWE	Full back
Archie GEMMILL	Midfielder	Jeff WEALANDS	Goalkeeper
Don GIVENS	Forward	Frank WORTHINGTON	Forward
Terry GOODE	Forward		

Season	League	League Position	P	W	D	L	F	A	Pts	3 Point Equivalent
1994–95	L2	1	46	25	7	14	84	37	89	1.782609
1991–92	Division 3	2	46	23	12	11	69	52	81	1.760870
1998–99	**L1**	**4**	**46**	**23**	**11**	**12**	**66**	**37**	**81**	**1.739130**
1997–98	L1	7	46	19	10	17	60	35	74	1.456522
1989–90	Division 3	7	46	18	12	16	60	59	66	1.434783
1990–91	Division 3	12	46	16	17	13	45	49	65	1.413043
1996–97	L1	10	46	17	14	15	52	48	66	1.413043
1995–96	L1	15	46	15	18	13	61	64	58	1.369565
1992–93	L1	19	46	13	21	12	50	72	51	1.304348
1993–94	L1	22	46	13	21	12	52	69	51	1.304348

SQUAD 1998–99   4TH IN FIRST DIVISION

Gary ABLETT	Defender
Dele ADEBOLA	Forward
Jon BASS	Defender
Ian BENNETT	Goalkeeper
Lee BRADBURY	Forward
Simon CHARLTON	Defender/Left back
Howard FORINTON	Forward
Nicky FORSTER	Forward
Paul FURLONG	Forward
Jerry GILL	Defender/Right back
Martin GRAINGER	Defender/Left back
David HOLDSWORTH	Defender/Centre back
Chris HOLLAND	Midfielder
Bryan HUGHES	Midfielder
Graham HYDE	Midfielder
Michael JOHNSON	Defender/Centre back
Andrew JOHNSON	Forward
Chris MARSDEN	Midfielder
Simon MARSH	Defender
Jon McCARTHY	Midfielder
Peter NDLOVU	Forward
Martin O'CONNOR	Midfielder
Kevin POOLE	Goalkeeper
Darren PURSE	Defender/Centre back
Steve ROBINSON	Midfielder
Gary ROWETT	Defender
Darren WASSELL	Defender

Season	League	League Position	P	W	D	L	F	A	Pts	3 Point Equivalent
2006–07	Championship	2	46	26	8	12	67	42	86	1.869565
2000–01	L1	5	46	23	14	9	59	48	78	1.804348
1999–2000	L1	5	46	22	13	11	65	44	77	1.717391
2001–02	L1	5	46	21	12	13	70	49	76	1.630435
2003–04	**Premier League**	**10**	**38**	**12**	**14**	**12**	**43**	**48**	**50**	**1.315789**
2002–03	Premier League	13	38	13	9	16	41	49	48	1.263158
2004–05	Premier League	12	38	11	12	15	40	46	45	1.184211
2005–06	Premier League	18	38	8	10	20	28	50	34	0.894737

SQUAD 2003–04   10TH IN THE PREMIER LEAGUE

Andrew BARROWMAN	Forward
Ian BENNETT	Goalkeeper
Darren CARTER	Midfielder
Aliou CISSE	Defender
Jamie CLAPHAM	Defender/Midfielder
Stephen CLEMENCE	Midfielder
Kenny CUNNINGHAM	Defender
Paul DEVLIN	Midfielder
Christophe DUGARRY	Forward
David DUNN	Midfielder
Lucho FIGUEROA	Forward
Mikael FORSSELL	Forward
Martin GRAINGER	Defender/Left back
Geoff HORSFIELD	Forward
Bryan HUGHES	Midfielder
Stern JOHN	Forward
Damien JOHNSON	Midfielder
Jeff KENNA	Defender/Right back
Jovan KIROVSKI	Midfielder/Forward
Stan LAZARIDIS	Midfielder
Clinton MORRISON	Forward
Darren PURSE	Defender/Centre back
Robbie SAVAGE	Midfielder
Maik TAYLOR	Goalkeeper
Martin TAYLOR	Defender/Centre back
Oliver TEBILY	Defender
Matthew UPSON	Defender/Centre back

BIRMINGHAM CITY

BLACKBURN ROVERS

Season	League	League Position	P	W	D	L	F	A	Pts	3 Point Equivalent
1953–54	Divison 2	3	42	23	9	10	86	50	55	1.857143
1957–58	**Divison 2**	**2**	**42**	**22**	**12**	**8**	**93**	**57**	**56**	**1.857143**
1956–57	Divison 2	4	42	21	10	11	83	75	52	1.738095
1954–55	Divison 2	6	42	22	6	14	114	79	50	1.714286
1955–56	Divison 2	4	42	21	6	15	84	65	48	1.642857
1950–51	Divison 2	6	42	19	8	15	65	66	46	1.547619
1952–53	Divison 2	9	42	18	8	16	68	65	44	1.476190
1958–59	Division 1	10	42	17	10	15	76	70	44	1.452381
1951–52	Divison 2	14	42	17	6	19	54	63	40	1.357143
1948–49	Divison 2	14	42	15	8	19	53	63	38	1.261905
1949–50	Divison 2	16	42	14	10	18	55	60	38	1.238095
1946–47	Division 1	17	42	14	8	20	45	53	36	1.190476
1947–48	Division 1	21	42	11	10	21	54	72	32	1.023810

SQUAD 1957–58   2ND IN DIVISION 2

Tommy BRIGGS	Centre forward	Ally MacLEOD	Winger
Ron CAIRNS	Inside forward	Mick McGRATH	Wing half
Ronnie CLAYTON	Wing half	Bill SMITH	Wing half/Inside forward
Peter DOBING	Inside forward	Roy STEPHENSON	Outside right
Bryan DOUGLAS	Outside right	Jack SWINDELLS	Centre forward
Billy ECKERSLEY	Full back	Ken TAYLOR	Full back
Roy ISHERWOOD	Outside right	Roy VERNON	Inside forward
Tom JOHNSTON	Centre forward	Dave WHELAN	Full back
Pat KENNEDY	Full back	Matt WOODS	Centre half
Harry LEYLAND	Goalkeeper		

Season	League	League Position	P	W	D	L	F	A	Pts	3 Point Equivalent
1966–67	Division 2	4	42	19	13	10	56	46	51	1.666667
1963–64	**Division 1**	**7**	**42**	**18**	**10**	**14**	**89**	**65**	**46**	**1.523810**
1967–68	Division 2	8	42	16	11	15	56	49	43	1.404762
1964–65	Division 1	10	42	16	10	16	83	79	42	1.380952
1960–61	Division 1	8	42	15	13	14	77	76	43	1.380952
1962–63	Division 1	11	42	15	12	15	79	71	42	1.357143
1961–62	Division 1	16	42	14	11	17	50	58	39	1.261905
1959–60	Division 1	17	42	16	5	21	60	70	37	1.261905
1968–69	Division 2	19	42	13	11	18	52	63	37	1.190476
1965–66	Division 1	22	42	8	4	30	57	88	20	0.666667

SQUAD 1963–64   7TH IN DIVISION 1

Reg BLORE	Winger	George JONES	Forward
Jack BRAY	Full back	Walter JOYCE	Wing half
John BYROM	Forward	Andy McEVOY	Inside forward
Ronnie CLAYTON	Wing half	Mick McGRATH	Wing half
Bryan DOUGLAS	Outside right	Keith NEWTON	Full back
Fred ELSE	Goalkeeper	Fred PICKERING	Centre forward
Mike ENGLAND	Centre half	Barrie RATCLIFFE	Outside left
Mike FERGUSON	Midfielder	Chris SIMS	Full back
Mike HARRISON	Outside left	Ken TAYLOR	Full back
Alan HOLDEN	Wing half		

Season	League	League Position	P	W	D	L	F	A	Pts	3 Point Equivalent
1974–75	Division 3	1	46	22	16	8	68	45	60	1.782609
1972–73	Division 3	3	46	20	15	11	57	47	55	1.630435
1969–70	**Division 2**	**8**	**42**	**20**	**7**	**15**	**54**	**50**	**47**	**1.595238**
1977–78	Division 2	5	42	16	13	13	56	60	45	1.452381
1971–72	Division 3	10	46	19	9	18	54	57	47	1.434783
1973–74	Division 3	13	46	18	10	18	62	64	46	1.391304
1976–77	Division 2	12	42	15	9	18	42	54	39	1.285714
1975–76	Division 2	15	42	12	14	16	45	50	38	1.190476
1978–79	Division 2	22	42	10	10	22	41	72	30	0.952381
1970–71	Division 2	21	42	6	15	21	37	69	27	0.785714

1970s

SQUAD 1969–70 — 8TH IN DIVISION 2

John BARTON	Goalkeeper	Roger JONES	Goalkeeper
Adam BLACKLAW	Goalkeeper	Ken KNIGHTON	Midfielder
Laurie CALLOWAY	Midfielder	Frank KOPEL	Full back
Ray CHARTER	Full back	Don MARTIN	Forward/Midfielder
John CODDINGTON	Centre half	Stuart METCALFE	Midfielder
John CONNELLY	Outside right	Dick MULVANEY	Central defender
Malcolm DARLING	Forward	Keith NEWTON	Full back
Tex ECCLES	Centre forward	Eamonn ROGERS	Winger
Jim FRYATT	Centre forward	Jeff WHALLEY	Winger
Freddie GOODWIN	Midfielder	Billy WILSON	Full back
Brian HILL	Outside left	Mick WOOD	Defender
Allan HUNTER	Central defender		

Season	League	League Position	P	W	D	L	F	A	Pts	3 Point Equivalent
1979–80	Division 3	2	46	25	9	12	58	36	59	1.826087
1987–88	**Division 2**	**5**	**44**	**21**	**14**	**9**	**68**	**52**	**77**	**1.750000**
1984–85	Division 2	5	42	21	10	11	66	41	73	1.738095
1988–89	Division 2	5	46	22	11	13	74	59	77	1.673913
1983–84	Division 2	6	42	17	16	9	57	46	67	1.595238
1980–81	Division 2	4	42	16	18	8	42	29	50	1.571429
1981–82	Division 2	10	42	16	11	15	47	43	59	1.404762
1982–83	Division 2	11	42	15	12	15	58	58	57	1.357143
1986–87	Division 2	12	42	15	10	17	45	55	55	1.309524
1985–86	Division 2	19	42	12	13	17	53	62	49	1.166667

1980s

SQUAD 1987–88 — 5TH IN DIVISION 2

Alan AINSCOW	Midfielder	Keith HILL	Defender/Centre back
Steve ARCHIBALD	Forward	Lenny JOHNROSE	Midfielder
Ossie ARDILES	Midfielder	David MAIL	Central defender
Simon BARKER	Midfielder	John MILLAR	Midfielder
Sean CURRY	Forward	Ian MILLER	Right Winger
Ally DAWSON	Central defender	Vince O'KEEFE	Goalkeeper
Tony DIAMOND	Forward	Mark PATTERSON	Midfielder
Simon GARNER	Forward	Chris PRICE	Right back
Howard GAYLE	Winger	Nicky REID	Defender/Midfielder
Terry GENNOE	Goalkeeper	Scott SELLARS	Midfielder
Colin HENDRY	Defender/Centre back	Chris SULLEY	Left back

BLACKBURN ROVERS

Season	League	League Position	P	W	D	L	F	A	Pts	3 Point Equivalent
1994–95	**Premier League**	**1**	**42**	**27**	**8**	**7**	**80**	**39**	**89**	**2.119048**
1993–94	Premier League	2	42	25	9	8	63	36	84	2.000000
1992–93	Premier League	4	42	20	11	11	68	46	71	1.690476
1989–90	Division 2	5	46	19	17	10	74	59	74	1.608696
1991–92	Division 2	6	46	21	11	14	70	53	74	1.608696
1995–96	Premier League	7	38	18	7	13	61	47	61	1.605263
1997–98	Premier League	6	38	16	10	12	57	52	58	1.526316
1990–91	Division 2	19	46	14	10	22	51	66	52	1.130435
1996–97	Premier League	13	38	9	15	14	42	43	42	1.105263
1998–99	Premier League	19	38	7	14	17	38	52	35	0.921053

SQUAD 1994–95

CHAMPIONS OF THE PREMIER LEAGUE

Mark ATKINS	Midfielder		Ian PEARCE	Defender/Centre back
David BATTY	Midfielder		Stuart RIPLEY	Midfielder
Henning BERG	Defender/Centre back		Alan SHEARER	Forward
Tim FLOWERS	Goalkeeper		Tim SHERWOOD	Midfielder
Tony GALE	Central defender		Robbie SLATER	Midfielder
Kevin GALLACHER	Forward		Chris SUTTON	Forward
Colin HENDRY	Defender/Centre back		Paul WARHURST	Defender/Midfielder
Jeff KENNA	Defender/Right back		Jason WILCOX	Midfielder
Graeme LE SAUX	Defender/Left back		Richard WITSCHGE	Midfielder
Bobby MIMMS	Goalkeeper		Alan WRIGHT	Defender/Left back
Mike NEWELL	Forward			

Season	League	League Position	P	W	D	L	F	A	Pts	3 Point Equivalent
2000–01	L1	2	46	26	7	13	76	39	91	1.847826
2005–06	**Premier League**	**6**	**38**	**19**	**6**	**13**	**51**	**42**	**63**	**1.657895**
2002–03	Premier League	6	38	16	12	10	52	43	60	1.578947
2006–07	Premier League	10	38	15	7	16	52	54	52	1.368421
1999–2000	L1	11	46	15	14	17	55	51	62	1.282609
2001–02	Premier League	10	38	12	10	16	55	51	46	1.210526
2003–04	Premier League	15	38	12	8	18	51	59	44	1.157895
2004–05	Premier League	15	38	9	15	14	32	43	42	1.105263

SQUAD 2005–06

6TH IN THE PREMIER LEAGUE

Craig BELLAMY	Forward		Dominic MATTEO	Defender/Midfielder
David BENTLEY	Forward		Aaron MOKOENA	Defender/Centre back
Paul DICKOV	Forward		Lucas NEILL	Defender/Midfielder
Brett EMERTON	Defender		Ryan NELSEN	Defender
Garry FLITCROFT	Midfielder		Morten Gamst PEDERSEN	Midfielder
Brad FRIEDEL	Goalkeeper		Sergio PETER	Midfielder
Paul GALLAGHER	Forward		Steven REID	Midfielder
Michael GRAY	Defender/Left back		Robbie SAVAGE	Midfielder
Vratislav GRESKO	Defender		Florent SINAMA-PONGOLLE	Forward
Matt JANSEN	Forward		David THOMPSON	Midfielder
Jemal JOHNSON	Forward		Andy TODD	Defender/Midfielder
Zurab KHIZANISHVILI	Defender		TUGAY Kerimoglu	Midfielder
Shefki KUQI	Forward			

BOLTON WANDERERS

Season	League	League Position	P	W	D	L	F	A	Pts	3 Point Equivalent
1958–59	**Division 1**	**4**	**42**	**20**	**10**	**12**	**79**	**66**	**50**	**1.666667**
1951–52	Division 1	5	42	19	10	13	65	61	48	1.595238
1953–54	Division 1	5	42	18	12	12	75	60	48	1.571429
1950–51	Division 1	8	42	19	7	16	64	61	45	1.523810
1955–56	Division 1	8	42	18	7	17	71	58	43	1.452381
1956–57	Division 1	9	42	16	12	14	65	65	44	1.428571
1952–53	Division 1	14	42	15	9	18	61	69	39	1.285714
1947–48	Division 1	17	42	16	5	21	46	58	37	1.261905
1954–55	Division 1	18	42	13	13	16	62	69	39	1.238095
1948–49	Division 1	14	42	14	10	18	59	68	38	1.238095
1957–58	Division 1	15	42	14	10	18	65	87	38	1.238095
1946–47	Division 1	18	42	13	8	21	57	69	34	1.119048
1949–50	Division 1	16	42	10	14	18	45	59	34	1.047619

1940s & 50s

SQUAD 1958–59   4TH IN DIVISION 1

Tommy BANKS	Full back	Derek HENNIN	Wing half
Neville BANNISTER	Outside right	John HIGGINS	Centre half
Brian BIRCH	Outside right	Freddie HILL	Inside forward
Peter DEAKIN	Inside forward	Doug HOLDEN	Outside right
Joe DEAN	Goalkeeper	Eddie HOPKINSON	Goalkeeper
Bryan EDWARDS	Wing half	Nat LOFTHOUSE	Centre forward
Gordon EDWARDS	Centre half	Ray PARRY	Inside forward
Malcolm EDWARDS	Left back	Brian RILEY	Outside left
Syd FARRIMOND	Left back	Graham STANLEY	Wing half
Ralph GUBBINS	Inside forward	Dennis STEVENS	Inside forward
Roy HARTLE	Full back		

Season	League	League Position	P	W	D	L	F	A	Pts	3 Point Equivalent
1964–65	Division 2	3	42	20	10	12	80	58	50	1.666667
1959–60	**Division 1**	**6**	**42**	**20**	**8**	**14**	**59**	**51**	**48**	**1.619048**
1961–62	Division 1	11	42	16	10	16	62	66	42	1.380952
1965–66	Division 2	9	42	16	9	17	62	59	41	1.357143
1966–67	Division 2	9	42	14	14	14	64	58	42	1.333333
1967–68	Division 2	12	42	13	13	16	60	63	39	1.238095
1968–69	Division 2	17	42	12	14	16	55	67	38	1.190476
1962–63	Division 1	18	42	15	5	22	55	75	35	1.190476
1960–61	Division 1	18	42	12	11	19	58	73	35	1.119048
1963–64	Division 1	21	42	10	8	24	48	80	28	0.904762

1960s

SQUAD 1959–60   6TH IN DIVISION 1

Tommy BANKS	Full back	Roy HARTLE	Full back
Neville BANNISTER	Outside right	Derek HENNIN	Wing half
Brian BIRCH	Outside right	John HIGGINS	Centre half
John BOLLANDS	Goalkeeper	Freddie HILL	Inside forward
Graham CUNLIFFE	Wing half	Doug HOLDEN	Outside right
Peter DEAKIN	Inside forward	Eddie HOPKINSON	Goalkeeper
Joe DEAN	Goalkeeper	Dick OXTOBY	Centre half
Bryan EDWARDS	Wing half	Ray PARRY	Inside forward
Malcolm EDWARDS	Left back	Ernie PHYTHIAN	Centre forward
Syd FARRIMOND	Left back	Graham STANLEY	Wing half
Ralph GUBBINS	Inside forward	Dennis STEVENS	Inside forward

Season	League	League Position	P	W	D	L	F	A	Pts	3 Point Equivalent
1977–78	Division 2	1	42	24	10	8	63	33	58	1.952381
1972–73	Division 3	1	46	25	11	10	73	39	61	1.869565
1975–76	Division 2	4	42	20	12	10	64	38	52	1.714286
1976–77	Division 2	4	42	20	11	11	75	54	51	1.690476
1971–72	Division 3	7	46	17	16	13	51	41	50	1.456522
1973–74	Division 2	11	42	15	12	15	44	40	42	1.357143
1974–75	Division 2	10	42	15	12	15	45	41	42	1.357143
1969–70	Division 2	16	42	12	12	18	54	61	36	1.142857
1978–79	Division 1	17	42	12	11	19	54	75	35	1.119048
1970–71	Division 2	22	42	7	10	25	35	74	24	0.738095

SQUAD 1977–78   CHAMPIONS OF DIVISION 2

Sam ALLARDYCE	Central defender	Peter NICHOLSON	Full back
Andy CLEMENTS	Central defender	Peter REID	Midfielder
Tony DUNNE	Left back	John RITSON	Right back
Alan GOWLING	Forward	Steve TAYLOR	Forward
Mike GRAHAM	Defender	Peter THOMPSON	Left winger
Roy GREAVES	Midfielder	Ray TRAIN	Midfielder
Garry JONES	Forward	Alan WALDRON	Midfielder
Paul JONES	Central defender	Mick WALSH	Central defender
Seamus McDONAGH	Goalkeeper	Neil WHATMORE	Forward
Willie MORGAN	Winger	Frank WORTHINGTON	Forward

Season	League	League Position	P	W	D	L	F	A	Pts	3 Point Equivalent
1987–88	Division 4	3	46	22	12	12	66	42	78	1.695652
1983–84	Division 3	10	46	18	10	18	56	60	64	1.391304
1988–89	Division 3	10	46	16	16	14	58	54	64	1.391304
1980–81	Division 2	18	42	14	10	18	61	66	38	1.238095
1984–85	Division 3	17	46	16	6	24	69	75	54	1.173913
1985–86	Division 3	17	46	15	8	23	54	68	53	1.152174
1981–82	Division 2	19	42	13	7	22	39	61	46	1.095238
1982–83	Division 2	22	42	11	11	20	42	61	44	1.047619
1986–87	Division 3	21	46	10	15	21	46	58	45	0.978261
1979–80	Division 1	22	42	5	15	22	38	73	25	0.714286

SQUAD 1980–81   18TH IN DIVISION 2

Michael BENNETT	Left back	Craig MOORES	Forward
Ian BRENNAN	Left back	Peter NICHOLSON	Full back
David BURKE	Left back	Dusan NIKOLIC	Winger
Len CANTELLO	Midfielder	Tad NOWAK	Winger
Mike CARTER	Winger	Dennis PEACOCK	Goalkeeper
Dave CLEMENT	Right back	Terry POOLE	Goalkeeper
Alan GOWLING	Forward	Peter REID	Midfielder
Mike GRAHAM	Defender	John THOMAS	Forward
David HOGGAN	Midfielder	Chris THOMPSON	Midfielder
Paul JONES	Central defender	Mick WALSH	Central defender
Brian KIDD	Forward	Neil WHATMORE	Forward
Gerry McELHINNEY	Central defender	Phil WILSON	Midfielder

	Season	League	League Position	P	W	D	L	F	A	Pts	3 Point Equivalent
1990s	1992–93	L2	2	46	27	10	9	80	41	90	1.978261
	1996–97	**L1**	**1**	**46**	**28**	**4**	**14**	**100**	**53**	**98**	**1.913043**
	1990–91	Division 3	4	46	24	11	11	64	50	83	1.804348
	1994–95	L1	3	46	21	11	14	67	45	77	1.608696
	1998–99	L1	6	46	20	10	16	78	59	76	1.521739
	1989–90	Division 3	6	46	18	15	13	59	48	69	1.500000
	1993–94	L1	14	46	15	17	14	63	64	59	1.347826
	1991–92	Division 3	13	46	14	17	15	57	56	59	1.282609
	1997–98	Premier League	18	38	9	13	16	41	61	40	1.052632
	1995–96	Premier League	20	38	8	5	25	39	71	29	0.763158

SQUAD 1996–97   CHAMPIONS OF FIRST DIVISION

Gudni BERGSSON	Defender/Centre back	Mixu PAATELAINEN	Forward
Nathan BLAKE	Forward	Jimmy PHILLIPS	Defender/Left back
Keith BRANAGAN	Goalkeeper	Jamie POLLOCK	Midfielder
Wayne BURNETT	Midfielder	Scott SELLARS	Midfielder
Chris FAIRCLOUGH	Centre back	John SHERIDAN	Midfielder
Per FRANDSEN	Midfielder	Bryan SMALL	Defender/Left back
Scott GREEN	Defender/Right back	Gerry TAGGART	Defender/Centre back
Michael JOHANSEN	Midfielder	Scott TAYLOR	Forward
David LEE	Forward	Alan THOMPSON	Midfielder
Steve McANESPIE	Midfielder	Andy TODD	Defender/Midfielder
John McGINLAY	Forward	Gavin WARD	Goalkeeper

	Season	League	League Position	P	W	D	L	F	A	Pts	3 Point Equivalent
2000s	2000–01	L1	3	46	24	7	15	76	45	87	1.717391
	1999–2000	L1	6	46	21	12	13	69	50	76	1.630435
	2004–05	**Premier League**	**6**	**38**	**16**	**10**	**12**	**49**	**44**	**58**	**1.526316**
	2005–06	Premier League	8	38	15	11	12	49	41	56	1.473684
	2006–07	Premier League	7	38	16	8	14	47	52	56	1.473684
	2003–04	Premier League	8	38	14	11	13	48	56	53	1.394737
	2002–03	Premier League	17	38	10	14	14	41	51	44	1.157895
	2001–02	Premier League	16	38	9	13	16	44	62	40	1.052632

SQUAD 2004–05   6TH IN THE PREMIER LEAGUE

Anthony BARNESS	Defender/Midfielder	Radhi JAIDI	Defender/Centre back
Tal BEN HAIM	Defender	Santos Correa JULIO CESAR	Defender/Centre back
Ivan CAMPO	Defender/Midfielder	Blessing KAKU	Midfielder
Vincent CANDELA	Defender/Left back	Bruno N'GOTTY	Defender/Centre back
Kevin DAVIES	Forward	Kevin NOLAN	Midfielder
El Hadji DIOUF	Forward	Andy OAKES	Goalkeeper
Khalilou FADIGA	Forward	Joey O'BRIEN	Midfielder
Les FERDINAND	Forward	Jay Jay OKOCHA	Midfielder
Ricardo GARDNER	Midfielder	Henrik PEDERSEN	Forward
Stelios GIANNAKOPOULOS	Midfielder	Kevin POOLE	Goalkeeper
Fernando HIERRO	Defender/Midfielder	Gary SPEED	Defender/Midfielder
Nicky HUNT	Defender	Ricardo VAZ TE	Forward
Jussi JAASKELAINEN	Goalkeeper		

BRADFORD CITY

Season	League	League Position	P	W	D	L	F	A	Pts	3 Point Equivalent
1957–58	**Division 3 North**	**3**	**46**	**21**	**15**	**10**	**73**	**49**	**57**	**1.695652**
1946–47	Division 3 North	5	42	20	10	12	62	47	50	1.666667
1953–54	Division 3 North	5	46	22	9	15	60	55	53	1.630435
1956–57	Division 3 North	9	46	22	8	16	78	68	52	1.608696
1950–51	Division 3 North	7	46	21	10	15	90	63	52	1.586957
1955–56	Division 3 North	8	46	18	13	15	78	64	49	1.456522
1958–59	Division 3	11	46	18	11	17	84	76	47	1.413043
1947–48	Division 3 North	14	42	15	10	17	65	66	40	1.309524
1952–53	Division 3 North	16	46	14	18	14	75	80	46	1.304348
1951–52	Division 3 North	15	46	16	10	20	61	68	42	1.260870
1954–55	Division 3 North	21	46	13	10	23	47	55	36	1.065217
1949–50	Division 3 North	19	42	12	8	22	61	76	32	1.047619
1948–49	Division 3 North	22	42	10	9	23	48	77	29	0.928571

SQUAD 1957–58   3RD IN DIVISION 3 NORTH

Martin BAKES	Outside left	George MULHOLLAND	Full back
Dave BOYLE	Inside forward	Jeff NUNDY	Centre half
Malcolm CURRIE	Defender	John REID	Inside forward
Tommy FLOCKETT	Full back	Willie ROBB	Wing half
Peter GLOVER	Wing half	Les SAMUELS	Inside forward
David JACKSON	Inside Forward/Wing half	Johnny SIMM	Winger
Peter JACKSON	Wing half	Geoff SMITH	Goalkeeper
James LAWLOR	Centre half	Derek STOKES	Centre forward
Ron LIVERSIDGE	Centre forward	Geoff WALKER	Outside left
Willie MARSHALL	Centre forward	Bobby WEBB	Outside right

Season	League	League Position	P	W	D	L	F	A	Pts	3 Point Equivalent
1963–64	**Division 4**	**5**	**46**	**25**	**6**	**15**	**76**	**62**	**56**	**1.760870**
1967–68	Division 4	5	46	23	11	12	72	51	57	1.739130
1961–62	Division 4	5	44	21	9	14	94	86	51	1.636364
1968–69	Division 4	4	46	18	20	8	65	46	56	1.608696
1966–67	Division 4	11	46	19	10	17	74	62	48	1.456522
1959–60	Division 3	19	46	15	12	19	66	74	42	1.239130
1965–66	Division 4	23	46	12	13	21	63	94	37	1.065217
1960–61	Division 3	22	46	11	14	21	65	87	36	1.021739
1964–65	Division 4	19	46	12	8	26	70	88	32	0.956522
1962–63	Division 4	23	46	11	10	25	64	93	32	0.934783

SQUAD 1963–64   5TH IN DIVISION 4

James BLACKER	Centre half	Brian REDFEARN	Outside left
Roy ELLAM	Centre half	Brian SAWYER	Centre forward
James FISHER	Goalkeeper	Mike SMITH	Centre half
Gavin FLETCHER	Inside forward	Stan STORTON	Full back
Harry GREEN	Centre forward	Bruce STOWELL	Wing half
John HALL	Outside right	Arthur THORPE	Outside left
Stan HARLAND	Wing half	Ray TONG	Winger
John HELLAWELL	Inside forward	John WEBSTER	Outside right
Brian KELLY	Full back	Peter WRAGG	Wing half/Inside forward
Tom PRICE	Inside forward		

Season	League	League Position	P	W	D	L	F	A	Pts	3 Point Equivalent
1976–77	**Division 4**	**4**	**46**	**23**	**13**	**10**	**78**	**51**	**59**	**1.782609**
1973–74	Division 4	8	46	17	14	15	58	52	48	1.413043
1974–75	Division 4	10	46	17	13	16	56	51	47	1.391304
1969–70	Division 3	10	46	17	12	17	57	50	46	1.369565
1978–79	Division 4	15	46	17	9	20	62	68	43	1.304348
1972–73	Division 4	16	46	16	11	19	61	65	43	1.282609
1975–76	Division 4	17	46	12	17	17	63	65	41	1.152174
1970–71	Division 3	19	46	13	14	19	49	62	40	1.152174
1977–78	Division 3	22	46	12	10	24	56	86	34	1.000000
1971–72	Division 3	24	46	11	10	25	45	77	32	0.934783

1970s

SQUAD 1976–77 — 4TH IN DIVISION 4

Joe COOKE	Central defender/Forward
Ian COOPER	Left back
Terry DOLAN	Midfielder
Peter DOWNSBOROUGH	Goalkeeper
Dave FRETWELL	Central defender
Dave HALL	Midfielder
Peter HARDCASTLE	Full back
Don HUTCHINS	Winger
Gerry INGRAM	Forward
Rod JOHNSON	Midfielder/Forward
Clive McFADZEAN	Forward
Billy McGINLEY	Winger
John MIDDLETON	Central defender
John NAPIER	Central defender
Phil NICHOLLS	Central defender
Ces PODD	Full back
Billy PUNTON	Goalkeeper
David RATCLIFFE	Central defender
Warren RAYNER	Winger
Alex SPARK	Central defender
Garry WATSON	Left back
Bernie WRIGHT	Forward

Season	League	League Position	P	W	D	L	F	A	Pts	3 Point Equivalent
1984–85	Division 3	1	46	28	10	8	77	45	94	2.043478
1981–82	Division 4	2	46	26	13	7	88	45	91	1.978261
1979–80	Division 4	5	46	24	12	10	77	50	60	1.826087
1987–88	**Division 2**	**4**	**44**	**22**	**11**	**11**	**74**	**54**	**77**	**1.750000**
1983–84	Division 3	7	46	20	11	15	73	65	71	1.543478
1982–83	Division 3	12	46	16	13	17	68	69	61	1.326087
1986–87	Division 2	10	42	15	10	17	62	62	55	1.309524
1985–86	Division 2	13	42	16	6	20	51	63	54	1.285714
1980–81	Division 4	14	46	14	16	16	53	60	44	1.260870
1988–89	Division 2	14	46	13	17	16	52	59	56	1.217391

1980s

SQUAD 1987–88 — 4TH IN DIVISION 2

Greg ABBOTT	Midfielder
Mark ELLIS	Winger
David EVANS	Central defender
Ron FUTCHER	Forward
Karl GODDARD	Midfielder/Left back
John HENDRIE	Right Winger
Mick KENNEDY	Midfielder
Mark LEONARD	Forward
Peter LITCHFIELD	Goalkeeper
Stuart McCALL	Midfielder
Brian MITCHELL	Right back
Gavin OLIVER	Central defender
Ian ORMONDROYD	Forward
Steve O'SHAUGHNESSY	Central defender/Midfielder
Leigh PALIN	Midfielder
Bob SAVAGE	Midfielder
Lee SINNOTT	Central defender
Steve STAUNTON	Defender
Adrian THORPE	Winger
Paul TOMLINSON	Goalkeeper
Chris WITHE	Left back

1990s

Season	League	League Position	P	W	D	L	F	A	Pts	3 Point Equivalent
1998–99	**L1**	**2**	**46**	**26**	**11**	**9**	**82**	**47**	**87**	**1.934783**
1995–96	L2	6	46	22	17	7	71	69	73	1.804348
1993–94	L2	7	46	19	14	13	61	53	70	1.543478
1990–91	Division 3	8	46	20	10	16	62	54	70	1.521739
1992–93	L2	10	46	18	14	14	69	67	68	1.478261
1994–95	L2	14	46	16	18	12	57	64	60	1.434783
1997–98	L1	13	46	14	17	15	46	59	57	1.282609
1991–92	Division 3	16	46	13	19	14	62	61	58	1.260870
1996–97	L1	21	46	12	22	12	47	72	48	1.260870
1989–90	Division 2	23	46	9	14	23	44	68	41	0.891304

SQUAD 1998–99 — 2ND IN FIRST DIVISION

Peter BEAGRIE	Midfielder	Nigel PEPPER	Midfielder
Robbie BLAKE	Forward	Craig RAMAGE	Midfielder
Paul BOLLAND	Midfielder	Isaiah RANKIN	Forward
John DREYER	Defender/Centre back	Lee SHARPE	Midfielder
Amaral EDINHO	Forward	Lee TODD	Defender/Full back
Gareth GRANT	Forward	Gary WALSH	Goalkeeper
Wayne JACOBS	Defender/Left back	Gordon WATSON	Forward
Jamie LAWRENCE	Midfielder	Ashley WESTWOOD	Defender/Centre back
Stuart McCALL	Midfielder	Gareth WHALLEY	Midfielder
Lee MILLS	Forward	Dean WINDASS	Forward
Darren MOORE	Defender/Centre back	Stephen WRIGHT	Defender/Right back
Andy O'BRIEN	Defender/Centre back		

2000s

Season	League	League Position	P	W	D	L	F	A	Pts	3 Point Equivalent
2001–02	L1	15	46	15	21	10	69	76	55	1.434783
2004–05	League 1	11	46	17	15	14	64	62	65	1.434783
2002–03	L1	19	46	14	22	10	51	73	52	1.391304
2005–06	League 1	11	46	14	19	13	51	49	61	1.326087
2003–04	L1	23	46	10	30	6	38	69	36	1.304348
2006–07	League 1	22	46	11	14	21	47	65	47	1.021739
1999–2000	**Premier League**	**17**	**38**	**9**	**9**	**20**	**38**	**68**	**36**	**0.947368**
2000–01	Premier League	20	38	5	11	22	30	70	26	0.684211

SQUAD 1999–2000 — 17TH IN THE PREMIER LEAGUE

Peter BEAGRIE	Midfielder	Andy O'BRIEN	Defender/Centre back
Robbie BLAKE	Forward	Isaiah RANKIN	Forward
Jorge Paulo CADETE	Striker	Neil REDFEARN	Midfielder
Matt CLARKE	Goalkeeper	Bruno RODRIGUEZ	Striker
Aidan DAVISON	Goalkeeper	Dean SAUNDERS	Forward
John DREYER	Defender/Centre back	Lee SHARPE	Midfielder
Gareth GRANT	Forward	Neville SOUTHALL	Goalkeeper
Gunnar HALLE	Full back	Gary WALSH	Goalkeeper
Wayne JACOBS	Defender/Left back	Ashley WESTWOOD	Defender/Centre back
Jamie LAWRENCE	Midfielder	David WETHERALL	Defender/Centre back
Stuart McCALL	Midfielder	Gareth WHALLEY	Midfielder
Lee MILLS	Forward	Dean WINDASS	Forward
Andy MYERS	Defender		

CHARLTON ATHLETIC

	Season	League	League Position	P	W	D	L	F	A	Pts	3 Point Equivalent
1940s & 50s	1957–58	Division 2	3	42	24	7	11	107	69	55	1.880952
	1952–53	**Division 1**	**5**	**42**	**19**	**11**	**12**	**77**	**63**	**49**	**1.619048**
	1953–54	Dvision 1	9	42	19	6	17	75	77	44	1.500000
	1951–52	Dvision 1	10	42	17	10	15	68	63	44	1.452381
	1958–59	Division 2	8	42	18	7	17	92	90	43	1.452381
	1948–49	Dvision 1	9	42	15	12	15	63	67	42	1.357143
	1955–56	Dvision 1	14	42	17	6	19	75	81	40	1.357143
	1947–48	Dvision 1	13	42	17	6	19	57	66	40	1.357143
	1954–55	Dvision 1	15	42	15	10	17	76	75	40	1.309524
	1950–51	Division 1	17	42	14	9	19	63	80	37	1.214286
	1949–50	Dvision 1	20	42	13	6	23	53	65	32	1.071429
	1946–47	Dvision 1	19	42	11	12	19	57	71	34	1.071429
	1956–57	Dvision 1	22	42	9	4	29	62	120	22	0.738095

SQUAD 1952–53 — 5TH IN DIVISION 1

Bobby AYRE	Outside right
Kevin BARRY	Outside left
Sam BARTRAM	Goalkeeper
Jock CAMPBELL	Full back
Ken CHAMBERLAIN	Centre half
Riley CULLUM	Inside forward
Chris DUFFY	Outside left
John EVANS	Inside forward
Benny FENTON	Wing half
Eddie FIRMANI	Inside forward
Cyril HAMMOND	Wing half
John HEWIE	Full back
Gordon HURST	Winger
Bert JOHNSON	Wing half
Billy KIERNAN	Outside left
Stuart LEARY	Centre forward
Frank LOCK	Left back
Syd O'LINN	Inside forward
Tony PAWSON	Winger
Albert POUNDER	Outside right
Derek UFTON	Centre half
Albert UYTENBOGARDT	Goalkeeper
Charlie VAUGHAN	Centre forward
Jimmy WALLS	Centre half

	Season	League	League Position	P	W	D	L	F	A	Pts	3 Point Equivalent
1960s	**1968–69**	**Division 2**	**3**	**42**	**18**	**14**	**10**	**61**	**52**	**50**	**1.619048**
	1963–64	Division 2	4	42	19	10	13	76	70	48	1.595238
	1959–60	Division 2	7	42	17	13	12	90	87	47	1.523810
	1960–61	Division 2	10	42	16	11	15	97	91	43	1.404762
	1961–62	Division 2	15	42	15	9	18	69	75	39	1.285714
	1965–66	Division 2	16	42	12	14	16	61	70	38	1.190476
	1967–68	Division 2	15	42	12	13	17	63	68	37	1.166667
	1966–67	Division 2	19	42	13	9	20	49	53	35	1.142857
	1964–65	Division 2	18	42	13	9	20	64	75	35	1.142857
	1962–63	Division 2	20	42	13	5	24	62	94	31	1.047619

SQUAD 1968–69 — 3RD IN DIVISION 2

Gordon BOLLAND	Inside forward
Dennis BOOTH	Midfielder
Jack BURKETT	Full back
Tony BURNS	Goalkeeper
Alan CAMPBELL	Midfielder
Ray CRAWFORD	Centre forward
Bob CURTIS	Defender
Harry GREGORY	Midfielder
Keith HAYWARD	Goalkeeper
Paul HINCE	Winger
John KEIRS	Centre half
Mike KENNING	Winger
Brian KINSEY	Left back
Graham MOORE	Midfielder
Jimmy MULLEN	Winger
Keith PEACOCK	Midfielder
Peter REEVES	Central defender
John STENSON	Midfielder
Matt TEES	Centre forward
Ray TREACY	Forward
Paul WENT	Central defender
Charlie WRIGHT	Goalkeeper

Season	League	League Position	P	W	D	L	F	A	Pts	3 Point Equivalent
1974–75	Division 3	3	46	22	11	13	76	61	55	1.673913
1976–77	**Division 2**	**7**	**42**	**16**	**16**	**10**	**71**	**58**	**48**	**1.523810**
1973–74	Division 3	14	46	19	8	19	66	73	46	1.413043
1975–76	Division 2	9	42	15	12	15	61	72	42	1.357143
1972–73	Division 3	11	46	17	11	18	69	67	45	1.347826
1977–78	Division 2	17	42	13	12	17	55	68	38	1.214286
1978–79	Division 2	19	42	11	13	18	60	69	35	1.095238
1971–72	Division 2	21	42	12	9	21	55	77	33	1.071429
1970–71	Division 2	20	42	8	14	20	41	65	30	0.904762
1969–70	Division 2	20	42	7	17	18	35	76	31	0.904762

SQUAD 1976–77   7TH IN DIVISION 2

Les BERRY	Central defender	Hughie McAULEY	Winger
Richie BOWMAN	Midfielder	Willie O'SULLIVAN	Winger
Tony BURMAN	Forward	Keith PEACOCK	Midfielder
Bob CURTIS	Central defender	Mark PENFOLD	Right back
Mike FLANAGAN	Forward	Colin POWELL	Winger
Jimmy GILES	Central defender	Dick TYDEMAN	Midfielder
Derek HALES	Forward	Phil WARMAN	Left back
Geoff HAMMOND	Full back	Jeff WOOD	Goalkeeper
George HOPE	Forward	Tony YOUNG	Midfielder
Peter HUNT	Midfielder	David YOUNG	Midfielder

180

Season	League	League Position	P	W	D	L	F	A	Pts	3 Point Equivalent
1985–86	**Division 2**	**2**	**42**	**22**	**11**	**9**	**78**	**45**	**77**	**1.833333**
1980–81	Division 3	3	46	25	9	12	63	44	59	1.826087
1983–84	Division 2	13	42	16	9	17	53	64	57	1.357143
1981–82	Division 2	13	42	13	12	17	50	65	51	1.214286
1982–83	Division 2	17	42	13	9	20	63	86	48	1.142857
1988–89	Division 1	14	38	10	12	16	44	58	42	1.105263
1984–85	Division 2	17	42	11	12	19	51	63	45	1.071429
1987–88	Division 1	17	40	9	15	16	38	52	42	1.050000
1986–87	Division 1	19	42	11	11	20	45	55	44	1.047619
1979–80	Division 2	22	42	6	10	26	39	78	22	0.666667

SQUAD 1985–86   2ND IN DIVISION 2

Mark AIZLEWOOD	Central defender	Rob LEE	Midfielder
Les BERRY	Central defender	Jimmy LOVERIDGE	Midfielder
Alan CURBISHLEY	Midfielder	Jim MELROSE	Forward
Alan DAVIES	Winger	John PEARSON	Forward
Mike FLANAGAN	Forward	John PENDER	Central defender
Paul FRIAR	Left back	Mark REID	Left back
Steve GRITT	Midfielder	George SHIPLEY	Midfielder
John HUMPHREY	Right back	Mark STUART	Midfielder
Nicky JOHNS	Goalkeeper	Steve THOMPSON	Central defender
Tony LANGE	Goalkeeper	Tony TOWNER	Winger

Season	League	League Position	P	W	D	L	F	A	Pts	3 Point Equivalent
1997–98	L1	4	46	26	10	10	80	49	88	1.913043
1993–94	L1	11	46	19	19	8	61	58	65	1.652174
1991–92	Division 2	7	46	20	11	15	54	48	71	1.543478
1994–95	L1	15	46	16	19	11	58	66	59	1.456522
1996–97	L1	15	46	16	19	11	52	66	59	1.456522
1992–93	L1	12	46	16	17	13	49	46	61	1.413043
1995–96	L1	6	46	17	9	20	57	45	71	1.304348
1990–91	Division 2	16	46	13	17	16	57	61	56	1.217391
1998–99	Premier League	18	38	8	12	18	41	56	36	0.947368
1989–90	Division 1	19	38	7	9	22	31	57	30	0.789474

SQUAD 1997–98   4TH IN FIRST DIVISION

Bradley ALLEN	Forward	Carl LEABURN	Forward
Stuart BALMER	Defender/Centre back	Kevin LISBIE	Forward
Anthony BARNESS	Defender/Midfielder	Clive MENDONCA	Forward
Mark BOWEN	Defender/Left back	Danny MILLS	Defender
Mark BRIGHT	Forward	Paul MORTIMER	Midfielder
Steve BROWN	Defender/Centre back	Shaun NEWTON	Midfielder
Phil CHAPPLE	Centre back	Kevin NICHOLLS	Midfielder
Paul EMBLEN	Midfielder	Scott PARKER	Midfielder
Neil HEANEY	Midfielder	Andy PETTERSON	Goalkeeper
Matty HOLMES	Midfielder	John ROBINSON	Midfielder
Sasa ILIC	Goalkeeper	Richard RUFUS	Defender/Centre back
Steve JONES	Forward	Mike SALMON	Goalkeeper
Keith JONES	Midfielder	Jamie STUART	Defender/Left back
Mark KINSELLA	Midfielder	Eddie YOUDS	Defender/Centre back
Paul KONCHESKY	Defender/Midfielder		

Season	League	League Position	P	W	D	L	F	A	Pts	3 Point Equivalent
1999–2000	L1	1	46	27	9	10	79	45	91	1.956522
2003–04	Premier League	7	38	14	11	13	51	51	53	1.394737
2000–01	Premier League	9	38	14	10	14	50	57	52	1.368421
2002–03	Premier League	12	38	14	7	17	45	56	49	1.289474
2005–06	Premier League	13	38	13	8	17	41	55	47	1.236842
2004–05	Premier League	11	38	12	10	16	42	58	46	1.210526
2001–02	Premier League	14	38	10	14	14	38	49	44	1.157895
2006–07	Premier League	19	38	8	10	20	34	60	34	0.894737

SQUAD 2003–04   7TH IN THE PREMIER LEAGUE

Shaun BARTLETT	Forward	Radostin KISHISHEV	Defender/Midfielder
Jamal CAMPBELL-RYCE	Midfielder	Paul KONCHESKY	Defender/Midfielder
Carlton COLE	Forward	Kevin LISBIE	Forward
Paolo DI CANIO	Forward	Scott PARKER	Midfielder
Jason EUELL	Midfielder/Forward	Chris PERRY	Defender/Centre back
Mark FISH	Defender/Centre back	Chris POWELL	Defender/Left back
Jonathan FORTUNE	Defender/Centre back	Gary ROWETT	Defender
Matt HOLLAND	Midfielder	Simon ROYCE	Goalkeeper
Hermann HREIDARSSON	Defender/Centre back	Graham STUART	Midfielder
Claus JENSEN	Midfielder	Matthias SVENSSON	Forward
Jonatan JOHANSSON	Forward	Jerome THOMAS	Midfielder
Dean KIELY	Goalkeeper	Luke YOUNG	Defender

CHARLTON ATHLETIC

CHELSEA

Season	League	League Position	P	W	D	L	F	A	Pts	3 Point Equivalent
1954–55	Division 1	1	42	20	12	10	81	57	52	1.714286
1953–54	Division 1	8	42	16	12	14	74	68	44	1.428571
1958–59	Division 1	14	42	18	4	20	77	98	40	1.380952
1957–58	Division 1	11	42	15	12	15	83	79	42	1.357143
1946–47	Division 1	15	42	16	7	19	69	84	39	1.309524
1955–56	Division 1	16	42	14	11	17	64	77	39	1.261905
1956–57	Division 1	12	42	13	13	16	73	73	39	1.238095
1949–50	Division 1	13	42	12	16	14	58	65	40	1.238095
1947–48	Division 1	18	42	14	9	19	53	71	37	1.214286
1948–49	Division 1	13	42	12	14	16	69	68	38	1.190476
1951–52	Division 1	19	42	14	8	20	52	72	36	1.190476
1952–53	Division 1	19	42	12	11	19	56	66	35	1.119048
1950–51	Division 1	20	42	12	8	22	53	65	32	1.047619

SQUAD 1954–55 — CHAMPIONS OF DIVISION 1

Ken ARMSTRONG	Wing half	Seamus O'CONNELL	Inside forward
Roy BENTLEY	Centre forward	Eric PARSONS	Outside right
Frank BLUNSTONE	Outside left	Bill ROBERTSON	Goalkeeper
Peter BRABROOK	Outside right	Derek SAUNDERS	Wing half
Alan DICKS	Wing half	Peter SILLETT	Full back
Bob EDWARDS	Inside forward	Bobby SMITH	Forward
Ron GREENWOOD	Centre half	Les STUBBS	Inside forward
John HARRIS	Defender	Chick THOMSON	Goalkeeper
Jim LEWIS	Centre forward	Stan WICKS	Centre half
Johnny McNICHOL	Inside forward	Stan WILLEMSE	Left back

Season	League	League Position	P	W	D	L	F	A	Pts	3 Point Equivalent
1964–65	Division 1	3	42	24	8	10	89	54	56	1.904762
1962–63	Division 2	2	42	24	4	14	81	42	52	1.809524
1965–66	Division 1	5	42	22	7	13	65	53	51	1.738095
1968–69	Division 1	5	42	20	10	12	73	53	50	1.666667
1963–64	Division 1	5	42	20	10	12	72	56	50	1.666667
1967–68	Division 1	6	42	18	12	12	62	68	48	1.571429
1966–67	Division 1	9	42	15	14	13	67	62	44	1.404762
1960–61	Division 1	12	42	15	7	20	98	100	37	1.238095
1959–60	Division 1	18	42	14	9	19	76	91	37	1.214286
1961–62	Division 1	22	42	9	10	23	63	94	28	0.880952

SQUAD 1964–65 — 3RD IN DIVISION 1

Peter BONETTI	Goalkeeper	Jim McCALLIOG	Midfielder
Johnny BOYLE	Midfielder	Eddie McCREADIE	Full back
Barry BRIDGES	Centre forward	John MORTIMORE	Centre half
John DUNN	Goalkeeper	Bert MURRAY	Outside right
George GRAHAM	Forward/Midfielder	Ken SHELLITO	Right back
Allan HARRIS	Left back	Billy SINCLAIR	Wing half
Ron HARRIS	Defender	Jimmy SMART	Winger
Marvin HINTON	Centre half	Bobby TAMBLING	Forward
John HOLLINS	Midfielder	Frank UPTON	Wing half
Peter HOUSEMAN	Winger	Terry VENABLES	Midfielder
Tommy KNOX	Outside left	Ian WATSON	Full back

	Season	League	League Position	P	W	D	L	F	A	Pts	3 Point Equivalent
1970s	1976–77	Division 2	2	42	21	13	8	73	53	55	1.809524
	1969–70	**Division 1**	**3**	**42**	**21**	**13**	**8**	**70**	**50**	**55**	**1.809524**
	1970–71	Division 1	6	42	18	15	9	52	42	51	1.642857
	1971–72	Division 1	7	42	18	12	12	58	49	48	1.571429
	1972–73	Division 1	12	42	13	14	15	49	51	40	1.261905
	1975–76	Division 2	11	42	12	16	14	53	54	40	1.238095
	1973–74	Division 1	17	42	12	13	17	56	60	37	1.166667
	1977–78	Division 1	16	42	11	14	17	46	69	36	1.119048
	1974–75	Division 1	21	42	9	15	18	42	72	33	1.000000
	1978–79	Division 1	22	42	5	10	27	44	92	20	0.595238

SQUAD 1969–70   3RD IN DIVISION 1

Tommy BALDWIN	Forward	Stewart HOUSTON	Defender
Alan BIRCHENALL	Midfielder	Alan HUDSON	Midfielder
Peter BONETTI	Goalkeeper	Tommy HUGHES	Goalkeeper
Johnny BOYLE	Midfielder	Ian HUTCHINSON	Centre forward
Charlie COOKE	Midfielder	Eddie McCREADIE	Full back
John DEMPSEY	Central defender	Paddy MULLIGAN	Right back
Ron HARRIS	Defender	Peter OSGOOD	Forward
Marvin HINTON	Centre half	Bobby TAMBLING	Forward
John HOLLINS	Midfielder	Dave WEBB	Defender
Peter HOUSEMAN	Winger		

	Season	League	League Position	P	W	D	L	F	A	Pts	3 Point Equivalent
1980s	1988–89	Division 2	1	46	29	12	5	96	50	99	2.152174
	1983–84	Division 2	1	42	25	13	4	90	40	88	2.095238
	1979–80	Division 2	4	42	23	7	12	66	52	53	1.809524
	1985–86	**Division 1**	**6**	**42**	**20**	**11**	**11**	**57**	**56**	**71**	**1.690476**
	1984–85	Division 1	6	42	18	12	12	63	48	66	1.571429
	1981–82	Division 2	12	42	15	12	15	60	60	57	1.357143
	1980–81	Division 2	12	42	14	12	16	46	41	40	1.285714
	1986–87	Division 1	14	42	13	13	16	53	64	52	1.238095
	1982–83	Division 2	18	42	11	14	17	51	61	47	1.119048
	1987–88	Division 1	18	40	9	15	16	50	68	42	1.050000

SQUAD 1985–86   6TH IN DIVISION 1

John BUMSTEAD	Midfielder	Kevin McALLISTER	Forward
Paul CANOVILLE	Winger	Joe McLAUGHLIN	Midfielder
Gareth DAVIES	Forward	John McNAUGHT	Midfielder
Kerry DIXON	Forward	John MILLAR	Midfielder
Keith DUBLIN	Defender	Jerry MURPHY	Left Midfielder
Gordon DURIE	Forward	Pat NEVIN	Forward
Steve FRANCIS	Goalkeeper	Eddie NIEDZWIECKI	Goalkeeper
Les FRIDGE	Goalkeeper	Colin PATES	Central defender
Tony GODDEN	Goalkeeper	Doug ROUGVIE	Defender
Micky HAZARD	Midfielder	Duncan SHEARER	Forward
Terry HOWARD	Defender	Nigel SPACKMAN	Midfielder
Robert ISAAC	Central defender	David SPEEDIE	Forward
Keith JONES	Midfielder	Darren WOOD	Midfielder
Colin LEE	Forward/Central defender		

1990s

Season	League	League Position	P	W	D	L	F	A	Pts	3 Point Equivalent
1998–99	Premier League	3	38	20	15	3	57	30	75	1.973684
1997–98	Premier League	4	38	20	3	15	71	43	63	1.657895
1989–90	Division 1	5	38	16	12	10	58	50	60	1.578947
1996–97	Premier League	6	38	16	11	11	58	55	59	1.552632
1992–93	Premier League	11	42	14	14	14	51	54	56	1.333333
1995–96	Premier League	11	38	12	14	12	46	44	50	1.315789
1990–91	Division 1	10	38	13	10	15	58	69	49	1.289474
1994–95	Premier League	11	42	13	15	14	50	55	54	1.285714
1991–92	Division 1	14	42	13	14	15	50	60	53	1.261905
1993–94	Premier League	14	42	13	12	17	49	53	51	1.214286

SQUAD 1998–99   3RD IN THE PREMIER LEAGUE

Celestine BABAYARO	Defender/Left back	Brian LAUDRUP	Forward
Pierluigi CASIRAGHI	Forward	Graeme LE SAUX	Defender/Left back
Ed DE GOEY	Goalkeeper	Frank LEBOEUF	Defender/Centre back
Marcel DESAILLY	Defender/Centre back	Jody MORRIS	Midfielder
Roberto DI MATTEO	Midfielder	Andy MYERS	Defender
Michael DUBERRY	Defender/Centre back	Eddie NEWTON	Midfielder
Albert FERRER	Full back	Mark NICHOLLS	Forward
Tore Andre FLO	Forward	Dan PETRESCU	Midfielder
Mikael FORSSELL	Forward	Gus POYET	Midfielder
Bjarne GOLDBAEK	Midfielder	John TERRY	Defender/Centre back
Kevin HITCHCOCK	Goalkeeper	Gianluca VIALLI	Forward
Dimitri KHARINE	Goalkeeper	Dennis WISE	Midfielder
Bernard LAMBOURDE	Defender/Centre back	Gianfranco ZOLA	Forward

2000s

Season	League	League Position	P	W	D	L	F	A	Pts	3 Point Equivalent
2004–05	Premier League	1	38	29	8	1	72	15	95	2.500000
2005–06	Premier League	1	38	29	4	5	72	22	91	2.394737
2006–07	Premier League	2	38	24	11	3	64	24	83	2.184211
2003–04	Premier League	2	38	24	7	7	67	30	79	2.078947
2002–03	Premier League	4	38	19	10	9	68	38	67	1.763158
1999–2000	Premier League	5	38	18	11	9	53	34	65	1.710526
2001–02	Premier League	6	38	17	13	8	66	38	64	1.684211
2000–01	Premier League	6	38	17	10	11	68	45	61	1.605263

SQUAD 2004–05   CHAMPIONS OF THE PREMIER LEAGUE

Celestine BABAYARO	Defender/Left back	Jiri JAROSIK	Midfielder
Wayne BRIDGE	Defender/Left back	Glen JOHNSON	Defender/Right back
Ricardo CARVALHO	Defender	Mateja KEZMAN	Forward
Petr CECH	Goalkeeper	Frank LAMPARD	Midfielder
Joe COLE	Midfielder	Claude MAKELELE	Midfielder
Carlo CUDICINI	Goalkeeper	Nuno MORAIS	Defender/Midfielder
Didier DROGBA	Forward	Adrian MUTU	Forward
Damien DUFF	Midfielder/Forward	Filipe de OLIVEIRA	Midfielder
Paulo FERREIRA	Defender	Scott PARKER	Midfielder
Mikael FORSSELL	Forward	Lenny PIDGELEY	Goalkeeper
William GALLAS	Defender	Arjen ROBBEN	Midfielder
Fotso Ndjitap GEREMI	Midfielder	Alexei SMERTIN	Midfielder
Anthony GRANT	Midfielder	John TERRY	Defender/Centre back
Eidur GUDJOHNSEN	Midfielder/Forward	Cardoso Mendes TIAGO	Midfielder
Robert HUTH	Defender/Centre back	Steven WATT	Defender/Centre back

COVENTRY CITY

Season	League	League Position	P	W	D	L	F	A	Pts	3 Point Equivalent
1958–59	Division 4	2	46	24	12	10	84	47	60	1.826087
1950–51	**Division 2**	**7**	**42**	**19**	**7**	**16**	**75**	**59**	**45**	**1.523810**
1952–53	Division 3 South	6	46	19	12	15	77	62	50	1.500000
1955–56	Division 3 South	8	46	20	9	17	73	60	49	1.500000
1946–47	Division 2	8	42	16	13	13	66	59	45	1.452381
1954–55	Division 3 South	9	46	18	11	17	67	59	47	1.413043
1953–54	Division 3 South	14	46	18	9	19	61	56	45	1.369565
1947–48	Division 2	10	42	14	13	15	59	52	41	1.309524
1956–57	Division 3 South	16	46	16	12	18	74	84	44	1.304348
1949–50	Division 2	12	42	13	13	16	55	55	39	1.238095
1948–49	Division 2	16	42	15	7	20	55	64	37	1.238095
1951–52	Division 2	21	42	14	6	22	59	82	34	1.142857
1957–58	Division 3 South	19	46	13	13	20	61	81	39	1.130435

SQUAD 1950–51 — 7TH IN DIVISION 2

Jim ALDERTON	Wing half	Ian JAMIESON	Wing half
Brynley ALLEN	Inside forward	Norman LOCKHART	Outside left
Harry BARRATT	Defender	Dick MASON	Full back
Joe BELL	Full back	Martin McDONNELL	Centre half
Tommy BRIGGS	Centre forward	Ted ROBERTS	Centre forward
Ken CHISHOLM	Inside forward	Noel SIMPSON	Wing half
Les COOK	Wing half	Terry SPRINGTHORPE	Full back
John EVANS	Centre forward	Peter TAYLOR	Goalkeeper
Harry HART	Inside forward	Charlie TIMMINS	Left back
Jimmy HILL	Outside left	Les WARNER	Outside right
Peter HILL	Inside forward	Alf WOOD	Goalkeeper

185

Season	League	League Position	P	W	D	L	F	A	Pts	3 Point Equivalent
1966–67	**Division 2**	**1**	**42**	**23**	**13**	**6**	**74**	**43**	**59**	**1.952381**
1963–64	Division 3	1	46	22	16	8	98	61	60	1.782609
1965–66	Division 2	3	42	20	13	9	73	53	53	1.738095
1959–60	Division 3	5	46	21	10	15	78	63	52	1.586957
1962–63	Division 3	4	46	18	17	11	83	69	53	1.543478
1964–65	Division 2	10	42	17	9	16	72	70	43	1.428571
1960–61	Division 3	15	46	16	12	18	80	83	44	1.304348
1961–62	Division 3	14	46	16	11	19	64	71	43	1.282609
1967–68	Division 1	20	42	9	15	18	51	71	33	1.000000
1968–69	Division 1	20	42	10	11	21	46	64	31	0.976190

SQUAD 1966–67 — CHAMPIONS OF DIVISION 2

Dietmar BRUCK	Full back	Johnny KEY	Outside right
David CLEMENTS	Left back	Brian LEWIS	Midfielder
Mick COOP	Right back	Barry LOWES	Outside right
George CURTIS	Centre half	Ernie MACHIN	Midfielder
Ron FARMER	Wing half	John MITTEN	Winger
Ian GIBSON	Midfielder	Pat MORRISSEY	Forward
Bill GLAZIER	Goalkeeper	Ray POINTER	Centre forward
Bobby GOULD	Forward	Ronnie REES	Winger
Brian HILL	Defender	Peter THOMAS	Goalkeeper
Mick KEARNS	Defender	John TUDOR	Forward

COVENTRY CITY

Season	League	League Position	P	W	D	L	F	A	Pts	3 Point Equivalent
1969–70	**Division 1**	**6**	**42**	**19**	**11**	**12**	**58**	**48**	**49**	**1.619048**
1977–78	Division 1	7	42	18	12	12	75	62	48	1.571429
1978–79	Division 1	10	42	14	16	12	58	68	44	1.380952
1970–71	Division 1	10	42	16	10	16	37	38	42	1.380952
1975–76	Division 1	14	42	13	14	15	47	57	40	1.261905
1973–74	Division 1	16	42	14	10	18	43	54	38	1.238095
1974–75	Division 1	14	42	12	15	15	51	62	39	1.214286
1972–73	Division 1	19	42	13	9	20	40	55	35	1.142857
1976–77	Division 1	19	42	10	15	17	48	59	35	1.071429
1971–72	Division 1	18	42	9	15	18	44	67	33	1.000000

SQUAD 1969–70 — 6TH IN DIVISION 1

Gerry BAKER	Centre forward	Brian HILL	Defender
Roy BARRY	Centre half	Ernie HUNT	Forward
Jeff BLOCKLEY	Central defender	Brian JOICEY	Forward
Dietmar BRUCK	Full back	Ernie MACHIN	Midfielder
Willie CARR	Midfielder	Neil MARTIN	Centre forward
Chris CATTLIN	Left back	Eric McMANUS	Goalkeeper
David CLEMENTS	Left back	Dennis MORTIMER	Midfielder
Mick COOP	Right back	John O'ROURKE	Centre forward
George CURTIS	Centre half	Graham PADDON	Midfielder
Ian GIBSON	Midfielder	Bobby PARKER	Defender
Bill GLAZIER	Goalkeeper	Billy RAFFERTY	Forward
Trevor GOULD	Midfielder	Maurice SETTERS	Wing half
Ernie HANNIGAN	Winger		

Season	League	League Position	P	W	D	L	F	A	Pts	3 Point Equivalent
1986–87	**Division 1**	**10**	**42**	**17**	**12**	**13**	**50**	**45**	**63**	**1.500000**
1988–89	Division 1	7	38	14	13	11	47	42	55	1.447368
1987–88	Division 1	10	40	13	14	13	46	53	53	1.325000
1979–80	Division 1	15	42	16	7	19	56	66	39	1.309524
1981–82	Division 1	14	42	13	11	18	56	62	50	1.190476
1983–84	Division 1	19	42	13	11	18	57	77	50	1.190476
1984–85	Division 1	18	42	15	5	22	47	64	50	1.190476
1980–81	Division 1	16	42	13	10	19	48	68	36	1.166667
1982–83	Division 1	19	42	13	9	20	48	59	48	1.142857
1985–86	Division 1	17	42	11	10	21	48	71	43	1.023810

SQUAD 1986–87 — 10TH IN DIVISION 1

Micky ADAMS	Left back	Martin LANE	Defender
David BENNETT	Winger	Steve LIVINGSTONE	Defender/Forward
Brian BORROWS	Right back	Lloyd McGRATH	Midfielder
Paul CULPIN	Forward	Steve OGRIZOVIC	Goalkeeper
Tony DOBSON	Defender/Full back	Ian PAINTER	Forward
Greg DOWNS	Left back	Trevor PEAKE	Central defender
Dean EMERSON	Midfielder	David PHILLIPS	Defender/Midfielder
Gareth EVANS	Striker	Nicky PICKERING	Midfielder
Gary GILLESPIE	Central defender	Cyrille REGIS	Forward
Micky GYNN	Midfielder	Graham RODGER	Central defender
Keith HOUCHEN	Forward	Les SEALEY	Goalkeeper
Brian KILCLINE	Central defender	Andy WILLIAMS	Midfielder

Season	League	League Position	P	W	D	L	F	A	Pts	3 Point Equivalent
1997–98	Premier League	11	38	12	16	10	46	44	52	1.368421
1993–94	Premier League	11	42	14	14	14	43	45	56	1.333333
1989–90	Division 1	12	38	14	7	17	39	59	49	1.289474
1992–93	Premier League	15	42	13	13	16	52	57	52	1.238095
1994–95	Premier League	16	42	12	14	16	44	62	50	1.190476
1990–91	Division 1	16	38	11	11	16	42	49	44	1.157895
1998–99	Premier League	15	38	11	9	18	39	51	42	1.105263
1996–97	Premier League	17	38	9	14	15	38	54	41	1.078947
1991–92	Division 1	19	42	11	11	20	35	44	44	1.047619
1995–96	Premier League	16	38	8	14	16	42	60	38	1.000000

SQUAD 1997–98 — 11TH IN THE PREMIER LEAGUE

George BOATENG	Midfielder
Willie BOLAND	Midfielder
Gary BREEN	Defender/Centre back
David BURROWS	Defender/Left back
Dion DUBLIN	Defender/Forward
Andy DUCROS	Forward
Marcus HALL	Defender/Left back
Simon HAWORTH	Forward
Magnus HEDMAN	Goalkeeper
Darren HUCKERBY	Forward
Martin JOHANSEN	Midfielder
Kyle LIGHTBOURNE	Forward
Gary McALLISTER	Midfielder
Viorel MOLDOVAN	Forward
Roland NILSSON	Defender/Right back
Steve OGRIZOVIC	Goalkeeper
Barry QUINN	Midfielder
Kevin RICHARDSON	Midfielder
John SALAKO	Midfielder
Richard SHAW	Defender/Centre back
Sam SHILTON	Midfielder
Trond Egil SOLTVEDT	Midfielder
Gavin STRACHAN	Midfielder
Paul TELFER	Midfielder
Noel WHELAN	Forward
Paul WILLIAMS	Defender/Centre back

Season	League	League Position	P	W	D	L	F	A	Pts	3 Point Equivalent
2001–02	L1	11	46	20	20	6	59	53	66	1.739130
2003–04	L1	12	46	17	14	14	67	54	65	1.434783
2005–06	Championship	8	46	16	15	15	62	65	63	1.369565
2004–05	Championship	19	46	13	20	13	61	73	52	1.282609
2002–03	L1	20	46	12	20	14	46	62	50	1.217391
2006–07	Championship	17	46	16	8	22	47	62	56	1.217391
1999–2000	Premier League	14	38	12	8	18	47	54	44	1.157895
2000–01	Premier League	19	38	8	10	20	36	63	34	0.894737

SQUAD 2001–02 — 11TH IN FIRST DIVISION

Tomas ANTONELIUS	Defender/Right back
Robert BETTS	Midfielder
Jay BOTHROYD	Forward
Gary BREEN	Defender/Centre back
Horacio CARBONARI	Defender/Centre back
Lee CARSLEY	Midfielder
Youssef CHIPPO	Midfielder
Calum DAVENPORT	Defender/Centre back
Laurent DELORGE	Midfielder
Marc EDWORTHY	Defender
John EUSTACE	Midfielder
Tim FLOWERS	Goalkeeper
Lee FOWLER	Midfielder
Andy GORAM	Goalkeeper
Mario Ivan GUERRERO	Defender/Left back
Marcus HALL	Defender/Left back
Colin HEALY	Midfielder
Magnus HEDMAN	Goalkeeper
Lee HUGHES	Forward
Julian JOACHIM	Forward
Chris KIRKLAND	Goalkeeper
Mo KONJIC	Defender/Centre back
Jairo MARTINEZ	Forward
Gary McSHEFFREY	Forward
Lee MILLS	Forward
Roland NILSSON	Defender/Right back
Runar NORMANN	Midfielder
Keith O'NEILL	Midfielder
Craig PEAD	Midfielder
Barry QUINN	Midfielder
Youssef SAFRI	Defender/Midfielder
Richard SHAW	Defender/Centre back
Gavin STRACHAN	Midfielder
David THOMPSON	Midfielder
Paul TROLLOPE	Defender/Midfielder
Paul WILLIAMS	Defender/Centre back
Ysrael ZUNIGA	Forward

COVENTRY CITY

CRYSTAL PALACE

1940s & 50s

Season	League	League Position	P	W	D	L	F	A	Pts	3 Point Equivalent
1958–59	Division 4	7	46	20	12	14	90	71	52	1.565217
1949–50	**Division 3 South**	**7**	**42**	**15**	**14**	**13**	**55**	**54**	**44**	**1.404762**
1957–58	Division 3 South	14	46	15	13	18	70	72	43	1.260870
1952–53	Division 3 South	13	46	15	13	18	66	82	43	1.260870
1947–48	Division 3 South	13	42	13	13	16	49	49	39	1.238095
1946–47	Division 3 South	18	42	13	11	18	49	62	37	1.190476
1951–52	Division 3 South	19	46	15	9	22	61	80	39	1.173913
1953–54	Division 3 South	22	46	14	12	20	60	86	40	1.173913
1956–57	Division 3 South	20	46	11	18	17	62	75	40	1.108696
1954–55	Division 3 South	20	46	11	16	19	52	80	38	1.065217
1955–56	Division 3 South	23	46	12	10	24	54	83	34	1.000000
1948–49	Division 3 South	22	42	8	11	23	38	76	27	0.833333
1950–51	Division 3 South	24	46	8	11	27	33	84	27	0.760870

SQUAD 1949–50   7TH IN DIVISION 3 SOUTH

Roy BAILEY	Goalkeeper	Wally HANLON	Outside left
Bill BLACKSHAW	Outside right	Ted HARDING	Full back
Ted BROUGHTON	Outside right	Ray HOWELLS	Outside left
Frank BUCKLEY	Wing half	Noel KELLY	Inside forward
Charlie BUMSTEAD	Goalkeeper	Fred KURZ	Centre forward
Charlie CHASE	Wing half	Jack LEWIS	Wing half
Geoff CHILVERS	Wing half	Peter MULHERON	Inside forward
Dave CLELLAND	Outside right	Joseph MURPHY	Full back
Fred DAWES	Left back	Ronnie ROOKE	Centre forward
Louis DELANEY	Full back	Alex ROSS	Wing half
Jack EDWARDS	Full back	Jack SHERWOOD	Wing half
Marcel GAILLARD	Winger	Hugh SURTEES	Winger
Ron GEORGE	Full back	John THOMAS	Centre forward
Dick GRAHAM	Goalkeeper	Jack WATSON	Centre half

1960s

Season	League	League Position	P	W	D	L	F	A	Pts	3 Point Equivalent
1960–61	Division 4	2	46	29	6	11	110	69	64	2.021739
1968–69	**Division 2**	**2**	**42**	**22**	**12**	**8**	**70**	**47**	**56**	**1.857143**
1963–64	Division 3	2	46	23	14	9	73	51	60	1.804348
1966–67	Division 2	7	42	19	10	13	61	55	48	1.595238
1959–60	Division 4	8	46	19	12	15	84	64	50	1.500000
1964–65	Division 2	7	42	16	13	13	55	51	45	1.452381
1962–63	Division 3	11	46	17	13	16	68	58	47	1.391304
1965–66	Division 2	11	42	14	13	15	47	52	41	1.309524
1967–68	Division 2	11	42	14	11	17	56	56	39	1.261905
1961–62	Division 3	15	46	14	14	18	83	80	42	1.217391

SQUAD 1968–69   2ND IN DIVISION 2

Jack BANNISTER	Wing half	John LOUGHLAN	Full back
Mel BLYTH	Central defender	John McCORMICK	Central defender
Trevor DAWKINS	Midfielder	David PAYNE	Defender
Phil HOADLEY	Central defender	Eddie PRESLAND	Full back
Roger HOY	Defender/Midfielder	John SEWELL	Full back
Cliff JACKSON	Forward	Brian SNOWDON	Centre half
John JACKSON	Goalkeeper	Tony TAYLOR	Left back
Steve KEMBER	Midfielder	Colin TAYLOR	Outside left
Mark LAZARUS	Winger	Bobby WOODRUFF	Midfielder
Terry LONG	Defender		

	Season	League	League Position	P	W	D	L	F	A	Pts	3 Point Equivalent
1970s	1978–79	Division 2	1	42	19	19	4	51	24	57	1.809524
	1976–77	Division 3	3	46	23	13	10	68	40	59	1.782609
	1975–76	Division 3	5	46	18	17	11	61	46	53	1.543478
	1974–75	Division 3	5	46	18	15	13	66	57	51	1.500000
	1977–78	Division 2	9	42	13	15	14	50	47	41	1.285714
	1970–71	Division 1	18	42	12	11	19	39	57	35	1.119048
	1973–74	Division 2	20	42	11	12	19	43	56	34	1.071429
	1972–73	Division 1	21	42	9	12	21	41	58	30	0.928571
	1971–72	Division 1	20	42	8	13	21	39	65	29	0.880952
	1969–70	Division 1	20	42	6	15	21	34	68	27	0.785714

SQUAD 1978–79   CHAMPIONS OF DIVISION 2

John BURRIDGE	Goalkeeper	Steve KEMBER	Midfielder
Jim CANNON	Central defender	Jerry MURPHY	Left Midfielder
Nicky CHATTERTON	Midfielder	Peter NICHOLAS	Midfielder
Mike ELWISS	Forward	Kenny SANSOM	Left back
Terry FENWICK	Defender	Tony SEALY	Forward
Billy GILBERT	Central defender	Barry SILKMAN	Midfielder
Tony HAZELL	Defender	Neil SMILLIE	Left winger
Vince HILAIRE	Left winger	Dave SWINDLEHURST	Forward
Paul HINSHELWOOD	Right back	Ian WALSH	Forward

	Season	League	League Position	P	W	D	L	F	A	Pts	3 Point Equivalent
1980s	1988–89	Division 2	3	46	23	12	11	71	49	81	1.760870
	1987–88	Division 2	6	44	22	9	13	86	59	75	1.704545
	1985–86	Division 2	5	42	19	9	14	57	52	66	1.571429
	1986–87	Division 2	6	42	19	5	18	51	53	62	1.476190
	1979–80	Division 1	13	42	12	16	14	41	50	40	1.238095
	1981–82	Division 2	15	42	13	9	20	34	45	48	1.142857
	1982–83	Division 2	15	42	12	12	18	43	52	48	1.142857
	1984–85	Division 2	15	42	12	12	18	46	65	48	1.142857
	1983–84	Division 2	18	42	12	11	19	42	52	47	1.119048
	1980–81	Division 1	22	42	6	7	29	47	83	19	0.595238

SQUAD 1979–80   13TH IN DIVISION 1

Terry BOYLE	Central defender	Vince HILAIRE	Left winger
Shaun BROOKS	Midfielder	Paul HINSHELWOOD	Right back
John BURRIDGE	Goalkeeper	Steve KEMBER	Midfielder
Jim CANNON	Central defender	Jerry MURPHY	Midfielder
Terry FENWICK	Defender	Peter NICHOLAS	Midfielder
Mike FLANAGAN	Forward	Kenny SANSOM	Left back
Gerry FRANCIS	Midfielder	Neil SMILLIE	Left winger
David FRY	Goalkeeper	Dave SWINDLEHURST	Forward
Billy GILBERT	Central defender	Ian WALSH	Forward
Gary GOODCHILD	Forward		

CRYSTAL PALACE

1990s

Season	League	League Position	P	W	D	L	F	A	Pts	3 Point Equivalent
1993–94	L1	1	46	27	10	9	73	46	90	1.978261
1990–91	**Division 1**	**3**	**38**	**20**	**9**	**9**	**50**	**41**	**69**	**1.815789**
1995–96	L1	3	46	20	11	15	67	48	75	1.543478
1996–97	L1	6	46	19	13	14	78	48	71	1.521739
1991–92	Division 1	10	42	14	15	13	53	61	57	1.357143
1989–90	Division 1	15	38	13	9	16	42	66	48	1.263158
1998–99	L1	14	46	14	16	16	58	71	58	1.260870
1992–93	Premier League	20	42	11	16	15	48	61	49	1.166667
1994–95	Premier League	19	42	11	12	19	34	49	45	1.071429
1997–98	Premier League	20	38	8	9	21	37	71	33	0.868421

SQUAD 1990–91 — 3RD IN DIVISION 1

Phil BARBER	Midfielder		Simon OSBORN	Midfielder
Paul BODIN	Left back		Alan PARDEW	Midfielder
Mark BRIGHT	Forward		John SALAKO	Midfielder
Stan COLLYMORE	Forward		Richard SHAW	Defender/Centre back
Mark DENNIS	Left back		Gareth SOUTHGATE	Defender/Centre back
Andy GRAY	Midfielder		Geoff THOMAS	Midfielder
Rudi HEDMAN	Defender		Garry THOMPSON	Forward
Glyn HODGES	Midfielder		Andy THORN	Central defender
John HUMPHREY	Right back		Ian WRIGHT	Forward
Nigel MARTYN	Goalkeeper		Eric YOUNG	Central defender
Eddie McGOLDRICK	Midfielder			

190

2000s

Season	League	League Position	P	W	D	L	F	A	Pts	3 Point Equivalent
2001–02	L1	10	46	20	20	6	70	62	66	1.739130
2003–04	**L1**	**6**	**46**	**21**	**15**	**10**	**72**	**61**	**73**	**1.695652**
2005–06	Championship	6	46	21	12	13	67	48	75	1.630435
2006–07	Championship	12	46	18	11	17	59	51	65	1.413043
1999–2000	L1	15	46	13	18	15	57	67	54	1.239130
2000–01	L1	21	46	12	21	13	57	70	49	1.239130
2002–03	L1	14	46	14	15	17	59	52	59	1.239130
2004–05	Premier League	18	38	7	12	19	41	62	33	0.868421

SQUAD 2003–04 — 6TH IN FIRST DIVISION

Cedric BERTHELIN	Goalkeeper		Andrew JOHNSON	Forward
Tommy BLACK	Forward		Mikele LEIGERTWOOD	Defender/Midfielder
Gary BORROWDALE	Defender/Left back		Hayden MULLINS	Midfielder
Danny BUTTERFIELD	Defender/Right back		Thomas MYHRE	Goalkeeper
Matt CLARKE	Goalkeeper		Tony POPOVIC	Defender/Centre back
Shaun DERRY	Defender/Midfielder		Darren POWELL	Defender/Centre back
Rob EDWARDS	Defender		Aki RIIHILAHTI	Midfielder
Curtis FLEMING	Defender/Right back		Wayne ROUTLEDGE	Midfielder
Dougie FREEDMAN	Forward		Neil SHIPPERLEY	Forward
Danny GRANVILLE	Defender/Midfielder		Jamie SMITH	Defender/Midfielder
Julian GRAY	Midfielder		Tom SOARES	Midfielder
Gavin HEEROO	Midfielder		Kit SYMONS	Defender/Centre back
Mark HUDSON	Defender		Nico VAESEN	Goalkeeper
Michael HUGHES	Midfielder/Forward		Ben WATSON	Midfielder

DERBY COUNTY

Season	League	League Position	P	W	D	L	F	A	Pts	3 Point Equivalent
1955–56	Division 3 North	2	46	28	7	11	110	55	63	1.978261
1956–57	Division 3 North	1	46	26	11	9	111	53	63	1.934783
1948–49	**Division 1**	**3**	**42**	**22**	**9**	**11**	**74**	**55**	**53**	**1.785714**
1947–48	Division 1	4	42	19	12	11	77	57	50	1.642857
1958–59	Division 2	7	42	20	8	14	74	71	48	1.619048
1949–50	Division 1	11	42	17	10	15	69	61	44	1.452381
1946–47	Division 1	14	42	18	5	19	73	79	41	1.404762
1950–51	Division 1	11	42	16	8	18	81	75	40	1.333333
1951–52	Division 1	17	42	15	7	20	63	80	37	1.238095
1957–58	Division 2	16	42	14	8	20	60	81	36	1.190476
1953–54	Division 2	18	42	12	11	19	64	82	35	1.119048
1952–53	Division 1	22	42	11	10	21	59	74	32	1.023810
1954–55	Division 2	22	42	7	9	26	53	82	23	0.714286

1940s & 50s

SQUAD 1948–49   3RD IN DIVISION 1

Frank BROOME	Centre forward	Jack PARRY	Inside forward
Ted CLAMP	Goalkeeper	John POPPITT	Full back
Dick CUSHLOW	Centre half	Tommy POWELL	Outside right
Reg HARRISON	Outside right	Jack STAMPS	Centre forward
Jack HOWE	Full back	Billy STEEL	Winger
Leon LEUTY	Centre half	Doug TAFT	Centre forward
Steve McLACHLAN	Wing half	Cyril THOMPSON	Centre forward
Johnny MORRIS	Inside forward	Bill TOWNSEND	Goalkeeper
Bert MOZLEY	Full back	Colin WALKER	Wing half
Walter MUSSON	Wing half	Tim WARD	Wing half
Allen OLIVER	Outside left	Timothy WARD	Wing half
Jack PARR	Full back	Terry WEBSTER	Goalkeeper

Season	League	League Position	P	W	D	L	F	A	Pts	3 Point Equivalent
1968–69	**Division 2**	**1**	**42**	**26**	**11**	**5**	**65**	**32**	**63**	**2.119048**
1964–65	Division 2	9	42	16	11	15	84	79	43	1.404762
1965–66	Division 2	8	42	16	11	15	71	68	43	1.404762
1960–61	Division 2	12	42	15	10	17	80	80	40	1.309524
1961–62	Division 2	16	42	14	11	17	68	75	39	1.261905
1963–64	Division 2	13	42	14	11	17	56	67	39	1.261905
1967–68	Division 2	18	42	13	10	19	71	78	36	1.166667
1959–60	Division 2	18	42	14	7	21	61	77	35	1.166667
1966–67	Division 2	17	42	12	12	18	68	72	36	1.142857
1962–63	Division 2	18	42	12	12	18	61	72	36	1.142857

1960s

SQUAD 1968–69   CHAMPIONS OF DIVISION 2

Richie BARKER	Forward	John McGOVERN	Midfielder
Willie CARLIN	Midfielder	John O'HARE	Forward
Peter DANIEL	Defender	John RICHARDSON	Full back
Alan DURBAN	Midfielder	John ROBSON	Full back
Les GREEN	Goalkeeper	Arthur STEWART	Wing half
Kevin HECTOR	Forward	Jim WALKER	Left back/Winger
Alan HINTON	Outside left	Ron WEBSTER	Right back/Wing half
Dave MACKAY	Left half	Frank WIGNALL	Centre forward
Roy McFARLAND	Central defender	Pat WRIGHT	Full back

1970s

Season	League	League Position	P	W	D	L	F	A	Pts	3 Point Equivalent
1971–72	**Division 1**	**1**	**42**	**24**	**10**	**8**	**69**	**33**	**58**	**1.952381**
1969–70	Division 1	4	42	22	9	11	64	37	53	1.785714
1974–75	Division 1	1	42	21	11	10	67	49	53	1.761905
1975–76	Division 1	4	42	21	11	10	75	58	53	1.761905
1973–74	Division 1	3	42	17	14	11	52	42	48	1.547619
1972–73	Division 1	7	42	19	8	15	56	54	46	1.547619
1970–71	Division 1	9	42	16	10	16	56	54	42	1.380952
1977–78	Division 1	12	42	14	13	15	54	59	41	1.309524
1976–77	Division 1	15	42	9	19	14	50	55	37	1.095238
1978–79	Division 1	19	42	10	11	21	44	71	31	0.976190

SQUAD 1971–72   CHAMPIONS OF DIVISION 1

Tony BAILEY	Central defender	John McGOVERN	Midfielder
Colin BOULTON	Goalkeeper	John O'HARE	Forward
Alan DURBAN	Midfielder	Steve POWELL	Midfielder/Defender
Archie GEMMILL	Midfielder	John ROBSON	Full back
Kevin HECTOR	Forward	Colin TODD	Central defender
Terry HENNESSEY	Central defender	Jim WALKER	Left back/Winger
Alan HINTON	Outside left	Ron WEBSTER	Right back/Wing half
Roy McFARLAND	Central defender	Frank WIGNALL	Centre forward

1980s

Season	League	League Position	P	W	D	L	F	A	Pts	3 Point Equivalent
1986–87	Division 2	1	42	25	9	8	64	38	84	2.000000
1985–86	Division 3	3	46	23	15	8	80	41	84	1.826087
1988–89	**Division 1**	**5**	**38**	**17**	**7**	**14**	**40**	**38**	**58**	**1.526316**
1984–85	Division 3	7	46	19	13	14	65	54	70	1.521739
1980–81	Division 2	6	42	15	15	12	57	52	45	1.428571
1982–83	Division 2	13	42	10	19	13	49	58	49	1.166667
1981–82	Division 2	16	42	12	12	18	53	68	48	1.142857
1987–88	Division 1	15	40	10	13	17	35	45	43	1.075000
1983–84	Division 2	20	42	11	9	22	36	72	42	1.000000
1979–80	Division 1	21	42	11	8	23	47	67	30	0.976190

SQUAD 1988–89   5TH IN DIVISION 1

Paul BLADES	Defender	Gary MICKLEWHITE	Midfielder
Nigel CALLAGHAN	Winger	Mark PATTERSON	Defender/Right back
John CHIEDOZIE	Winger	David PENNEY	Midfielder
Steve CROSS	Midfielder/Full back	Nick PICKERING	Midfielder
Mike FORSYTH	Left back	Mel SAGE	Right back
Phil GEE	Forward	Dean SAUNDERS	Forward
Paul GODDARD	Forward	Peter SHILTON	Goalkeeper
Trevor HEBBERD	Midfielder	Geraint WILLIAMS	Midfielder
Rob HINDMARCH	Central defender	Mark WRIGHT	Central defender
Ted McMINN	Winger		

Season	League	League Position	P	W	D	L	F	A	Pts	3 Point Equivalent
1991–92	Division 2	3	46	23	9	14	69	51	78	1.695652
1992–93	L1	8	46	19	18	9	68	57	66	1.630435
1993–94	L1	6	46	20	15	11	73	68	71	1.630435
1995–96	L1	2	46	21	9	16	71	51	79	1.565217
1994–95	L1	9	46	18	16	12	66	51	66	1.521739
1997–98	**Premier League**	**9**	**38**	**16**	**7**	**15**	**52**	**49**	**55**	**1.447368**
1998–99	Premier League	8	38	13	13	12	40	45	52	1.368421
1989–90	Division 1	16	38	13	7	18	43	40	46	1.210526
1996–97	Premier League	12	38	11	13	14	45	58	46	1.210526
1990–91	Division 1	20	38	5	9	24	37	75	24	0.631579

1990s

SQUAD 1997–98 — 9TH IN THE PREMIER LEAGUE

Aljosa ASANOVIC	Midfielder	Mart POOM	Goalkeeper
Francesco BAIANO	Striker	Chris POWELL	Defender/Left back
Lars BOHINEN	Midfielder	Darryl POWELL	Midfielder
Deon BURTON	Forward	Gary ROWETT	Defender
Matt CARBON	Defender/Centre back	Paul SIMPSON	Midfielder
Lee CARSLEY	Midfielder	Mauricio SOLIS	Midfielder
Christian DAILLY	Defender/Centre back	Igor STIMAC	Centre back
Rory DELAP	Defender/Midfielder	Dean STURRIDGE	Forward
Steve ELLIOTT	Defender/Centre back	Paul TROLLOPE	Defender/Midfielder
Stefano ERANIO	Midfielder	Robin VAN DER LAAN	Midfielder
Russell HOULT	Goalkeeper	Paulo WANCHOPE	Forward
Jonathan HUNT	Midfielder	Ashley WARD	Forward
Rob KOZLUK	Defender/Midfielder	Ron WILLEMS	Forward
Jacob LAURSEN	Defender/Centre back	Dean YATES	Centre back

Season	League	League Position	P	W	D	L	F	A	Pts	3 Point Equivalent
2006–07	**Championship**	**3**	**46**	**25**	**9**	**12**	**62**	**46**	**84**	**1.826087**
2004–05	Championship	4	46	22	14	10	71	60	76	1.739130
2002–03	L1	18	46	15	24	7	55	74	52	1.500000
2003–04	League 1	20	46	13	20	13	53	67	52	1.282609
2000–01	Premier League	17	38	10	12	16	37	59	42	1.105263
2005–06	Championship	20	46	10	20	16	53	67	50	1.086957
1999–2000	Premier League	16	38	9	11	18	44	57	38	1.000000
2001–02	Premier League	19	38	8	6	24	33	63	30	0.789474

2000s

SQUAD 2006–07 — 3RD IN THE CHAMPIONSHIP

Giles BARNES	Forward	David JONES	Midfielder
Morten BISGAARD	Defender/Midfielder	Dean LEACOCK	Defender
Paul BOERTIEN	Defender/Midfielder	Arturo LUPOLI	Forward
Adam BOLDER	Midfielder	Jonathan MACKEN	Forward
Stephen BYWATER	Goalkeeper	Bob MALCOLM	Defender/Midfielder
Mo CAMARA	Defender/Left back	Jay McEVELEY	Defender
Lee CAMP	Goalkeeper	Tyrone MEARS	Defender/Midfielder
Darren CURRIE	Midfielder	Darren MOORE	Defender/Centre back
Marc EDWORTHY	Defender	Lewin NYATANGA	Defender/Centre back
Craig FAGAN	Forward	Matt OAKLEY	Midfielder
Lee GRANT	Goalkeeper	Stephen PEARSON	Midfielder
Steve HOWARD	Forward	Paul PESCHISOLIDO	Forward
Inigo IDIAKEZ	Midfielder	Ryan SMITH	Midfielder
Richard JACKSON	Defender	Tommy SMITH	Midfielder/Forward
Michael JOHNSON	Defender/Centre back	Jon STEAD	Forward
Seth JOHNSON	Midfielder	Gary TEALE	Forward

193

DERBY COUNTY

EVERTON

Season	League	League Position	P	W	D	L	F	A	Pts	3 Point Equivalent
1953–54	Division 2	2	42	20	16	6	92	58	56	1.809524
1951–52	Division 2	7	42	17	10	15	64	58	44	1.452381
1946–47	Division 1	10	42	17	9	16	62	67	43	1.428571
1954–55	**Division 1**	**11**	**42**	**16**	**10**	**16**	**62**	**68**	**42**	**1.380952**
1947–48	Division 1	14	42	17	6	19	52	66	40	1.357143
1958–59	Division 1	15	42	17	4	21	71	87	38	1.309524
1955–56	Division 1	15	42	15	10	17	55	69	40	1.309524
1956–57	Division 1	15	42	14	10	18	61	79	38	1.238095
1952–53	Division 2	16	42	12	14	16	71	75	38	1.190476
1957–58	Division 1	16	42	13	11	18	65	75	37	1.190476
1948–49	Division 1	18	42	13	11	18	41	63	37	1.190476
1949–50	Division 1	18	42	10	14	18	42	66	34	1.047619
1950–51	Division 1	22	42	12	8	22	48	86	32	1.047619

SQUAD 1954–55   11TH IN DIVISION 1

Ted BUCKLE	Winger	Harry LEYLAND	Goalkeeper
Don DONOVAN	Full back	Tony McNAMARA	Outside right
Tommy EGLINTON	Outside left	Eric MOORE	Full back
Alec FARRALL	Wing half	Jimmy O'NEILL	Goalkeeper
Peter FARRELL	Wing half	John PARKER	Midfielder
Wally FIELDING	Inside forward	Harry POTTS	Inside forward
Jackie GRANT	Wing half	George RANKIN	Full back
Dave HICKSON	Centre forward	Ron SAUNDERS	Centre forward
Tommy JONES	Centre half	Jimmy TANSEY	Full back
Cyril LELLO	Wing half	Eddie WAINWRIGHT	Inside forward
Gwyn LEWIS	Centre forward	Matt WOODS	Centre half

194

Season	League	League Position	P	W	D	L	F	A	Pts	3 Point Equivalent
1962–63	**Division 1**	**1**	**42**	**25**	**11**	**6**	**84**	**42**	**61**	**2.047619**
1968–69	Division 1	3	42	21	15	6	77	36	57	1.857143
1967–68	Division 1	5	42	23	6	13	67	40	52	1.785714
1963–64	Division 1	3	42	21	10	11	84	64	52	1.738095
1960–61	Division 1	5	42	22	6	14	87	69	50	1.714286
1961–62	Division 1	4	42	20	11	11	88	54	51	1.690476
1966–67	Division 1	6	42	19	10	13	65	46	48	1.595238
1964–65	Division 1	4	42	17	15	10	69	60	49	1.571429
1965–66	Division 1	11	42	15	11	16	56	62	41	1.333333
1959–60	Division 1	15	42	13	11	18	73	78	37	1.190476

SQUAD 1962–63   CHAMPIONS OF DIVISION 1

Billy BINGHAM	Outside right	Alex SCOTT	Outside right
Albert DUNLOP	Goalkeeper	George SHARPLES	Wing half
Jimmy GABRIEL	Wing half	Dennis STEVENS	Inside forward
Brian HARRIS	Wing half	Derek TEMPLE	Outside left
George HESLOP	Centre half	George THOMSON	Full back
Tony KAY	Left half	Ray VEALL	Outside left
Brian LABONE	Centre half	Roy VERNON	Inside forward
Mick MEAGAN	Full back	Gordon WEST	Goalkeeper
Johnny MORRISSEY	Outside left	Frank WIGNALL	Centre forward
Alex PARKER	Right back	Alex YOUNG	Forward

	Season	League	League Position	P	W	D	L	F	A	Pts	3 Point Equivalent
1970s	1969–70	Division 1	1	42	29	8	5	72	34	66	2.261905
	1977–78	Division 1	3	42	22	11	9	76	45	55	1.833333
	1978–79	Division 1	4	42	17	17	8	52	40	51	1.619048
	1974–75	Division 1	4	42	16	18	8	56	42	50	1.571429
	1973–74	Division 1	7	42	16	12	14	50	48	44	1.428571
	1975–76	Division 1	11	42	15	12	15	60	66	42	1.357143
	1976–77	Division 1	9	42	14	14	14	62	64	42	1.333333
	1972–73	Division 1	17	42	13	11	18	41	49	37	1.190476
	1970–71	Division 1	14	42	12	13	17	54	60	37	1.166667
	1971–72	Division 1	15	42	9	18	15	37	48	36	1.071429

SQUAD 1969–70 — CHAMPIONS OF DIVISION 1

Alan BALL	Midfielder	Roger KENYON	Central defender
Sandy BROWN	Full back	Brian LABONE	Centre half
Frank D'ARCY	Full back	John MORRISSEY	Outside left
Colin HARVEY	Midfielder	Keith NEWTON	Full back
Gerry HUMPHREYS	Winger	Joe ROYLE	Forward
John HURST	Central defender	Gordon WEST	Goalkeeper
Jimmy HUSBAND	Forward	Alan WHITTLE	Forward/Midfielder
Tommy JACKSON	Midfielder	Tommy WRIGHT	Full back
Howard KENDALL	Midfielder		

	Season	League	League Position	P	W	D	L	F	A	Pts	3 Point Equivalent
1980s	1984–85	Division 1	1	42	28	6	8	88	43	90	2.142857
	1985–86	Division 1	2	42	26	8	8	87	41	86	2.047619
	1986–87	Division 1	1	42	26	8	8	76	31	86	2.047619
	1987–88	Division 1	4	40	19	13	8	53	27	70	1.750000
	1981–82	Division 1	8	42	17	13	12	56	50	64	1.523810
	1982–83	Division 1	7	42	18	10	14	66	48	64	1.523810
	1983–84	Division 1	7	42	16	14	12	44	42	62	1.476190
	1988–89	Division 1	8	38	14	12	12	50	45	54	1.421053
	1980–81	Division 1	15	42	13	10	19	55	58	36	1.166667
	1979–80	Division 1	19	42	9	17	16	43	51	35	1.047619

SQUAD 1984–85 — CHAMPIONS OF DIVISION 1

Ian ATKINS	Defender/Midfielder	Peter REID	Midfielder
John BAILEY	Left back	Kevin RICHARDSON	Midfielder
Paul BRACEWELL	Midfielder	Neill RIMMER	Midfielder
Terry CURRAN	Winger	Graeme SHARP	Forward
Jason DANSKIN	Midfielder	Kevin SHEEDY	Midfielder
Andy GRAY	Forward	Neville SOUTHALL	Goalkeeper
Alan HARPER	Defender/Midfielder	Trevor STEVEN	Midfielder
Adrian HEATH	Forward	Gary STEVENS	Right back
Darren HUGHES	Left back/Midfielder	Pat VAN DEN HAUWE	Full back
John MORRISSEY	Right winger	Rob WAKENSHAW	Forward
Derek MOUNTFIELD	Central defender	Derek WALSH	Midfielder/Right back
Darren OLDROYD	Right back	Paul WILKINSON	Forward
Kevin RATCLIFFE	Central defender		

EVERTON

Season	League	League Position	P	W	D	L	F	A	Pts	3 Point Equivalent
1995–96	**Premier League**	**6**	**38**	**17**	**10**	**11**	**64**	**44**	**61**	**1.605263**
1989–90	Division 1	6	38	17	8	13	57	46	59	1.552632
1990–91	Division 1	9	38	13	12	13	50	46	51	1.342105
1991–92	Division 1	12	42	13	14	15	52	51	53	1.261905
1992–93	Premier League	13	42	15	8	19	53	55	53	1.261905
1994–95	Premier League	15	42	11	17	14	44	51	50	1.190476
1998–99	Premier League	14	38	11	10	17	42	47	43	1.131579
1996–97	Premier League	15	38	10	12	16	44	57	42	1.105263
1997–98	Premier League	17	38	9	13	16	41	56	40	1.052632
1993–94	Premier League	17	42	12	8	22	42	63	44	1.047619

SQUAD 1995–96　　　　　6TH IN THE PREMIER LEAGUE

Gary ABLETT	Defender	Matt JACKSON	Defender/Centre back
Daniel AMOKACHI	Forward	Andrei KANCHELSKIS	Midfielder
Stuart BARLOW	Forward	Anders LIMPAR	Midfielder
Earl BARRETT	Defender	Jon O'CONNOR	Defender/Centre back
Michael BRANCH	Forward	Joe PARKINSON	Midfielder
John EBBRELL	Midfielder	Paul RIDEOUT	Forward
Duncan FERGUSON	Forward	Vinny SAMWAYS	Midfielder
Tony GRANT	Midfielder	Craig SHORT	Defender/Centre back
Gerard HENNIGAN	Midfielder	Neville SOUTHALL	Goalkeeper
Andy HINCHCLIFFE	Full back	Graham STUART	Midfielder
Paul HOLMES	Defender/Full back	David UNSWORTH	Defender
Barry HORNE	Midfielder	Dave WATSON	Defender/Centre back
Marc HOTTIGER	Right back		

Season	League	League Position	P	W	D	L	F	A	Pts	3 Point Equivalent
2004–05	**Premier League**	**4**	**38**	**18**	**7**	**13**	**45**	**46**	**61**	**1.605263**
2002–03	Premier League	7	38	17	8	13	48	49	59	1.552632
2006–07	Premier League	6	38	15	13	10	52	36	58	1.526316
1999–2000	Premier League	13	38	12	14	12	59	49	50	1.315789
2005–06	Premier League	11	38	14	8	16	34	49	50	1.315789
2001–02	Premier League	15	38	11	10	17	45	57	43	1.131579
2000–01	Premier League	16	38	11	9	18	45	59	42	1.105263
2003–04	Premier League	17	38	9	12	17	45	57	39	1.026316

SQUAD 2004–05　　　　　4TH IN THE PREMIER LEAGUE

Mikel ARTETA	Midfielder	Nigel MARTYN	Goalkeeper
James BEATTIE	Forward	James McFADDEN	Midfielder/Forward
Marcus BENT	Forward	Gary NAYSMITH	Defender/Midfielder
Tim CAHILL	Midfielder	Leon OSMAN	Midfielder
Kevin CAMPBELL	Forward	Alessandro PISTONE	Defender
Lee CARSLEY	Midfielder	Alan STUBBS	Defender/Centre back
Nick CHADWICK	Forward	James VAUGHAN	Forward
Duncan FERGUSON	Forward	Steve WATSON	Defender
Thomas GRAVESEN	Midfielder	David WEIR	Defender
Tony HIBBERT	Midfielder	Richard WRIGHT	Goalkeeper
Kevin KILBANE	Midfielder	Joseph YOBO	Defender/Midfielder

FULHAM

Season	League	League Position	P	W	D	L	F	A	Pts	3 Point Equivalent
1958–59	**Division 2**	**2**	**42**	**27**	**6**	**9**	**96**	**61**	**60**	**2.071429**
1948–49	Division 2	1	42	24	9	9	77	37	57	1.928571
1957–58	Division 2	5	42	20	12	10	97	59	52	1.714286
1955–56	Division 2	9	42	20	6	16	89	79	46	1.571429
1953–54	Division 2	8	42	17	10	15	98	85	44	1.452381
1952–53	Division 2	8	42	17	10	15	81	71	44	1.452381
1956–57	Division 2	11	42	19	4	19	84	76	42	1.452381
1947–48	Division 2	11	42	15	10	17	47	46	40	1.309524
1946–47	Division 2	15	42	15	9	18	63	74	39	1.285714
1954–55	Division 2	14	42	14	11	17	76	79	39	1.261905
1950–51	Division 1	18	42	13	11	18	52	68	37	1.190476
1949–50	Division 1	17	42	10	14	18	41	54	34	1.047619
1951–52	Division 1	22	42	8	11	23	58	77	27	0.833333

1940s & 50s

SQUAD 1958–59   2ND IN DIVISION 2

Tony BARTON	Outside right	Johnny KEY	Outside right
Roy BENTLEY	Centre forward	Derek LAMPE	Centre half
Trevor CHAMBERLAIN	Outside left	Jimmy LANGLEY	Left back
George COHEN	Right back	Robin LAWLER	Defender
Ken COLLINS	Full back	Graham LEGGAT	Winger
Maurice COOK	Centre forward	Eddie LOWE	Wing half
John DOHERTY	Centro forward	Tony MACEDO	Goalkeeper
David EDWARDS	Wing half	Alan MULLERY	Wing half
Johnny HAYNES	Inside forward	Brian O'CONNELL	Outside left
Ken HEWKINS	Goalkeeper	Joe STAPLETON	Centre half
Jimmy HILL	Inside forward	Arthur STEVENS	Outside right
Mick JOHNSON	Winger		

Season	League	League Position	P	W	D	L	F	A	Pts	3 Point Equivalent
1959–60	**Division 1**	**10**	**42**	**17**	**10**	**15**	**73**	**80**	**44**	**1.452381**
1963–64	Division 1	15	42	13	13	16	58	65	39	1.238095
1962–63	Division 1	16	42	14	10	18	50	71	38	1.238095
1960–61	Division 1	17	42	14	8	20	72	95	36	1.190476
1965–66	Division 1	20	42	14	7	21	67	85	35	1.166667
1961–62	Division 1	20	42	13	7	22	66	74	33	1.095238
1966–67	Division 1	18	42	11	12	19	71	83	34	1.071429
1964–65	Division 1	20	42	11	12	19	60	78	34	1.071429
1967–68	Division 1	22	42	10	7	25	56	98	27	0.880952
1968–69	Division 2	22	42	7	11	24	40	81	25	0.761905

1960s

SQUAD 1959–60   10TH IN DIVISION 1

Roy BENTLEY	Centre forward	Jimmy LANGLEY	Left back
Trevor CHAMBERLAIN	Outside left	Robin LAWLER	Defender
George COHEN	Right back	Graham LEGGAT	Winger
Maurice COOK	Centre forward	Eddie LOWE	Wing half
John DOHERTY	Centre forward	Tony MACEDO	Goalkeeper
Johnny HAYNES	Inside forward	Alan MULLERY	Wing half
Ken HEWKINS	Goalkeeper	Brian O'CONNELL	Outside left
Jimmy HILL	Inside forward	Joe STAPLETON	Centre half
Mick JOHNSON	Winger	Alfie STOKES	Inside forward
Alan JONES	Centre forward	Reg STRATTON	Centre forward
Johnny KEY	Outside right	Brian SULLIVAN	Inside forward
Derek LAMPE	Centre half		

1970s

Season	League	League Position	P	W	D	L	F	A	Pts	3 Point Equivalent
1970–71	Division 3	2	46	24	12	10	68	41	60	1.826087
1969–70	Division 3	4	46	20	15	11	81	55	55	1.630435
1972–73	**Division 2**	**9**	**42**	**16**	**12**	**14**	**58**	**49**	**44**	**1.428571**
1973–74	Division 2	13	42	16	10	16	39	43	42	1.380952
1974–75	Division 2	9	42	13	16	13	44	39	42	1.309524
1977–78	Division 2	10	42	14	13	15	49	49	41	1.309524
1978–79	Division 2	10	42	13	15	14	50	47	41	1.285714
1975–76	Division 2	12	42	13	14	15	45	47	40	1.261905
1976–77	Division 2	17	42	11	13	18	54	61	35	1.095238
1971–72	Division 2	20	42	12	10	20	45	68	34	1.095238

SQUAD 1972–73 — 9TH IN DIVISION 2

Les BARRETT	Outside left	Barry LLOYD	Midfielder
Stan BROWN	Wing half	Reg MATTHEWSON	Centre half
Fred CALLAGHAN	Left back	Peter MELLOR	Goalkeeper
Dave CARLTON	Midfielder	John MITCHELL	Forward
Jimmy CONWAY	Outside right	Dave MORELINE	Full back
John CONWAY	Winger	Alan MULLERY	Wing half
Roger CROSS	Forward	Mike PENTECOST	Full back
John CUTBUSH	Right back	Alan PINKNEY	Midfielder
Jimmy DUNNE	Central defender	John RICHARDSON	Central defender
Steve EARLE	Forward	Paul SHRUBB	Defender/Midfielder
John FRASER	Right back	Les STRONG	Left back
Stan HORNE	Midfielder	Malcolm WEBSTER	Goalkeeper
John LACY	Central defender	Paul WENT	Central defender

198

1980s

Season	League	League Position	P	W	D	L	F	A	Pts	3 Point Equivalent
1981–82	Division 3	3	46	21	15	10	77	51	78	1.695652
1982–83	**Division 2**	**4**	**42**	**20**	**9**	**13**	**64**	**47**	**69**	**1.642857**
1988–89	Division 3	4	46	22	9	15	69	67	75	1.630435
1984–85	Division 2	9	42	19	8	15	68	64	65	1.547619
1987–88	Division 3	9	46	19	9	18	69	60	66	1.434783
1983–84	Division 2	11	42	15	12	15	60	53	57	1.357143
1980–81	Division 3	13	46	15	13	18	57	64	43	1.260870
1986–87	Division 3	18	46	12	17	17	59	77	53	1.152174
1979–80	Division 2	20	42	11	7	24	42	74	29	0.952381
1985–86	Division 2	22	42	10	6	26	45	69	36	0.857143

SQUAD 1982–83 — 4TH IN DIVISION 2

Roger BROWN	Central defender	Sean O'DRISCOLL	Winger
Cliff CARR	Left back	Peter O'SULLIVAN	Midfielder
Dean CONEY	Forward	Paul PARKER	Defender
Gordon DAVIES	Forward	Gerry PEYTON	Goalkeeper
Tony GALE	Central defender	John REEVES	Midfielder
Jeff HOPKINS	Central defender	Leroy ROSENIOR	Forward
Ray HOUGHTON	Midfielder	Les STRONG	Left back
Ray LEWINGTON	Midfielder	Dale TEMPEST	Forward
Kevin LOCK	Defender	Andy THOMAS	Midfielder/Forward
Brian McDERMOTT	Winger	Robert WILSON	Midfielder

Season	League	League Position	P	W	D	L	F	A	Pts	3 Point Equivalent
1998–99	L2	1	46	31	7	8	79	32	101	2.173913
1996–97	L3	1	46	25	9	12	72	38	87	1.826087
1997–98	League 2	6	46	20	16	10	60	43	70	1.652174
1991–92	Division 3	9	46	19	13	14	57	53	70	1.521739
1994–95	L3	8	42	16	12	14	60	54	62	1.428571
1993–94	L2	21	46	14	22	10	50	63	52	1.391304
1992–93	L2	12	46	16	13	17	57	55	65	1.326087
1995–96	L3	17	46	12	17	17	57	63	53	1.152174
1989–90	Division 3	20	46	12	15	19	55	66	51	1.108696
1990–91	Division 3	21	46	10	16	20	41	56	46	1.000000

SQUAD 1998–99 — CHAMPIONS OF SECOND DIVISION

Philippe ALBERT	Defender/Centre back		Matt LAWRENCE	Defender
Peter BEARDSLEY	Forward		Dirk LEHMANN	Forward
Kevin BETSY	Forward		Steve McANESPIE	Midfielder
Paul BRACEWELL	Midfielder		Paul MOODY	Forward
Matt BRAZIER	Midfielder		Simon MORGAN	Defender/Centre back
Rufus BREVETT	Defender/Left back		Alan NEILSON	Defender
Paul BROOKER	Midfielder/Forward		Paul PESCHISOLIDO	Forward
Chris COLEMAN	Defender/Centre back		John SALAKO	Midfielder
Wayne COLLINS	Midfielder		Rob SCOTT	Defender/Forward
Luke CORNWALL	Forward		Neil SMITH	Midfielder
Sean DAVIS	Midfielder		Jamie SMITH	Defender/Midfielder
Steve FINNAN	Defender/Right back		Kit SYMONS	Defender/Centre back
Barry HAYLES	Forward		Maik TAYLOR	Goalkeeper
Steve HAYWARD	Midfielder		Paul TROLLOPE	Defender/Midfielder
Geoff HORSFIELD	Forward		Gus UHLENBEEK	Defender/Midfielder
Francois KELLER	Midfielder			

Season	League	League Position	P	W	D	L	F	A	Pts	3 Point Equivalent
2000–01	L1	1	46	30	5	11	90	32	101	2.065217
1999–2000	L1	9	46	17	13	16	49	41	67	1.391304
2003–04	**Premier League**	**9**	**38**	**14**	**10**	**14**	**52**	**46**	**52**	**1.368421**
2002–03	Premier League	14	38	13	9	16	41	50	48	1.263158
2005–06	Premier League	12	38	14	6	18	48	58	48	1.263158
2001–02	Premier League	13	38	10	14	14	36	44	44	1.157895
2004–05	Premier League	13	38	12	8	18	52	60	44	1.157895
2006–07	Premier League	16	38	8	15	15	38	60	39	1.026316

SQUAD 2003–04 — 9TH IN THE PREMIER LEAGUE

Luis BOA MORTE	Forward		Dean LEACOCK	Defender
Carlos BOCANEGRA	Defender/Centre back		Sylvain LEGWINSKI	Midfielder
Jerome BONNISSEL	Defender		Steed MALBRANQUE	Midfielder
Malik BUARI	Midfielder		Steve MARLET	Forward
Lee CLARK	Midfielder		Brian McBRIDE	Forward
Mark CROSSLEY	Goalkeeper		Andy MELVILLE	Defender/Centre back
Sean DAVIS	Midfielder		Ian PEARCE	Defender/Centre back
Martin DJETOU	Defender/Midfielder		Mark PEMBRIDGE	Midfielder
Alain GOMA	Defender/Centre back		Bobby PETTA	Midfielder
Adam GREEN	Defender/Left back		Darren PRATLEY	Midfielder
Jon HARLEY	Defender/Midfielder		Zesh REHMAN	Defender/Centre back
Barry HAYLES	Forward		Louis SAHA	Forward
Junichi INAMOTO	Midfielder		Facundo SAVA	Forward
Collins JOHN	Forward		Edwin VAN DER SAR	Goalkeeper
Zat KNIGHT	Defender/Centre back		Moritz VOLZ	Defender/Right back

FULHAM

IPSWICH TOWN

Season	League	League Position	P	W	D	L	F	A	Pts	3 Point Equivalent
1953–54	Division 3 South	1	46	27	10	9	82	51	64	1.978261
1955–56	Division 3 South	3	46	25	14	7	106	60	64	1.934783
1956–57	Division 3 South	1	46	25	9	12	101	54	59	1.826087
1947–48	Division 3 South	4	42	23	3	16	67	61	49	1.714286
1950–51	Division 3 South	8	46	23	6	17	69	58	52	1.630435
1948–49	Division 3 South	7	42	18	9	15	78	77	45	1.500000
1946–47	Division 3 South	6	42	16	14	12	61	53	46	1.476190
1957–58	**Division 2**	**8**	**42**	**16**	**12**	**14**	**68**	**69**	**44**	**1.428571**
1958–59	Division 2	16	42	17	6	19	62	77	40	1.357143
1951–52	Division 3 South	17	46	16	9	21	63	74	41	1.239130
1952–53	Division 3 South	16	46	13	15	18	60	69	41	1.173913
1949–50	Division 3 South	17	42	12	11	19	57	86	35	1.119048
1954–55	Division 2	21	42	11	6	25	57	92	28	0.928571

SQUAD 1957–58 — 8TH IN DIVISION 2

Basil ACRES	Full back	Ken MALCOLM	Full back
Roy BAILEY	Goalkeeper	George McMILLAN	Goalkeeper
Ron BLACKMAN	Centre forward	Doug MILLWARD	Inside forward
Larry CARBERRY	Right back	Neil MYLES	Wing half
David DEACON	Full back	Ted PHILLIPS	Inside forward
John ELSWORTHY	Wing half	Reg PICKETT	Wing half
Tommy GARNEYS	Centre forward	Billy REED	Outside right
Bobby JOHNSTONE	Wing half	Derek REES	Outside left
Jimmy LEADBETTER	Outside left	Doug REES	Centre half
Colin LUNDSTRUM	Winger	Brian SIDDALL	Inside forward
George MacLUCKIE	Outside left	Vic SNELL	Full back

Season	League	League Position	P	W	D	L	F	A	Pts	3 Point Equivalent
1960–61	Division 2	1	42	26	7	9	100	55	59	2.023810
1967–68	Division 2	1	42	22	15	5	79	44	59	1.928571
1961–62	**Division 1**	**1**	**42**	**24**	**8**	**10**	**93**	**67**	**56**	**1.904762**
1966–67	Division 2	5	42	17	16	9	70	54	50	1.595238
1959–60	Division 2	11	42	19	6	17	78	68	44	1.500000
1964–65	Division 2	5	42	15	17	10	74	67	47	1.476190
1968–69	Division 1	12	42	15	11	16	59	60	41	1.333333
1965–66	Division 2	15	42	15	9	18	58	66	39	1.285714
1962–63	Division 1	17	42	12	11	19	59	78	35	1.119048
1963–64	Division 1	22	42	9	7	26	56	121	25	0.809524

SQUAD 1961–62 — CHAMPIONS OF DIVISION 1

Roy BAILEY	Goalkeeper	Jimmy LEADBETTER	Outside left
Bill BAXTER	Centre half	Ken MALCOLM	Full back
Larry CARBERRY	Right back	Doug MORAN	Inside forward
John COMPTON	Left back	Andy NELSON	Centre half
Ray CRAWFORD	Centre forward	Aled OWEN	Winger
Dermot CURTIS	Centre forward	Ted PHILLIPS	Inside forward
John ELSWORTHY	Wing half	Reg PICKETT	Wing half
Wilf HALL	Goalkeeper	Roy STEPHENSON	Outside right

Season	League	League Position	P	W	D	L	F	A	Pts	3 Point Equivalent
1974–75	Division 1	3	42	23	5	14	66	44	51	1.761905
1976–77	**Division 1**	**3**	**42**	**22**	**8**	**12**	**66**	**39**	**52**	**1.761905**
1978–79	Division 1	6	42	20	9	13	63	49	49	1.642857
1973–74	Division 1	4	42	18	11	13	67	58	47	1.547619
1972–73	Division 1	4	42	17	14	11	55	45	48	1.547619
1975–76	Division 1	6	42	16	14	12	54	48	46	1.476190
1971–72	Division 1	13	42	11	16	15	39	53	38	1.166667
1977–78	Division 1	18	42	11	13	18	47	61	35	1.095238
1970–71	Division 1	19	42	12	10	20	42	48	34	1.095238
1969–70	Division 1	18	42	10	11	21	40	63	31	0.976190

1970s

SQUAD 1976–77 — 3RD IN DIVISION 1

Kevin BEATTIE	Central defender	John PEDDELTY	Central defender
Keith BERTSCHIN	Forward	Dale ROBERTS	Central defender
George BURLEY	Right back	Pat SHARKEY	Midfielder
Paul COOPER	Goalkeeper	Laurie SIVELL	Goalkeeper
Eric GATES	Forward	Brian TALBOT	Midfielder
David GEDDIS	Forward	Les TIBBOTT	Full back
Allan HUNTER	Central defender	Robin TURNER	Forward
Mick LAMBERT	Winger	John WARK	Midfielder
Paul MARINER	Forward	Trevor WHYMARK	Forward
Mick MILLS	Full back	Clive WOODS	Winger
Roger OSBORNE	Midfielder		

Season	League	League Position	P	W	D	L	F	A	Pts	3 Point Equivalent
1981–82	**Division 1**	**2**	**42**	**26**	**5**	**11**	**75**	**53**	**83**	**1.976190**
1980–81	Division 1	2	42	23	10	9	77	43	56	1.880952
1979–80	Division 1	3	42	22	9	11	68	39	53	1.785714
1988–89	Division 2	8	46	22	7	17	71	61	73	1.586957
1986–87	Division 2	5	42	17	13	12	59	43	64	1.523810
1987–88	Division 2	8	44	19	9	16	61	52	66	1.500000
1982–83	Division 1	9	42	15	13	14	64	50	58	1.380952
1983–84	Division 1	12	42	15	8	19	55	57	53	1.261905
1984–85	Division 1	17	42	13	11	18	46	57	50	1.190476
1985–86	Division 1	20	42	11	8	23	32	55	41	0.976190

1980s

SQUAD 1981–82 — 2ND IN DIVISION 1

Alan BRAZIL	Forward	Mick MILLS	Full back
George BURLEY	Right back	Arnold MUHREN	Midfielder
Terry BUTCHER	Central defender	Kevin O'CALLAGHAN	Winger
Paul COOPER	Goalkeeper	Russell OSMAN	Central defender
Mich D'AVRAY	Forward	Tommy PARKIN	Midfielder
Eric GATES	Forward	Laurie SIVELL	Goalkeeper
Irvin GERNON	Defender	Kevin STEGGLES	Defender
John JACKSON	Goalkeeper	Frans THIJSSEN	Midfielder
Paul MARINER	Forward	Robin TURNER	Forward
Steve McCALL	Midfielder	John WARK	Midfielder

IPSWICH TOWN

Season	League	League Position	P	W	D	L	F	A	Pts	3 Point Equivalent
1990–99	L1	3	46	26	12	8	69	32	86	1.956522
1991–92	Division 2	1	46	24	12	10	70	50	84	1.826087
1997–98	L1	5	46	23	9	14	77	43	83	1.695652
1995–96	L1	7	46	19	15	12	79	69	69	1.565217
1996–97	L1	4	46	20	12	14	68	50	74	1.565217
1989–90	Division 2	9	46	19	12	15	67	66	69	1.500000
1990–91	Division 2	14	46	13	18	15	60	68	57	1.239130
1992–93	Premier League	16	42	12	16	14	50	55	52	1.238095
1993–94	Premier League	19	42	9	16	17	35	58	43	1.023810
1994–95	Premier League	22	42	7	6	29	36	93	27	0.642857

SQUAD 1998–99   3RD IN FIRST DIVISION

Samassi ABOU	Forward		Alex MATHIE	Forward
Titus BRAMBLE	Defender/Centre back		Tony MOWBRAY	Defender/Centre back
Wayne BROWN	Defender/Centre back		Richard NAYLOR	Defender/Forward
Jamie CLAPHAM	Defender/Midfielder		Bobby PETTA	Midfielder
Jason CUNDY	Defender/Centre back		Jamie SCOWCROFT	Midfielder/Forward
Kieron DYER	Midfielder		Danny SONNER	Midfielder
Marlon HAREWOOD	Forward		Micky STOCKWELL	Midfielder
Lee HODGES	Forward		Adam TANNER	Midfielder
Matt HOLLAND	Midfielder		Mauricio TARICCO	Defender/Left back
Marco HOLSTER	Midfielder		Manuel THETIS	Centre back
Jonathan HUNT	Midfielder		Mark VENUS	Defender/Centre back
David JOHNSON	Forward		Paolo VERNAZZA	Midfielder
John KENNEDY	Midfielder		Fabian WILNIS	Defender/Midfielder
Richard LOGAN	Forward		Richard WRIGHT	Goalkeeper
Jim MAGILTON	Midfielder			

Season	League	League Position	P	W	D	L	F	A	Pts	3 Point Equivalent
1999–2000	L1	3	46	25	9	12	71	42	87	1.826087
2004–05	Championship	3	46	24	9	13	85	56	85	1.760870
2000–01	**Premier League**	**5**	**38**	**20**	**6**	**12**	**57**	**42**	**66**	**1.736842**
2003–04	L1	6	46	21	15	10	84	72	73	1.695652
2002–03	L1	7	46	19	14	13	80	64	70	1.543478
2006–07	Championship	14	46	18	8	20	64	59	62	1.347826
2005–06	Championship	15	46	14	14	18	53	66	56	1.217391
2001–02	Premier League	18	38	9	9	20	41	64	36	0.947368

SQUAD 2000–01   5TH IN THE PREMIER LEAGUE

Nabil ABIDALLAH	Midfielder		Chris MAKIN	Defender
Alun ARMSTRONG	Forward		John McGREAL	Defender
Titus BRAMBLE	Defender/Centre back		Richard NAYLOR	Defender/Forward
Keith BRANAGAN	Goalkeeper		Martijn REUSER	Midfielder
Wayne BROWN	Defender/Centre back		John SCALES	Defender/Centre back
Mark BURCHILL	Forward		Jamie SCOWCROFT	Midfielder/Forward
Jamie CLAPHAM	Defender/Midfielder		Marcus STEWART	Forward
Gary CROFT	Defender/Left back		Mark VENUS	Defender/Centre back
Matt HOLLAND	Midfielder		Fabian WILNIS	Defender/Midfielder
Hermann HREIDARSSON	Defender/Centre back		Jermaine WRIGHT	Defender/Midfielder
David JOHNSON	Forward		Richard WRIGHT	Goalkeeper
Jim MAGILTON	Midfielder			

LEEDS UNITED

<table>
<tr><td rowspan="14">1940s & 50s</td></tr>
</table>

Season	League	League Position	P	W	D	L	F	A	Pts	3 Point Equivalent
1954–55	Division 2	4	42	23	7	12	70	53	53	1.809524
1955–56	Division 2	2	42	23	6	13	80	60	52	1.785714
1950–51	Division 2	5	42	20	8	14	63	55	48	1.619048
1951–52	Division 2	6	42	18	11	13	59	57	47	1.547619
1949–50	Division 2	5	42	17	13	12	54	45	47	1.523810
1956–57	**Division 1**	**8**	**42**	**15**	**14**	**13**	**72**	**63**	**44**	**1.404762**
1953–54	Division 2	10	42	15	13	14	89	81	43	1.380952
1952–53	Division 2	10	42	14	15	13	71	63	43	1.357143
1958–59	Division 1	15	42	15	9	18	57	74	39	1.285714
1957–58	Division 1	17	42	14	9	19	51	63	37	1.214286
1947–48	Division 2	18	42	14	8	20	62	72	36	1.190476
1948–49	Division 2	15	42	12	13	17	55	63	37	1.166667
1946–47	Division 1	22	42	6	6	30	45	90	18	0.571429

SQUAD 1956–57   8TH IN DIVISION 1

Harold BROOK	Centre forward	Jack MARSDEN	Centre half
John CHARLES	Centre forward	Frank McKENNA	Winger
Jack CHARLTON	Centre half	George MEEK	Winger
Chris CROWE	Inside forward	Albert NIGHTINGALE	Inside forward
Jimmy DUNN	Full back	George O'BRIEN	Inside forward
Bobby FORREST	Inside forward	Jack OVERFIELD	Outside left
Archie GIBSON	Wing half	Keith RIPLEY	Wing half
Grenville HAIR	Full back	Roy WOOD	Goalkeeper
Eric KERFOOT	Wing half		

Season	League	League Position	P	W	D	L	F	A	Pts	3 Point Equivalent
1968–69	**Division 1**	**1**	**42**	**27**	**13**	**2**	**66**	**26**	**67**	**2.238095**
1963–64	Division 2	1	42	24	15	3	71	34	63	2.071429
1964–65	Division 1	2	42	26	9	7	83	52	61	2.071429
1965–66	Division 1	2	42	23	9	10	79	38	55	1.857143
1966–67	Division 1	4	42	22	11	9	62	42	55	1.833333
1967–68	Division 1	4	42	22	9	11	71	41	53	1.785714
1962–63	Division 2	5	42	19	10	13	79	53	48	1.595238
1960–61	Division 2	14	42	14	10	18	75	83	38	1.238095
1961–62	Division 2	19	42	12	12	18	50	61	36	1.142857
1959–60	Division 1	21	42	12	10	20	65	92	34	1.095238

<table>
<tr><td rowspan="10">1960s</td></tr>
</table>

SQUAD 1968–69   CHAMPIONS OF DIVISION 1

Mick BATES	Midfielder	Norman HUNTER	Central defender
Rod BELFITT	Centre forward	Albert JOHANNESON	Outside left
Billy BREMNER	Midfielder	Mick JONES	Centre forward
Jack CHARLTON	Centre half	Peter LORIMER	Forward
Terry COOPER	Left back	Paul MADELEY	Midfielder/Defender
Johnny GILES	Midfielder	Mike O'GRADY	Outside left
Eddie GRAY	Winger	Paul REANEY	Right back
Jimmy GREENHOFF	Forward	Gary SPRAKE	Goalkeeper
Terry HIBBITT	Midfielder		

Season	League	League Position	P	W	D	L	F	A	Pts	3 Point Equivalent
1970–71	Division 1	2	42	27	10	5	72	30	64	2.166667
1973–74	**Division 1**	**1**	**42**	**24**	**14**	**4**	**66**	**31**	**62**	**2.047619**
1971–72	Division 1	2	42	24	9	9	73	31	57	1.928571
1969–70	Division 1	2	42	21	15	6	84	49	57	1.857143
1972–73	Division 1	3	42	21	11	10	71	45	53	1.761905
1975–76	Division 1	5	42	21	9	12	65	46	51	1.714286
1978–79	Division 1	5	42	18	14	10	70	52	50	1.619048
1977–78	Division 1	9	42	18	10	14	63	53	46	1.523810
1974–75	Division 1	9	42	16	13	13	57	49	45	1.452381
1976–77	Division 1	10	42	15	12	15	48	51	42	1.357143

SQUAD 1973–74   CHAMPIONS OF DIVISION 1

Mick BATES	Midfielder	Norman HUNTER	Central defender
Billy BREMNER	Midfielder	Mick JONES	Centre forward
Trevor CHERRY	Defender	Joe JORDAN	Forward
Allan CLARKE	Forward	Gary LIDDELL	Forward
Terry COOPER	Left back	Peter LORIMER	Forward
Roy ELLAM	Centre half	Paul MADELEY	Midfielder/Defender
Johnny GILES	Midfielder	Gordon McQUEEN	Central defender
Eddie GRAY	Winger	Paul REANEY	Right back
Frank GRAY	Left back	David STEWART	Goalkeeper
David HARVEY	Goalkeeper	Terry YORATH	Midfielder

Season	League	League Position	P	W	D	L	F	A	Pts	3 Point Equivalent
1984–85	Division 2	7	42	19	12	11	66	43	69	1.642857
1986–87	Division 2	4	42	19	11	12	58	44	68	1.619048
1987–88	Division 2	7	44	19	12	13	61	51	69	1.568182
1988–89	Division 2	10	46	17	16	13	59	50	67	1.456522
1980–81	**Division 1**	**9**	**42**	**17**	**10**	**15**	**39**	**47**	**44**	**1.452381**
1982–83	Division 2	8	42	13	21	8	51	46	60	1.428571
1983–84	Division 2	10	42	16	12	14	55	56	60	1.428571
1979–80	Division 1	11	42	13	14	15	46	50	40	1.261905
1985–86	Division 2	14	42	15	8	19	56	72	53	1.261905
1981–82	Division 1	20	42	10	12	20	39	61	42	1.000000

SQUAD 1980–81   9TH IN DIVISION 1

Aidan BUTTERWORTH	Forward	Gary HAMSON	Midfielder
Jeff CHANDLER	Winger	Carl HARRIS	Winger
Trevor CHERRY	Defender	Paul HART	Central defender
Terry CONNOR	Forward	Kevin HIRD	Midfielder
Alan CURTIS	Forward/Midfielder	John LUKIC	Goalkeeper
Martin DICKINSON	Central defender	Paul MADELEY	Midfielder/Defender
Neil FIRM	Central defender	Keith PARKINSON	Central defender
Brian FLYNN	Midfielder	Derek PARLANE	Forward
Arthur GRAHAM	Winger	Alex SABELLA	Midfielder
Eddie GRAY	Winger	Byron STEVENSON	Midfielder
Brian GREENHOFF	Central defender	Gwyn THOMAS	Midfielder

Season	League	League Position	P	W	D	L	F	A	Pts	3 Point Equivalent
1991–92	Division 1	1	42	22	16	4	74	37	82	1.952381
1989–90	Division 2	1	46	24	13	9	79	52	85	1.847826
1998–99	Premier League	4	38	18	13	7	62	34	67	1.763158
1994–95	Premier League	5	42	20	13	9	59	38	73	1.738095
1990–91	Division 1	4	38	19	7	12	65	47	64	1.684211
1993–94	Premier League	5	42	18	16	8	65	39	70	1.666667
1997–98	Premier League	5	38	17	8	13	57	46	59	1.552632
1992–93	Premier League	17	42	12	15	15	57	62	51	1.214286
1996–97	Premier League	11	38	11	13	14	28	38	46	1.210526
1995–96	Premier League	13	38	12	7	19	40	57	43	1.131579

1990s

SQUAD 1991–92 — CHAMPIONS OF DIVISION 1

Tony AGANA	Forward	John McCLELLAND	Central defender
David BATTY	Midfielder	Jon NEWSOME	Centre back
Eric CANTONA	Forward	Carl SHUTT	Forward
Lee CHAPMAN	Forward	Gary SPEED	Defender/Midfielder
Bobby DAVISON	Forward	Mel STERLAND	Right back
Tony DORIGO	Full back	Gordon STRACHAN	Midfielder
Chris FAIRCLOUGH	Centre back	Imre VARADI	Forward
Steve HODGE	Midfielder	Rodney WALLACE	Forward
Chris KAMARA	Midfielder	David WETHERALL	Defender/Centre back
Garry KELLY	Defender/Right back	Mike WHITLOW	Defender
John LUKIC	Goalkeeper	Chris WHYTE	Central defender
Gary McALLISTER	Midfielder		

Season	League	League Position	P	W	D	L	F	A	Pts	3 Point Equivalent
1999–2000	Premier League	3	38	21	6	11	58	43	69	1.815789
2000–01	Premier League	4	38	20	8	10	64	43	68	1.789474
2001–02	Premier League	5	38	18	12	8	53	37	66	1.736842
2005–06	Championship	5	46	21	15	10	57	38	78	1.695652
2002–03	Premier League	15	38	14	5	19	58	57	47	1.236842
2004–05	Championship	14	46	14	14	18	49	52	60	1.217391
2006–07	Championship	24	46	13	7	26	46	72	36	1.000000
2003–04	Premier League	19	38	8	9	21	40	79	33	0.868421

2000s

SQUAD 1999–2000 — 3RD IN THE PREMIER LEAGUE

Eirik BAKKE	Midfielder	Matthew JONES	Midfielder
David BATTY	Midfielder	Garry KELLY	Defender/Right back
Lee BOWYER	Midfielder	Harry KEWELL	Midfielder/Forward
Michael BRIDGES	Forward	Nigel MARTYN	Goalkeeper
Michael DUBERRY	Defender/Centre back	Stephen McPHAIL	Midfielder
Alfe-Inge HAALAND	Defender/Midfielder	Danny MILLS	Defender
Ian HARTE	Defender/Left back	Lucas RADEBE	Defender/Centre back
Martin HIDEN	Defender/Full back	Alan SMITH	Forward
David HOPKIN	Midfielder	Jason WILCOX	Midfielder
Darren HUCKERBY	Forward	Jonathan WOODGATE	Defender/Centre back

LEEDS UNITED

LEICESTER CITY

Season	League	League Position	P	W	D	L	F	A	Pts	3 Point Equivalent
1956–57	**Division 2**	**1**	**42**	**25**	**11**	**6**	**109**	**67**	**61**	**2.047619**
1953–54	Division 2	1	42	23	10	9	97	60	56	1.880952
1955–56	Division 2	5	42	21	6	15	94	78	48	1.642857
1951–52	Division 2	5	42	19	9	14	78	64	47	1.571429
1952–53	Division 2	5	42	18	12	12	89	74	48	1.571429
1946–47	Division 2	9	42	18	7	17	69	64	43	1.452381
1947–48	Division 2	9	42	16	11	15	60	57	43	1.404762
1950–51	Division 2	14	42	15	11	16	68	58	41	1.333333
1949–50	Division 2	15	42	12	15	15	55	65	39	1.214286
1954–55	Division 1	21	42	12	11	19	74	86	35	1.119048
1957–58	Division 1	18	42	14	5	23	91	112	33	1.119048
1948–49	Division 2	19	42	10	16	16	62	79	36	1.095238
1958–59	Division 1	19	42	11	10	21	67	98	32	1.023810

1940s & 50s

SQUAD 1956–57 | CHAMPIONS OF DIVISION 2

John ANDERSON	Goalkeeper	Stan MILBURN	Full back
Colin APPLETON	Wing half	Jimmy MORAN	Inside forward
Willie CUNNINGHAM	Full back	Johnny MORRIS	Inside forward
Jack FROGGATT	Outside left/Half back	John OGILVIE	Full back
Willie GARDINER	Centre forward	Arthur ROWLEY	Inside forward
Derek HINES	Centre forward	Harry SINCLAIR	Goalkeeper
Derek HOGG	Outside left	Jimmy WALSH	Centre forward
Dave MacLAREN	Goalkeeper	Pat WARD	Wing half
Thomas McDONALD	Outside right	Bill WEBB	Full back
Ian McNEILL	Inside forward	Billy WRIGHT	Outside left

206

Season	League	League Position	P	W	D	L	F	A	Pts	3 Point Equivalent
1962–63	**Division 1**	**4**	**42**	**20**	**12**	**10**	**79**	**53**	**52**	**1.714286**
1965–66	Division 1	7	42	21	7	14	80	65	49	1.666667
1960–61	Division 1	6	42	18	9	15	87	70	45	1.500000
1966–67	Division 1	8	42	18	8	16	78	71	44	1.476190
1963–64	Division 1	11	42	16	11	15	61	58	43	1.404762
1961–62	Division 1	14	42	17	6	19	72	71	40	1.357143
1959–60	Division 1	12	42	13	13	16	66	75	39	1.238095
1967–68	Division 1	13	42	13	12	17	64	69	38	1.214286
1964–65	Division 1	18	42	11	13	18	69	85	35	1.095238
1968–69	Division 1	21	42	9	12	21	39	68	30	0.928571

1960s

SQUAD 1962–63 | 4TH IN DIVISION 1

Colin APPLETON	Wing half	Ian KING	Centre half
Gordon BANKS	Goalkeeper	Billy McDERMENT	Wing half
Len CHALMERS	Right back	Frank McLINTOCK	Central defender
Albert CHEESEBROUGH	Inside forward	Richie NORMAN	Left back
Graham CROSS	Central defender	Howard RILEY	Outside right
Davie GIBSON	Inside forward	John SJOBERG	Defender
Terry HEATH	Midfielder	Mike STRINGFELLOW	Outside left
George HEYES	Goalkeeper	Jimmy WALSH	Centre forward
Ken KEYWORTH	Centre forward/Wing half		

Season	League	League Position	P	W	D	L	F	A	Pts	3 Point Equivalent
1970–71	Division 2	1	42	23	13	6	57	30	59	1.952381
1969–70	Division 2	3	42	19	13	10	64	50	51	1.666667
1975–76	**Division 1**	**7**	**42**	**13**	**19**	**10**	**48**	**51**	**45**	**1.380952**
1973–74	Division 1	9	42	13	16	13	51	41	42	1.309524
1976–77	Division 1	11	42	12	18	12	47	60	42	1.285714
1971–72	Division 1	12	42	13	13	16	41	46	39	1.238095
1974–75	Division 1	18	42	12	12	18	46	60	36	1.142857
1978–79	Division 2	17	42	10	17	15	43	52	37	1.119048
1972–73	Division 1	16	42	10	17	15	40	46	37	1.119048
1977–78	Division 1	22	42	5	12	25	26	70	22	0.642857

SQUAD 1975–76 — 7TH IN DIVISION 1

Brian ALDERSON	Winger	Dennis ROFE	Left back
Alan BIRCHENALL	Midfielder	Jon SAMMELS	Midfielder
Jeff BLOCKLEY	Central defender	Steve SIMS	Central defender
Graham CROSS	Central defender	David TOMLIN	Winger
Steve EARLE	Forward	Mark WALLINGTON	Goalkeeper
Chris GARLAND	Forward	Keith WELLER	Midfielder/Winger
Len GLOVER	Winger	Steve WHITWORTH	Right back
Steve KEMBER	Midfielder	Alan WOOLLETT	Defender
Bob LEE	Forward	Frank WORTHINGTON	Forward

Season	League	League Position	P	W	D	L	F	A	Pts	3 Point Equivalent
1979–80	**Division 2**	**1**	**42**	**21**	**13**	**8**	**58**	**38**	**55**	**1.809524**
1982–83	Division 2	3	42	20	10	12	72	44	70	1.666667
1981–82	Division 2	8	42	18	12	12	56	48	66	1.571429
1987–88	Division 2	13	44	16	11	17	62	61	59	1.340909
1983–84	Division 1	15	42	13	12	17	65	68	51	1.214286
1984–85	Division 1	15	42	15	6	21	65	73	51	1.214286
1988–89	Division 2	15	46	13	16	17	56	63	55	1.195652
1980–81	Division 1	21	42	13	6	23	40	67	32	1.071429
1985–86	Division 1	19	42	10	12	20	54	76	42	1.000000
1986–87	Division 1	20	42	11	9	22	54	76	42	1.000000

SQUAD 1979–80 — CHAMPIONS OF DIVISION 2

David BUCHANAN	Forward	Andy PEAKE	Midfielder
Pat BYRNE	Midfielder	Dennis ROFE	Left back
Mick DUFFY	Midfielder	Geoff SCOTT	Defender
Paul EDMUNDS	Winger	Bobby SMITH	Left back
Mark GOODWIN	Midfielder	Gregor STEVENS	Central defender
Martin HENDERSON	Forward	Derek STRICKLAND	Forward
Eddie KELLY	Midfielder	Mark WALLINGTON	Goalkeeper
Alan LEE	Winger	Peter WELSH	Defender
Gary LINEKER	Forward	Tommy WILLIAMS	Defender
Larry MAY	Central defender	Ian WILSON	Midfielder
John O'NEILL	Central defender	Alan YOUNG	Forward

1990s

Season	League	League Position	P	W	D	L	F	A	Pts	3 Point Equivalent
1992–93	L1	6	46	22	14	10	71	64	76	1.739130
1991–92	Division 2	4	46	23	8	15	62	55	77	1.673913
1995–96	L1	5	46	19	13	14	66	60	71	1.521739
1993–94	L1	4	46	19	11	16	72	59	73	1.478261
1997–98	**Premier League**	**10**	**38**	**13**	**14**	**11**	**51**	**41**	**53**	**1.394737**
1998–99	Premier League	10	38	12	13	13	40	46	49	1.289474
1989–90	Division 2	13	46	15	14	17	67	79	59	1.282609
1996–97	Premier League	9	38	12	11	15	46	54	47	1.236842
1990–91	Division 2	22	46	14	8	24	60	83	50	1.086957
1994–95	Premier League	21	42	6	11	25	45	80	29	0.690476

SQUAD 1997–98   10TH IN THE PREMIER LEAGUE

Pegguy ARPHEXAD	Goalkeeper	Neil LENNON	Midfielder
Stuart CAMPBELL	Midfielder	Ian MARSHALL	Forward
Steve CLARIDGE	Forward	Sam McMAHON	Midfielder
Tony COTTEE	Forward	Garry PARKER	Midfielder
Matt ELLIOTT	Defender/Centre back	Spencer PRIOR	Defender/Centre back
Graham FENTON	Forward	Robbie SAVAGE	Midfielder
Steve GUPPY	Midfielder	Rob ULLATHORNE	Defender
Emile HESKEY	Forward	Steve WALSH	Defender/Centre back
Muzzy IZZET	Midfielder	Julian WATTS	Defender/Centre back
Pontus KAAMARK	Defender/Centre back	Stuart WILSON	Midfielder/Forward
Kasey KELLER	Goalkeeper	Theo ZAGORAKIS	Midfielder

2000s

Season	League	League Position	P	W	D	L	F	A	Pts	3 Point Equivalent
2002–03	L1	2	46	26	6	14	73	40	92	1.826087
1999–2000	**Premier League**	**8**	**38**	**16**	**7**	**15**	**55**	**55**	**55**	**1.447368**
2000–01	Premier League	13	38	14	6	18	39	51	48	1.263158
2005–06	Championship	16	46	13	15	18	51	59	54	1.173913
2006–07	Championship	19	46	13	14	19	49	64	53	1.152174
2004–05	Championship	15	46	12	13	21	49	46	57	1.065217
2003–04	Premier League	18	38	6	15	17	48	65	33	0.868421
2001–02	Premier League	20	38	5	13	20	30	64	28	0.736842

SQUAD 1999–2000   8TH IN THE PREMIER LEAGUE

Pegguy ARPHEXAD	Goalkeeper	Emile HESKEY	Forward
Stuart CAMPBELL	Midfielder	Andy IMPEY	Midfielder
Stan COLLYMORE	Forward	Muzzy IZZET	Midfielder
Tony COTTEE	Forward	Neil LENNON	Midfielder
Lawrie DUDFIELD	Forward	Ian MARSHALL	Forward
Darren EADIE	Midfielder	Stefan OAKES	Midfielder
Matt ELLIOTT	Defender/Centre back	Robbie SAVAGE	Midfielder
Graham FENTON	Forward	Frank SINCLAIR	Defender/Centre back
Tim FLOWERS	Goalkeeper	Jordan STEWART	Midfielder
Phil GILCHRIST	Defender/Centre back	Scott TAYLOR	Midfielder
Tommy GOODWIN	Defender/Full back	Danny THOMAS	Midfielder
Arnar GUNNLAUGSSON	Forward	Steve WALSH	Defender/Centre back
Steve GUPPY	Midfielder	Theo ZAGORAKIS	Midfielder

LIVERPOOL

Season	League	League Position	P	W	D	L	F	A	Pts	3 Point Equivalent
1946–47	**Division 1**	**1**	**42**	**25**	**7**	**10**	**84**	**52**	**57**	**1.952381**
1958–59	Division 2	4	42	24	5	13	87	62	53	1.833333
1957–58	Division 2	4	42	22	10	10	79	54	54	1.809524
1956–57	Division 2	3	42	21	11	10	82	54	53	1.761905
1955–56	Division 2	3	42	21	6	15	85	63	48	1.642857
1949–50	Division 1	8	42	17	14	11	64	54	48	1.547619
1950–51	Division 1	9	42	16	11	15	53	59	43	1.404762
1947–48	Division 1	11	42	16	10	16	65	61	42	1.380952
1954–55	Division 2	11	42	16	10	16	92	96	42	1.380952
1951–52	Division 1	11	42	12	19	11	57	61	43	1.309524
1948–49	Division 1	12	42	13	14	15	53	43	40	1.261905
1952–53	Division 1	17	42	14	8	20	61	82	36	1.190476
1953–54	Division 1	22	42	9	10	23	68	97	28	0.880952

1940s & 50s

SQUAD 1946–47 — CHAMPIONS OF DIVISION 1

Charlie ASHCROFT	Goalkeeper	Billy LIDDELL	Forward
Jack BALMER	Inside forward	Tommy McLEOD	Inside forward
Tom BUSH	Centre half	Ray MINSHULL	Goalkeeper
Len CARNEY	Inside forward	Berry NIEUWENHUYS	Outside right
Cyril DONE	Centre forward	Bob PAISLEY	Wing half
John EASDALE	Centre half	Stan PALK	Wing half/Inside forward
Harry EASTHAM	Inside forward	Bob PRIDAY	Winger
Willie FAGAN	Inside forward	Barney RAMSDEN	Full back
James HARLEY	Full back	Cyril SIDLOW	Goalkeeper
Laurie HUGHES	Centre half	Eddie SPICER	Full back
Bill JONES	Wing half	Albert STUBBINS	Centre forward
Harry KAYE	Wing half	Phil TAYLOR	Inside forward/Wing half
Ray LAMBERT	Full back	Billy WATKINSON	Centre forward

209

Season	League	League Position	P	W	D	L	F	A	Pts	3 Point Equivalent
1961–62	Division 2	1	42	27	8	7	99	43	62	2.119048
1965–66	**Division 1**	**1**	**42**	**26**	**9**	**7**	**79**	**34**	**61**	**2.071429**
1968–69	Division 1	2	42	25	11	6	63	24	61	2.047619
1963–64	Division 1	1	42	26	5	11	92	45	57	1.976190
1967–68	Division 1	3	42	22	11	9	71	40	55	1.833333
1960–61	Division 2	3	42	21	10	11	87	58	52	1.738095
1959–60	Division 2	3	42	20	10	12	90	66	50	1.666667
1966–67	Division 1	5	42	19	13	10	64	47	51	1.666667
1962–63	Division 1	8	42	17	10	15	71	59	44	1.452381
1964–65	Division 1	7	42	17	10	15	67	73	44	1.452381

1960s

SQUAD 1965–66 — CHAMPIONS OF DIVISION 1

Alf ARROWSMITH	Centre forward	Gordon MILNE	Wing half
Gerry BYRNE	Left back	Tommy SMITH	Defender
Ian CALLAGHAN	Outside right	Ian ST JOHN	Forward/Midfielder
Bobby GRAHAM	Forward	Willie STEVENSON	Wing half
Roger HUNT	Forward	Geoff STRONG	Inside forward
Chris LAWLER	Right back	Peter THOMPSON	Winger
Tommy LAWRENCE	Goalkeeper	Ron YEATS	Centre half

Season	League	League Position	P	W	D	L	F	A	Pts	3 Point Equivalent
1978–79	**Division 1**	**1**	**42**	**30**	**8**	**4**	**85**	**16**	**68**	**2.333333**
1972–73	Division 1	1	42	25	10	7	72	42	60	2.023810
1975–76	Division 1	1	42	23	14	5	66	31	60	1.976190
1977–78	Division 1	2	42	24	9	9	65	34	57	1.928571
1971–72	Division 1	3	42	24	9	9	64	30	57	1.928571
1976–77	Division 1	1	42	23	11	8	62	33	57	1.904762
1973–74	Division 1	2	42	22	13	7	52	31	57	1.880952
1974–75	Division 1	2	42	20	11	11	60	39	51	1.690476
1969–70	Division 1	5	42	20	11	11	65	42	51	1.690476
1970–71	Division 1	5	42	17	17	8	42	24	51	1.619048

SQUAD 1978–79 — CHAMPIONS OF DIVISION 1

Jimmy CASE	Midfielder
Ray CLEMENCE	Goalkeeper
Kenny DALGLISH	Forward
David FAIRCLOUGH	Forward
Alan HANSEN	Defender/Centre back
Steve HEIGHWAY	Winger
Emlyn HUGHES	Defender/Midfielder
David JOHNSON	Forward
Alan KENNEDY	Left back
Ray KENNEDY	Midfielder/Forward
Sammy LEE	Midfielder
Terry McDERMOTT	Midfielder
Phil NEAL	Defender/Right back
Graeme SOUNESS	Midfielder
Phil THOMPSON	Central defender

Season	League	League Position	P	W	D	L	F	A	Pts	3 Point Equivalent
1987–88	**Division 1**	**1**	**40**	**26**	**12**	**2**	**87**	**24**	**90**	**2.250000**
1985–86	Division 1	1	42	26	10	6	89	37	88	2.095238
1981–82	Division 1	1	42	26	9	7	80	32	87	2.071429
1979–80	Division 1	1	42	25	10	7	81	30	60	2.023810
1988–89	Division 1	2	38	22	10	6	65	28	76	2.000000
1982–83	Division 1	1	42	24	10	8	87	37	82	1.952381
1983–84	Division 1	1	42	22	14	6	73	32	80	1.904762
1984–85	Division 1	2	42	22	11	9	68	35	77	1.833333
1986–87	Division 1	2	42	23	8	11	72	42	77	1.833333
1980–81	Division 1	5	42	17	17	8	62	42	51	1.619048

SQUAD 1987–88 — CHAMPIONS OF DIVISION 1

Gary ABLETT	Defender
John ALDRIDGE	Forward
John BARNES	Forward
Peter BEARDSLEY	Forward
Kenny DALGLISH	Forward
Gary GILLESPIE	Central defender
Bruce GROBBELAAR	Goalkeeper
Alan HANSEN	Defender/Centre back
Mike HOOPER	Goalkeeper
Ray HOUGHTON	Midfielder
Craig JOHNSTON	Forward/Winger
Mark LAWRENSON	Defender
Kevin MacDONALD	Midfielder
Steve McMAHON	Midfielder
Jan MOLBY	Midfielder
Steve NICOL	Defender
Nigel SPACKMAN	Midfielder
Steve STAUNTON	Defender
Paul WALSH	Forward
John WARK	Midfielder
Alex WATSON	Defender/Centre back
Ronnie WHELAN	Midfielder

Season	League	League Position	P	W	D	L	F	A	Pts	3 Point Equivalent
1989–90	**Division 1**	**1**	**38**	**23**	**10**	**5**	**78**	**37**	**79**	**2.078947**
1990–91	Division 1	2	38	23	7	8	77	40	76	2.000000
1995–96	Premier League	3	38	20	11	7	70	34	71	1.868421
1996–97	Premier League	4	38	19	11	8	62	37	68	1.789474
1994–95	Premier League	4	42	21	11	10	65	37	74	1.761905
1997–98	Premier League	3	38	18	11	9	68	42	65	1.710526
1991–92	Division 1	6	42	16	16	10	47	40	64	1.523810
1993–94	Premier League	8	42	17	9	16	59	55	60	1.428571
1998–99	Premier League	7	38	15	9	14	68	49	54	1.421053
1992–93	Premier League	6	42	16	11	15	62	55	59	1.404762

1990s

SQUAD 1989–90   CHAMPIONS OF DIVISION 1

Gary ABLETT	Defender
John ALDRIDGE	Forward
John BARNES	Forward
Peter BEARDSLEY	Forward
David BURROWS	Defender/Left back
Kenny DALGLISH	Forward
Gary GILLESPIE	Central defender
Bruce GROBBELAAR	Goalkeeper
Alan HANSEN	Defender/Centre back
Ray HOUGHTON	Midfielder
Glenn HYSEN	Central defender
Mike MARSH	Midfielder
Steve McMAHON	Midfielder
Jan MOLBY	Midfielder
Steve NICOL	Defender
Ronny ROSENTHAL	Forward
Ian RUSH	Forward
Steve STAUNTON	Defender
Nick TANNER	Central defender
Barry VENISON	Right back
Ronnie WHELAN	Midfielder

Season	League	League Position	P	W	D	L	F	A	Pts	3 Point Equivalent
2005–06	Premier League	3	38	25	7	6	57	25	82	2.157895
2001–02	**Premier League**	**2**	**38**	**24**	**8**	**6**	**67**	**30**	**80**	**2.105263**
2000–01	Premier League	3	38	20	9	9	71	39	69	1.815789
2006–07	Premier League	3	38	20	8	10	57	27	68	1.789474
1999–2000	Premier League	4	38	19	10	9	51	30	67	1.763158
2002–03	Premier League	5	38	18	10	10	61	41	64	1.684211
2003–04	Premier League	4	38	16	12	10	55	37	60	1.578947
2004–05	Premier League	5	38	17	7	14	52	41	58	1.526316

2000s

SQUAD 2001–02   2ND IN THE PREMIER LEAGUE

Nicolas ANELKA	Forward
Pegguy ARPHEXAD	Goalkeeper
Markus BABBEL	Defender
Nick BARMBY	Midfielder/Forward
Patrik BERGER	Midfielder
Igor BISCAN	Midfielder
Jamie CARRAGHER	Defender/Midfielder
Jerzy DUDEK	Goalkeeper
Robbie FOWLER	Forward
Steven GERRARD	Midfielder
Dietmar HAMANN	Midfielder
Stephane HENCHOZ	Defender/Centre back
Emile HESKEY	Forward
Sami HYYPIA	Defender/Centre back
Chris KIRKLAND	Goalkeeper
Jari LITMANEN	Midfielder
Danny MURPHY	Midfielder
Michael OWEN	Forward
Jamie REDKNAPP	Midfielder
John Arne RIISE	Defender
Vladimir SMICER	Midfielder
Gregory VIGNAL	Defender/Left back
Sander WESTERVELD	Goalkeeper
Abel XAVIER	Defender/Midfielder

Season	League	League Position	P	W	D	L	F	A	Pts	3 Point Equivalent
1946–47	Division 2	1	42	26	10	6	78	35	62	2.095238
1950–51	Division 2	2	42	19	14	9	89	61	52	1.690476
1957–58	**Division 1**	**5**	**42**	**22**	**5**	**15**	**104**	**100**	**49**	**1.690476**
1955–56	Division 1	4	42	18	10	14	82	69	46	1.523810
1954–55	Division 1	7	42	18	10	14	76	69	46	1.523810
1948–49	Division 1	7	42	15	15	12	47	51	45	1.428571
1947–48	Division 1	10	42	15	12	15	52	47	42	1.357143
1951–52	Division 1	15	42	13	13	16	58	61	39	1.238095
1953–54	Division 1	17	42	14	9	19	62	77	37	1.214286
1952–53	Division 1	20	42	14	7	21	72	87	35	1.166667
1956–57	Division 1	18	42	13	9	20	78	88	35	1.142857
1958–59	Division 1	20	42	11	9	22	64	95	31	1.000000
1949–50	Division 1	21	42	8	13	21	36	68	29	0.880952

SQUAD 1957–58 — 5TH IN DIVISON 1

Colin BARLOW	Outside right	Bill LEIVERS	Full back
Ken BARNES	Wing half	Roy LITTLE	Full back
Ken BRANAGAN	Full back	Keith MARSDEN	Centre forward
Roy CHEETHAM	Defender	Billy McADAMS	Centre forward
Roy CLARKE	Outside left	John McCLELLAND	Outside right
Dave EWING	Centre half	Jack McTAVISH	Centre half
Paddy FAGAN	Winger	Ron PHOENIX	Wing half
Dennis FIDLER	Outside left	Ray SAMBROOK	Winger
Steve FLEET	Goalkeeper	John SAVAGE	Goalkeeper
Johnny HART	Inside forward	Cliff SEAR	Left back
Joe HAYES	Inside forward	Ken TAYLOR	Full back
Bobby JOHNSTONE	Inside forward	Bert TRAUTMANN	Goalkeeper
Alan KIRKMAN	Inside forward	Roy WARHURST	Wing half

Season	League	League Position	P	W	D	L	F	A	Pts	3 Point Equivalent
1967–68	**Division 1**	**1**	**42**	**26**	**6**	**10**	**86**	**43**	**58**	**2.000000**
1965–66	Division 2	1	42	22	15	5	76	44	59	1.928571
1963–64	Division 2	6	42	18	10	14	84	66	46	1.523810
1961–62	Division 1	12	42	17	7	18	78	81	41	1.380952
1964–65	Division 2	11	42	16	9	17	63	62	41	1.357143
1968–69	Division 1	13	42	15	10	17	64	55	40	1.309524
1959–60	Division 1	16	42	17	3	22	78	84	37	1.285714
1966–67	Division 1	15	42	12	15	15	43	52	39	1.214286
1960–61	Division 1	13	42	13	11	18	79	90	37	1.190476
1962–63	Division 1	21	42	10	11	21	58	102	31	0.976190

SQUAD 1967–68 — CHAMPIONS OF DIVISION 1

Colin BELL	Midfielder	Paul HINCE	Winger
Tony BOOK	Full back	Stan HORNE	Midfielder
Stan BOWLES	Midfielder	Chris JONES	Forward
Roy CHEETHAM	Defender	Bobby KENNEDY	Full back
John CLAY	Inside forward	Franny LEE	Forward
Tony COLEMAN	Outside left	Ken MULHEARN	Goalkeeper
Dave CONNOR	Full back	Alan OAKES	Midfielder
Joe CORRIGAN	Goalkeeper	Alan OGLEY	Goalkeeper
Harry DOWD	Goalkeeper	Glyn PARDOE	Left back
Mike DOYLE	Central defender	Mike SUMMERBEE	Winger
George HESLOP	Centre half	Neil YOUNG	Forward

Season	League	League Position	P	W	D	L	F	A	Pts	3 Point Equivalent
1971–72	**Division 1**	**4**	**42**	**23**	**11**	**8**	**77**	**45**	**57**	**1.904762**
1976–77	Division 1	2	42	21	14	7	60	34	56	1.833333
1977–78	Division 1	4	42	20	12	10	74	51	52	1.714286
1974–75	Division 1	8	42	18	10	14	54	54	46	1.523810
1975–76	Division 1	8	42	16	11	15	64	46	43	1.404762
1969–70	Division 1	10	42	16	11	15	55	48	43	1.404762
1972–73	Division 1	11	42	15	11	16	57	60	41	1.333333
1973–74	Division 1	14	42	14	12	16	39	46	40	1.285714
1970–71	Division 1	11	42	12	17	13	47	42	41	1.261905
1978–79	Division 1	15	42	13	13	16	58	56	39	1.238095

SQUAD 1971–72   4TH IN DIVISION 1

Colin BELL	Midfielder	George HESLOP	Centre half
Tony BOOK	Full back	Freddie HILL	Inside forward
Tommy BOOTH	Central defender	Derek JEFFRIES	Central defender
Steve CARTER	Winger	Jeff JOHNSON	Midfielder
Dave CONNOR	Full back	Franny LEE	Forward
Joe CORRIGAN	Goalkeeper	Rodney MARSH	Forward
Wyn DAVIES	Forward	Ian MELLOR	Winger
Willie DONACHIE	Left back	Alan OAKES	Midfielder
Mike DOYLE	Central defender	Mike SUMMERBEE	Winger
Ron HEALEY	Goalkeeper	Tony TOWERS	Midfielder
Phil HENSON	Midfielder	Neil YOUNG	Forward

213

Season	League	League Position	P	W	D	L	F	A	Pts	3 Point Equivalent
1988–89	Division 2	2	46	23	13	10	77	53	82	1.782609
1984–85	Division 2	3	42	21	11	10	66	40	74	1.761905
1983–84	Division 2	4	42	20	10	12	66	48	70	1.666667
1987–88	Division 2	9	44	19	8	17	80	60	65	1.477273
1981–82	**Division 1**	**10**	**42**	**15**	**13**	**14**	**49**	**50**	**58**	**1.380952**
1980–81	Division 1	12	42	14	11	17	56	59	39	1.261905
1979–80	Division 1	17	42	12	13	17	43	66	37	1.166667
1982–83	Division 1	20	42	13	8	21	47	70	47	1.119048
1985–86	Division 1	15	42	11	12	19	43	57	45	1.071429
1986–87	Division 1	21	42	8	15	19	36	57	39	0.928571

SQUAD 1981–82   10TH IN DIVISION 1

Kevin BOND	Central defender	Steve KINSEY	Winger
Tommy BOOTH	Central defender	Andy MAY	Midfielder
Phil BOYER	Forward	Bobby McDONALD	Left back
Tommy CATON	Central defender	Martin O'NEILL	Midfielder
Joe CORRIGAN	Goalkeeper	Paul POWER	Midfielder
Andy ELLIOTT	Midfielder	Ray RANSON	Right back
Trevor FRANCIS	Forward	Kevin REEVES	Forward
Gerry GOW	Midfielder	Nicky REID	Defender/Midfielder
Aage HAREIDE	Defender	John RYAN	Midfielder/Right back
Asa HARTFORD	Midfielder	Dennis TUEART	Winger
Tony HENRY	Midfielder	Alex WILLIAMS	Goalkeeper
Tommy HUTCHISON	Winger	Clive WILSON	Defender/Midfielder
Gary JACKSON	Midfielder		

MANCHESTER CITY

Season	League	League Position	P	W	D	L	F	A	Pts	3 Point Equivalent
1991–92	Division 1	5	42	20	10	12	61	48	70	1.666667
1990–91	Division 1	5	38	17	11	10	64	53	62	1.631579
1998–99	L2	3	46	22	8	16	69	33	82	1.608696
1996–97	L1	14	46	17	19	10	59	60	61	1.521739
1992–93	**Premier League**	**9**	**42**	**15**	**12**	**15**	**56**	**51**	**57**	**1.357143**
1989–90	Division 1	14	38	12	12	14	43	52	48	1.263158
1997–98	L1	22	46	12	22	12	56	57	48	1.260870
1994–95	Premier League	17	42	12	13	17	53	64	49	1.166667
1993–94	Premier League	16	42	9	18	15	38	49	45	1.071429
1995–96	Premier League	18	38	9	11	18	33	58	38	1.000000

SQUAD 1992–93   9TH IN THE PREMIER LEAGUE

David BRIGHTWELL	Defender/Centre back	Steve McMAHON	Midfielder
Ian BRIGHTWELL	Defender/Right back	Adie MIKE	Forward
Tony COTON	Goalkeeper	Terry PHELAN	Defender/Left back
Keith CURLE	Defender/Centre back	Michael QUIGLEY	Midfielder
Andy DIBBLE	Goalkeeper	Niall QUINN	Forward
Garry FLITCROFT	Midfielder	Ray RANSON	Right back
Andy HILL	Right back	Peter REID	Midfielder
Rick HOLDEN	Winger	Mike SHERON	Forward
Kaare INGEBRIGTSEN	Midfielder	Fitzroy SIMPSON	Midfielder
David KERR	Midfielder	Michel VONK	Central defender
Paul LAKE	Midfielder	David WHITE	Forward
Martyn MARGETSON	Goalkeeper		

Season	League	League Position	P	W	D	L	F	A	Pts	3 Point Equivalent
2001–02	League 1	1	46	31	9	6	108	52	99	2.217391
1999–2000	L1	2	46	26	9	11	78	40	89	1.891304
2004–05	**Premier League**	**8**	**38**	**13**	**13**	**12**	**47**	**39**	**52**	**1.368421**
2002–03	Premier League	9	38	15	6	17	47	54	51	1.342105
2005–06	Premier League	15	38	13	4	21	43	48	43	1.131579
2006–07	Premier League	14	38	11	9	18	29	44	42	1.105263
2003–04	Premier League	16	38	9	14	15	55	54	41	1.078947
2000–01	Premier League	18	38	8	10	20	41	65	34	0.894737

SQUAD 2004–05   8TH IN THE PREMIER LEAGUE

Nicolas ANELKA	Forward	Kiki MUSAMPA	Midfielder
Joey BARTON	Midfielder	Christian NEGOUAI	Midfielder
Paul BOSVELT	Midfielder	Nedum ONUOHA	Defender
Lee CROFT	Midfielder	Claudio REYNA	Midfielder
Sylvain DISTIN	Defender	Antoine SIBIERSKI	Midfielder
Richard DUNNE	Defender/Centre back	Trevor SINCLAIR	Midfielder
Willo FLOOD	Midfielder	David SOMMEIL	Defender
Robbie FOWLER	Forward	Sun JIHAI	Defender
David JAMES	Goalkeeper	Ben THATCHER	Defender/Left back
Stephen JORDAN	Defender	Nicky WEAVER	Goalkeeper
Jonathan MACKEN	Forward	Bradley WRIGHT-PHILLIPS	Forward
Steve McMANAMAN	Midfielder	Shaun WRIGHT-PHILLIPS	Midfielder/Forward
Danny MILLS	Defender		

MANCHESTER UNITED

Season	League	League Position	P	W	D	L	F	A	Pts	3 Point Equivalent
1956–57	Division 1	1	42	28	8	6	103	54	64	2.190476
1955–56	Division 1	1	42	25	10	7	83	51	60	2.023810
1950–51	Division 1	2	42	24	8	10	74	40	56	1.904762
1951–52	Division 1	1	42	23	11	8	95	52	57	1.904762
1958–59	Division 1	2	42	24	7	11	103	66	55	1.880952
1946–47	Division 1	2	42	22	12	8	95	54	56	1.857143
1948–49	Division 1	2	42	21	11	10	77	44	53	1.761905
1947–48	Division 1	2	42	19	14	9	81	48	52	1.690476
1949–50	Division 1	4	42	18	14	10	69	44	50	1.619048
1954–55	Division 1	5	42	20	7	15	84	74	47	1.595238
1953–54	Division 1	4	42	18	12	12	73	58	48	1.571429
1952–53	Division 1	8	42	18	10	14	69	72	46	1.523810
1957–58	Division 1	9	42	16	11	15	85	75	43	1.404762

1940s & 50s

SQUAD 1956–57 — CHAMPIONS OF DIVISION 1

Geoff BENT	Full back	Freddie GOODWIN	Wing half
Johnny BERRY	Outside right	Ian GREAVES	Full back
Jackie BLANCHFLOWER	Centre half	Tony HAWKSWORTH	Goalkeeper
Roger BYRNE	Full back	Mark JONES	Centre half
Bobby CHARLTON	Centre forward	Wilf McGUINNESS	Wing half
Gordon CLAYTON	Goalkeeper	David PEGG	Outside left
Eddie COLMAN	Wing half	Albert SCANLON	Outside left
Ron COPE	Centre half	Tommy TAYLOR	Centre forward
Alex DAWSON	Centre forward	Dennis VIOLLET	Centre forward
John DOHERTY	Inside forward	Colin WEBSTER	Centre forward
Duncan EDWARDS	Wing half	Liam WHELAN	Inside forward
Bill FOULKES	Defender	Ray WOOD	Goalkeeper

Season	League	League Position	P	W	D	L	F	A	Pts	3 Point Equivalent
1964–65	Division 1	1	42	26	9	7	89	39	61	2.071429
1966–67	Division 1	1	42	24	12	6	84	45	60	2.000000
1967–68	Division 1	2	42	24	8	10	89	55	56	1.904762
1963–64	Division 1	2	42	23	7	12	90	62	53	1.809524
1965–66	Division 1	4	42	18	15	9	84	59	51	1.642857
1959–60	Division 1	7	42	19	7	16	102	80	45	1.523810
1960–61	Division 1	7	42	18	9	15	88	76	45	1.500000
1968–69	Division 1	11	42	15	12	15	57	53	42	1.357143
1961–62	Division 1	15	42	15	9	18	72	75	39	1.285714
1962–63	Division 1	19	42	12	10	20	67	81	34	1.095238

1960s

SQUAD 1964–65 — CHAMPIONS OF DIVISION 1

John ASTON	Outside left	John FITZPATRICK	Wing half
George BEST	Midfielder/Forward	Bill FOULKES	Defender
Shay BRENNAN	Full back	David GASKELL	Goalkeeper
Noel CANTWELL	Left back	David HERD	Centre forward
Bobby CHARLTON	Centre forward	Denis LAW	Inside forward
John CONNELLY	Outside right	Ian MOIR	Winger
Paddy CRERAND	Right half	David SADLER	Central defender
Tony DUNNE	Left back	Maurice SETTERS	Wing half
Pat DUNNE	Goalkeeper	Nobby STILES	Wing half

Season	League	League Position	P	W	D	L	F	A	Pts	3 Point Equivalent
1974–75	Division 2	1	42	26	9	7	66	30	61	2.071429
1975–76	**Division 1**	**3**	**42**	**23**	**10**	**9**	**68**	**42**	**56**	**1.880952**
1971–72	Division 1	8	42	19	10	13	69	61	48	1.595238
1976–77	Division 1	6	42	18	11	13	71	62	47	1.547619
1978–79	Division 1	9	42	15	15	12	60	63	45	1.428571
1969–70	Division 1	8	42	14	17	11	66	61	45	1.404762
1970–71	Division 1	8	42	16	11	15	65	66	43	1.404762
1977–78	Division 1	10	42	16	10	16	67	63	42	1.380952
1972–73	Division 1	18	42	12	13	17	44	60	37	1.166667
1973–74	Division 1	21	42	10	12	20	38	48	32	1.000000

SQUAD 1975–76 — 3RD IN DIVISION 1

Arthur ALBISTON	Left back	Tommy JACKSON	Midfielder
Martin BUCHAN	Central defender	Jimmy KELLY	Midfielder
Steve COPPELL	Winger	Lou MACARI	Forward
Peter COYNE	Forward	David McCREERY	Midfielder
Gerry DALY	Midfielder	Sammy McILROY	Midfielder
Alex FORSYTH	Left back	Jimmy NICHOLL	Right back
Brian GREENHOFF	Central defender	Stuart PEARSON	Forward
Tony GRIMSHAW	Midfielder	Paddy ROCHE	Goalkeeper
Gordon HILL	Winger	Alex STEPNEY	Goalkeeper
Stewart HOUSTON	Defender	Tony YOUNG	Midfielder

Season	League	League Position	P	W	D	L	F	A	Pts	3 Point Equivalent
1987–88	**Division 1**	**2**	**40**	**23**	**12**	**5**	**71**	**38**	**81**	**2.025000**
1979–80	Division 1	2	42	24	10	8	65	35	58	1.952381
1981–82	Division 1	3	42	22	12	8	59	29	78	1.857143
1984–85	Division 1	4	42	22	10	10	77	47	76	1.809524
1985–86	Division 1	4	42	22	10	10	70	36	76	1.809524
1983–84	Division 1	4	42	20	14	8	71	41	74	1.761905
1982–83	Division 1	3	42	19	13	10	56	38	70	1.666667
1980–81	Division 1	8	42	15	18	9	51	36	48	1.500000
1988–89	Division 1	11	38	13	12	13	45	35	51	1.342105
1986–87	Division 1	11	42	14	14	14	52	45	56	1.333333

SQUAD 1987–88 — 2ND IN DIVISION 1

Arthur ALBISTON	Left back	Brian McCLAIR	Midfielder
Viv ANDERSON	Right back	Paul McGRATH	Central defender/Midfielder
Clayton BLACKMORE	Midfielder/Full back	Kevin MORAN	Central defender
Steve BRUCE	Central defender	Remi MOSES	Midfielder
Peter DAVENPORT	Forward	Liam O'BRIEN	Midfielder
Mike DUXBURY	Full back/Midfielder	Jesper OLSEN	Left Winger
Billy GARTON	Central defender	Bryan ROBSON	Midfielder
Colin GIBSON	Left back/Midfielder	Gordon STRACHAN	Right Midfielder
Deiniol GRAHAM	Forward	Chris TURNER	Goalkeeper
Graeme HOGG	Defender/Centre back	Gary WALSH	Goalkeeper
Lee MARTIN	Left back	Norman WHITESIDE	Midfielder/Forward

Season	League	League Position	P	W	D	L	F	A	Pts	3 Point Equivalent
1993–94	**Premier League**	1	42	27	11	4	80	38	92	2.190476
1995–96	Premier League	1	38	25	7	6	73	35	82	2.157895
1994–95	Premier League	2	42	26	10	6	77	28	88	2.095238
1998–99	Premier League	1	38	22	13	3	80	37	79	2.078947
1997–98	Premier League	2	38	23	8	7	73	26	77	2.026316
1992–93	Premier League	1	42	24	12	6	67	31	84	2.000000
1996–97	Premier League	1	38	21	12	5	76	44	75	1.973684
1991–92	Division 1	2	42	21	15	6	63	33	78	1.857143
1990–91	Division 1	6	38	16	12	10	58	45	59	1.578947
1989–90	Division 1	13	38	13	9	16	46	47	48	1.263158

SQUAD 1993–94 — CHAMPIONS OF THE PREMIER LEAGUE

Steve BRUCE	Central defender	Brian McCLAIR	Midfielder
Nicky BUTT	Midfielder	Colin McKEE	Forward
Eric CANTONA	Forward	Gary NEVILLE	Defender/Right back
Dion DUBLIN	Defender/Forward	Gary PALLISTER	Defender/Centre back
Darren FERGUSON	Midfielder	Paul PARKER	Defender
Ryan GIGGS	Midfielder	Mike PHELAN	Midfielder
Mark HUGHES	Forward	Bryan ROBSON	Midfielder
Paul INCE	Midfielder	Peter SCHMEICHEL	Goalkeeper
Denis IRWIN	Defender/Full back	Lee SHARPE	Midfielder
Andrei KANCHELSKIS	Midfielder	Ben THORNLEY	Forward
Roy KEANE	Midfielder	Gary WALSH	Goalkeeper
Lee MARTIN	Left back		

Season	League	League Position	P	W	D	L	F	A	Pts	3 Point Equivalent
1999–2000	**Premier League**	1	38	28	7	3	97	45	91	2.394737
2006–07	Premier League	1	38	28	5	5	83	27	89	2.342105
2002–03	Premier League	1	38	25	8	5	74	34	83	2.184211
2005–06	Premier League	2	38	25	8	5	72	34	83	2.184211
2000–01	Premier League	1	38	24	8	6	79	31	80	2.105263
2001–02	Premier League	3	38	24	5	9	87	45	77	2.026316
2004–05	Premier League	3	38	22	11	5	58	26	77	2.026316
2003–04	Premier League	3	38	23	6	9	64	35	75	1.973684

SQUAD 1999–2000 — CHAMPIONS OF THE PREMIER LEAGUE

David BECKHAM	Midfielder	Roy KEANE	Midfielder
Henning BERG	Defender/Centre back	David MAY	Defender/Centre back
Mark BOSNICH	Goalkeeper	Gary NEVILLE	Defender/Right back
Nicky BUTT	Midfielder	Phil NEVILLE	Defender/Midfielder
Michael CLEGG	Defender	Paul SCHOLES	Midfielder
Andrew COLE	Forward	Teddy SHERINGHAM	Forward
Jordi CRUYFF	Midfielder	Mikael SILVESTRE	Defender
Nick CULKIN	Goalkeeper	Ole Gunnar SOLSKJAER	Forward
John CURTIS	Defender/Right back	Jaap STAM	Defender/Centre back
Quinton FORTUNE	Midfielder	Massimo TAIBI	Goalkeeper
Ryan GIGGS	Midfielder	Raimond VAN DER GOUW	Goalkeeper
Jonathan GREENING	Midfielder	Ronnie WALLWORK	Midfielder
Danny HIGGINBOTHAM	Defender/Left back	Mark WILSON	Midfielder
Denis IRWIN	Defender/Full back	Dwight YORKE	Forward
Ronny JOHNSEN	Defender/Centre back		

MIDDLESBROUGH

Season	League	League Position	P	W	D	L	F	A	Pts	3 Point Equivalent
1956–57	Division 2	6	42	19	10	13	84	60	48	1.595238
1949–50	**Division 1**	**9**	**42**	**20**	**7**	**15**	**59**	**48**	**47**	**1.595238**
1950–51	Division 1	6	42	18	11	13	76	65	47	1.547619
1957–58	Division 2	7	42	19	7	16	83	74	45	1.523810
1954–55	Division 2	12	42	18	6	18	73	82	42	1.428571
1946–47	Division 1	11	42	17	8	17	73	68	42	1.404762
1955–56	Division 2	14	42	16	8	18	76	78	40	1.333333
1958–59	Division 2	13	42	15	10	17	87	71	40	1.309524
1952–53	Division 1	13	42	14	11	17	70	77	39	1.261905
1947–48	Division 1	16	42	14	9	19	71	73	37	1.214286
1951–52	Division 1	18	42	15	6	21	64	88	36	1.214286
1948–49	Division 1	19	42	11	12	19	46	57	34	1.071429
1953–54	Division 1	21	42	10	10	22	60	91	30	0.952381

SQUAD 1949–50   9TH IN DIVISION 1

Harry BELL	Wing half	John HODGSON	Goalkeeper
Tommy BLENKINSOPP	Defender	Billy LINACRE	Forward
Joe BROWN	Wing half	Wilf MANNION	Inside forward
Lindy DELAPENHA	Forward	Alex McCRAE	Inside forward
Peter DESMOND	Inside forward	Peter McKENNAN	Inside forward
Ronnie DICKS	Wing half	Martin REAGAN	Winger
Harold DOBBIE	Centre forward	Stan RICKABY	Full back
Mick FENTON	Centre forward	Dick ROBINSON	Full back
Arthur FITZSIMONS	Inside forward	Johnny SPUHLER	Centre forward
Jimmy GORDON	Wing half	Rolando UGOLINI	Goalkeeper
George HARDWICK	Full back	Geoff WALKER	Outside left
Jimmy HARTNETT	Outside left	Billy WHITAKER	Centre half
Gordon HEPPLE	Full back	Tom WOODWARD	Outside right

Season	League	League Position	P	W	D	L	F	A	Pts	3 Point Equivalent
1966–67	Division 3	2	46	23	9	14	87	64	55	1.695652
1962–63	**Division 2**	**4**	**42**	**20**	**9**	**13**	**86**	**85**	**49**	**1.642857**
1968–69	Division 2	4	42	19	11	12	58	49	49	1.619048
1959–60	Division 2	5	42	19	10	13	90	64	48	1.595238
1960–61	Division 2	5	42	18	12	12	83	74	48	1.571429
1967–68	Division 2	6	42	17	12	13	60	54	46	1.500000
1963–64	Division 2	10	42	15	11	16	67	52	41	1.333333
1961–62	Division 2	12	42	16	7	19	76	72	39	1.309524
1964–65	Division 2	17	42	13	9	20	70	76	35	1.142857
1965–66	Division 2	21	42	10	13	19	58	86	33	1.023810

SQUAD 1962–63   4TH IN DIVISION 2

Bob APPLEBY	Goalkeeper	Cyril KNOWLES	Left back
Ron BURBECK	Winger	Arthur LIGHTENING	Goalkeeper
Neville CHAPMAN	Right back	Joe LIVINGSTONE	Centre forward
Morris EMMERSON	Goalkeeper	Mick McNEIL	Full back
Bill GATES	Centre half	Dick NEAL	Wing half
Ian GIBSON	Midfielder	Mel NURSE	Centre half
Bill HARRIS	Inside forward/Wing half	Bryan ORRITT	Inside forward
Billy HORNER	Defender	Alan PEACOCK	Centre forward
Bobby HUME	Outside left	Bill POVEY	Winger
Gordon JONES	Full back	Ken THOMSON	Centre half
Arthur KAYE	Outside right	Ray YEOMAN	Wing half

Season	League	League Position	P	W	D	L	F	A	Pts	3 Point Equivalent
1973–74	Division 2	1	42	27	11	4	77	30	65	2.190476
1969–70	Division 2	4	42	20	10	12	55	45	50	1.666667
1974–75	**Division 1**	**7**	**42**	**18**	**12**	**12**	**54**	**40**	**48**	**1.571429**
1970–71	Division 2	7	42	17	14	11	60	43	48	1.547619
1971–72	Division 2	9	42	19	8	15	50	48	46	1.547619
1972–73	Division 2	4	42	17	13	12	46	43	47	1.523810
1975–76	Division 1	13	42	15	10	17	46	45	40	1.309524
1976–77	Division 1	12	42	14	13	15	40	45	41	1.309524
1978–79	Division 1	12	42	15	10	17	57	50	40	1.309524
1977–78	Division 1	14	42	12	15	15	42	54	39	1.214286

1970s

SQUAD 1974–75   7TH IN DIVISION 1

David ARMSTRONG	Midfielder	David MILLS	Forward
Stuart BOAM	Central defender	Bobby MURDOCH	Midfielder
Peter BRINE	Midfielder	Tom PATERSON	Forward
Harry CHARLTON	Midfielder	Jim PLATT	Goalkeeper
Terry COOPER	Left back	Malcolm SMITH	Forward
John CRAGGS	Right back	Graeme SOUNESS	Midfielder
Alan FOGGON	Winger	Frank SPRAGGON	Defender
John HICKTON	Forward	Brian TAYLOR	Central defender
Willie MADDREN	Central defender	Alan WILLEY	Forward
Tony McANDREW	Central defender	Billy WOOF	Forward

Season	League	League Position	P	W	D	L	F	A	Pts	3 Point Equivalent
1986–87	Division 3	2	46	28	10	8	67	30	94	2.043478
1987–88	Division 2	3	44	22	12	10	63	36	78	1.772727
1979–80	**Division 1**	**9**	**42**	**16**	**12**	**14**	**50**	**44**	**44**	**1.428571**
1980–81	Division 1	14	42	16	5	21	53	61	37	1.261905
1983–84	Division 2	17	42	12	13	17	41	47	49	1.166667
1982–83	Division 2	16	42	11	15	16	46	67	48	1.142857
1985–86	Division 2	21	42	12	9	21	44	53	45	1.071429
1988–89	Division 1	18	38	9	12	17	44	61	39	1.026316
1984–85	Division 2	19	42	10	10	22	41	57	40	0.952381
1981–82	Division 1	22	42	8	15	19	34	52	39	0.928571

1980s

SQUAD 1979–80   9TH IN DIVISION 1

Mike ANGUS	Midfielder	Bozo JANKOVIC	Forward
David ARMSTRONG	Midfielder	Peter JOHNSON	Left back
Billy ASHCROFT	Forward	Craig JOHNSTON	Forward/Winger
Billy ASKEW	Midfielder	Tony McANDREW	Central defender
Ian BAILEY	Left back	Irving NATTRASS	Right back
Ian BELL	Midfielder	Jeff PETERS	Left back
Micky BURNS	Forward	Jim PLATT	Goalkeeper
Terry COCHRANE	Winger	Mark PROCTOR	Midfielder
John CRAGGS	Right back	Alan RAMAGE	Central defender
Stan CUMMINS	Midfielder	Dave SHEARER	Forward
Graeme HEDLEY	Midfielder	Jim STEWART	Goalkeeper
David HODGSON	Forward	Billy WOOF	Forward

Season	League	League Position	P	W	D	L	F	A	Pts	3 Point Equivalent
1997–98	L1	2	46	27	9	10	77	41	91	1.956522
1991–92	Division 2	2	46	23	11	12	58	41	80	1.739130
1994–95	L1	1	46	23	10	13	67	40	82	1.717391
1990–91	Division 2	7	46	20	9	17	66	47	69	1.500000
1993–94	L1	9	46	18	15	13	66	54	67	1.500000
1998–99	**Premier League**	**9**	**38**	**12**	**15**	**11**	**48**	**54**	**51**	**1.342105**
1995–96	Premier League	12	38	11	10	17	35	50	43	1.131579
1996–97	Premier League	19	38	10	12	16	51	60	39	1.105263
1989–90	Division 2	21	46	13	11	22	52	63	50	1.086957
1992–93	Premier League	21	42	11	11	20	54	75	44	1.047619

SQUAD 1998–99   9TH IN THE PREMIER LEAGUE

Alun ARMSTRONG	Forward		Vladimir KINDER	Defender
Steve BAKER	Defender		Neil MADDISON	Midfielder
Mikkel BECK	Forward		Paul MERSON	Midfielder
Marlon BERESFORD	Goalkeeper		Alan MOORE	Midfielder
Marco BRANCA	Centre forward		Robbie MUSTOE	Midfielder
Andy CAMPBELL	Forward		Keith O'NEILL	Midfielder
Colin COOPER	Defender/Centre back		Gary PALLISTER	Defender/Centre back
Michael CUMMINS	Midfielder		Hamilton RICARD	Forward
Brian DEANE	Forward		Mark SCHWARZER	Goalkeeper
Gianluca FESTA	Centre back		Phil STAMP	Midfielder
Curtis FLEMING	Defender/Right back		Robbie STOCKDALE	Defender/Right back
Paul GASCOIGNE	Midfielder		Mark SUMMERBELL	Midfielder
Jason GAVIN	Defender/Centre back		Andy TOWNSEND	Midfielder
Dean GORDON	Defender/Left back		Steve VICKERS	Centre back
Craig HARRISON	Defender/Left back			

Season	League	League Position	P	W	D	L	F	A	Pts	3 Point Equivalent
2004–05	**Premier League**	**7**	**38**	**14**	**13**	**11**	**53**	**46**	**55**	**1.447368**
1999–2000	Premier League	12	38	14	10	14	46	52	52	1.368421
2002–03	Premier League	11	38	13	10	15	48	44	49	1.289474
2003–04	Premier League	11	38	13	9	16	44	52	48	1.263158
2006–07	Premier League	12	38	12	10	16	44	49	46	1.210526
2001–02	Premier League	12	38	12	9	17	35	47	45	1.184211
2005–06	Premier League	14	38	12	9	17	48	58	45	1.184211
2000–01	Premier League	14	38	9	15	14	44	44	42	1.105263

SQUAD 2004–05   7TH IN THE PREMIER LEAGUE

Matthew BATES	Defender/Centre back		Gaizka MENDIETA	Midfielder
George BOATENG	Midfielder		James MORRISON	Midfielder
Malcolm CHRISTI E	Forward		Carlo NASH	Goalkeeper
Colin COOPER	Defender/Centre back		Szilard NEMETH	Forward
Andrew DAVIES	Defender/Centre back		Ray PARLOUR	Midfielder
Dorival Guidoni Junior DORIVA	Midfielder		Stuart PARNABY	Defender/Midfielder
Stewart DOWNING	Midfielder		Franck QUEUDRUE	Defender/Left back
Ugo EHIOGU	Defender/Centre back		Michael REIZIGER	Defender/Right Back
Danny GRAHAM	Forward		Chris RIGGOTT	Defender/Centre back
Jimmy Floyd HASSELBAINK	Forward		Mark SCHWARZER	Goalkeeper
Joseph-Desire JOB	Forward		Gareth SOUTHGATE	Defender/Centre back
Brad JONES	Goalkeeper		Mark VIDUKA	Forward
Jason KENNEDY	Midfielder		Bolo ZENDEN	Midfielder
Tony McMAHON	Defender/Right back			

NEWCASTLE UNITED

Season	League	League Position	P	W	D	L	F	A	Pts	3 Point Equivalent
1947–48	Division 2	2	42	24	8	10	72	41	56	1.904762
1948–49	**Division 1**	**4**	**42**	**20**	**12**	**10**	**70**	**56**	**52**	**1.714286**
1949–50	Division 1	5	42	19	12	11	77	55	50	1.642857
1946–47	Division 2	5	42	19	10	13	95	62	48	1.595238
1950–51	Division 1	4	42	18	13	11	62	53	49	1.595238
1951–52	Division 1	8	42	18	9	15	98	73	45	1.500000
1954–55	Division 1	8	42	17	9	16	89	77	43	1.428571
1955–56	Division 1	11	42	17	7	18	85	70	41	1.380952
1958–59	Division 1	11	42	17	7	18	80	80	41	1.380952
1953–54	Division 1	15	42	14	10	18	72	77	38	1.238095
1952–53	Division 1	16	42	14	9	19	59	70	37	1.214286
1956–57	Division 1	17	42	14	8	20	67	87	36	1.190476
1957–58	Division 1	19	42	12	8	22	73	81	32	1.047619

SQUAD 1948–49 — 4TH IN DIVISION 1

Ron BATTY	Left back	Joe HARVEY	Wing half
Frank BRENNAN	Centre half	Frank HOUGHTON	Inside forward/Wing half
Albert CLARK	Wing half	George LOWRIE	Centre forward
Bobby COWELL	Full back	William McCALL	Outside left
Benny CRAIG	Full back	Jackie MILBURN	Centre forward
Norman DODGIN	Wing half	Bobby MITCHELL	Outside left
Andy DONALDSON	Centre forward	George ROBLEDO	Inside forward
Jack FAIRBROTHER	Goalkeeper	Albert SIBLEY	Outside right
Bob FRASER	Centre half	George STOBBART	Inside forward
Eric GARBUTT	Goalkeeper	Ernie TAYLOR	Inside forward
Colin GIBSON	Outside right	Tommy THOMPSON	Inside forward
Doug GRAHAM	Full back	Tommy WALKER	Outside right
George HAIR	Outside left		

Season	League	League Position	P	W	D	L	F	A	Pts	3 Point Equivalent
1964–65	Division 2	1	42	24	9	9	81	45	57	1.928571
1962–63	Division 2	7	42	18	11	13	79	59	47	1.547619
1963–64	Division 2	8	42	20	5	17	74	69	45	1.547619
1959–60	**Division 1**	**8**	**42**	**18**	**8**	**16**	**82**	**78**	**44**	**1.476190**
1968–69	Division 1	9	42	15	14	13	61	55	44	1.404762
1961–62	Division 2	11	42	15	9	18	64	58	39	1.285714
1967–68	Division 1	10	42	13	15	14	54	67	41	1.285714
1965–66	Division 1	15	42	14	9	19	50	63	37	1.214286
1966–67	Division 1	20	42	12	9	21	39	81	33	1.071429
1960–61	Division 1	21	42	11	10	21	86	109	32	1.023810

SQUAD 1959–60 — 8TH IN DIVISION 1

Ivor ALLCHURCH	Inside forward	Alf McMICHAEL	Full back
Jackie BELL	Wing half	Bobby MITCHELL	Outside left
George EASTHAM	Inside forward	Stewart MITCHELL	Goalkeeper
Bobby FERGUSON	Full back	John MITTEN	Winger
Albert FRANKS	Wing half	Malcolm SCOTT	Centre half
Bobby GILFILLAN	Forward	Jimmy SCOULAR	Wing half
Ken HALE	Inside forward	Ronnie SIMPSON	Goalkeeper
Bryan HARVEY	Goalkeeper	Bob STOKOE	Centre half
George HESLOP	Centre half	Alex TAIT	Centre forward
Gordon HUGHES	Outside right	John TAYLOR	Outside right
Dick KEITH	Right back	Len WHITE	Centre forward
George LUKE	Outside left	Bob WHITEHEAD	Full back
John McGUIGAN	Inside forward	Brian WRIGHT	Wing half
Bill McKINNEY	Right back		

Season	League	League Position	P	W	D	L	F	A	Pts	3 Point Equivalent
1976–77	**Division 1**	5	42	18	13	11	64	49	49	1.595238
1969–70	Division 1	7	42	17	13	12	57	35	47	1.523810
1972–73	Division 1	9	42	16	13	13	60	51	45	1.452381
1978–79	Division 2	8	42	17	8	17	51	55	42	1.404762
1971–72	Division 1	11	42	15	11	16	49	52	41	1.333333
1970–71	Division 1	12	42	14	13	15	44	46	41	1.309524
1974–75	Division 1	15	42	15	9	18	59	72	39	1.285714
1975–76	Division 1	15	42	15	9	18	71	62	39	1.285714
1973–74	Division 1	15	42	13	12	17	49	48	38	1.214286
1977–78	Division 1	21	42	6	10	26	42	78	22	0.666667

1970s

SQUAD 1976–77   5TH IN DIVISION 1

Stewart BARROWCLOUGH	Winger	Pat HOWARD	Central defender
John BIRD	Central defender	Ray HUDSON	Midfielder
Ray BLACKHALL	Right back	Alan KENNEDY	Left back
Micky BURNS	Forward	Mick MAHONEY	Goalkeeper
Paul CANNELL	Forward	Aiden McCAFFREY	Central defender
Tommy CASSIDY	Midfielder	Kenny MITCHELL	Central defender
David CRAIG	Right back	Irving NATTRASS	Right back
Tommy CRAIG	Midfielder	Geoff NULTY	Midfielder
Alan GOWLING	Forward	Graham OATES	Defender/Midfielder
Alan GUY	Midfielder	John TUDOR	Forward

Season	League	League Position	P	W	D	L	F	A	Pts	3 Point Equivalent
1983–84	Division 2	3	42	24	8	10	85	53	80	1.904762
1982–83	Division 2	5	42	18	13	11	75	53	67	1.595238
1985–86	**Division 1**	11	42	17	12	13	67	72	63	1.500000
1981–82	Division 2	9	42	18	8	16	52	50	62	1.476190
1979–80	Division 2	9	42	15	14	13	53	49	44	1.404762
1987–88	Division 1	8	40	14	14	12	55	53	56	1.400000
1980–81	Division 2	11	42	14	14	14	30	45	42	1.333333
1984–85	Division 1	14	42	13	13	16	55	70	52	1.238095
1986–87	Division 1	17	42	12	11	19	47	65	47	1.119048
1988–89	Division 1	20	38	7	10	21	32	63	31	0.815789

1980s

SQUAD 1985–86   11TH IN DIVISION 1

John ANDERSON	Defender	David McKELLAR	Goalkeeper
John BAILEY	Left back	Robert McKINNON	Defender
Peter BEARDSLEY	Forward	Gary MEGSON	Midfielder
Jeff CLARKE	Central defender	George REILLY	Forward
Tony CUNNINGHAM	Forward	Glenn ROEDER	Central defender
Alan DAVIES	Winger	Paul STEPHENSON	Midfielder
Paul GASCOIGNE	Midfielder	Ian STEWART	Winger
Peter HADDOCK	Defender	Martin THOMAS	Goalkeeper
Chris HEDWORTH	Defender	Kenny WHARTON	Left back/Midfielder
David McCREERY	Midfielder	Billy WHITEHURST	Forward
Neil McDONALD	Right back/Midfielder		

Season	League	League Position	P	W	D	L	F	A	Pts	3 Point Equivalent
1992–93	L1	1	46	29	8	9	92	38	96	2.065217
1995–96	**Premier League**	**2**	**38**	**24**	**6**	**8**	**66**	**37**	**78**	**2.052632**
1993–94	Premier League	3	42	23	8	11	82	41	77	1.833333
1996–97	Premier League	2	38	19	11	8	73	40	68	1.789474
1989–90	Division 2	3	46	22	14	10	80	55	80	1.739130
1994–95	Premier League	6	42	20	12	10	67	47	72	1.714286
1990–91	Division 2	11	46	14	17	15	49	56	59	1.282609
1998–99	Premier League	13	38	11	13	14	48	54	46	1.210526
1997–98	Premier League	13	38	11	11	16	35	44	44	1.157895
1991–92	Division 2	20	46	13	13	20	66	84	52	1.130435

SQUAD 1995–96 — 2ND IN THE PREMIER LEAGUE

Philippe ALBERT	Defender/Centre back
Faustino ASPRILLA	Forward
Warren BARTON	Defender/Right back
David BATTY	Midfielder
Peter BEARDSLEY	Forward
John BERESFORD	Defender/Left back
Lee CLARK	Midfielder
Robbie ELLIOTT	Defender/Midfielder
Les FERDINAND	Forward
Ruel FOX	Midfielder
Keith GILLESPIE	Midfielder
David GINOLA	Midfielder
Shaka HISLOP	Goalkeeper
Marc HOTTIGER	Right back
Steve HOWEY	Defender/Centre back
Darren HUCKERBY	Forward
Paul KITSON	Forward
Rob LEE	Midfielder
Darren PEACOCK	Defender/Centre back
Scott SELLARS	Midfielder
Pavel SRNICEK	Goalkeeper
Steve WATSON	Defender

Season	League	League Position	P	W	D	L	F	A	Pts	3 Point Equivalent
2001–02	**Premier League**	**4**	**38**	**21**	**8**	**9**	**74**	**52**	**71**	**1.868421**
2002–03	Premier League	3	38	21	6	11	63	48	69	1.815789
2005–06	Premier League	7	38	17	7	14	47	42	58	1.526316
2003–04	Premier League	5	38	13	17	8	52	40	56	1.473684
1999–2000	Premier League	11	38	14	10	14	63	54	52	1.368421
2000–01	Premier League	11	38	14	9	15	44	50	51	1.342105
2004–05	Premier League	14	38	10	14	14	47	57	44	1.157895
2006–07	Premier League	13	38	11	10	17	38	47	43	1.131579

SQUAD 2001–02 — 4TH IN THE PREMIER LEAGUE

Clarence ACUNA	Midfielder
Shola AMEOBI	Forward
Warren BARTON	Defender/Right back
Christian BASSEDAS	Midfielder
Craig BELLAMY	Forward
Olivier BERNARD	Defender/Left back
Carl CORT	Forward
Nikos DABIZAS	Defender/Centre back
Sylvain DISTIN	Defender
Kieron DYER	Midfielder
Robbie ELLIOTT	Defender/Midfielder
Shay GIVEN	Goalkeeper
Andy GRIFFIN	Defender/Right back
Aaron HUGHES	Defender
Jermaine JENAS	Midfielder
Rob LEE	Midfielder
Lomano Tresor LUA LUA	Forward
Jamie McCLEN	Midfielder
Andy O'BRIEN	Defender/Centre back
Laurent ROBERT	Midfielder
Alan SHEARER	Forward
Nolberto SOLANO	Midfielder
Gary SPEED	Defender/Midfielder

NORWICH CITY

1940s & 50s

Season	League	League Position	P	W	D	L	F	A	Pts	3 Point Equivalent
1950–51	Division 3 South	2	46	25	14	7	82	45	64	1.934783
1951–52	Division 3 South	3	46	26	9	11	89	50	61	1.891304
1952–53	Division 3 South	4	46	25	10	11	99	55	60	1.847826
1958–59	Division 3	4	46	22	13	11	89	62	57	1.717391
1957–58	Division 3 South	8	46	19	15	12	75	70	53	1.565217
1953–54	Division 3 South	7	46	20	11	15	73	66	51	1.543478
1955–56	Division 3 South	7	46	19	13	14	86	82	51	1.521739
1948–49	Division 3 South	10	42	16	12	14	67	49	44	1.428571
1954–55	Division 3 South	12	46	18	10	18	60	60	46	1.391304
1949–50	Division 3 South	11	42	16	10	16	65	63	42	1.380952
1947–48	Division 3 South	21	42	13	8	21·	61	76	34	1.119048
1946–47	Division 3 South	21	42	10	8	24	64	100	28	0.904762
1956–57	Division 3 South	24	46	8	15	23	61	94	31	0.847826

SQUAD 1950–51 — 2ND IN DIVISION 3 SOUTH

Eric ARNOLD	Full back	Roy HOLLIS	Centre forward
Ron ASHMAN	Defender	Bert HOLMES	Centre half
Jack BRADLEY	Inside forward	Noel KINSEY	Inside forward
Tom DOCHERTY	Outside left	Bill LEWIS	Full back
John DUFFY	Full back	Dennis MORGAN	Full back
Len DUTTON	Wing half	Ken NETHERCOTT	Goalkeeper
George EPHGRAVE	Goalkeeper	Les OWENS	Centre forward
Les EYRE	Inside forward	Don PICKWICK	Wing half
Reg FOULKES	Centre half	Johnny SUMMERS	Forward
Johnny GAVIN	Outside right	Maurice TOBIN	Left back

224

1960s

Season	League	League Position	P	W	D	L	F	A	Pts	3 Point Equivalent
1959–60	Division 3	2	46	24	11	11	82	54	59	1.804348
1960–61	Division 2	4	42	20	9	13	70	53	49	1.642857
1964–65	Division 2	6	42	20	7	15	61	57	47	1.595238
1962–63	Division 2	13	42	17	8	17	80	79	42	1.404762
1967–68	Division 2	9	42	16	11	15	60	65	43	1.404762
1968–69	Division 2	13	42	15	10	17	53	56	40	1.309524
1966–67	Division 2	11	42	13	14	15	49	55	40	1.261905
1961–62	Division 2	17	42	14	11	17	61	70	39	1.261905
1965–66	Division 2	13	42	12	15	15	52	52	39	1.214286
1963–64	Division 2	17	42	11	13	18	64	80	35	1.095238

SQUAD 1960–61 — 4TH IN DIVISION 2

Terry ALLCOCK	Inside forward	Derrick LYTHGOE	Winger
Ron ASHMAN	Defender	Roy McCROHAN	Wing half
Ollie BURTON	Wing half	Bill PUNTON	Outside left
Barry BUTLER	Centre half	Dick SCOTT	Wing half/Inside forward
Errol CROSSAN	Outside right	Ron SPELMAN	Outside right
Matt CROWE	Wing half	Bryan THURLOW	Right back
Jimmy HILL	Inside forward	George WAITES	Winger
Neil KENNON	Goalkeeper	Brian WHITEHOUSE	Inside forward
Bunny LARKIN	Wing half/Inside forward		

	Season	League	League Position	P	W	D	L	F	A	Pts	3 Point Equivalent
1970s	1971–72	Division 2	1	42	21	15	6	60	36	57	1.857143
	1974–75	Division 2	3	42	20	13	9	58	37	53	1.738095
	1969–70	Division 2	11	42	16	11	15	49	46	43	1.404762
	1970–71	Division 2	10	42	15	14	13	54	52	44	1.404762
	1975–76	**Division 1**	**10**	**42**	**16**	**10**	**16**	**58**	**58**	**42**	**1.380952**
	1976–77	Division 1	16	42	14	9	19	47	64	37	1.214286
	1977–78	Division 1	13	42	11	18	13	52	66	40	1.214286
	1978–79	Division 1	16	42	7	23	12	51	57	37	1.047619
	1972–73	Division 1	20	42	11	10	21	36	63	32	1.023810
	1973–74	Division 1	22	42	7	15	20	37	62	29	0.857143

SQUAD 1975–76   10TH IN DIVISION 1

Kevin BOND	Central defender	Mel MACHIN	Midfielder
Phil BOYER	Forward	John MILLER	Winger
Geoff BUTLER	Defender	Peter MORRIS	Midfielder
Neil DAVIDS	Central defender	Martin PETERS	Midfielder
Duncan FORBES	Central defender	Tony POWELL	Central defender
Steve GRAPES	Midfielder	Billy STEELE	Midfielder
David JONES	Central defender	Dave STRINGER	Defender
Kevin KEELAN	Goalkeeper	Colin SUGGETT	Midfielder
Ted McDOUGALL	Forward	Colin SULLIVAN	Left back
Mick McGUIRE	Midfielder	Paul WILSON	Midfielder

225

	Season	League	League Position	P	W	D	L	F	A	Pts	3 Point Equivalent
1980s	1985–86	Division 2	1	42	25	9	8	84	37	84	2.000000
	1981–82	Division 2	3	42	22	5	15	64	50	71	1.690476
	1988–89	**Division 1**	**4**	**38**	**17**	**11**	**10**	**48**	**45**	**62**	**1.631579**
	1986–87	Division 1	5	42	17	17	8	53	51	68	1.619048
	1982–83	Division 1	14	42	14	12	16	52	58	54	1.285714
	1979–80	Division 1	12	42	13	14	15	58	66	40	1.261905
	1983–84	Division 1	14	42	12	15	15	48	49	51	1.214286
	1984–85	Division 1	20	42	13	10	19	46	64	49	1.166667
	1987–88	Division 1	14	40	12	9	19	40	52	45	1.125000
	1980–81	Division 1	20	42	13	7	22	49	73	33	1.095238

SQUAD 1988–89   4TH IN DIVISION 1

Malcolm ALLEN	Forward	Bryan GUNN	Goalkeeper
Mark BOWEN	Defender/Left back	Andy LINIGHAN	Defender/Centre back
Ian BUTTERWORTH	Central defender	Mike PHELAN	Midfielder
Dean CONEY	Forward	Trevor PUTNEY	Midfielder
Paul COOK	Midfielder	Robert ROSARIO	Forward
Ian CROOK	Midfielder	Jon SHEFFIELD	Goalkeeper
Robert FLECK	Forward	Alan TAYLOR	Forward
Ruel FOX	Midfielder	Andy TOWNSEND	Midfielder
Dale GORDON	Winger		

Season	League	League Position	P	W	D	L	F	A	Pts	3 Point Equivalent
1992–93	**Premier League**	**3**	**42**	**21**	**9**	**12**	**61**	**65**	**72**	**1.714286**
1996–97	L1	13	46	17	17	12	63	68	63	1.478261
1989–90	Division 1	10	38	13	14	11	44	42	53	1.394737
1997–98	L1	15	46	14	19	13	52	69	55	1.326087
1995–96	L1	16	46	14	17	15	59	55	57	1.282609
1998–99	L1	9	46	15	14	17	62	61	62	1.282609
1993–94	Premier League	12	42	12	17	13	65	61	53	1.261905
1990–91	Division 1	15	38	13	6	19	41	64	45	1.184211
1991–92	Division 1	18	42	11	12	19	47	63	45	1.071429
1994–95	Premier League	20	42	10	13	19	37	54	43	1.023810

SQUAD 1992–93   3RD IN THE PREMIER LEAGUE

Darren BECKFORD	Forward	Jason MINETT	Midfielder
Mark BOWEN	Defender/Left back	Rob NEWMAN	Defender/Forward
Ian BUTTERWORTH	Central defender	David PHILLIPS	Defender/Midfielder
Ian CROOK	Midfielder	John POLSTON	Defender/Centre back
Ian CULVERHOUSE	Right back	Lee POWER	Forward
Efan EKOKU	Forward	Mark ROBINS	Forward
Ruel FOX	Midfielder	Dave SMITH	Midfielder
Jeremy GOSS	Midfielder	Daryl SUTCH	Defender
Bryan GUNN	Goalkeeper	Chris SUTTON	Defender/Forward
Andy JOHNSON	Midfielder	Colin WOODTHORPE	Defender/Left back
Gary MEGSON	Midfielder		

Season	League	League Position	P	W	D	L	F	A	Pts	3 Point Equivalent
2003–04	**L1**	**1**	**46**	**28**	**8**	**10**	**79**	**39**	**94**	**2.000000**
2001–02	L1	6	46	22	9	15	60	51	75	1.760870
2002–03	L1	8	46	19	15	12	60	49	69	1.565217
2000–01	L1	15	46	14	20	12	46	58	54	1.347826
2005–06	Championship	9	46	18	8	20	56	65	62	1.347826
1999–2000	L1	12	46	14	17	15	45	50	57	1.282609
2006–07	Championship	16	46	16	9	21	56	71	57	1.239130
2004–05	Premier League	19	38	7	12	19	42	77	33	0.868421

SQUAD 2003–04   CHAMPIONS OF FIRST DIVISION

Zema ABBEY	Forward	Gary HOLT	Midfielder
Jim BRENNAN	Defender	Darren HUCKERBY	Forward
Keith BRIGGS	Defender/Midfielder	Ryan JARVIS	Forward
Kevin COOPER	Midfielder	Malky MACKAY	Defender/Centre back
Peter CROUCH	Forward	Leon McKENZIE	Forward
Adam DRURY	Defender/Left back	Paul McVEIGH	Forward
Clint EASTON	Midfielder	Phil MULRYNE	Midfielder
Marc EDWORTHY	Defender	David NIELSEN	Forward
Craig FLEMING	Defender/Centre back	Alex NOTMAN	Forward
Damien FRANCIS	Midfielder	Mark RIVERS	Forward
Robert GREEN	Goalkeeper	Iwan ROBERTS	Forward
Elvis HAMMOND	Forward	Jason SHACKELL	Defender/Centre back
Kevin HARPER	Midfielder	Matthias SVENSSON	Forward
Ian HENDERSON	Forward		

NOTTINGHAM FOREST

Season	League	League Position	P	W	D	L	F	A	Pts	3 Point Equivalent
1950–51	Division 3 South	1	46	30	10	6	110	40	70	2.173913
1956–57	Division 2	2	42	22	10	10	94	55	54	1.809524
1953–54	Division 2	4	42	20	12	10	86	59	52	1.714286
1949–50	Division 3 South	4	42	20	9	13	67	39	49	1.642857
1951–52	Division 2	4	42	18	13	11	77	62	49	1.595238
1955–56	Division 2	7	42	19	9	14	68	63	47	1.571429
1952–53	Division 2	7	42	18	8	16	77	67	44	1.476190
1957–58	**Division 1**	**10**	**42**	**16**	**10**	**16**	**69**	**63**	**42**	**1.380952**
1958–59	Division 1	13	42	17	6	19	71	74	40	1.357143
1954–55	Division 2	15	42	16	7	19	58	62	39	1.309524
1946–47	Division 2	11	42	15	10	17	69	74	40	1.309524
1948–49	Division 2	21	42	14	7	21	50	54	35	1.166667
1947–48	Division 2	19	42	12	11	19	54	60	35	1.119048

1940s & 50s

SQUAD 1957–58   10TH IN DIVISION 1

Eddie BAILY	Inside left	Arthur LIGHTENING	Goalkeeper
Jim BARRETT	Forward	Bob McKINLAY	Centre half
Jack BURKITT	Wing half	Bill MORLEY	Wing half
Fay COYLE	Centre forward	John QUIGLEY	Inside forward
Ron FARMER	Wing half	Harry SHARRATT	Goalkeeper
Billy GRAY	Winger	Ken SIMCOE	Centre forward
Peter HIGHAM	Centre forward	Geoff THOMAS	Full back
Jack HUTCHINSON	Full back	Chick THOMSON	Goalkeeper
Stuart IMLACH	Outside left	Peter WATSON	Centre half
Eric JONES	Winger	Bill WHARE	Right back
Chris JOYCE	Inside forward	Tommy WILSON	Centre forward

Season	League	League Position	P	W	D	L	F	A	Pts	3 Point Equivalent
1966–67	**Division 1**	**2**	**42**	**23**	**10**	**9**	**64**	**41**	**56**	**1.880952**
1964–65	Division 1	5	42	17	13	12	71	67	47	1.523810
1962–63	Division 1	9	42	17	10	15	67	69	44	1.452381
1963–64	Division 1	13	42	16	9	17	64	68	41	1.357143
1967–68	Division 1	11	42	14	11	17	52	64	39	1.261905
1960–61	Division 1	14	42	14	9	19	62	78	37	1.214286
1965–66	Division 1	18	42	14	8	20	56	72	36	1.190476
1961–62	Division 1	19	42	13	10	19	63	79	36	1.166667
1959–60	Division 1	20	42	13	9	20	50	74	35	1.142857
1968–69	Division 1	18	42	10	13	19	45	57	33	1.023810

1960s

SQUAD 1966–67   2ND IN DIVISION 1

Colin ADDISON	Inside forward	Mike KEAR	Outside right
Joe BAKER	Centre forward	Barry LYONS	Winger
John BARNWELL	Wing half	Bob McKINLAY	Centre half
Sammy CHAPMAN	Central defender	Henry NEWTON	Midfielder/Left back
Chris CROWE	Inside forward	David STAINWRIGHT	Centre forward
Peter GRUMMITT	Goalkeeper	Ian STOREY-MOORE	Winger
Terry HENNESSEY	Central defender	Jeff WHITEFOOT	Wing half
Peter HINDLEY	Right back	Frank WIGNALL	Centre forward
Alan HINTON	Outside left	John WINFIELD	Left back

Season	League	League Position	P	W	D	L	F	A	Pts	3 Point Equivalent
1977–78	**Division 1**	**1**	**42**	**25**	**14**	**3**	**69**	**24**	**64**	**2.119048**
1978–79	Division 1	2	42	21	18	3	61	26	60	1.928571
1976–77	Division 2	3	42	21	10	11	77	43	52	1.738095
1975–76	Division 2	8	42	17	12	13	55	40	46	1.500000
1973–74	Division 2	7	42	15	15	12	57	43	45	1.428571
1972–73	Division 2	14	42	14	12	16	47	52	40	1.285714
1974–75	Division 2	16	42	12	14	16	43	55	38	1.190476
1970–71	Division 1	16	42	14	8	20	42	61	36	1.190476
1969–70	Division 1	15	42	10	18	14	50	71	38	1.142857
1971–72	Division 1	21	42	8	9	25	47	81	25	0.785714

SQUAD 1977–78 — CHAMPIONS OF DIVISION 1

Viv ANDERSON	Right back	John MIDDLETON	Goalkeeper
Colin BARRETT	Full back	Dave NEEDHAM	Central defender
Ian BOWYER	Midfielder	John O'HARE	Forward
Kenny BURNS	Central defender	Martin O'NEILL	Midfielder
Frank CLARK	Left back	John ROBERTSON	Winger
Archie GEMMILL	Midfielder	Peter SHILTON	Goalkeeper
Larry LLOYD	Central defender	Peter WITHE	Forward
John McGOVERN	Midfielder	Tony WOODCOCK	Forward

Season	League	League Position	P	W	D	L	F	A	Pts	3 Point Equivalent
1987–88	**Division 1**	**3**	**40**	**20**	**13**	**7**	**67**	**39**	**73**	**1.825000**
1983–84	Division 1	3	42	22	8	12	76	45	74	1.761905
1988–89	Division 1	3	38	17	13	8	64	43	64	1.684211
1980–81	Division 1	7	42	19	12	11	62	44	50	1.642857
1982–83	Division 1	5	42	20	9	13	62	50	69	1.642857
1979–80	Division 1	5	42	20	8	14	63	43	48	1.619048
1985–86	Division 1	8	42	19	11	12	69	53	68	1.619048
1986–87	Division 1	8	42	18	11	13	64	51	65	1.547619
1984–85	Division 1	9	42	19	7	16	56	48	64	1.523810
1981–82	Division 1	12	42	15	12	15	42	48	57	1.357143

SQUAD 1987–88 — 3RD IN DIVISION 1

Dave CAMPBELL	Midfielder	Calvin PLUMMER	Winger
Franz CARR	Winger	Brian RICE	Winger
Steve CHETTLE	Defender/Centre back	Hans SEGERS	Goalkeeper
Nigel CLOUGH	Midfielder	Phil STARBUCK	Forward
Gary CROSBY	Midfielder	Steve SUTTON	Goalkeeper
Gary FLEMING	Full back	Des WALKER	Defender/Centre back
Colin FOSTER	Central defender	Darren WASSELL	Defender
Tommy GAYNOR	Forward	Neil WEBB	Midfielder
Lee GLOVER	Forward	Paul WILKINSON	Forward
Kjetil OSVOLD	Winger	Brett WILLIAMS	Left back
Garry PARKER	Midfielder	Terry WILSON	Midfielder
Stuart PEARCE	Defender		

Season	League	League Position	P	W	D	L	F	A	Pts	3 Point Equivalent
1997–98	L1	1	46	28	8	10	82	42	94	2.000000
1994–95	**Premier League**	**3**	**42**	**22**	**11**	**9**	**72**	**43**	**77**	**1.833333**
1993–94	L1	2	46	23	9	14	74	49	83	1.695652
1995–96	Premier League	9	38	15	13	10	50	54	58	1.526316
1989–90	Division 1	9	38	15	9	14	55	47	54	1.421053
1990–91	Division 1	8	38	14	12	12	65	50	54	1.421053
1991–92	Division 1	8	42	16	11	15	60	58	59	1.404762
1992–93	Premier League	22	42	10	10	22	41	62	40	0.952381
1996–97	Premier League	20	38	6	16	16	31	59	34	0.894737
1998–99	Premier League	20	38	7	9	22	35	69	30	0.789474

SQUAD 1994–95 — 3RD IN THE PREMIER LEAGUE

Kingsley BLACK	Midfielder
Lars BOHINEN	Midfielder
Garry BULL	Forward
Steve CHETTLE	Defender/Centre back
Stan COLLYMORE	Forward
Colin COOPER	Defender/Centre back
Mark CROSSLEY	Goalkeeper
Scot GEMMILL	Midfielder
Alfe-Inge HAALAND	Defender/Midfielder
Jason LEE	Forward
Des LYTTLE	Defender/Right back
Paul McGREGOR	Forward
Stuart PEARCE	Defender
David PHILLIPS	Defender/Midfielder
Robert ROSARIO	Forward
Bryan ROY	Forward
Steve STONE	Midfielder
Carl TILER	Defender/Centre back
Vance WARNER	Central defender
Ian WOAN	Midfielder
Tommy WRIGHT	Goalkeeper

229

Season	League	League Position	P	W	D	L	F	A	Pts	3 Point Equivalent
2006–07	League 1	4	46	23	13	10	65	41	82	1.782609
2000–01	**L1**	**11**	**46**	**20**	**18**	**8**	**55**	**53**	**68**	**1.695652**
2002–03	L1	6	46	20	12	14	82	50	74	1.565217
2005–06	League 1	7	46	19	12	15	67	52	69	1.500000
2003–04	L1	14	46	15	16	15	61	58	60	1.326087
1999–2000	L1	14	46	14	18	14	53	55	56	1.304348
2001–02	L1	16	46	12	16	18	50	51	54	1.130435
2004–05	Championship	23	46	9	20	17	42	66	44	1.021739

SQUAD 2000–2001 — 11TH IN FIRST DIVISION

Chris BART-WILLIAMS	Midfielder
Dave BEASANT	Goalkeeper
Francis BENALI	Defender
Robbie BLAKE	Forward
Jim BRENNAN	Defender
Colin CALDERWOOD	Defender/Centre back
Richard COOPER	Defender/Midfielder
Kevin DAWSON	Defender/Centre back
Chris DOIG	Defender/Centre back
Gareth EDDS	Defender/Right back
Christian EDWARDS	Defender/Centre back
Keith FOY	Defender/Midfielder
Dougie FREEDMAN	Forward
David FREEMAN	Forward
Andy GRAY	Midfielder/Forward
Marlon HAREWOOD	Forward
Jon-Olav HJELDE	Defender/Centre back
Jermaine JENAS	Midfielder
Stern JOHN	Forward
Andy JOHNSON	Midfielder
David JOHNSON	Forward
Gary JONES	Defender/Midfielder/Forward
Jack LESTER	Forward
Matthieu LOUIS-JEAN	Defender/Right back
Ben OLSEN	Midfielder
David PLATT	Midfielder
David PRUTTON	Midfielder
Andy REID	Midfielder/Forward
Barry ROCHE	Goalkeeper
Alan ROGERS	Defender/Midfielder
Riccardo SCIMECA	Defender/Midfielder
Matthew UPSON	Defender/Centre back
Tony VAUGHAN	Defender
Gareth WILLIAMS	Midfielder

NOTTINGHAM FOREST

OLDHAM ATHLETIC

Season	League	League Position	P	W	D	L	F	A	Pts	3 Point Equivalent
1952–53	**Division 3 North**	1	46	22	15	9	77	45	59	**1.760870**
1951–52	Division 3 North	4	46	24	9	13	90	61	57	1.760870
1948–49	Division 3 North	6	42	18	9	15	75	67	45	1.500000
1954–55	Division 3 North	10	46	19	10	17	74	68	48	1.456522
1949–50	Division 3 North	11	42	16	11	15	58	63	43	1.404762
1947–48	Division 3 North	11	42	14	13	15	63	64	41	1.309524
1957–58	Division 3 North	15	46	14	17	15	72	84	45	1.282609
1950–51	Division 3 North	15	46	16	8	22	73	73	40	1.217391
1958–59	Division 4	21	46	16	4	26	59	84	36	1.130435
1956–57	Division 3 North	19	46	12	15	19	66	74	39	1.108696
1946–47	Division 3 North	19	42	12	8	22	55	80	32	1.047619
1955–56	Division 3 North	20	46	10	18	18	76	86	38	1.043478
1953–54	Division 2	22	42	8	9	25	40	89	25	0.785714

SQUAD 1952–53 — CHAMPIONS OF DIVISION 3 NORTH

Ken BRIERLEY	Outside left	Tommy LOWRIE	Wing half
Lewis BROOK	Full back	Billy McGLEN	Wing half
George BURNETT	Goalkeeper	Bobby McILVENNY	Inside forward
Alf CLARKE	Centre forward	Peter McKENNAN	Inside forward
Ian CRAWFORD	Forward	Jimmy MUNRO	Outside right
Ron FAWLEY	Outside left/Left back	Bill NAYLOR	Full back
Eric GEMMELL	Centre forward	Fred OGDEN	Goalkeeper
George HARDWICK	Full back	Billy ORMOND	Outside left
Joe HARRIS	Centre forward	Les SMITH	Right half
Harry HOULAHAN	Inside left	Bob WHELAN	Right half
Harry JACKSON	Forward	Archie WHYTE	Centre half
Bob JACKSON	Right back/Wing half		

Season	League	League Position	P	W	D	L	F	A	Pts	3 Point Equivalent
1962–63	Division 4	2	46	24	11	11	95	60	59	1.804348
1963–64	**Division 3**	9	46	20	8	18	73	70	48	**1.478261**
1966–67	Division 3	10	46	19	10	17	80	63	48	1.456522
1961–62	Division 4	11	44	17	12	15	77	70	46	1.431818
1960–61	Division 4	12	46	19	7	20	79	88	45	1.391304
1967–68	Division 3	17	46	18	7	21	60	65	43	1.326087
1964–65	Division 3	20	46	13	10	23	61	83	36	1.065217
1965–66	Division 3	20	46	12	13	21	55	81	37	1.065217
1968–69	Division 3	24	46	13	9	24	50	83	35	1.043478
1959–60	Division 4	23	46	8	12	26	41	83	28	0.782609

SQUAD 1963–64 — 9TH IN DIVISION 3

Colin BARLOW	Outside right	Bob LEDGER	Outside right
John BOLLANDS	Goalkeeper	Bert LISTER	Centre forward
Jim BOWIE	Midfielder	Billy MARSHALL	Full back
Ken BRANAGAN	Full back	Peter McCALL	Wing half
John BURDESS	Inside forward	Billy McGINN	Full back
John COLQUHOUN	Midfielder	Jimmy SCOTT	Wing half
Bobby CRAIG	Inside forward	George SIEWRIGHT	Wing half
Jimmy FRIZZELL	Inside forward/Wing half	Alan SWINBURNE	Goalkeeper
Alan HALSALL	Goalkeeper	Barry TAYLOR	Full back
Albert JACKSON	Centre half	Colin WHITAKER	Outside left
Bobby JOHNSTONE	Inside forward	Alan WILLIAMS	Centre half

	Season	League	League Position	P	W	D	L	F	A	Pts	3 Point Equivalent
1970s	1973–74	Division 3	1	46	25	12	9	83	47	62	1.891304
	1970–71	Division 4	3	46	24	11	11	88	63	59	1.804348
	1972–73	Division 3	4	46	19	16	11	72	54	54	1.586957
	1971–72	Division 3	11	46	17	11	18	59	63	45	1.347826
	1977–78	**Division 2**	**8**	**42**	**13**	**16**	**13**	**54**	**58**	**42**	**1.309524**
	1976–77	Division 2	13	42	14	10	18	52	64	38	1.238095
	1978–79	Division 2	14	42	13	13	16	52	61	39	1.238095
	1975–76	Division 2	17	42	13	12	17	57	68	38	1.214286
	1969–70	Division 4	19	46	13	13	20	60	65	39	1.130435
	1974–75	Division 2	18	42	10	15	17	40	48	35	1.071429

SQUAD 1977–78 — 8TH IN DIVISION 2

Graham BELL	Midfielder
Mike BERNARD	Midfielder
Ronnie BLAIR	Defender
Les CHAPMAN	Midfielder
Paul EDWARDS	Central defender
Steve EDWARDS	Defender
Steve GARDNER	Midfielder
Alan GROVES	Winger
Vic HALOM	Forward
Paul HEATON	Midfielder
Keith HICKS	Central defender
Mark HILTON	Midfielder

David HOLT	Defender
Garry HOOLICKIN	Defender
John HURST	Central defender
David IRVING	Forward
Chris OGDEN	Goalkeeper
John PLATT	Goalkeeper
Dave SHAW	Forward
Steve TAYLOR	Forward
Carl VALENTINE	Winger
Ian WOOD	Full back
Alan YOUNG	Forward

	Season	League	League Position	P	W	D	L	F	A	Pts	3 Point Equivalent
1980s	**1986–87**	**Division 2**	**3**	**42**	**22**	**9**	**11**	**65**	**44**	**75**	**1.785714**
	1987–88	Division 2	10	44	18	11	15	72	64	65	1.477273
	1982–83	Division 2	7	42	14	19	9	64	47	61	1.452381
	1985–86	Division 2	8	42	17	9	16	62	61	60	1.428571
	1979–80	Division 2	11	42	16	11	15	49	53	43	1.404762
	1981–82	Division 2	11	42	15	14	13	50	51	59	1.404762
	1984–85	Division 2	14	42	15	8	19	49	67	53	1.261905
	1980–81	Division 2	15	42	12	15	15	39	48	39	1.214286
	1988–89	Division 2	16	46	11	21	14	75	72	54	1.173913
	1983–84	Division 2	19	42	13	8	21	47	73	47	1.119048

SQUAD 1986–87 — 3RD IN DIVISION 2

Andy BARLOW	Left back
Aaron CALLAGHAN	Central defender
Mike CECERE	Forward
Bob COLVILLE	Forward
Willie DONACHIE	Left back
Neil EDMONDS	Midfielder
Tony ELLIS	Forward
Ron FUTCHER	Forward
Andy GORAM	Goalkeeper
Andy GORTON	Goalkeeper
Tony HENRY	Midfielder
Garry HOOLICKIN	Defender

Denis IRWIN	Defender/Full back
Paul JONES	Central defender
Andy LINIGHAN	Defender/Centre back
Darren McDONOUGH	Defender/Midfielder
Mick McGUIRE	Midfielder
Mike MILLIGAN	Midfielder
Kevin MOORE	Central defender
Ian ORMONDROYD	Forward
Roger PALMER	Forward
John RYAN	Left back/Midfielder
Gary WILLIAMS	Full back
Tommy WRIGHT	Left winger

OLDHAM ATHLETIC

Season	League	League Position	P	W	D	L	F	A	Pts	3 Point Equivalent
1990–91	Division 2	1	46	25	13	8	83	53	88	1.913043
1989–90	Division 2	8	46	19	14	13	70	57	71	1.543478
1994–95	L1	14	46	16	17	13	60	60	61	1.413043
1998–99	L2	20	46	14	23	9	48	66	51	1.413043
1995–96	L1	18	46	14	18	14	54	50	56	1.304348
1997–98	L2	13	46	15	15	16	62	54	61	1.304348
1991–92	Division 1	17	42	14	9	19	63	67	51	1.214286
1992–93	Premier League	19	42	13	10	19	63	74	49	1.166667
1996–97	L1	23	46	10	23	13	51	66	43	1.152174
1993–94	Premier League	21	42	9	13	20	42	68	40	0.952381

SQUAD 1990–91   CHAMPIONS OF DIVISION 2

Neil ADAMS	Defender/Midfielder	Andy HOLDEN	Central defender
Andy BARLOW	Left back	Rick HOLDEN	Winger
Earl BARRETT	Defender	Richard JOBSON	Defender/Centre back
Paul BERNARD	Midfielder	Paul KANE	Defender/Midfielder
Derek BRAZIL	Central defender	Ian MARSHALL	Forward
David CURRIE	Forward	Paul MOULDEN	Forward
Willie DONACHIE	Left back	Roger PALMER	Forward
Mike FILLERY	Midfielder	Neil REDFEARN	Midfielder
Gunnar HALLE	Full back	Andy RITCHIE	Forward
Jon HALLWORTH	Goalkeeper	Paul WARHURST	Defender/Midfielder
Nick HENRY	Midfielder	Gary WILLIAMS	Full back

Season	League	League Position	P	W	D	L	F	A	Pts	3 Point Equivalent
2006–07	League 1	6	46	21	12	13	69	47	75	1.630435
2002–03	L2	5	46	22	8	16	68	38	82	1.608696
1999–2000	L2	14	46	16	18	12	50	55	60	1.434783
2001–02	L2	9	46	18	12	16	77	65	70	1.434783
2005–06	League 1	10	46	18	11	17	58	60	65	1.413043
2004–05	League 1	19	46	14	22	10	60	73	52	1.391304
2000–01	League 2	15	46	15	18	13	53	65	58	1.369565
2003–04	L2	15	46	12	13	21	66	60	57	1.065217

SQUAD 2006–07   6TH IN LEAGUE 1

Hasney ALJOFREE	Defender/Midfielder	Michael PEARSON	Defender
Alan BLAYNEY	Goalkeeper	Les POGLIACOMI	Goalkeeper
Simon CHARLTON	Defender/Left back	Chris PORTER	Forward
Leon CLARKE	Forward	Craig ROCASTLE	Midfielder
Tomasz CYWKA	Midfielder	Miki ROQUE	Defender
Neal EARDLEY	Defender	Deane SMALLEY	Midfielder
Paul EDWARDS	Midfielder	Terry SMITH	Goalkeeper
Luigi GLOMBARD	Forward	Stefan STAM	Defender
Lewis GRABBAN	Forward	Chris SWAILES	Defender/Centre back
Sean GREGAN	Defender/Midfielder	Chris TAYLOR	Midfielder
Will HAINING	Defender/Centre back	Marc TIERNEY	Defender
Chris HALL	Forward	Neal TROTMAN	Defender
Chris HOWARTH	Goalkeeper	Ben TURNER	Defender/Centre back
David KNIGHT	Goalkeeper	Paul WARNE	Forward
Andy LIDDELL	Forward	Richie WELLENS	Midfielder
Kelvin LOMAX	Midfielder	Matthew WOLFENDEN	Forward
Gary McDONALD	Midfielder	Neil WOOD	Forward
Maheta MOLANGO	Forward		

PORTSMOUTH

Season	League	League Position	P	W	D	L	F	A	Pts	3 Point Equivalent
1948–49	**Division 1**	1	42	25	8	9	84	42	58	1.976190
1949–50	Division 1	1	42	22	9	11	74	38	53	1.785714
1951–52	Division 1	4	42	20	8	14	68	58	48	1.619048
1954–55	Division 1	3	42	18	12	12	74	62	48	1.571429
1947–48	Division 1	8	42	19	7	16	68	50	45	1.523810
1950–51	Division 1	7	42	16	15	11	71	68	47	1.500000
1946–47	Division 1	12	42	16	9	17	66	60	41	1.357143
1955–56	Division 1	12	42	16	9	17	78	85	41	1.357143
1953–54	Division 1	14	42	14	11	17	81	89	39	1.261905
1952–53	Division 1	15	42	14	10	18	74	83	38	1.238095
1957–58	Division 1	20	42	12	8	22	73	88	32	1.047619
1956–57	Division 1	19	42	10	13	19	62	92	33	1.023810
1958–59	Division 1	22	42	6	9	27	64	112	21	0.642857

SQUAD 1948–49 — CHAMPIONS OF DIVISION 1

Bert BARLOW	Inside forward	Peter HARRIS	Outside right
Gerry BOWLER	Centre half	Billy HINDMARSH	Full back
Ernie BUTLER	Goalkeeper	Cliff PARKER	Outside left
Ike CLARKE	Inside forward	Len PHILLIPS	Inside forward
Lindy DELAPENHA	Forward	Duggie REID	Inside forward
Jimmy DICKINSON	Wing half	Phil ROOKES	Full back
Harry FERRIER	Full back	Jimmy SCOULAR	Wing half
Reg FLEWIN	Centre half	Bill THOMPSON	Wing half
Jack FROGGATT	Outside left/Half back	Jasper YOUELL	Full back

233

Season	League	League Position	P	W	D	L	F	A	Pts	3 Point Equivalent
1961–62	Division 3	1	46	27	11	8	87	47	65	2.000000
1967–68	**Division 2**	5	42	18	13	11	68	55	49	1.595238
1963–64	Division 2	9	42	16	11	15	79	70	43	1.404762
1965–66	Division 2	12	42	16	8	18	74	78	40	1.333333
1966–67	Division 2	14	42	13	13	16	59	70	39	1.238095
1968–69	Division 2	15	42	12	14	16	58	58	38	1.190476
1962–63	Division 2	16	42	13	11	18	63	79	37	1.190476
1964–65	Division 2	20	42	12	10	20	56	77	34	1.095238
1960–61	Division 2	21	42	11	11	20	64	91	33	1.047619
1959–60	Division 2	20	42	10	12	20	59	77	32	1.000000

SQUAD 1967–68 — 5TH IN DIVISION 2

Dennis EDWARDS	Inside forward	John MILKINS	Goalkeeper
Harry HARRIS	Inside forward/Wing half	Roy PACK	Full back
Frank HAYDOCK	Centre half	Ray POINTER	Centre forward
Ray HIRON	Forward	Cliff PORTWOOD	Inside forward
Nicky JENNINGS	Outside left	Ray POTTER	Goalkeeper
Bobby KELLARD	Midfielder	George SMITH	Midfielder
George LEY	Left back	Ron TINDALL	Defender/Centre forward
Albert McCANN	Inside forward	Mike TRAVERS	Midfielder
John McCLELLAND	Outside right	Mike TREBILCOCK	Centre forward

Season	League	League Position	P	W	D	L	F	A	Pts	3 Point Equivalent
1978–79	Division 4	7	46	20	12	14	62	48	52	1.565217
1973–74	**Division 2**	**15**	**42**	**14**	**12**	**16**	**45**	**62**	**40**	**1.285714**
1974–75	Division 2	17	42	12	13	17	44	54	37	1.166667
1971–72	Division 2	16	42	12	13	17	59	68	37	1.166667
1969–70	Division 2	17	42	13	9	20	66	80	35	1.142857
1972–73	Division 2	17	42	12	11	19	42	59	35	1.119048
1970–71	Division 2	16	42	10	14	18	46	61	34	1.047619
1976–77	Division 3	20	46	11	14	21	53	70	36	1.021739
1977–78	Division 3	24	46	7	17	22	41	75	31	0.826087
1975–76	Division 2	22	42	9	7	26	32	61	25	0.809524

SQUAD 1973–74　　　　　　　　　　　　　　　15TH IN DIVISION 2

David BEST	Goalkeeper
John COLLINS	Full back
Ron DAVIES	Centre forward
Peter ELLIS	Central defender
Ken FOGGO	Outside right
Eoin HAND	Central defender
Ray HIRON	Forward
Nicky JENNINGS	Outside Left
Bobby KELLARD	Midfielder
Brian LEWIS	Midfielder
Albert McCANN	Inside forward
Malcolm MANLEY	Central defender
Peter MARINELLO	Winger

Micky MELLOWS	Midfielder
John MILKINS	Goalkeeper
David MUNKS	Defender
Norman PIPER	Midfielder
Peter PRICE	Forward
Dick REYNOLDS	Midfielder/Forward
Phil ROBERTS	Right back
Paul SMITH	Midfielder
Alan STEPHENSON	Centre half
Andy STEWART	Forward
Ron TILSED	Goalkeeper
Paul WENT	Central defender
Billy WILSON	Full back

Season	League	League Position	P	W	D	L	F	A	Pts	3 Point Equivalent
1982–83	Division 3	1	46	27	10	9	74	41	91	1.978261
1986–87	**Division 2**	**2**	**42**	**23**	**9**	**10**	**53**	**28**	**78**	**1.857143**
1979–80	Division 4	4	46	24	12	10	91	49	60	1.826087
1984–85	Division 2	4	42	20	14	8	69	50	74	1.761905
1985–86	Division 2	4	42	22	7	13	69	41	73	1.738095
1980–81	Division 3	6	46	22	9	15	55	47	53	1.630435
1981–82	Division 3	13	46	14	19	13	56	51	61	1.326087
1983–84	Division 2	16	42	14	7	21	73	64	49	1.166667
1988–89	Division 2	20	46	13	12	21	53	62	51	1.108696
1987–88	Division 1	19	40	7	14	19	36	66	35	0.875000

SQUAD 1986–87　　　　　　　　　　　　　　　2ND IN DIVISION 2

Kevin BALL	Midfielder
Noel BLAKE	Defender/Centre back
Eamonn COLLINS	Midfielder
Liam DAISH	Defender/Centre back
Kevin DILLON	Midfielder
Billy GILBERT	Central defender
Paul HARDYMAN	Left back
Vince HILAIRE	Winger
Mick KENNEDY	Midfielder
Alan KNIGHT	Goalkeeper

Paul MARINER	Forward
Nicky MORGAN	Forward
Kevin O'CALLAGHAN	Winger
Mick QUINN	Forward
Kenny RUSSELL	Midfielder
Kenny SWAIN	Right back
Mick TAIT	Midfielder/Defender
Michael THOMAS	Midfielder
Paul WOOD	Forward

Season	League	League Position	P	W	D	L	F	A	Pts	3 Point Equivalent
1992–93	L1	3	46	26	10	10	80	46	88	1.913043
1996–97	L1	7	46	20	18	8	59	53	68	1.695652
1991–92	Division 2	9	46	19	12	15	65	51	69	1.500000
1993–94	L1	17	46	15	18	13	52	58	58	1.369565
1994–95	L1	18	46	15	18	13	53	63	58	1.369565
1997–98	L1	20	46	13	23	10	51	63	49	1.347826
1989–90	Division 2	12	46	15	16	15	62	65	61	1.326087
1995–96	L1	21	46	13	20	13	61	69	52	1.282609
1998–99	L1	19	46	11	21	14	57	73	47	1.173913
1990–91	Division 2	17	46	14	11	21	58	70	53	1.152174

SQUAD 1992–93   3RD IN FIRST DIVISION

Steve AGNEW	Midfielder	George LAWRENCE	Winger
Warren ASPINALL	Midfielder	Gavin MAGUIRE	Central defender
Andy AWFORD	Defender	Alan McLOUGHLIN	Midfielder
Chris BURNS	Midfielder	Shaun MURRAY	Midfielder
Guy BUTTERS	Defender/Centre back	Warren NEILL	Right back
Mark CHAMBERLAIN	Winger	Darryl POWELL	Midfielder
Colin CLARKE	Forward	Chris PRICE	Right back
Ray DANIEL	Left back	Lee RUSSELL	Defender/Centre back
Stuart DOLING	Midfielder	Mark STIMSON	Defender
Alan KNIGHT	Goalkeeper	Kit SYMONS	Defender
Bjorn KRISTENSEN	Centre back	Paul WALSH	Forward
Martin KUHL	Midfielder	Guy WHITTINGHAM	Forward

Season	League	League Position	P	W	D	L	F	A	Pts	3 Point Equivalent
2002–03	L1	1	46	29	6	11	97	45	96	2.021739
2006–07	Premier League	9	38	14	12	12	45	42	54	1.421053
1999–2000	L1	18	46	13	21	12	55	66	51	1.304348
2001–02	L1	17	46	13	19	14	60	72	53	1.260870
2003–04	Premier League	13	38	12	9	17	47	54	45	1.184211
2004–05	Premier League	16	38	10	9	19	43	59	39	1.026316
2000–01	L1	20	46	10	17	19	47	59	49	1.021739
2005–06	Premier League	17	38	10	8	20	37	62	38	1.000000

SQUAD 2006–07   9TH IN THE PREMIER LEAGUE

Sol CAMPBELL	Defender/Centre back	Lomano Tresor LUA LUA	Forward
Andrew COLE	Forward	Pedro MENDES	Midfielder
Sean DAVIS	Midfielder	Arnold MVUEMBA	Midfielder
Rudolph DOUALA M'BELA	Forward	Benjani MWARUWARI	Forward
Manuel FERNANDES	Midfielder	Andy O'BRIEN	Defender/Centre back
Andy GRIFFIN	Defender/Right back	Gary O'NEIL	Midfielder
Richard HUGHES	Midfielder	Noe PAMAROT	Defender/Right back
David JAMES	Goalkeeper	Linvoy PRIMUS	Defender/Centre back
Glen JOHNSON	Defender/Right back	Frank SONGO'O	Forward
Nwankwo KANU	Forward	Dejan STEFANOVIC	Defender
Dean KIELY	Goalkeeper	Matthew TAYLOR	Defender/Midfielder
Ognjen KOROMAN	Midfielder	David THOMPSON	Midfielder
Niko KRANJCAR	Midfielder	Svetoslav TODOROV	Forward
Bissan Etame-Mayer LAUREN	Defender/Midfielder	Djimi TRAORE	Defender

QUEENS PARK RANGERS

Season	League	League Position	P	W	D	L	F	A	Pts	3 Point Equivalent
1947–48	**Division 3 South**	**1**	**42**	**26**	**9**	**7**	**74**	**37**	**61**	**2.071429**
1946–47	Division 3 South	2	42	23	11	8	74	40	57	1.904762
1957–58	Division 3 South	10	46	18	14	14	64	65	50	1.478261
1956–57	Division 3 South	10	46	18	11	17	61	60	47	1.413043
1958–59	Division 3	13	46	19	8	19	74	77	46	1.413043
1950–51	Division 2	16	42	15	10	17	71	82	40	1.309524
1954–55	Division 3 South	15	46	15	14	17	69	75	44	1.282609
1948–49	Division 2	13	42	14	11	17	44	62	39	1.261905
1953–54	Division 3 South	18	46	16	10	20	60	68	42	1.260870
1955–56	Division 3 South	18	46	14	11	21	64	86	39	1.152174
1952–53	Division 3 South	20	46	12	15	19	61	82	39	1.108696
1949–50	Division 2	20	42	11	12	19	40	57	34	1.071429
1951–52	Division 2	22	42	11	12	19	52	81	34	1.071429

SQUAD 1947–48   CHAMPIONS OF DIVISION 3 SOUTH

Ernie ADAMS	Winger	Don MILLS	Inside forward
Bert ADDINALL	Centre forward	Alf PARKINSON	Wing half
Reg ALLEN	Goalkeeper	Johnny PATTISON	Outside left
Danny BOXSHALL	Winger	George POWELL	Full back
Reg CHAPMAN	Centre half	Ivor POWELL	Wing half
Harry DANIELS	Left half	Fred RAMSCAR	Inside forward
Reg DUDLEY	Full back	Ted REAY	Left back
Fred DURRANT	Centre forward	Alf RIDYARD	Centre half
Johnny HARTBURN	Outside left	Jack ROSE	Right back
Cyril HATTON	Inside forward	Reg SAPHIN	Goalkeeper
Bill HEATH	Full back	Albert SMITH	Wing half
Arthur JEFFERSON	Full back	George SMITH	Centre half
Billy McEWAN	Outside right	George STEWART	Inside forward

Season	League	League Position	P	W	D	L	F	A	Pts	3 Point Equivalent
1966–67	Division 3	1	46	26	15	5	103	38	67	2.021739
1967–68	**Division 2**	**2**	**42**	**25**	**8**	**9**	**67**	**36**	**58**	**1.976190**
1960–61	Division 3	3	46	25	10	11	93	60	60	1.847826
1961–62	Division 3	4	46	24	11	11	111	73	59	1.804348
1965–66	Division 3	3	46	24	9	13	95	65	57	1.760870
1959–60	Division 3	8	46	18	13	15	73	54	49	1.456522
1963–64	Division 3	15	46	18	9	19	76	78	45	1.369565
1964–65	Division 3	14	46	17	12	17	72	80	46	1.369565
1962–63	Division 3	13	46	17	11	18	85	76	45	1.347826
1968–69	Division 1	22	42	4	10	28	39	95	18	0.523810

SQUAD 1967–68   2ND IN DIVISION 2

Leslie ALLEN	Centre forward	Mick LEACH	Midfielder
Frank CLARKE	Forward	Rodney MARSH	Forward
Dave CLEMENT	Right back	Mick McGOVERN	Midfielder
Bobby FINCH	Full back	Ian MORGAN	Winger
Allan HARRIS	Left back	Roger MORGAN	Winger
Tony HAZELL	Defender	Keith SANDERSON	Inside forward
Ron HUNT	Centre half	Frank SIBLEY	Wing half
Mike KEEN	Wing half	Ron SPRINGETT	Goalkeeper
Bobby KEETCH	Centre half	Ian WATSON	Full back
Mike KELLY	Goalkeeper	Alan WILKS	Forward
Mark LAZARUS	Winger		

Season	League	League Position	P	W	D	L	F	A	Pts	3 Point Equivalent
1972–73	Division 2	2	42	24	13	5	81	37	61	2.023810
1975–76	**Division 1**	**2**	**42**	**24**	**11**	**7**	**67**	**33**	**59**	**1.976190**
1971–72	Division 2	4	42	20	14	8	57	28	54	1.761905
1969–70	Division 2	9	42	17	11	14	66	57	45	1.476190
1970–71	Division 2	11	42	16	11	15	58	53	43	1.404762
1974–75	Division 1	11	42	16	10	16	54	54	42	1.380952
1973–74	Division 1	8	42	13	17	12	56	52	43	1.333333
1976–77	Division 1	14	42	13	12	17	47	52	38	1.214286
1977–78	Division 1	19	42	9	15	18	47	64	33	1.000000
1978–79	Division 1	20	42	6	13	23	45	73	25	0.738095

1970s

SQUAD 1975–76   2ND IN DIVISION 1

Ron ABBOTT	Central defender	Don MASSON	Midfielder
John BECK	Midfielder	Frank McLINTOCK	Central defender
Stan BOWLES	Midfielder	Phil NUTT	Forward
Dave CLEMENT	Right back	Phil PARKES	Goalkeeper
Gerry FRANCIS	Midfielder	Don SHANKS	Full back
Ian GILLARD	Left back	Tony TAGG	Central defender
Don GIVENS	Forward	Dave THOMAS	Winger
John HOLLINS	Midfielder	Dave WEBB	Defender
Mick LEACH	Midfielder		

Season	League	League Position	P	W	D	L	F	A	Pts	3 Point Equivalent
1982–83	Division 2	1	42	26	7	9	77	36	85	2.023810
1983–84	**Division 1**	**5**	**42**	**22**	**7**	**13**	**67**	**37**	**73**	**1.738095**
1987–88	Division 1	5	40	19	10	11	48	38	67	1.675000
1981–82	Division 2	5	42	21	6	15	65	43	69	1.642857
1979–80	Division 2	5	42	18	13	11	75	53	49	1.595238
1988–89	Division 1	9	38	14	11	13	43	37	53	1.394737
1980–81	Division 2	8	42	15	13	14	56	46	43	1.380952
1985–86	Division 1	13	42	15	7	20	53	64	52	1.238095
1984–85	Division 1	19	42	13	11	18	53	72	50	1.190476
1986–87	Division 1	16	42	13	11	18	48	64	50	1.190476

1980s

SQUAD 1983–84   5TH IN DIVISION 1

Clive ALLEN	Forward	Peter HUCKER	Goalkeeper
Steve BURKE	Winger	Alan McDONALD	Central defender
Jeremy CHARLES	Forward	Gary MICKLEWHITE	Midfielder
Ian DAWES	Left back	Warren NEILL	Right back
Terry FENWICK	Defender	Glenn ROEDER	Central defender
Wayne FEREDAY	Winger	Tony SEALY	Forward
Mike FILLERY	Midfielder	Simon STAINROD	Forward
Mike FLANAGAN	Forward	Ian STEWART	Winger
John GREGORY	Midfielder	Gary WADDOCK	Midfielder
Bob HAZELL	Central defender	Steve WICKS	Central defender

Season	League	League Position	P	W	D	L	F	A	Pts	3 Point Equivalent
1996–97	L1	9	46	18	16	12	64	60	66	1.521739
1992–93	**Premier League**	**5**	**42**	**17**	**12**	**13**	**63**	**55**	**63**	**1.500000**
1993–94	Premier League	9	42	16	12	14	62	61	60	1.428571
1994–95	Premier League	8	42	17	9	16	61	59	60	1.428571
1989–90	Division 1	11	38	13	11	14	45	44	50	1.315789
1991–92	Division 1	11	42	12	18	12	48	47	54	1.285714
1998–99	L1	20	46	12	23	11	52	61	47	1.282609
1990–91	Division 1	12	38	12	10	16	44	53	46	1.210526
1997–98	L1	21	46	10	17	19	51	63	49	1.021739
1995–96	Premier League	19	38	9	6	23	38	57	33	0.868421

SQUAD 1992–93 — 5TH IN THE PREMIER LEAGUE

Bradley ALLEN	Forward	Michael MEAKER	Midfielder
Dennis BAILEY	Forward	Darren PEACOCK	Defender/Centre back
David BARDSLEY	Defender	Gary PENRICE	Forward
Simon BARKER	Midfielder	Karl READY	Defender/Centre back
Rufus BREVETT	Defender/Left back	Tony ROBERTS	Goalkeeper
Justin CHANNING	Defender	Andy SINTON	Midfielder
Maurice DOYLE	Midfielder	Jan STEJSKAL	Goalkeeper
Les FERDINAND	Forward	Garry THOMPSON	Forward
Ian HOLLOWAY	Winger	Devon WHITE	Forward
Andy IMPEY	Midfielder	Ray WILKINS	Midfielder
Danny MADDIX	Defender/Centre back	Clive WILSON	Defender/Midfielder
Alan McDONALD	Central defender		

Season	League	League Position	P	W	D	L	F	A	Pts	3 Point Equivalent
2002–03	L2	4	46	24	11	11	69	45	83	1.804348
2003–04	L2	2	46	22	7	17	80	45	83	1.586957
2001–02	L2	8	46	19	13	14	60	49	71	1.521739
2004–05	**Championship**	**11**	**46**	**17**	**18**	**11**	**54**	**58**	**62**	**1.500000**
1999–2000	L1	10	46	16	12	18	62	53	66	1.304348
2006–07	Championship	18	46	14	11	21	54	68	53	1.152174
2005–06	Championship	21	46	12	14	20	50	65	50	1.086957
2000–01	L1	23	46	7	20	19	45	75	40	0.891304

SQUAD 2004–05 — 11TH IN THE CHAMPIONSHIP

Gareth AINSWORTH	Midfielder	Arthur GNOHERE	Defender/Centre back
Shabazz BAIDOO	Forward	Lewis HAMILTON	Defender
Stefan BAILEY	Midfielder	Richard JOHNSON	Midfielder
Marcus BEAN	Midfielder	Pat KANYUKA	Defender/Centre back
Leon BEST	Forward	Kevin McLEOD	Midfielder
Marcus BIGNOT	Defender/Midfielder	Adam MILLER	Defender/Midfielder
Marc BIRCHAM	Defender/Midfielder	Scott MULHOLLAND	Midfielder
Serge BRANCO	Midfielder	Gino PADULA	Defender/Left back
Aaron BROWN	Midfielder	Matthew ROSE	Defender/Midfielder
Lee COOK	Forward	Generoso ROSSI	Goalkeeper
Jamie CURETON	Forward	Martin ROWLANDS	Midfielder
Andrew DAVIES	Defender/Centre back	Simon ROYCE	Goalkeeper
Chris DAY	Goalkeeper	Georges SANTOS	Defender/Midfielder
Scott DONNELLY	Forward	Danny SHITTU	Defender/Centre back
Richard EDGHILL	Defender/Right back	Frankie SIMEK	Defender
Terrell FORBES	Defender	Dean STURRIDGE	Forward
Paul FURLONG	Forward	Tony THORPE	Forward
Kevin GALLEN	Forward	Luke TOWNSEND	Forward

READING

1940s & 50s

Season	League	League Position	P	W	D	L	F	A	Pts	3 Point Equivalent
1951–52	Division 3 South	2	46	29	3	14	112	60	61	1.956522
1948–49	Division 3 South	2	42	25	5	12	77	50	55	1.904762
1950–51	Division 3 South	3	46	21	15	10	88	53	57	1.695652
1957–58	Division 3 South	5	46	21	13	12	79	51	55	1.652174
1958–59	Division 3	6	46	21	8	17	78	63	50	1.543478
1953–54	Division 3 South	8	46	20	9	17	86	73	49	1.500000
1952–53	Division 3 South	11	46	19	8	19	69	64	46	1.413043
1946–47	Division 3 South	9	42	16	11	15	83	74	43	1.404762
1949–50	Division 3 South	10	42	17	8	17	70	64	42	1.404762
1956–57	Division 3 South	13	46	18	9	19	80	81	45	1.369565
1947–48	Division 3 South	10	42	15	11	16	56	58	41	1.333333
1954–55	Division 3 South	18	46	13	15	18	65	73	41	1.173913
1955–56	Division 3 South	17	46	15	9	22	70	79	39	1.173913

SQUAD 1951–52   2ND IN DIVISION 3 SOUTH

Bill AMOR	Outside right	Jimmy JOHNSTON	Wing half
Ken BAINBRIDGE	Outside left	Jack LEWIS	Wing half
Doug BARTON	Full back	Bill LIVINGSTONE	Centre half
Ron BLACKMAN	Centre forward	George MARKS	Goalkeeper
Gordon BRICE	Centre half	John McBRIDE	Goalkeeper
Johnny BROOKS	Inside forward	Peter McLEAN	Wing half
Maurice EDELSTON	Centre forward	Ron MOYSE	Full back
Doug FARQUHAR	Wing half	Les OWENS	Centre forward
Freddie FISHER	Outside right	Bill PARKER	Outside left
David GRIEVE	Winger	Dennis SIMPSON	Outside right
Les HENLEY	Inside forward	Stan WICKS	Centre half
Len HODGES	Inside right		

1960s

Season	League	League Position	P	W	D	L	F	A	Pts	3 Point Equivalent
1966–67	Division 3	4	46	22	9	15	76	57	53	1.630435
1961–62	Division 3	7	46	22	9	15	77	66	53	1.630435
1963–64	Division 3	6	46	21	10	15	79	62	52	1.586957
1967–68	Division 3	5	46	21	9	16	70	60	51	1.565217
1965–66	Division 3	8	46	19	13	14	70	63	51	1.521739
1959–60	Division 3	11	46	18	10	18	84	77	46	1.391304
1964–65	Division 3	13	46	16	14	16	70	70	46	1.347826
1968–69	Division 3	14	46	15	13	18	67	66	43	1.260870
1962–63	Division 3	20	46	16	8	22	74	78	40	1.217391
1960–61	Division 3	18	46	14	12	20	72	83	40	1.173913

SQUAD 1966–67   4TH IN DIVISION 3

Dennis ALLEN	Inside forward	Alan SCARROTT	Winger
Dave BACUZZI	Full back	Peter SILVESTER	Forward
Ron BAYLISS	Defender	Roger SMEE	Centre forward
John CHAPMAN	Defender	Dick SPIERS	Centre half
Ray DEAN	Centre half	Pat TERRY	Centre forward
Mike DIXON	Goalkeeper	Rod THORNHILL	Wing half
Maurice EVANS	Wing half	Mike TRAVERS	Midfielder
Brian FAULKES	Full back	Duggie WEBB	Inside forward
Ron FOSTER	Inside forward	Jimmy WHEELER	Inside forward
George HARRIS	Outside left	Arthur WILKIE	Goalkeeper
Colin MELDRUM	Left back	Ernie YARD	Forward
Jimmy MULLEN	Winger		

1970s

Season	League	League Position	P	W	D	L	F	A	Pts	3 Point Equivalent
1978–79	Division 4	1	46	26	13	7	76	35	65	1.978261
1975–76	Division 4	3	46	24	12	10	70	51	60	1.826087
1969–70	**Division 3**	**8**	**46**	**21**	**11**	**14**	**87**	**77**	**53**	**1.608696**
1974–75	Division 4	7	46	21	10	15	63	47	52	1.586957
1972–73	Division 4	7	46	17	18	11	51	38	52	1.500000
1977–78	Division 4	8	46	18	14	14	55	52	50	1.478261
1973–74	Division 4	6	46	16	19	11	58	37	51	1.456522
1971–72	Division 4	16	46	17	8	21	56	76	42	1.282609
1970–71	Division 3	21	46	14	11	21	48	85	39	1.152174
1976–77	Division 3	21	46	13	9	24	49	73	35	1.043478

SQUAD 1969–70 — 8TH IN DIVISION 3

Dennis ALLEN	Inside forward
Terry BELL	Forward
Paul BENCE	Midfielder
Roy BROWN	Goalkeeper
Dennis G BUTLER	Wing half
Dennis M BUTLER	Left back
Les CHAPPELL	Midfielder
Gordon CUMMING	Midfielder
Steve DEATH	Goalkeeper
Will DIXON	Right back
John DOCHERTY	Outside right
Dick HABBIN	Midfielder
John HARLEY	Midfielder
George HARRIS	Outside left
Alan HITCHCOCK	Full back
Tom JENKINS	Outside left
Colin MELDRUM	Left back
Stuart MORGAN	Central defender
John SAINTY	Forward/Midfielder
Freddie SHARPE	Centre half
Peter SILVESTER	Forward
Roger SMEE	Centre forward
Dick SPIERS	Centre half
Rod THORNHILL	Wing half
Barry WAGSTAFF	Midfielder
Tony WAGSTAFF	Midfielder
Bobby WILLIAMS	Inside forward

1980s

Season	League	League Position	P	W	D	L	F	A	Pts	3 Point Equivalent
1985–86	Division 3	1	46	29	7	10	67	51	94	2.043478
1983–84	Division 4	3	46	22	16	8	84	56	82	1.782609
1984–85	Division 3	9	46	19	12	15	68	62	69	1.500000
1979–80	Division 3	7	46	16	16	14	66	65	48	1.391304
1980–81	Division 3	10	46	18	10	18	62	62	46	1.391304
1981–82	Division 3	12	46	17	11	18	67	75	62	1.347826
1986–87	**Division 2**	**13**	**42**	**14**	**11**	**17**	**52**	**59**	**53**	**1.261905**
1988–89	Division 3	18	46	15	11	20	68	72	56	1.217391
1982–83	Division 3	21	46	12	17	17	64	79	53	1.152174
1987–88	Division 2	22	44	10	12	22	44	70	42	0.954545

SQUAD 1986–87 — 13TH IN DIVISION 2

Colin BAILIE	Midfielder
Paul BARRON	Goalkeeper
Stuart BEAVON	Midfielder
Kevin BREMNER	Forward
Paul CANOVILLE	Winger
Dean CROMBIE	Defender
Steve FRANCIS	Goalkeeper
Michael GILKES	Midfielder
Bob HAZELL	Central defender
Martin HICKS	Central defender
Dean HORRIX	Forward
Terry HURLOCK	Midfielder
Gary PETERS	Defender
Steve RICHARDSON	Left back
Andy ROGERS	Left Winger
Trevor SENIOR	Forward
Neil SMILLIE	Winger
Les TAYLOR	Midfielder
Nigel VAUGHAN	Midfielder
Gary WESTWOOD	Goalkeeper
Mark WHITE	Full back/Midfielder
Jerry WILLIAMS	Midfielder
Steve WOOD	Central defender

Season	League	League Position	P	W	D	L	F	A	Pts	3 Point Equivalent
1993–94	L2	1	46	26	9	11	81	44	89	1.891304
1994–95	**L1**	**2**	**46**	**23**	**13**	**10**	**58**	**44**	**79**	**1.782609**
1992–93	L2	8	46	18	13	15	66	51	69	1.456522
1998–99	L2	11	46	16	17	13	54	63	61	1.413043
1989–90	Division 3	10	46	15	19	12	57	53	64	1.391304
1996–97	L1	18	46	15	19	12	58	67	57	1.391304
1991–92	Division 3	12	46	16	13	17	59	62	61	1.326087
1990–91	Division 3	15	46	17	8	21	53	66	59	1.282609
1997–98	L1	24	46	11	26	9	39	78	42	1.282609
1995–96	L1	19	46	13	16	17	54	63	56	1.195652

SQUAD 1994–95 — 2ND IN FIRST DIVISION

Darren BARNARD	Defender/Left back
Andy BERNAL	Defender
Alan CAREY	Forward
Michael GILKES	Midfielder
Mick GOODING	Midfielder
Uwe HARTENBERGER	Forward
Shaka HISLOP	Goalkeeper
Paul HOLSGROVE	Midfielder
Jeff HOPKINS	Central defender
Tommy JONES	Midfielder
Dylan KERR	Defender/Full back
Jamie LAMBERT	Midfielder
Stuart LOVELL	Midfielder
Keith McPHERSON	Centre back
Mick MURPHY	Defender/Forward
Lee NOGAN	Forward
Simon OSBORN	Midfielder
Phil PARKINSON	Midfielder
Jimmy QUINN	Forward
Scott TAYLOR	Midfielder
Adrian VIVEASH	Defender/Centre back
Dariusz WDOWCZYK	Central defender
Adrian WILLIAMS	Defender/Centre back

Season	League	League Position	P	W	D	L	F	A	Pts	3 Point Equivalent
2005–06	Championship	1	46	31	13	2	99	32	106	2.304348
2002–03	L1	4	46	25	17	4	61	46	79	2.000000
2000–01	L2	3	46	25	10	11	86	52	86	1.847826
2001–02	L2	2	46	23	8	15	70	43	84	1.673913
2003–04	L1	9	46	20	16	10	55	57	70	1.652174
2004–05	Championship	7	46	19	14	13	51	44	70	1.543478
2006–07	**Premier League**	**8**	**38**	**16**	**7**	**15**	**52**	**47**	**55**	**1.447368**
1999–2000	L2	10	46	16	16	14	57	63	62	1.391304

SQUAD 2006–07 — 8TH IN THE PREMIER LEAGUE

Andre BIKEY OMOGU	Defender
Bobby CONVEY	Midfielder
Ulises DE LA CRUZ	Defender/Midfielder
Kevin DOYLE	Forward
Michael DUBERRY	Defender/Centre back
Adam FEDERICI	Goalkeeper
Brynjar GUNNARSSON	Defender/Centre back
Marcus HAHNEMANN	Goalkeeper
Greg HALFORD	Defender
James HARPER	Midfielder
Steve HUNT	Midfielder
Ivar INGIMARSSON	Defender/Midfielder
Seol KI HYEON	Forward
Dave KITSON	Forward
Leroy LITA	Forward
Glen LITTLE	Midfielder
Shane LONG	Forward
Graham MURTY	Defender/Midfielder
John OSTER	Midfielder
Nicky SHOREY	Defender/Left back
Steve SIDWELL	Midfielder
Sam SODJE	Defender/Centre back
Ibrahima SONKO	Defender/Centre back

READING

1940s & 50s

Season	League	League Position	P	W	D	L	F	A	Pts	3 Point Equivalent
1952–53	Division 2	1	42	25	10	7	97	55	60	2.023810
1958–59	Division 2	3	42	23	7	12	82	48	53	1.809524
1957–58	Division 2	6	42	21	10	11	75	50	52	1.738095
1949–50	Division 2	3	42	19	14	9	68	49	52	1.690476
1946–47	**Division 1**	**6**	**42**	**21**	**7**	**14**	**89**	**75**	**49**	**1.666667**
1956–57	Division 2	7	42	19	8	15	87	76	46	1.547619
1950–51	Division 2	8	42	16	12	14	72	62	44	1.428571
1951–52	Division 2	11	42	18	5	19	90	76	41	1.404762
1947–48	Division 1	12	42	16	10	16	65	70	42	1.380952
1954–55	Division 1	13	42	17	7	18	70	86	41	1.380952
1955–56	Division 1	22	42	12	9	21	63	77	33	1.071429
1953–54	Division 1	20	42	11	11	20	69	90	33	1.047619
1948–49	Division 1	22	42	11	11	20	57	78	33	1.047619

SQUAD 1946–47 — 6TH IN DIVISION 1

Harold BROOK	Centre forward	Albert NIGHTINGALE	Inside forward
Colin COLLINDRIDGE	Outside left	John PICKERING	Inside forward
Albert COX	Full back	Bobby REID	Outside left
Alex FORBES	Wing half	Walter RICKETT	Outside right
Fred FURNISS	Full back	Eddie SHIMWELL	Full back
Jimmy HAGAN	Inside forward	John SMITH	Goalkeeper
Ernie JACKSON	Wing half	Charlie THOMPSON	Centre forward
George JONES	Outside left	Dennis THOMPSON	Forward
Harry LATHAM	Centre half	Roy WARHURST	Wing half
Stan MACHENT	Inside forward	Dick YOUNG	Centre half
Harry MILLS	Forward		

1960s

Season	League	League Position	P	W	D	L	F	A	Pts	3 Point Equivalent
1960–61	Division 2	2	42	26	6	10	81	51	58	2.000000
1959–60	Division 2	4	42	19	12	11	68	51	50	1.642857
1961–62	**Division 1**	**5**	**42**	**19**	**9**	**14**	**61**	**69**	**47**	**1.571429**
1962–63	Division 1	10	42	16	12	14	58	60	44	1.428571
1968–69	Division 2	9	42	16	11	15	61	50	43	1.404762
1963–64	Division 1	12	42	16	11	15	61	64	43	1.404762
1965–66	Division 2	9	42	16	11	15	56	59	43	1.404762
1966–67	Division 1	10	42	16	10	16	52	59	42	1.380952
1964–65	Division 1	19	42	12	11	19	50	64	35	1.119048
1967–68	Division 1	21	42	11	10	21	49	70	32	1.023810

SQUAD 1961–62 — 5TH IN DIVISION 1

Len ALLCHURCH	Outside right	Harry ORR	Wing half
Cecil COLDWELL	Right back	Derek PACE	Centre forward
John DOCHERTY	Outside right	Brian RICHARDSON	Wing half
Denis FINNIGAN	Centre half	Billy RUSSELL	Inside forward
Barry HARTLE	Outside left/Left back	Graham SHAW	Left back
Alan HODGKINSON	Goalkeeper	Joe SHAW	Centre half
Billy HODGSON	Inside forward	Dennis SHIELS	Centre forward
Keith KETTLEBOROUGH	Inside forward	Ron SIMPSON	Outside left
Ken MALLENDER	Defender	Gerry SUMMERS	Wing half
Cliff MASON	Full back	Des THOMPSON	Goalkeeper
Reg MATTHEWSON	Centre half	Bob WIDDOWSON	Goalkeeper

	Season	League	League Position	P	W	D	L	F	A	Pts	3 Point Equivalent
1970s	1970–71	Division 2	2	42	21	14	7	73	39	56	1.833333
	1969–70	Division 2	6	42	22	5	15	73	38	49	1.690476
	1974–75	**Division 1**	**6**	**42**	**18**	**13**	**11**	**58**	**51**	**49**	**1.595238**
	1971–72	Division 1	10	42	17	12	13	61	60	46	1.500000
	1977–78	Division 2	12	42	16	8	18	62	73	40	1.333333
	1972–73	Division 1	14	42	15	10	17	51	59	40	1.309524
	1973–74	Division 1	13	42	14	12	16	44	49	40	1.285714
	1976–77	Division 2	11	42	14	12	16	54	63	40	1.285714
	1978–79	Division 2	20	42	11	12	19	52	69	34	1.071429
	1975–76	Division 1	22	42	6	10	26	33	82	22	0.666667

SQUAD 1974–75   6TH IN DIVISION 1

Len BADGER	Right back	Gary FRANCE	Centre forward
David BRADFORD	Midfielder	Colin FRANKS	Central defender
Jim BROWN	Goalkeeper	Terry GARBETT	Midfielder
Steve CAMMACK	Forward	Steve GOULDING	Full back
Eddie COLQUHOUN	Central defender	Ted HEMSLEY	Defender
Tony CURRIE	Midfielder	Garry JONES	Forward
Billy DEARDEN	Forward	Ian MacKENZIE	Defender
Keith EDDY	Midfielder	Terry NICHOLL	Midfielder
Steve FAULKNER	Central defender	Mick SPEIGHT	Midfielder
Tony FIELD	Forward	Alan WOODWARD	Winger
John FLYNN	Central defender		

	Season	League	League Position	P	W	D	L	F	A	Pts	3 Point Equivalent
1980s	1981–82	Division 4	1	46	27	15	4	94	41	96	2.086957
	1988–89	Division 3	2	46	25	9	12	93	54	84	1.826087
	1983–84	Division 3	3	46	24	11	11	86	53	83	1.804348
	1985–86	**Division 2**	**7**	**42**	**17**	**11**	**14**	**64**	**63**	**62**	**1.476190**
	1979–80	Division 3	12	46	18	10	18	60	66	46	1.391304
	1982–83	Division 3	11	46	19	7	20	62	64	64	1.391304
	1986–87	Division 2	9	42	15	13	14	50	49	58	1.380952
	1980–81	Division 3	21	46	14	12	20	65	63	40	1.173913
	1984–85	Division 2	18	42	10	14	18	54	66	44	1.047619
	1987–88	Division 2	21	44	13	7	24	45	74	46	1.045455

SQUAD 1985–86   7TH IN DIVISION 2

Kevin ARNOTT	Midfielder	Paddy McGEENEY	Midfielder
Russell BLACK	Forward	Ken McNAUGHT	Central defender
Joe BOLTON	Left back	Colin MORRIS	Winger
John BURRIDGE	Goalkeeper	Tony PHILLISKIRK	Forward
Glenn COCKERILL	Midfielder	Brian SMITH	Defender
Jeff ECKHARDT	Defender	Paul SMITH	Forward/Right back
Keith EDWARDS	Forward	Paul STANCLIFFE	Central defender
Mel EVES	Forward	Phil THOMPSON	Central defender
Steve FOLEY	Midfielder	Lee WALSHAW	Midfielder
David FRAIN	Midfielder	Steve WIGLEY	Winger
Tony KENWORTHY	Central defender	Peter WITHE	Forward
Roy LEWINGTON	Midfielder		

Season	League	League Position	P	W	D	L	F	A	Pts	3 Point Equivalent
1989–90	Division 2	2	46	24	13	9	78	58	85	1.847826
1996–97	**L1**	**5**	**46**	**20**	**13**	**13**	**75**	**52**	**73**	**1.586957**
1998–99	L1	8	46	18	15	13	71	66	67	1.500000
1997–98	L1	6	46	19	10	17	69	54	74	1.456522
1995–96	L1	9	46	16	16	14	57	54	62	1.391304
1994–95	L1	8	46	17	12	17	74	55	68	1.369565
1991–92	Division 1	9	42	16	9	17	65	63	57	1.357143
1992–93	Premier League	14	42	14	10	18	54	53	52	1.238095
1990–91	Division 1	13	38	13	7	18	36	55	46	1.210526
1993–94	Premier League	20	42	8	18	16	42	60	42	1.000000

SQUAD 1996–97 — 5TH IN FIRST DIVISION

Graham ANTHONY	Midfielder
Mark BEARD	Defender
Chris BETTNEY	Midfielder
John EBBRELL	Midfielder
Jan-Aage FJORTOFT	Forward
Charlie HARTFIELD	Midfielder/Full back
Steve HAWES	Midfielder
Nick HENRY	Midfielder
Doug HODGSON	Central defender
David HOLDSWORTH	Defender/Centre back
Don HUTCHISON	Midfielder
Petr KATCHURO	Forward
Alan KELLY	Goalkeeper
Lance KEY	Goalkeeper
Roger NILSEN	Defender
Paul PARKER	Defender
Mark PATTERSON	Midfielder
Lee SANDFORD	Defender/Centre back
Andy SCOTT	Forward
Chris SHORT	Defender
Paul SIMPSON	Midfielder
Nigel SPACKMAN	Midfielder
Phil STARBUCK	Forward
Gareth TAYLOR	Forward
Simon TREACY	Goalkeeper
Michel VONK	Central defender
Andy HUNT	Forward
Mitch WARD	Midfielder
David WHITE	Forward
Dane WHITEHOUSE	Midfielder

Season	League	League Position	P	W	D	L	F	A	Pts	3 Point Equivalent
2005–06	**Championship**	**2**	**46**	**26**	**12**	**8**	**76**	**46**	**90**	**1.956522**
2002–03	L1	3	46	23	12	11	72	52	80	1.760870
2003–04	L1	8	46	20	15	11	65	56	71	1.630435
2000–01	L1	10	46	19	16	11	52	49	68	1.586957
2004–05	Championship	8	46	18	15	13	57	56	67	1.500000
2001–02	L1	13	46	15	16	15	53	54	60	1.326087
1999–2000	L1	16	46	13	18	15	59	71	54	1.239130
2006–07	Premier League	18	38	10	8	20	32	55	38	1.000000

SQUAD 2005–06 — 2ND IN THE CHAMPIONSHIP

Ade AKINBIYI	Forward
Chris ARMSTRONG	Defender/Left back
Leigh BROMBY	Defender/Centre back
Neil COLLINS	Defender/Centre back
Brian DEANE	Forward
Bruce DYER	Forward
Garry FLITCROFT	Midfielder
Jonathan FORTE	Forward
Simon FRANCIS	Defender/Midfielder
Derek GEARY	Defender/Centre back
Keith GILLESPIE	Midfielder
Andy GRAY	Midfielder/Forward
Jon HARLEY	Defender/Midfielder
Geoff HORSFIELD	Forward
Paul IFILL	Midfielder
Phil JAGIELKA	Defender/Midfielder
Steven KABBA	Forward
Paddy KENNY	Goalkeeper
Rob KOZLUK	Defender/Midfielder
Chris LUCKETTI	Defender/Centre back
Nick MONTGOMERY	Midfielder
Chris MORGAN	Defender/Centre back
Lilian NALIS	Midfielder
Vincent PERICARD	Forward
Alan QUINN	Midfielder
Paul SHAW	Forward
Neil SHIPPERLEY	Forward
Craig SHORT	Defender/Centre back
Michael TONGE	Midfielder
David UNSWORTH	Defender
Danny WEBBER	Forward

SHEFFIELD WEDNESDAY

Season	League	League Position	P	W	D	L	F	A	Pts	3 Point Equivalent
1958–59	Division 2	1	42	28	6	8	106	48	62	2.142857
1955–56	Division 2	1	42	21	13	8	101	62	55	1.809524
1951–52	Division 2	1	42	21	11	10	100	66	53	1.761905
1947–48	Division 2	4	42	20	11	11	66	53	51	1.690476
1949–50	Division 2	2	42	18	16	8	67	48	52	1.666667
1948–49	Division 2	8	42	15	13	14	63	56	43	1.380952
1956–57	**Division 1**	**14**	**42**	**16**	**6**	**20**	**82**	**88**	**38**	**1.285714**
1953–54	Division 1	19	42	15	6	21	70	91	36	1.214286
1952–53	Division 1	18	42	12	11	19	62	72	35	1.119048
1950–51	Division 1	21	42	12	8	22	64	83	32	1.047619
1946–47	Division 2	20	42	12	8	22	67	88	32	1.047619
1957–58	Division 1	22	42	12	7	23	69	92	31	1.023810
1954–55	Division 1	22	42	8	10	24	63	100	26	0.809524

1940s & 50s

SQUAD 1956–57 — 14TH IN DIVISION 1

Walter BINGLEY	Full back	Don McEVOY	Centre half
Albert BROADBENT	Outside left	David McINTOSH	Goalkeeper
Dave CARGILL	Outside left	Jack MARTIN	Full back
Norman CURTIS	Full back	Ralph O'DONNELL	Centre half
Keith ELLIS	Centre forward	Charlie PLLU	Goalkeeper
Alan FINNEY	Outside right	Albert QUIXALL	Inside forward
Redfern FROGGATT	Inside forward	Roy SHINER	Centre forward
Don GIBSON	Wing half	Ron STANIFORTH	Full back
Ron GREENSMITH	Outside left	Peter SWAN	Centre half
Brian HILL	Full back	Terry WHITHAM	Wing half
Alan HINCHCLIFFE	Goalkeeper	Derek WILKINSON	Outside right
Jimmy McANEARNEY	Inside forward	Les WILLIAMS	Goalkeeper
Tom McANEARNEY	Wing half	Gerry YOUNG	Wing half

Season	League	League Position	P	W	D	L	F	A	Pts	3 Point Equivalent
1960–61	**Division 1**	**2**	**42**	**23**	**12**	**7**	**78**	**47**	**58**	**1.928571**
1959–60	Division 1	5	42	19	11	12	80	59	49	1.619048
1963–64	Division 1	6	42	19	11	12	84	67	49	1.619048
1962–63	Division 1	6	42	19	10	13	77	63	48	1.595238
1961–62	Division 1	6	42	20	6	16	72	58	46	1.571429
1964–65	Division 1	8	42	16	11	15	57	55	43	1.404762
1966–67	Division 1	11	42	14	13	15	56	47	41	1.309524
1965–66	Division 1	17	42	14	8	20	56	66	36	1.190476
1968–69	Division 1	15	42	10	16	16	41	54	36	1.095238
1967–68	Division 1	19	42	11	12	19	51	63	34	1.071429

1960s

SQUAD 1960–61 — 2ND IN DIVISION 1

Bobby CRAIG	Inside forward	Tom McANEARNEY	Wing half
Keith ELLIS	Centre forward	Roy McLAREN	Goalkeeper
Johnny FANTHAM	Inside forward	Don MEGSON	Left back
Alan FINNEY	Outside right	John MEREDITH	Winger
Bill GRIFFIN	Inside forward	Ralph O'DONNELL	Centre half
Brian HILL	Full back	John QUINN	Midfielder
Peter JOHNSON	Right back	Ron SPRINGETT	Goalkeeper
Tony KAY	Left half	Peter SWAN	Centre half
Bobby LODGE	Outside right	Derek WILKINSON	Outside right
Jack MARTIN	Full back	Gerry YOUNG	Wing half

Season	League	League Position	P	W	D	L	F	A	Pts	3 Point Equivalent
1976–77	Division 3	8	46	22	9	15	65	55	53	1.630435
1972–73	**Division 2**	**10**	**42**	**17**	**10**	**15**	**59**	**55**	**44**	**1.452381**
1977–78	Division 3	14	46	15	16	15	50	52	46	1.326087
1978–79	Division 3	14	46	13	19	14	53	53	45	1.260870
1971–72	Division 2	14	42	13	12	17	51	58	38	1.214286
1970–71	Division 2	15	42	12	12	18	51	69	36	1.142857
1975–76	Division 3	20	46	12	16	18	48	59	40	1.130435
1973–74	Division 2	19	42	12	11	19	51	63	35	1.119048
1969–70	Division 1	22	42	8	9	25	40	71	25	0.785714
1974–75	Division 2	22	42	5	11	26	29	64	21	0.619048

SQUAD 1972–73   10TH IN DIVISION 2

David CLEMENTS	Left back	Colin PROPHETT	Central defender
Roy COYLE	Midfielder	Eddie PRUDHAM	Forward
Jim CRAIG	Full back	Peter RODRIGUES	Right back
Tommy CRAIG	Midfielder	John SINCLAIR	Winger
Peter EUSTACE	Midfielder	John SISSONS	Outside left
Peter FOX	Goalkeeper	Peter SPRINGETT	Goalkeeper
Peter GRUMMITT	Goalkeeper	David SUNLEY	Forward
Willie HENDERSON	Winger	Peter SWAN	Centre half
John HOLSGROVE	Central defender	Paul TAYLOR	Midfielder
Brian JOICEY	Forward	Allan THOMPSON	Central defender
Jimmy MULLEN	Central defender	Sam TODD	Defender
Eric POTTS	Winger	Rodger WYLDE	Forward
Mike PRENDERGAST	Forward		

Season	League	League Position	P	W	D	L	F	A	Pts	3 Point Equivalent
1983–84	Division 2	2	42	26	10	6	72	34	88	2.095238
1985–86	**Division 1**	**5**	**42**	**21**	**10**	**11**	**63**	**54**	**73**	**1.738095**
1979–80	Division 3	3	46	21	16	9	81	47	58	1.717391
1981–82	Division 2	4	42	20	10	12	55	51	70	1.666667
1984–85	Division 1	8	42	17	14	11	58	45	65	1.547619
1982–83	Division 2	6	42	16	15	11	60	47	63	1.500000
1980–81	Division 2	10	42	17	8	17	53	51	42	1.404762
1987–88	Division 1	11	40	15	8	17	52	66	53	1.325000
1986–87	Division 1	13	42	13	13	16	58	59	52	1.238095
1988–89	Division 1	15	38	10	12	16	34	51	42	1.105263

SQUAD 1985–86   5TH IN DIVISION 1

Andy BLAIR	Midfielder	Gary MEGSON	Midfielder
Mark CHAMBERLAIN	Winger	Chris MORRIS	Full back
Lee CHAPMAN	Forward	Gary SHELTON	Midfielder
Tony GREGORY	Midfielder	Peter SHIRTLIFF	Central defender
Paul HART	Central defender	Carl SHUTT	Forward
Martin HODGE	Goalkeeper	Mark SMITH	Central defender
Sigurdur JONSSON	Defender	Glynn SNODIN	Left back/Winger
Ian KNIGHT	Central defender	Simon STAINROD	Forward
Mick LYONS	Central defender	Mel STERLAND	Right back
Lawrie MADDEN	Central defender	Garry THOMPSON	Forward
Brian MARWOOD	Winger	Nigel WORTHINGTON	Midfielder

Season	League	League Position	P	W	D	L	F	A	Pts	3 Point Equivalent
1991–92	**Division 1**	**3**	**42**	**21**	**12**	**9**	**62**	**49**	**75**	**1.785714**
1990–91	Division 2	3	46	22	16	8	80	51	82	1.782609
1993–94	Premier League	7	42	16	16	10	76	54	64	1.523810
1996–97	Premier League	7	38	14	15	9	50	51	57	1.500000
1992–93	Premier League	7	42	15	14	13	55	51	59	1.404762
1994–95	Premier League	13	42	13	12	17	49	57	51	1.214286
1998–99	Premier League	12	38	13	7	18	41	42	46	1.210526
1997–98	Premier League	16	38	12	8	18	52	67	44	1.157895
1989–90	Division 1	18	38	11	10	17	35	51	43	1.131579
1995–96	Premier League	15	38	10	10	18	48	61	40	1.052632

SQUAD 1991–92   3RD IN DIVISION 1

Viv ANDERSON	Right back	Carlton PALMER	Midfielder
Chris BART-WILLIAMS	Midfielder	Nigel PEARSON	Central defender
Trevor FRANCIS	Forward	Kevin PRESSMAN	Goalkeeper
John HARKES	Right back/Midfielder	John SHERIDAN	Midfielder
David HIRST	Forward	Peter SHIRTLIFF	Central defender
Graham HYDE	Midfielder	Paul WARHURST	Defender/Midfielder
Nigel JEMSON	Forward	Gordon WATSON	Forward
David JOHNSON	Forward	Paul WILLIAMS	Forward
Phil KING	Left back	Danny WILSON	Midfielder
Steve MacKENZIE	Midfielder	Chris WOODS	Goalkeeper
Roland NILSSON	Defender/Right back	Nigel WORTHINGTON	Midfielder

Season	League	League Position	P	W	D	L	F	A	Pts	3 Point Equivalent
2006–07	**Championship**	**9**	**46**	**20**	**11**	**15**	**70**	**66**	**71**	**1.543478**
2004–05	League 1	5	46	19	12	15	77	59	72	1.500000
2000–01	L1	17	46	15	23	8	52	71	53	1.478261
2003–04	L2	16	46	13	19	14	48	64	53	1.260870
2001–02	L1	20	46	12	20	14	49	71	50	1.217391
2005–06	Championship	19	46	13	13	20	39	52	52	1.130435
2002–03	L1	22	46	10	20	16	56	73	46	1.086957
1999–2000	Premier League	19	38	8	7	23	38	70	31	0.815789

SQUAD 2006–07   9TH IN THE CHAMPIONSHIP

Steve ADAMS	Defender	Brad JONES	Goalkeeper
Chris ADAMSON	Goalkeeper	Rocky LEKEJ	Midfielder
Wayne ANDREWS	Forward	Kenny LUNT	Midfielder
Mark BEEVERS	Defender/Centre back	Steven MacLEAN	Forward
Luke BODEN	Forward	Sean McALLISTER	Midfielder
Madjid BOUGHERRA	Defender/Centre back	Rory McARDLE	Defender/Centre back
Chris BRUNT	Midfielder	Burton O'BRIEN	Midfielder
Lee BULLEN	Defender	Lloyd SAM	Midfielder
Deon BURTON	Forward	Frankie SIMEK	Defender
Leon CLARKE	Forward	Wade SMALL	Forward
Barry CORR	Forward	Tommy SPURR	Defender/Midfielder
Graham COUGHLAN	Defender/Centre back	Drew TALBOT	Forward
Mark CROSSLEY	Goalkeeper	Marcus TUDGAY	Forward
Yoann FOLLY	Midfielder	Iain TURNER	Goalkeeper
Peter GILBERT	Defender/Left back	Steve WATSON	Defender
David GRAHAM	Forward	Glenn WHELAN	Midfielder
John HILLS	Defender/Left back	Richard WOOD	Defender/Centre back
Jermaine JOHNSON	Midfielder		

247

SHEFFIELD WEDNESDAY

SOUTHAMPTON

Season	League	League Position	P	W	D	L	F	A	Pts	3 Point Equivalent
1948–49	**Division 2**	**3**	**42**	**23**	**9**	**10**	**69**	**36**	**55**	**1.857143**
1954–55	Division 3 South	3	46	24	11	11	75	51	59	1.804348
1947–48	Division 2	3	42	21	10	11	71	53	52	1.738095
1949–50	Division 2	4	42	19	14	9	64	48	52	1.690476
1957–58	Division 3 South	6	46	22	10	14	112	72	54	1.652174
1956–57	Division 3 South	4	46	22	10	14	76	52	54	1.652174
1953–54	Division 3 South	6	46	22	7	17	76	63	51	1.586957
1950–51	Division 2	12	42	15	13	14	66	73	43	1.380952
1955–56	Division 3 South	14	46	18	8	20	91	81	44	1.347826
1958–59	Division 3	14	46	17	11	18	88	80	45	1.347826
1951–52	Division 2	13	42	15	11	16	61	73	41	1.333333
1946–47	Division 2	14	42	15	9	18	69	76	39	1.285714
1952–53	Division 2	21	42	10	13	19	68	85	33	1.023810

SQUAD 1948–49   3RD IN DIVISION 2

Ted BATES	Inside forward	Albie ROLES	Full back
Ian BLACK	Goalkeeper	Tommy RUDKIN	Outside left
George CURTIS	Inside forward	Aug SCOTT	Inside forward
Eric DAY	Outside right	George SMITH	Wing half
Billy ELLERINGTON	Full back	Len STANSBRIDGE	Goalkeeper
Jose GALLEGO	Outside left	Bobby VECK	Outside left
Wilf GRANT	Centre forward	Charlie WAYMAN	Centre forward
Bill HEATON	Outside left	Eric WEBBER	Centre half
Joe MALLETT	Wing half	Roland WHEATLEY	Wing half
Alf RAMSEY	Full back	Len WILKINS	Full back
Bill ROCHFORD	Full back		

Season	League	League Position	P	W	D	L	F	A	Pts	3 Point Equivalent
1959–60	Division 3	1	46	26	9	11	106	75	61	1.891304
1965–66	Division 2	2	42	22	10	10	85	56	54	1.809524
1963–64	Division 2	5	42	19	9	14	100	73	47	1.571429
1964–65	Division 2	4	42	17	14	11	83	63	48	1.547619
1961–62	Division 2	6	42	18	9	15	77	62	45	1.500000
1960–61	Division 2	8	42	18	8	16	84	81	44	1.476190
1968–69	**Division 1**	**7**	**42**	**16**	**13**	**13**	**57**	**48**	**45**	**1.452381**
1962–63	Division 2	11	42	17	8	17	72	67	42	1.404762
1967–68	Division 1	16	42	13	11	18	66	83	37	1.190476
1966–67	Division 1	19	42	14	6	22	74	92	34	1.142857

SQUAD 1968–69   7TH IN DIVISION 1

Tony BYRNE	Defender	Joe KIRKUP	Full back
Mick CHANNON	Forward	Eric MARTIN	Goalkeeper
Ron DAVIES	Centre forward	Bob McCARTHY	Right back
Hugh FISHER	Midfielder	John McGRATH	Centre half
Jimmy GABRIEL	Wing half	Jimmy MELIA	Midfielder
Gerry GURR	Goalkeeper	Terry PAINE	Winger
Dennis HOLLYWOOD	Left back	Frank SAUL	Forward
Ken JONES	Full back	Bobby STOKES	Forward
Mick JUDD	Forward	John SYDENHAM	Outside left
Fred KEMP	Midfielder	David WALKER	Central defender

Season	League	League Position	P	W	D	L	F	A	Pts	3 Point Equivalent
1977–78	Division 2	2	42	22	13	7	70	39	57	1.880952
1975–76	Division 2	6	42	21	7	14	66	50	49	1.666667
1970–71	**Division 1**	**7**	**42**	**17**	**12**	**13**	**56**	**44**	**46**	**1.500000**
1976–77	Division 2	9	42	17	10	15	72	67	44	1.452381
1974–75	Division 2	13	42	15	11	16	53	54	41	1.333333
1978–79	Division 1	14	42	12	16	14	47	53	40	1.238095
1972–73	Division 1	13	42	11	18	13	47	52	40	1.214286
1973–74	Division 1	20	42	11	14	17	47	68	36	1.119048
1971–72	Division 1	19	42	12	7	23	52	80	31	1.023810
1969–70	Division 1	19	42	6	17	19	46	67	29	0.833333

SQUAD 1970–71 — 7TH IN DIVISION 1

Tony BYRNE	Defender		Joe KIRKUP	Full back
Mick CHANNON	Forward		Eric MARTIN	Goalkeeper
Sandy DAVIE	Goalkeeper		John McGRATH	Centre half
Ron DAVIES	Centre forward		Gerry O'BRIEN	Winger
Hugh FISHER	Midfielder		Brian O'NEIL	Midfielder
Roger FRY	Left back		Terry PAINE	Winger
Jimmy GABRIEL	Wing half		Bobby STOKES	Forward
Les HARFIELD	Winger		Dave THOMPSON	Outside right
Dennis HOLLYWOOD	Left back		David WALKER	Central defender
Tom JENKINS	Outside left			

Season	League	League Position	P	W	D	L	F	A	Pts	3 Point Equivalent
1983–84	**Division 1**	**2**	**42**	**22**	**11**	**9**	**66**	**38**	**77**	**1.833333**
1980–81	Division 1	6	42	20	10	12	76	56	50	1.666667
1984–85	Division 1	5	42	19	11	12	56	47	68	1.619048
1981–82	Division 1	7	42	19	9	14	72	67	66	1.571429
1979–80	Division 1	8	42	18	9	15	65	53	45	1.500000
1982–83	Division 1	12	42	15	12	15	54	58	57	1.357143
1987–88	Division 1	12	40	12	14	14	49	53	50	1.250000
1986–87	Division 1	12	42	14	10	18	69	68	52	1.238095
1988–89	Division 1	13	38	10	15	13	52	66	45	1.184211
1985–86	Division 1	14	42	12	10	20	51	62	46	1.095238

SQUAD 1983–84 — 2ND IN DIVISION 1

Reuben AGBOOLA	Left back		Mick MILLS	Full back
David ARMSTRONG	Midfielder		Steve MORAN	Forward
Ken ARMSTRONG	Central defender		Dave PUCKETT	Forward
Ian BAIRD	Forward		Dennis ROFE	Left back
Steve BAKER	Midfielder		Peter SHILTON	Goalkeeper
Alan CURTIS	Forward/Midfielder		Danny WALLACE	Forward
Mark DENNIS	Left back		Mark WHITLOCK	Central defender
Martin FOYLE	Forward		Steve WILLIAMS	Midfielder
Ivan GOLAC	Full back		Frank WORTHINGTON	Forward
Nick HOLMES	Midfielder		Mark WRIGHT	Central defender
Ian JURYEFF	Forward			

1990s

Season	League	League Position	P	W	D	L	F	A	Pts	3 Point Equivalent
1989–90	Division 1	7	38	15	10	13	71	63	55	1.447368
1994–95	Premier League	10	42	12	18	12	61	63	54	1.285714
1997–98	Premier League	12	38	14	6	18	50	55	48	1.263158
1991–92	Division 1	16	42	14	10	18	39	55	52	1.238095
1992–93	Premier League	18	42	13	11	18	54	61	50	1.190476
1990–91	Division 1	14	38	12	9	17	58	69	45	1.184211
1996–97	Premier League	16	38	10	11	17	50	56	41	1.078947
1998–99	Premier League	17	38	11	8	19	37	64	41	1.078947
1993–94	Premier League	18	42	12	7	23	49	66	43	1.023810
1995–96	Premier League	17	38	9	11	18	34	52	38	1.000000

SQUAD 1989–90   7TH IN DIVISION 1

Micky ADAMS	Left back	Barry HORNE	Midfielder
Ian ANDREWS	Goalkeeper	Matt LE TISSIER	Midfielder
Graham BAKER	Midfielder	Sammy LEE	Midfielder
Francis BENALI	Defender	Neil MADDISON	Midfielder
Jimmy CASE	Midfielder	Kevin MOORE	Central defender
Alexei CHEREDNIK	Right back	Russell OSMAN	Central defender
Glenn COCKERILL	Midfielder	Paul RIDEOUT	Forward
Andy COOK	Defender/Left back	Neil RUDDOCK	Defender/Centre back
Steve DAVIS	Defender/Centre back	Alan SHEARER	Forward
Jason DODD	Defender/Right back	Rodney WALLACE	Forward
Tim FLOWERS	Goalkeeper	Danny WALLACE	Forward
Gerry FORREST	Right back	Ray WALLACE	Defender

2000s

Season	League	League Position	P	W	D	L	F	A	Pts	3 Point Equivalent
2006–07	Championship	6	46	21	12	13	77	53	75	1.630435
2000–01	Premier League	10	38	14	10	14	40	48	52	1.368421
2002–03	Premier League	8	38	13	13	12	43	46	52	1.368421
2005–06	Championship	12	46	13	19	14	49	50	58	1.260870
2003–04	Premier League	12	38	12	11	15	44	45	47	1.236842
2001–02	Premier League	11	38	12	9	17	46	54	45	1.184211
1999–2000	Premier League	15	38	12	8	18	45	62	44	1.157895
2004–05	Premier League	20	38	6	14	18	45	66	32	0.842105

SQUAD 2000–01   10TH IN THE PREMIER LEAGUE

James BEATTIE	Forward	Claus LUNDEKVAM	Defender/Centre back
Francis BENALI	Defender	Chris MARSDEN	Midfielder
Imants BLEIDELIS	Midfielder	Garry MONK	Defender/Centre back
Wayne BRIDGE	Defender/Left back	Neil MOSS	Goalkeeper
Kevin DAVIES	Forward	Matt OAKLEY	Midfielder
Jason DODD	Defender/Right back	Marian PAHARS	Forward
Mark DRAPER	Midfielder	Dan PETRESCU	Midfielder
Tahar EL KHALEJ	Defender/Midfielder	Dean RICHARDS	Defender/Centre back
Kevin GIBBENS	Midfielder	Stuart RIPLEY	Midfielder
Paul JONES	Goalkeeper	Uwe ROSLER	Forward
Hassan KACHLOUL	Midfielder	Trond Egil SOLTVEDT	Midfielder
Matt LE TISSIER	Midfielder	Jo TESSEM	Midfielder

SUNDERLAND

Season	League	League Position	P	W	D	L	F	A	Pts	3 Point Equivalent
1949–50	**Division 1**	**3**	**42**	**21**	**10**	**11**	**83**	**62**	**52**	**1.738095**
1954–55	Division 1	4	42	15	18	9	64	54	48	1.500000
1946–47	Division 1	9	42	18	8	16	65	66	44	1.476190
1955–56	Division 1	9	42	17	9	16	80	95	43	1.428571
1952–53	Division 1	9	42	15	13	14	68	82	43	1.380952
1951–52	Division 1	12	42	15	12	15	70	61	42	1.357143
1958–59	Division 2	15	42	16	8	18	64	75	40	1.333333
1948–49	Division 1	8	42	13	17	12	49	58	43	1.333333
1950–51	Division 1	12	42	12	16	14	63	73	40	1.238095
1953–54	Division 1	18	42	14	8	20	81	89	36	1.190476
1947–48	Division 1	20	42	13	10	19	56	67	36	1.166667
1956–57	Division 1	20	42	12	8	22	67	88	32	1.047619
1957–58	Division 1	21	42	10	12	20	54	97	32	1.000000

SQUAD 1949–50 — 3RD IN DIVISION 1

Name	Position	Name	Position
Ivor BROADIS	Inside forward	Tommy REYNOLDS	Outside right
Norman CASE	Centre forward	Bobby ROBINSON	Goalkeeper
Bobby CRAIG	Full back	Reg SCOTSON	Wing half
Dick DAVIS	Centre forward	Len SHACKLETON	Inside forward
Len DUNS	Outside right	Jack STELLING	Full back
Fred HALL	Centre half	Billy WALSH	Centre half
Arthur HUDGELL	Full back	Willie WATSON	Wing half
Harry KIRTLEY	Inside forward	Bill WOOD	Full back
John MAPSON	Goalkeeper	Arthur WRIGHT	Wing half
Tommy McLAIN	Wing half/Centre forward	Tommy WRIGHT	Outside right

Season	League	League Position	P	W	D	L	F	A	Pts	3 Point Equivalent
1963–64	**Division 2**	**2**	**42**	**25**	**11**	**6**	**81**	**37**	**61**	**2.047619**
1961–62	Division 2	3	42	22	9	11	85	50	53	1.785714
1962–63	Division 2	3	42	20	12	10	84	55	52	1.714286
1960–61	Division 2	6	42	17	13	12	75	60	47	1.523810
1964–65	Division 1	15	42	14	9	19	64	74	37	1.214286
1967–68	Division 1	15	42	13	11	18	51	61	37	1.190476
1966–67	Division 1	17	42	14	8	20	58	72	36	1.190476
1965–66	Division 1	19	42	14	8	20	51	72	36	1.190476
1959–60	Division 2	16	42	12	12	18	52	65	36	1.142857
1968–69	Division 1	17	42	11	12	19	43	67	34	1.071429

SQUAD 1963–64 — 2ND IN DIVISION 2

Name	Position	Name	Position
Stan ANDERSON	Wing half	Andy KERR	Centre forward
Len ASHURST	Left back	Jim McNAB	Wing half
Johnny CROSSAN	Inside forward	Tommy MITCHINSON	Midfielder
Dave ELLIOTT	Midfielder	Jim MONTGOMERY	Goalkeeper
Ambrose FOGARTY	Inside forward	George MULHALL	Outside left
Martin HARVEY	Wing half	Colin NELSON	Full back
George HERD	Inside forward	Nick SHARKEY	Centre forward
Charlie HURLEY	Centre half	Brian USHER	Outside right
Cecil IRWIN	Right back		

251

Season	League	League Position	P	W	D	L	F	A	Pts	3 Point Equivalent
1975–76	**Division 2**	**1**	**42**	**24**	**8**	**10**	**67**	**36**	**56**	**1.904762**
1978–79	Division 2	4	42	22	11	9	70	44	55	1.833333
1974–75	Division 2	4	42	19	13	10	65	35	51	1.666667
1971–72	Division 2	5	42	17	16	9	67	57	50	1.595238
1973–74	Division 2	6	42	19	9	14	58	44	47	1.571429
1972–73	Division 2	6	42	17	12	13	59	49	46	1.500000
1977–78	Division 2	6	42	14	16	12	67	59	44	1.380952
1970–71	Division 2	13	42	15	12	15	52	54	42	1.357143
1976–77	Division 1	20	42	11	12	19	46	54	34	1.071429
1969–70	Division 1	21	42	6	14	22	30	68	26	0.761905

1970s

SQUAD 1975–76   CHAMPIONS OF DIVISION 2

Jack ASHURST	Central defender	Dennis LONGHORN	Midfielder
Joe BOLTON	Left back	Dick MALONE	Right back
Jeff CLARKE	Central defender	Bobby MITCHELL	Midfielder
Tom FINNEY	Midfielder	Bobby MONCUR	Central defender
Tommy GIBB	Midfielder	Jim MONTGOMERY	Goalkeeper
Roy GREENWOOD	Winger	Ian PORTERFIELD	Midfielder
Vic HALOM	Forward	Bryan ROBSON	Forward
Mike HENDERSON	Right back/Midfielder	Gary ROWELL	Winger
Mel HOLDEN	Forward	Trevor SWINBURNE	Goalkeeper
Billy HUGHES	Forward	Tony TOWERS	Midfielder
Bobby KERR	Midfielder	Ray TRAIN	Midfielder

252

Season	League	League Position	P	W	D	L	F	A	Pts	3 Point Equivalent
1987–88	Division 3	1	46	27	12	7	92	48	93	2.021739
1979–80	Division 2	2	42	21	12	9	69	42	54	1.785714
1988–89	Division 2	11	46	16	15	15	60	60	63	1.369565
1983–84	**Division 1**	**13**	**42**	**13**	**13**	**16**	**42**	**53**	**52**	**1.238095**
1982–83	Division 1	16	42	12	14	16	48	61	50	1.190476
1985–86	Division 2	18	42	13	11	18	47	61	50	1.190476
1980–81	Division 1	17	42	14	7	21	52	53	35	1.166667
1986–87	Division 2	20	42	12	12	18	49	59	48	1.142857
1981–82	Division 1	19	42	11	11	20	38	58	44	1.047619
1984–85	Division 1	21	42	10	10	22	40	62	40	0.952381

1980s

SQUAD 1983–84   13TH IN DIVISION 1

Ian ATKINS	Defender/Midfielder	Jamie MURRAY	Left back
Paul ATKINSON	Winger	Nicky PICKERING	Midfielder
Paul BRACEWELL	Midfielder	Mark PROCTOR	Midfielder
Lee CHAPMAN	Forward	Bryan ROBSON	Forward
Gordon CHISHOLM	Central defender	Gary ROWELL	Winger
John COOKE	Winger	Chris TURNER	Goalkeeper
Shaun ELLIOTT	Central defender	Barry VENISON	Right back
Rob HINDMARCH	Central defender	Nigel WALKER	Midfielder
Leighton JAMES	Winger	Colin WEST	Forward
Iain MUNRO	Left back		

Season	League	League Position	P	W	D	L	F	A	Pts	3 Point Equivalent
1998–99	L1	1	46	31	3	12	91	28	105	**2.086957**
1997–98	L1	3	46	26	8	12	86	50	90	1.869565
1993–94	L1	12	46	19	19	8	54	57	65	1.652174
1989–90	Division 2	6	46	20	14	12	70	64	74	1.608696
1995–96	L1	1	46	22	7	17	59	33	83	1.586957
1992–93	L1	21	46	13	22	11	50	64	50	1.326087
1991–92	Division 2	18	46	14	11	21	61	65	53	1.152174
1994–95	L1	20	46	12	16	18	41	45	54	1.130435
1996–97	Premier League	18	38	10	10	18	35	53	40	1.052632
1990–91	Division 1	19	38	8	10	20	38	60	34	0.894737

1990s

SQUAD 1998–99   CHAMPIONS OF LEAGUE 1

Sam AISTON	Midfielder	Andy MELVILLE	Defender/Centre back
Kevin BALL	Midfielder	John MULLIN	Midfielder/Forward
Michael BRIDGES	Forward	Kevin PHILLIPS	Forward
Paul BUTLER	Defender/Centre back	Niall QUINN	Forward
Lee CLARK	Midfielder	Alex RAE	Midfielder
Jody CRADDOCK	Defender/Centre back	Martin SCOTT	Left back
Danny DICHIO	Forward	Martin SMITH	Forward
Michael GRAY	Defender/Left back	Thomas SORENSEN	Goalkeeper
Darren HOLLOWAY	Defender/Midfielder	Nicky SUMMERBEE	Midfielder
Allan JOHNSTON	Midfielder	Paul THIRLWELL	Midfielder
Chris MAKIN	Defender	Neil WAINWRIGHT	Midfielder
Andy MARRIOTT	Goalkeeper	Darren WILLIAMS	Defender/Midfielder
Gavin McCANN	Midfielder		

Season	League	League Position	P	W	D	L	F	A	Pts	3 Point Equivalent
2004–05	Championship	1	46	29	10	7	76	41	94	2.108696
2006–07	Championship	1	46	27	7	12	76	47	88	1.913043
2003–04	L1	3	46	22	11	13	62	45	79	1.673913
1999–2000	**Premier League**	**7**	**38**	**16**	**10**	**12**	**57**	**56**	**58**	**1.526316**
2000–01	Premier League	7	38	15	12	11	46	41	57	1.500000
2001–02	Premier League	17	38	10	10	18	29	51	40	1.052632
2002–03	Premier League	20	38	4	7	27	21	65	19	0.500000
2005–06	Premier League	20	38	3	6	29	26	69	15	0.394737

2000s

SQUAD 1999–2000   7TH IN THE PREMIER LEAGUE

Kevin BALL	Midfielder	Gavin McCANN	Midfielder
Steve BOULD	Centre back	Milton NUNEZ	Forward
Thomas BUTLER	Midfielder	John OSTER	Midfielder
Paul BUTLER	Defender/Centre back	Kevin PHILLIPS	Forward
Jody CRADDOCK	Defender/Centre back	Niall QUINN	Forward
Danny DICHIO	Forward	Alex RAE	Midfielder
Carsten FREDGAARD	Forward	Michael REDDY	Forward
Michael GRAY	Defender/Left back	Eric ROY	Midfielder
Thomas HELMER	Centre back	Stefan SCHWARZ	Midfielder
Darren HOLLOWAY	Defender/Midfielder	Thomas SORENSEN	Goalkeeper
Kevin KILBANE	Midfielder	Nicky SUMMERBEE	Midfielder
Chris LUMSDON	Midfielder	Paul THIRLWELL	Midfielder
Chris MAKIN	Defender	Darren WILLIAMS	Defender/Midfielder
Andy MARRIOTT	Goalkeeper		

1940s & 50s

Season	League	League Position	P	W	D	L	F	A	Pts	3 Point Equivalent
1957–58	Division 3 South	4	46	21	15	10	79	50	57	1.695652
1948–49	Division 3 South	4	42	18	15	9	64	56	51	1.642857
1946–47	Division 3 South	4	42	19	11	12	84	73	49	1.619048
1949–50	Division 3 South	14	42	15	11	16	59	62	41	1.333333
1958–59	Division 3	15	46	16	13	17	59	57	45	1.326087
1950–51	Division 3 South	17	46	18	4	24	55	67	40	1.260870
1951–52	Division 3 South	16	46	14	14	18	51	68	42	1.217391
1953–54	Division 3 South	20	46	15	10	21	67	70	40	1.195652
1952–53	Division 3 South	18	46	14	12	20	64	79	40	1.173913
1956–57	Division 3 South	23	46	15	6	25	66	96	36	1.108696
1947–48	Division 3 South	16	42	10	16	16	41	46	36	1.095238
1954–55	Division 3 South	21	46	11	15	20	46	64	37	1.043478
1955–56	Division 3 South	24	46	8	14	24	34	78	30	0.826087

SQUAD 1957–58   4TH IN DIVISION 3 SOUTH

Walter BINGLEY	Full back	Jim KELLY	Centre forward
Sam BURTON	Goalkeeper	Jimmy LEE	Full back
Duncan CAMERON	Outside right	Gordon McDONALD	Left back
Peter CHAMBERLAIN	Centre half	Andy MICKLEWRIGHT	Inside forward
Lewis CLAYTON	Wing half	Alan MOORE	Outside right
Jimmy CROSS	Right half	John NEAL	Full back
Arnold D'ARCY	Outside left	Frank O'MAHONY	Centre forward
Brian DONALDSON	Outside right	Maurice OWEN	Centre forward/Centre half
Stan EARL	Full back	John RICHARDS	Inside forward
Bob EDWARDS	Inside forward	Bill ROOST	Inside forward
Jack FOUNTAIN	Wing half	Johnny SKULL	Outside right
Garth HUDSON	Centre half	Fred THOMPSON	Wing half
George HUNT	Right back		

1960s

Season	League	League Position	P	W	D	L	F	A	Pts	3 Point Equivalent
1968–69	Division 3	2	46	27	10	9	71	35	64	1.978261
1962–63	Division 3	2	46	22	14	10	87	56	58	1.739130
1965–66	Division 3	7	46	19	13	14	74	48	51	1.521739
1966–67	Division 3	8	46	20	10	16	81	59	50	1.521739
1961–62	Division 3	9	46	17	15	14	78	71	49	1.434783
1967–68	Division 3	10	46	16	17	13	74	51	49	1.413043
1959–60	Division 3	16	46	19	8	19	69	78	46	1.413043
1960–61	Division 3	16	46	14	15	17	62	55	43	1.239130
1963–64	Division 2	14	42	14	10	18	57	69	38	1.238095
1964–65	Division 2	21	42	14	5	23	63	81	33	1.119048

SQUAD 1968–69   2ND IN DIVISION 3

Michael BLICK	Centre half	Roy JONES	Goalkeeper
Frank BURROWS	Centre half	Peter NOBLE	Midfielder/Forward
Joe BUTLER	Midfielder	Willie PENMAN	Midfielder
David DANGERFIELD	Midfielder	Don ROGERS	Winger
Owen DAWSON	Full back	Roger SMART	Midfielder
Peter DOWNSBOROUGH	Goalkeeper	John SMITH	Inside forward
Stan HARLAND	Wing half	Rod THOMAS	Right back
Don HEATH	Winger	John TROLLOPE	Left back
Chris JONES	Forward		

Season	League	League Position	P	W	D	L	F	A	Pts	3 Point Equivalent
1978–79	Division 3	5	46	25	7	14	74	52	57	1.782609
1974–75	Division 3	4	46	21	11	14	64	58	53	1.608696
1969–70	**Division 2**	**5**	**42**	**17**	**16**	**9**	**57**	**47**	**50**	**1.595238**
1977–78	Division 3	10	46	16	16	14	67	60	48	1.391304
1970–71	Division 2	12	42	15	12	15	61	51	42	1.357143
1971–72	Division 2	11	42	15	12	15	47	47	42	1.357143
1976–77	Division 3	11	46	15	15	16	68	75	45	1.304348
1975–76	Division 3	19	46	16	8	22	62	75	40	1.217391
1972–73	Division 2	16	42	10	16	16	46	60	36	1.095238
1973–74	Division 2	22	42	7	11	24	36	72	25	0.761905

1970s

SQUAD 1969–70   5TH IN DIVISION 2

Michael BLICK	Centre half
Frank BURROWS	Central defender
Joe BUTLER	Midfielder
David DANGERFIELD	Midfielder
Owen DAWSON	Full back
David DOWN	Centre forward
Peter DOWNSBOROUGH	Goalkeeper
Stan HARLAND	Wing half
Don HEATH	Winger
Arthur HORSFIELD	Forward
Chris JONES	Forward
Peter NOBLE	Midfielder/Forward
Willie PENMAN	Midfielder
Don ROGERS	Winger
Roger SMART	Midfielder
John SMITH	Inside forward
Rod THOMAS	Right back
John TROLLOPE	Left back

Season	League	League Position	P	W	D	L	F	A	Pts	3 Point Equivalent
1985–86	Division 4	1	46	32	6	8	82	43	102	2.217391
1986–87	Division 3	3	46	25	12	9	77	47	87	1.891304
1988–89	**Division 2**	**6**	**46**	**20**	**16**	**10**	**68**	**53**	**76**	**1.652174**
1984–85	Division 4	8	46	21	9	16	62	58	72	1.565217
1982–83	Division 4	8	46	19	11	16	61	54	68	1.478261
1979–80	Division 3	10	46	19	8	19	71	63	46	1.413043
1987–88	Division 2	12	44	16	11	17	73	60	59	1.340909
1983–84	Division 4	17	46	15	13	18	58	56	58	1.260870
1980–81	Division 3	17	46	13	15	18	51	56	41	1.173913
1981–82	Division 3	22	46	13	13	20	55	71	52	1.130435

1980s

SQUAD 1988–89   6TH IN DIVISION 2

Leigh BARNARD	Midfielder
Bobby BARNES	Forward
Paul BODIN	Left back
Colin CALDERWOOD	Central defender
John CORNWELL	Midfielder/Winger
Peter COYNE	Forward
Fraser DIGBY	Goalkeeper
Steve FOLEY	Midfielder
David GEDDIS	Forward
Jon GITTENS	Defender
Charlie HENRY	Midfielder
Dave HOCKADAY	Full back
Tommy JONES	Midfielder
Phil KING	Left back
Ross MacLAREN	Central defender/Midfielder
Alan McLOUGHLIN	Midfielder
Tim PARKIN	Central defender
Duncan SHEARER	Forward
Fitzroy SIMPSON	Midfielder
Steve WHITE	Forward

255

SWINDON TOWN

Season	League	League Position	P	W	D	L	F	A	Pts	3 Point Equivalent
1995–96	L2	1	46	25	4	17	71	34	92	1.717391
1992–93	**L1**	**5**	**46**	**21**	**12**	**13**	**74**	**59**	**76**	**1.630435**
1989–90	Division 2	4	46	20	14	12	79	59	74	1.608696
1991–92	Division 2	8	46	18	15	13	69	55	69	1.500000
1996–97	L1	19	46	15	22	9	52	71	54	1.456522
1997–98	L1	18	46	14	22	10	42	73	52	1.391304
1998–99	L1	17	46	13	22	11	59	81	50	1.326087
1994–95	L1	21	46	12	22	12	54	73	48	1.260870
1990–91	Division 2	21	46	12	14	20	65	73	50	1.086957
1993–94	Premier League	22	42	5	15	22	47	100	30	0.714286

SQUAD 1992–93 — 5TH IN FIRST DIVISION

Paul BODIN	Left back	David KERSLAKE	Defender
Colin CALDERWOOD	Defender/Centre back	Martin LING	Midfielder
Shaun CLOSE	Forward	Ross MacLAREN	Central defender/Midfielder
Fraser DIGBY	Goalkeeper	Brian MARWOOD	Winger
Andy GRAY	Midfielder	Craig MASKELL	Forward
Nicky HAMMOND	Goalkeeper	Dave MITCHELL	Forward
Chris HAMON	Forward	John MONCUR	Midfielder
Micky HAZARD	Midfielder	Nicky SUMMERBEE	Midfielder
Glenn HODDLE	Midfielder	Shaun TAYLOR	Defender/Centre back
Kevin HORLOCK	Midfielder	Adrian VIVEASH	Defender/Centre back
Paul HUNT	Forward	Steve WHITE	Forward

Season	League	League Position	P	W	D	L	F	A	Pts	3 Point Equivalent
2006–07	League 2	3	46	25	10	11	58	38	85	1.847826
2003–04	**L2**	**5**	**46**	**20**	**13**	**13**	**76**	**58**	**73**	**1.586957**
2004–05	League 1	12	46	17	17	12	66	68	63	1.478261
2002–03	L2	10	46	16	18	12	59	63	60	1.434783
2001–02	L2	13	46	15	17	14	46	56	59	1.347826
2000–01	L2	20	46	13	20	13	47	65	52	1.282609
1999–2000	L1	24	46	8	26	12	38	77	36	1.086957
2005–06	League 1	23	46	11	15	20	46	65	48	1.043478

SQUAD 2003–04 — 5TH IN SECOND DIVISION

Deon BURTON	Forward	Junior LEWIS	Midfielder
David DUKE	Midfielder	Stefani MIGLIORANZI	Midfielder
Rhys EVANS	Goalkeeper	James MILNER	Midfielder
Rory FALLON	Forward	Tommy MOONEY	Forward
Craig FARR	Goalkeeper	Andrew NICHOLAS	Defender/Left back
Luke GARRARD	Defender	Sean O'HANLON	Defender
Bart GRIEMINK	Goalkeeper	Sam PARKIN	Forward
Andy GURNEY	Defender/Midfielder	Alan REEVES	Defender
Ian HERRING	Midfielder	Steve ROBINSON	Midfielder
Matt HEWLETT	Midfielder	Sebastien RUSTER	Midfielder
Matt HEYWOOD	Defender/Centre back	Grant SMITH	Midfielder
Brian HOWARD	Midfielder	Jon STEVENSON	Midfielder
Jerel IFIL	Defender/Centre back	Adrian VIVEASH	Defender/Centre back
Sammy IGOE	Midfielder		

TOTTENHAM HOTSPUR

	Season	League	League Position	P	W	D	L	F	A	Pts	3 Point Equivalent
1940s & 50s	1949–50	Division 2	1	42	27	7	8	81	35	61	2.095238
	1950–51	**Division 1**	**1**	**42**	**25**	**10**	**7**	**82**	**44**	**60**	**2.023810**
	1956–57	Division 1	2	42	22	12	8	104	56	56	1.857143
	1951–52	Division 1	2	42	22	9	11	76	51	53	1.785714
	1957–58	Division 1	3	42	21	9	12	93	77	51	1.714286
	1948–49	Division 2	5	42	17	16	9	72	44	50	1.595238
	1946–47	Division 2	6	42	17	14	11	65	53	48	1.547619
	1947–48	Division 2	8	42	15	14	13	56	43	44	1.404762
	1952–53	Division 1	10	42	15	11	16	78	69	41	1.333333
	1954–55	Division 1	16	42	16	8	18	72	73	40	1.333333
	1953–54	Division 1	16	42	16	5	21	65	76	37	1.261905
	1955–56	Division 1	18	42	15	7	20	61	71	37	1.238095
	1958–59	Division 1	18	42	13	10	19	85	95	36	1.166667

SQUAD 1950–51   CHAMPIONS OF DIVISION 1

Eddie BAILY	Inside left	Billy NICHOLSON	Wing half
Les BENNETT	Inside forward	Alf RAMSEY	Full back
Colin BRITTAN	Wing half	Jimmy SCARTH	Inside forward
Ron BURGESS	Wing half	Syd TICKRIDGE	Full back
Harry CLARKE	Centre half	Dennis UPHILL	Centre forward
Ted DITCHBURN	Goalkeeper	Sonny WALTERS	Winger
Len DUQUEMIN	Centre forward	Arthur WILLIS	Full back
Sid McCLELLAN	Inside forward	Charlie WITHERS	Full back
Les MEDLEY	Outside left	Alex WRIGHT	Inside forward
Peter MURPHY	Inside forward		

257

	Season	League	League Position	P	W	D	L	F	A	Pts	3 Point Equivalent
1960s	**1960–61**	**Division 1**	**1**	**42**	**31**	**4**	**7**	**115**	**55**	**66**	**2.309524**
	1966–67	Division 1	3	42	24	8	10	71	48	56	1.904762
	1962–63	Division 1	2	42	23	9	10	111	62	55	1.857143
	1959–60	Division 1	3	42	21	11	10	86	50	53	1.761905
	1961–62	Division 1	3	42	21	10	11	88	69	52	1.738095
	1963–64	Division 1	4	42	22	7	13	97	81	51	1.738095
	1967–68	Division 1	7	42	19	9	14	70	59	47	1.571429
	1964–65	Division 1	6	42	19	7	16	87	71	45	1.523810
	1965–66	Division 1	8	42	16	12	14	75	66	44	1.428571
	1968–69	Division 1	6	42	14	17	11	61	51	45	1.404762

SQUAD 1960–61   CHAMPIONS OF DIVISION 1

Leslie ALLEN	Centre forward	Dave MACKAY	Left half
Peter BAKER	Full back	Tony MARCHI	Wing half
Ken BARTON	Full back	Terry MEDWIN	Winger
Danny BLANCHFLOWER	Midfielder	Maurice NORMAN	Centre half
Bill BROWN	Goalkeeper	Frank SAUL	Forward
Terry DYSON	Outside left	John SMITH	Inside forward
Ron HENRY	Left back	Bobby SMITH	Forward
John HOLLOWBREAD	Goalkeeper	John WHITE	Inside forward
Cliff JONES	Winger		

Season	League	League Position	P	W	D	L	F	A	Pts	3 Point Equivalent
1977–78	Division 2	3	42	20	16	6	83	49	56	1.809524
1970–71	**Division 1**	**3**	**42**	**19**	**14**	**9**	**54**	**33**	**52**	**1.690476**
1971–72	Division 1	6	42	19	13	10	63	42	51	1.666667
1972–73	Division 1	8	42	16	13	13	58	48	45	1.452381
1969–70	Division 1	11	42	17	9	16	54	55	43	1.428571
1975–76	Division 1	9	42	14	15	13	63	63	43	1.357143
1973–74	Division 1	11	42	14	14	14	45	50	42	1.333333
1978–79	Division 1	11	42	13	15	14	48	61	41	1.285714
1974–75	Division 1	19	42	13	8	21	52	63	34	1.119048
1976–77	Division 1	22	42	12	9	21	48	72	33	1.071429

1970s

SQUAD 1970–71   3RD IN DIVISION 1

Phil BEAL	Defender	Cyril KNOWLES	Left back
Dennis BOND	Midfielder	Roger MORGAN	Winger
Martin CHIVERS	Forward	Alan MULLERY	Wing half
Peter COLLINS	Centre half	Terry NAYLOR	Central defender
Mike ENGLAND	Centre half	Jimmy NEIGHBOUR	Winger
Ray EVANS	Right back	Jimmy PEARCE	Winger
Alan GILZEAN	Centre forward	Steve PERRYMAN	Midfielder
Ken HANCOCK	Goalkeeper	Martin PETERS	Midfielder
Pat JENNINGS	Goalkeeper	John PRATT	Midfielder
Neil JOHNSON	Winger	Tony WANT	Left back
Joe KINNEAR	Right back		

258

Season	League	League Position	P	W	D	L	F	A	Pts	3 Point Equivalent
1984–85	**Division 1**	**3**	**42**	**23**	**8**	**11**	**78**	**51**	**77**	**1.833333**
1981–82	Division 1	4	42	20	11	11	67	48	71	1.690476
1986–87	Division 1	3	42	21	8	13	68	43	71	1.690476
1982–83	Division 1	4	42	20	9	13	65	50	69	1.642857
1985–86	Division 1	10	42	19	8	15	74	52	65	1.547619
1988–89	Division 1	6	38	15	12	11	60	46	57	1.500000
1983–84	Division 1	8	42	17	10	15	64	65	61	1.452381
1980–81	Division 1	10	42	14	15	13	70	68	43	1.357143
1979–80	Division 1	14	42	15	10	17	52	62	40	1.309524
1987–88	Division 1	13	40	12	11	17	38	48	47	1.175000

1980s

SQUAD 1984–85   3RD IN DIVISION 1

Clive ALLEN	Forward	Micky HAZARD	Midfielder
Ossie ARDILES	Midfielder	Glenn HODDLE	Midfielder
Mark BOWEN	Defender/Left back	Chris HUGHTON	Full back
Garry BROOKE	Winger	David LEWORTHY	Forward
John CHIEDOZIE	Winger	Gary MABBUTT	Central defender
Ray CLEMENCE	Goalkeeper	Paul MILLER	Central defender
Ian CROOK	Midfielder	Steve PERRYMAN	Midfielder
Garth CROOKS	Forward	Graham ROBERTS	Central defender
Ally DICK	Winger	Gary STEVENS	Right back/Midfielder
Mark FALCO	Forward	Danny THOMAS	Full back
Tony GALVIN	Winger		

Season	League	League Position	P	W	D	L	F	A	Pts	3 Point Equivalent
1989–90	**Division 1**	**3**	**38**	**19**	**6**	**13**	**59**	**47**	**63**	**1.657895**
1995–96	Premier League	8	38	16	13	9	50	38	61	1.605263
1994–95	Premier League	7	42	16	14	12	66	58	62	1.476190
1992–93	Premier League	8	42	16	11	15	60	66	59	1.404762
1990–91	Division 1	10	38	11	16	11	51	50	49	1.289474
1991–92	Division 1	15	42	15	7	20	58	63	52	1.238095
1998–99	Premier League	11	38	11	14	13	47	50	47	1.236842
1996–97	Premier League	10	38	13	7	18	44	51	46	1.210526
1997–98	Premier League	14	38	11	11	16	44	56	44	1.157895
1993–94	Premier League	15	42	11	12	19	54	59	45	1.071429

SQUAD 1989–90 — 3RD IN DIVISION 1

Paul ALLEN	Midfielder	Mohamed NAYIM	Midfielder
Gudni BERGSSON	Defender/Centre back	John POLSTON	Defender/Centre back
Guy BUTTERS	Defender/Centre back	Andy POLSTON	Central defender
Terry FENWICK	Defender	Mark ROBSON	Winger
Paul GASCOIGNE	Midfielder	Vinny SAMWAYS	Midfielder
David HOWELLS	Midfielder	Steve SEDGLEY	Centre back
Chris HUGHTON	Full back	Gary STEVENS	Right back/Midfielder
Gary LINEKER	Forward	Paul STEWART	Forward/Midfielder
Gary MABBUTT	Central defender	Mitchell THOMAS	Defender/Centre back
Bobby MIMMS	Goalkeeper	Erik THORSTVEDT	Goalkeeper
John MONCUR	Midfielder	Pat VAN DEN HAUWE	Full back
Paul MORAN	Forward	Paul WALSH	Forward

Season	League	League Position	P	W	D	L	F	A	Pts	3 Point Equivalent
2005–06	**Premier League**	**5**	**38**	**18**	**11**	**9**	**53**	**38**	**65**	**1.710526**
2006–07	Premier League	5	38	17	9	12	57	54	60	1.578947
1999–2000	Premier League	10	38	15	8	15	57	49	53	1.394737
2004–05	Premier League	9	38	14	10	14	47	41	52	1.368421
2001–02	Premier League	9	38	14	8	16	49	53	50	1.315789
2002–03	Premier League	10	38	14	8	16	51	62	50	1.315789
2000–01	Premier League	12	38	13	10	15	47	54	49	1.289474
2003–04	Premier League	14	38	13	6	19	47	57	45	1.184211

SQUAD 2005–06 — 5TH IN THE PREMIER LEAGUE

Lee BARNARD	Forward	Ledley KING	Defender/Midfielder
Michael BROWN	Midfielder	Young Pyo LEE	Defender/Midfielder
Michael CARRICK	Midfielder	Aaron LENNON	Midfielder/Forward
Calum DAVENPORT	Defender/Centre back	Pedro MENDES	Midfielder
Edgar DAVIDS	Midfielder	Ahmed Hossam MIDO	Forward
Michael DAWSON	Defender/Centre back	Danny MURPHY	Midfielder
Jermaine DEFOE	Forward	Nourredine NAYBET	Defender/Centre back
Erik EDMAN	Defender/Left back	Noe PAMAROT	Defender/Right back
Anthony GARDNER	Defender	Grzegorz RASIAK	Forward
Tom HUDDLESTONE	Defender/Midfielder	Andy REID	Midfielder/Forward
Johnnie JACKSON	Midfielder	Paul ROBINSON	Goalkeeper
Jermaine JENAS	Midfielder	Wayne ROUTLEDGE	Midfielder
Frederic KANOUTE	Forward	Paul STALTERI	Defender/Midfielder
Robbie KEANE	Forward	Teemu TAINIO	Midfielder
Stephen KELLY	Defender		

Season	League	League Position	P	W	D	L	F	A	Pts	3 Point Equivalent
1953–54	**Division 3 South**	**4**	**46**	**21**	**10**	**15**	**85**	**69**	**52**	**1.586957**
1954–55	Division 3 South	7	46	18	14	14	71	62	50	1.478261
1949–50	Division 3 South	6	42	16	13	13	45	35	45	1.452381
1956–57	Division 3 South	11	46	18	10	18	72	75	46	1.391304
1952–53	Division 3 South	10	46	15	17	14	62	63	47	1.347826
1946–47	Division 3 South	16	42	17	5	20	61	76	39	1.333333
1958–59	Division 4	15	46	16	10	20	81	79	42	1.260870
1947–48	Division 3 South	15	42	14	10	18	57	79	38	1.238095
1957–58	Division 3 South	16	46	13	16	17	59	77	42	1.195652
1955–56	Division 3 South	21	46	13	11	22	52	85	37	1.086957
1948–49	Division 3 South	17	42	10	15	17	41	54	35	1.071429
1951–52	Division 3 South	21	46	13	10	23	57	81	36	1.065217
1950–51	Division 3 South	23	46	9	11	26	54	88	29	0.826087

SQUAD 1953–54   4TH IN DIVISION 3 SOUTH

Chris ADAMS	Outside left	Frank MITCHELL	Wing half
Ted BENNETT	Goalkeeper	Phil NOLAN	Centre half
Dave BEWLEY	Wing half	Ralph OELOFSE	Wing half
Jimmy BOWIE	Inside forward	Tommy PATERSON	Inside forward
Roy BROWN	Centre half/Centre forward	Johnny PATON	Outside left
Tommy BROWN	Inside forward	Harold PHIPPS	Centre half
Maurice COOK	Centre forward	Reg SAPHIN	Goalkeeper
Charlie GALLOGLY	Full back	Bill SHIPWRIGHT	Centre half
Tony HAPGOOD	Outside right	Eddie SMITH	Inside forward
Jimmy JONES	Full back	Dave UNDERWOOD	Goalkeeper
Jimmy KELLY	Wing half	Jimmy WILSON	Wing half/Inside forward
John MEADOWS	Inside forward/Wing half		

Season	League	League Position	P	W	D	L	F	A	Pts	3 Point Equivalent
1968–69	**Division 3**	**1**	**46**	**27**	**10**	**9**	**74**	**34**	**64**	**1.978261**
1959–60	Division 4	4	46	24	9	13	92	67	57	1.760870
1963–64	Division 3	3	46	23	12	11	79	59	58	1.760870
1966–67	Division 3	3	46	20	14	12	61	46	54	1.608696
1960–61	Division 3	4	46	20	12	14	85	72	52	1.565217
1967–68	Division 3	6	46	21	8	17	74	50	50	1.543478
1964–65	Division 3	9	46	17	16	13	71	64	50	1.456522
1965–66	Division 3	12	46	17	13	16	55	51	47	1.391304
1962–63	Division 3	17	46	17	8	21	82	85	42	1.282609
1961–62	Division 3	17	46	14	13	19	63	74	41	1.195652

SQUAD 1968–69   CHAMPIONS OF DIVISION 3

Barry DYSON	Inside forward	Brian OWEN	Winger
Keith EDDY	Midfielder	Mike PACKER	Defender
Barry ENDEAN	Forward	Stewart SCULLION	Winger
Terry GARBETT	Midfielder	Roy SINCLAIR	Midfielder
Brian GARVEY	Defender	Bert SLATER	Goalkeeper
Rod GREEN	Centre forward	Mike WALKER	Goalkeeper
Dixie HALE	Wing half	Tom WALLEY	Midfielder
Walter LEES	Central defender	Duncan WELBOURNE	Defender
Bernie LEWIS	Outside left	Johnny WILLIAMS	Left back
Roy LOW	Inside forward		

Season	League	League Position	P	W	D	L	F	A	Pts	3 Point Equivalent
1977–78	Division 4	1	46	30	11	5	85	38	71	2.195652
1978–79	**Division 3**	**2**	**46**	**24**	**12**	**10**	**83**	**52**	**60**	**1.826087**
1975–76	Division 4	8	46	22	6	18	62	62	50	1.565217
1973–74	Division 3	7	46	19	12	15	64	56	50	1.500000
1976–77	Division 4	7	46	18	15	13	67	50	51	1.500000
1972–73	Division 3	19	46	12	17	17	43	48	41	1.152174
1970–71	Division 2	18	42	10	13	19	38	60	33	1.023810
1974–75	Division 3	23´	46	10	17	19	52	75	37	1.021739
1969–70	Division 2	19	42	9	13	20	44	57	31	0.952381
1971–72	Division 2	22	42	5	9	28	24	75	19	0.571429

SQUAD 1978–79   2ND IN DIVISION 3

Luther BLISSETT	Forward	Alan MAYES	Forward
Ian BOLTON	Central defender	Keith MERCER	Forward
Dennis BOOTH	Midfielder	Brian POLLARD	Winger
Keith CASSELLS	Forward	Keith PRITCHETT	Left back
Bobby DOWNES	Winger	Andy RANKIN	Goalkeeper
Sam ELLIS	Central defender	Steve SHERWOOD	Goalkeeper
Alan GARNER	Central defender	Steve SIMS	Central defender
Steve HARRISON	Left back	John STIRK	Right back
Ross JENKINS	Forward	Ray TRAIN	Midfielder
Roger JOSLYN	Midfielder		

261

Season	League	League Position	P	W	D	L	F	A	Pts	3 Point Equivalent
1981–82	Division 2	2	42	23	11	8	76	42	80	1.904762
1988–89	Division 2	4	46	22	12	12	74	48	78	1.695652
1982–83	**Division 1**	**2**	**42**	**22**	**5**	**15**	**74**	**57**	**71**	**1.690476**
1986–87	Division 1	9	42	18	9	15	67	54	63	1.500000
1980–81	Division 2	9	42	16	11	15	50	45	43	1.404762
1985–86	Division 1	12	42	16	11	15	69	62	59	1.404762
1983–84	Division 1	11	42	16	9	17	68	77	57	1.357143
1984–85	Division 1	11	42	14	13	15	81	71	55	1.309524
1979–80	Division 2	18	42	12	13	17	39	46	37	1.166667
1987–88	Division 1	20	40	7	11	22	27	51	32	0.800000

SQUAD 1982–83   2ND IN DIVISION 1

Gerry ARMSTRONG	Forward	David JOHNSON	Winger
John BARNES	Forward	Jan LOHMAN	Winger
Luther BLISSETT	Forward	Martin PATCHING	Midfielder
Ian BOLTON	Central defender	Pat RICE	Right back
Nigel CALLAGHAN	Winger	Wilf ROSTRON	Left back
Paul FRANKLIN	Central defender	Steve SHERWOOD	Goalkeeper
Jimmy GILLIGAN	Forward	Steve SIMS	Central defender
Kenny JACKETT	Midfielder/Left back	Worrell STERLING	Winger
Ross JENKINS	Forward	Les TAYLOR	Midfielder
Richard JOBSON	Defender/Centre back	Steve TERRY	Central defender

Season	League	League Position	P	W	D	L	F	A	Pts	3 Point Equivalent
1997–98	L2	1	46	24	6	16	67	41	88	1.695652
1998–99	**League 1**	**5**	**46**	**21**	**11**	**14**	**65**	**56**	**77**	**1.608696**
1994–95	L1	7	46	19	14	13	52	46	70	1.543478
1993–94	L1	19	46	15	22	9	66	80	54	1.456522
1991–92	Division 2	10	46	18	11	17	51	48	65	1.413043
1992–93	L1	16	46	14	19	13	57	71	55	1.326087
1996–97	L2	13	46	16	11	19	45	38	67	1.282609
1989–90	Division 2	15	46	14	15	17	58	60	57	1.239130
1990–91	Division 2	20	46	12	15	19	45	59	51	1.108696
1995–96	L1	23	46	10	18	18	62	70	48	1.043478

SQUAD 1998–99   5TH IN LEAGUE 1

Darren BAZELEY	Defender/Midfielder	Tommy MOONEY	Forward
Alex BONNOT	Midfielder	Michel NGONGE	Forward
Alec CHAMBERLAIN	Goalkeeper	Gifton NOEL-WILLIAMS	Forward
Tony DALEY	Midfielder	Robert PAGE	Defender/Centre back
Clint EASTON	Midfielder	Steve PALMER	Defender/Centre back
Nigel GIBBS	Defender	David PERPETUINI	Midfielder
Johann GUDMUNDSSON	Midfielder	Paul ROBINSON	Defender/Left back
Aion HAZAN	Midfielder	Ronny ROSENTHAL	Forward
Micah HYDE	Midfielder	Allan SMART	Forward
Ben IROHA	Midfielder	Tommy SMITH	Midfielder/Forward
Richard JOHNSON	Midfielder	Darren WARD	Defender/Centre back
Peter KENNEDY	Midfielder	Guy WHITTINGHAM	Forward
Jason LEE	Forward	Nick WRIGHT	Midfielder
Keith MILLEN	Defender/Centre back	Dean YATES	Centre back

Season	League	League Position	P	W	D	L	F	A	Pts	3 Point Equivalent
2005–06	**Championship**	**3**	**46**	**22**	**15**	**9**	**77**	**53**	**81**	**1.760870**
2000–01	L1	9	46	20	17	9	76	67	69	1.673913
2002–03	L1	13	46	17	20	9	54	70	60	1.543478
2001–02	L1	14	46	16	19	11	62	56	59	1.456522
2003–04	L1	16	46	15	19	12	54	68	57	1.391304
2004–05	Championship	18	46	12	18	16	52	59	52	1.173913
2006–07	Premier League	20	38	5	13	20	29	59	28	0.736842
1999–2000	Premier League	20	38	6	6	26	35	77	24	0.631579

SQUAD 2005–06   3RD IN THE CHAMPIONSHIP

Gabriel AGBONLOHOR	Forward	Ben FOSTER	Goalkeeper
Al BANGURA	Midfielder	Fran FRANCIS	Forward
Trevor BENJAMIN	Forward	Joel GRANT	Forward
Dominic BLIZZARD	Midfielder	Darius HENDERSON	Forward
Hameur BOUAZZA	Forward	Marlon KING	Forward
Clarke CARLISLE	Defender/Centre back	Malky MACKAY	Defender/Centre back
Alec CHAMBERLAIN	Goalkeeper	Gavin MAHON	Midfielder
James CHAMBERS	Defender	Adrian MARIAPPA	Defender/Centre back
Jay DeMERIT	Defender/Centre back	Anthony McNAMEE	Midfielder
Paul DEVLIN	Midfielder	Junior OSBORNE	Defender
Toumani DIAGOURAGA	Midfielder	Theo ROBINSON	Midfielder
Lloyd DOYLEY	Defender/Right back	Matthew SPRING	Midfielder
Chris EAGLES	Midfielder	Jordan STEWART	Midfielder
Carl FLETCHER	Midfielder	Ashley YOUNG	Midfielder/Forward

WEST BROMWICH ALBION

1940s & 50s

Season	League	League Position	P	W	D	L	F	A	Pts	3 Point Equivalent
1948–49	Division 2	2	42	24	8	10	69	39	56	1.904762
1953–54	**Division 1**	**2**	**42**	**22**	**9**	**11**	**86**	**63**	**53**	**1.785714**
1952–53	Division 1	4	42	21	8	13	66	60	50	1.690476
1957–58	Division 1	4	42	18	14	10	92	70	50	1.619048
1946–47	Division 2	7	42	20	8	14	88	75	48	1.619048
1958–59	Division 1	5	42	18	13	11	88	68	49	1.595238
1947–48	Division 2	7	42	18	9	15	63	58	45	1.500000
1955–56	Division 1	13	42	18	5	19	58	70	41	1.404762
1956–57	Division 1	11	42	14	14	14	59	61	42	1.333333
1954–55	Division 1	17	42	16	8	18	76	96	40	1.333333
1951–52	Division 1	13	42	14	13	15	74	77	41	1.309524
1949–50	Division 1	14	42	14	12	16	47	53	40	1.285714
1950–51	Division 1	16	42	13	11	18	53	61	37	1.190476

SQUAD 1953–54 — 2ND IN DIVISION 1

Ronnie ALLEN	Centre forward
Ray BARLOW	Wing half
Billy BROOKES	Wing half
Wilf CARTER	Inside forward
Freddie COX	Winger
Reg CUTLER	Winger
Reg DAVIES	Goalkeeper
Jim DUDLEY	Wing half
Jimmy DUGDALE	Centre half
Frank GRIFFIN	Outside right
Norman HEATH	Goalkeeper
Ken HODGKISSON	Inside forward
Grenville JONES	Outside right
Joe KENNEDY	Centre half
George LEE	Outside left
Len MILLARD	Full back
Johnny NICHOLLS	Inside forward
Stan RICKABY	Full back
Reg RYAN	Inside forward
Jim SANDERS	Goalkeeper
Stuart WILLIAMS	Full back

1960s

Season	League	League Position	P	W	D	L	F	A	Pts	3 Point Equivalent
1965–66	**Division 1**	**6**	**42**	**19**	**12**	**11**	**91**	**69**	**50**	**1.642857**
1959–60	Division 1	4	42	19	11	12	83	57	49	1.619048
1967–68	Division 1	8	42	17	12	13	75	62	46	1.500000
1963–64	Division 1	10	42	16	11	15	70	61	43	1.404762
1968–69	Division 1	10	42	16	11	15	64	67	43	1.404762
1960–61	Division 1	10	42	18	5	19	67	71	41	1.404762
1961–62	Division 1	9	42	15	13	14	83	67	43	1.380952
1966–67	Division 1	13	42	16	7	19	77	73	39	1.309524
1962–63	Division 1	14	42	16	7	19	71	79	39	1.309524
1964–65	Division 1	14	42	13	13	16	70	65	39	1.238095

SQUAD 1965–66 — 6TH IN DIVISION 1

Jeff ASTLE	Centre forward
Tony BROWN	Midfielder
Danny CAMPBELL	Centre half
Geoff CARTER	Outside left
Clive CLARK	Outside left
Dennis CLARKE	Full back
Ian COLLARD	Midfielder
Bobby CRAM	Right back
Campbell CRAWFORD	Full back
Ray CRAWFORD	Centre forward
Ray FAIRFAX	Full back
Ken FOGGO	Outside right
Duggie FRASER	Defender
Micky FUDGE	Inside forward
Bobby HOPE	Midfielder
Gerry HOWSHALL	Wing half
Stan JONES	Centre half
John KAYE	Defender/Centre forward
Dick KRZYWICKI	Winger
Graham LOVETT	Midfielder
Mick MASON	Inside forward
Ray POTTER	Goalkeeper
Dick SHEPPARD	Goalkeeper
Terry SIMPSON	Wing half
Kenny STEPHENS	Winger
Ray TREACY	Forward
Graham WILLIAMS	Left back
Bill WILLIAMS	Centre half
Ray WILSON	Left back

Season	League	League Position	P	W	D	L	F	A	Pts	3 Point Equivalent
1978–79	Division 1	3	42	24	11	7	72	35	59	1.976190
1975–76	Division 2	3	42	20	13	9	50	33	53	1.738095
1977–78	Division 1	6	42	18	14	10	62	53	50	1.619048
1974–75	Division 2	6	42	18	9	15	54	42	45	1.500000
1976–77	Division 1	7	42	16	13	13	62	56	45	1.452381
1973–74	Division 2	8	42	14	16	12	48	45	44	1.380952
1969–70	Division 1	16	42	14	9	19	58	66	37	1.214286
1971–72	Division 1	16	42	12	11	19	42	54	35	1.119048
1970–71	Division 1	17	42	10	15	17	58	75	35	1.071429
1972–73	Division 1	22	42	9	10	23	38	62	28	0.880952

SQUAD 1978–79   3RD IN DIVISION 1

Brendan BATSON	Right back	David MILLS	Forward
Martyn BENNETT	Central defender	Cyrille REGIS	Forward
Ally BROWN	Forward	Aly ROBERTSON	Central defender
Tony BROWN	Midfielder	Bryan ROBSON	Midfielder
Len CANTELLO	Midfielder	Derek STATHAM	Left back
Laurie CUNNINGHAM	Winger	Kevin SUMMERFIELD	Midfielder
Tony GODDEN	Goalkeeper	John TREWICK	Midfielder
Willie JOHNSTON	Winger	John WILE	Central defender
Mick MARTIN	Midfielder		

Season	League	League Position	P	W	D	L	F	A	Pts	3 Point Equivalent
1980–81	Division 1	4	42	20	12	10	60	42	52	1.714286
1988–89	Division 2	9	46	18	18	10	65	41	72	1.565217
1982–83	Division 1	11	42	15	12	15	51	49	57	1.357143
1984–85	Division 1	12	42	16	7	19	58	62	55	1.309524
1979–80	Division 1	10	42	11	19	12	54	50	41	1.238095
1983–84	Division 1	17	42	14	9	19	48	62	51	1.214286
1986–87	Division 2	15	42	13	12	17	51	49	51	1.214286
1987–88	Division 2	20	44	12	11	21	50	69	47	1.068182
1981–82	Division 1	17	42	11	11	20	46	57	44	1.047619
1985–86	Division 1	22	42	4	12	26	35	89	24	0.571429

SQUAD 1980–81   4TH IN DIVISION 1

Peter BARNES	Winger	Derek MONAGHAN	Forward
Brendan BATSON	Right back	Remi MOSES	Midfielder
Ian BENJAMIN	Forward	Gary OWEN	Midfielder
Martyn BENNETT	Central defender	Cyrille REGIS	Forward
Ally BROWN	Forward	Aly ROBERTSON	Central defender
Barry COWDRILL	Full back	Bryan ROBSON	Midfielder
Nicky CROSS	Forward	Derek STATHAM	Left back
John DEEHAN	Forward	John TREWICK	Midfielder
Tony GODDEN	Goalkeeper	John WILE	Central defender
David MILLS	Forward		

Season	League	League Position	P	W	D	L	F	A	Pts	3 Point Equivalent
1992–93	L2	4	46	25	11	10	88	54	85	1.869565
1991–92	Division 3	7	46	19	14	13	64	49	71	1.543478
1994–95	L1	19	46	16	20	10	51	57	58	1.478261
1998–99	L1	12	46	16	19	11	69	76	59	1.456522
1995–96	L1	11	46	16	18	12	60	68	60	1.434783
1997–98	L1	10	46	16	17	13	50	56	61	1.413043
1993–94	L1	21	46	13	21	12	60	69	51	1.304348
1996–97	L1	16	46	14	17	15	68	72	57	1.282609
1989–90	Division 2	20	46	12	15	19	67	71	51	1.108696
1990–91	Division 2	23	46	10	18	18	52	61	48	1.043478

SQUAD 1994–95   19TH IN FIRST DIVISION

Paul AGNEW	Left back	Steve LILWALL	Left back
Lee ASHCROFT	Forward	Paul MARDON	Centre back
Jeroen BOERE	Forward	Bernard McNALLY	Midfielder
Darren BRADLEY	Midfielder	Micky MELLON	Midfielder
Daryl BURGESS	Defender/Centre back	Stuart NAYLOR	Goalkeeper
Stacy COLDICOTT	Midfielder	Kieran O'REGAN	Defender/Midfielder
Scott DARTON	Central defender	Neil PARSLEY	Full back
Kevin DONOVAN	Midfielder	Mike PHELAN	Midfielder
Paul EDWARDS	Left back	Paul RAVEN	Defender/Centre back
Ian HAMILTON	Midfielder	Tony REES	Forward
Carl HEGGS	Forward	David SMITH	Midfielder
Craig HERBERT	Defender/Centre back	Gary STRODDER	Defender/Centre back
Andy HUNT	Forward	Bob TAYLOR	Forward
Tony LANGE	Goalkeeper		

Season	League	League Position	P	W	D	L	F	A	Pts	3 Point Equivalent
2001–02	L1	2	46	27	11	8	61	29	89	2.000000
2003–04	L1	2	46	25	10	11	64	42	86	1.847826
2000–01	L1	6	46	21	14	11	60	52	74	1.673913
2006–07	Championship	4	46	22	10	14	81	55	76	1.652174
1999–2000	L1	21	46	10	17	19	43	60	49	1.021739
2004–05	Premier League	17	38	6	16	16	36	61	34	0.894737
2005–06	Premier League	19	38	7	9	22	31	58	30	0.789474
2002–03	Premier League	19	38	6	8	24	29	65	26	0.684211

SQUAD 2001–02   2ND IN FIRST DIVISION

Michael APPLETON	Midfielder	Brian JENSEN	Goalkeeper
Igor BALIS	Midfielder	Andy JOHNSON	Midfielder
Trevor BENJAMIN	Forward	Adelino JORDAO	Midfielder
Tony BUTLER	Defender/Centre back	Des LYTTLE	Defender/Right back
James CHAMBERS	Defender	Derek McINNES	Midfielder
Adam CHAMBERS	Defender	Darren MOORE	Defender/Centre back
Neil CLEMENT	Defender/Midfielder	James QUINN	Midfielder/Forward
Warren CUMMINGS	Defender/Left back	Jason ROBERTS	Forward
Danny DICHIO	Forward	Uwe ROSLER	Forward
Scott DOBIE	Forward	Larus SIGURDSSON	Defender
Ruel FOX	Midfielder	Bob TAYLOR	Forward
Phil GILCHRIST	Defender/Centre back	Stanislav VARGA	Defender/Centre back
Russell HOULT	Goalkeeper		

WEST HAM UNITED

Season	League	League Position	P	W	D	L	F	A	Pts	3 Point Equivalent
1957–58	Division 2	1	42	23	11	8	101	54	57	1.904762
1958–59	**Division 1**	**6**	**42**	**21**	**6**	**15**	**85**	**70**	**48**	**1.642857**
1956–57	Division 2	8	42	19	8	15	59	63	46	1.547619
1954–55	Division 2	8	42	18	10	14	74	70	46	1.523810
1948–49	Division 2	7	42	18	10	14	56	58	46	1.523810
1947–48	Division 2	6	42	16	14	12	55	53	46	1.476190
1950–51	Division 2	13	42	16	10	16	68	69	42	1.380952
1946–47	Division 2	12	42	16	8	18	70	76	40	1.333333
1951–52	Division 2	12	42	15	11	16	67	77	41	1.333333
1953–54	Division 2	13	42	15	9	18	67	69	39	1.285714
1955–56	Division 2	16	42	14	11	17	74	69	39	1.261905
1952–53	Division 2	14	42	13	13	16	58	60	39	1.238095
1949–50	Division 2	19	42	12	12	18	53	61	36	1.142857

(margin label) 1940s & 50s

SQUAD 1958–59 — 6TH IN DIVISION 1

John BOND	Full back	Billy LANSDOWNE	Wing half
Ken BROWN	Centre half	Andy MALCOLM	Wing half
Noel CANTWELL	Left back	Bobby MOORE	Central defender
Billy DARE	Centre forward	Malcolm MUSGROVE	Outside left
John DICK	Inside forward	Andy NELSON	Centre half
Noel DWYER	Goalkeeper	Harry OBENEY	Wing half/Centre forward
Ernie GREGORY	Goalkeeper	Andy SMILLIE	Inside forward
Mike GRICE	Winger	John SMITH	Inside forward
Vic KEEBLE	Centre forward	Phil WOOSNAM	Inside forward
Joe KIRKUP	Full back	Doug WRAGG	Outside right

Season	League	League Position	P	W	D	L	F	A	Pts	3 Point Equivalent
1964–65	**Division 1**	**9**	**42**	**19**	**4**	**19**	**82**	**71**	**42**	**1.452381**
1961–62	Division 1	8	42	17	10	15	76	82	44	1.452381
1968–69	Division 1	8	42	13	18	11	66	50	44	1.357143
1962–63	Division 1	12	42	14	12	16	73	69	40	1.285714
1963–64	Division 1	14	42	14	12	16	69	74	40	1.285714
1965–66	Division 1	12	42	15	9	18	70	83	39	1.285714
1959–60	Division 1	14	42	16	6	20	75	91	38	1.285714
1967–68	Division 1	12	42	14	10	18	73	69	38	1.238095
1966–67	Division 1	16	42	14	8	20	80	84	36	1.190476
1960–61	Division 1	16	42	13	10	19	77	88	36	1.166667

(margin label) 1960s

SQUAD 1964–65 — 9TH IN DIVISION 1

Peter BENNETT	Midfielder	Brian DEAR	Centre forward
Dave BICKLES	Centre half	Geoff HURST	Forward
John BOND	Full back	Joe KIRKUP	Full back
Eddie BOVINGTON	Wing half	Bobby MOORE	Central defender
Ronnie BOYCE	Midfielder	Martin PETERS	Midfielder
Peter BRABROOK	Outside right	Eddie PRESLAND	Full back
Ken BROWN	Centre half	Tony SCOTT	Winger
Jack BURKETT	Full back	Alan SEALEY	Outside right
Johnny BYRNE	Centre forward	John SISSONS	Outside left
John CHARLES	Full back	Jim STANDEN	Goalkeeper
Trevor DAWKINS	Midfielder		

	Season	League	League Position	P	W	D	L	F	A	Pts	3 Point Equivalent
1970s	1978–79	Division 2	5	42	18	14	10	70	39	50	1.619048
	1972–73	**Division 1**	**6**	**42**	**17**	**12**	**13**	**67**	**53**	**46**	**1.500000**
	1974–75	Division 1	13	42	13	13	16	58	59	39	1.238095
	1975–76	Division 1	18	42	13	10	19	48	71	36	1.166667
	1973–74	Division 1	18	42	11	15	16	55	60	37	1.142857
	1971–72	Division 1	14	42	12	12	18	47	51	36	1.142857
	1969–70	Division 1	17	42	12	12	18	51	60	36	1.142857
	1976–77	Division 1	17	42	11	14	17	46	65	36	1.119048
	1977–78	Division 1	20	42	12	8	22	52	69	32	1.047619
	1970–71	Division 1	20	42	10	14	18	47	60	34	1.047619

SQUAD 1972–73 — 6TH IN DIVISION 1

John AYRIS	Winger	Frank LAMPARD	Full back
Clyde BEST	Centre forward	Kevin LOCK	Defender
Billy BONDS	Central defender	Bert LUTTON	Winger
Ronnie BOYCE	Midfielder	Ted McDOUGALL	Forward
Trevor BROOKING	Midfielder	John McDOWELL	Right back
Clive CHARLES	Full back	Bobby MOORE	Central defender
Ade COKER	Forward	Bryan ROBSON	Forward
Bobby FERGUSON	Goalkeeper	Tommy TAYLOR	Central defender
Peter GROTIER	Goalkeeper	Dudley TYLER	Winger
Pat HOLLAND	Winger		

	Season	League	League Position	P	W	D	L	F	A	Pts	3 Point Equivalent
1980s	1980–81	Division 2	1	42	28	10	4	79	29	66	2.238095
	1985–86	**Division 1**	**3**	**42**	**26**	**6**	**10**	**74**	**40**	**84**	**2.000000**
	1979–80	Division 2	7	42	20	7	15	54	43	47	1.595238
	1982–83	Division 1	8	42	20	4	18	68	62	64	1.523810
	1983–84	Division 1	9	42	17	9	16	60	55	60	1.428571
	1981–82	Division 1	9	42	14	16	12	66	57	58	1.380952
	1986–87	Division 1	15	42	14	10	18	52	67	52	1.238095
	1984–85	Division 1	16	42	13	12	17	51	68	51	1.214286
	1987–88	Division 1	18	40	9	15	16	40	52	42	1.050000
	1988–89	Division 1	19	38	10	8	20	37	62	38	1.000000

SQUAD 1985–86 — 3RD IN DIVISION 1

Bobby BARNES	Forward	Frank McAVENNIE	Forward
Greg CAMPBELL	Forward	Neil ORR	Central defender
Tony COTTEE	Forward	Phil PARKES	Goalkeeper
Alan DEVONSHIRE	Midfielder	George PARRIS	Midfielder
Alan DICKENS	Midfielder	Geoff PIKE	Midfielder
Tony GALE	Central defender	Steve POTTS	Defender/Right back
Paul GODDARD	Forward	Ray STEWART	Right back
Paul HILTON	Central defender/Forward	Steve WALFORD	Defender
Alvin MARTIN	Central defender	Mark WARD	Winger

1990s

Season	League	League Position	P	W	D	L	F	A	Pts	3 Point Equivalent
1992–93	L1	2	46	26	10	10	81	41	88	1.913043
1990–91	Division 2	2	46	24	15	7	60	34	87	1.891304
1989–90	Division 2	7	46	20	12	14	80	57	72	1.565217
1998–99	**Premier League**	**5**	**38**	**16**	**9**	**13**	**46**	**53**	**57**	**1.500000**
1997–98	Premier League	8	38	16	8	14	56	57	56	1.473684
1995–96	Premier League	10	38	14	9	15	43	52	51	1.342105
1993–94	Premier League	13	42	13	13	16	47	58	52	1.238095
1994–95	Premier League	14	42	13	11	18	44	48	50	1.190476
1996–97	Premier League	14	38	10	12	16	39	48	42	1.105263
1991–92	Division 1	22	42	9	11	22	37	59	38	0.904762

SQUAD 1998–99 — 5TH IN THE PREMIER LEAGUE

Samassi ABOU	Forward	Marc KELLER	Midfielder
Eyal BERKOVIC	Midfielder	Paul KITSON	Forward
Tim BREACKER	Full back	Frank LAMPARD	Midfielder
Joe COLE	Midfielder	Stan LAZARIDIS	Midfielder
Chris COYNE	Defender/Centre back	Steve LOMAS	Midfielder
Paolo DI CANIO	Forward	Javier MARGAS	Centre back
Julian DICKS	Defender	Scott MINTO	Defender/Left back
Rio FERDINAND	Defender/Centre back	John MONCUR	Midfielder
Marc-Vivien FOE	Midfielder	Manny OMOYINMI	Midfielder
Craig FORREST	Goalkeeper	Ian PEARCE	Defender/Centre back
John HARTSON	Forward	Steve POTTS	Defender/Right back
Shaka HISLOP	Goalkeeper	Neil RUDDOCK	Defender/Centre back
Lee HODGES	Forward	Trevor SINCLAIR	Midfielder
Gavin HOLLIGAN	Forward	Ian WRIGHT	Forward
Andy IMPEY	Midfielder		

2000s

Season	League	League Position	P	W	D	L	F	A	Pts	3 Point Equivalent
2004–05	Championship	6	46	21	15	10	66	56	73	1.695652
2003–04	L1	4	46	19	10	17	67	45	74	1.456522
1999–2000	Premier League	9	38	15	10	13	52	53	55	1.447368
2005–06	Premier League	9	38	16	7	15	52	55	55	1.447368
2001–02	**Premier League**	**7**	**38**	**15**	**8**	**15**	**48**	**57**	**53**	**1.394737**
2000–01	Premier League	15	38	10	12	16	45	50	42	1.105263
2002–03	Premier League	18	38	10	12	16	42	59	42	1.105263
2006–07	Premier League	15	38	12	5	21	35	59	41	1.078947

SQUAD 2001–02 — 7TH IN THE PREMIER LEAGUE

Shaun BYRNE	Defender/Midfielder	Paul KITSON	Forward
Titi CAMARA	Forward	Vladimir LABANT	Defender
Michael CARRICK	Midfielder	Steve LOMAS	Midfielder
Joe COLE	Midfielder	Grant McCANN	Midfielder
Laurent COURTOIS	Midfielder	Scott MINTO	Defender/Left back
Christian DAILLY	Defender/Centre back	John MONCUR	Midfielder
Jermaine DEFOE	Forward	Ian PEARCE	Defender/Centre back
Paolo DI CANIO	Forward	Tomas REPKA	Defender/Centre back
Hayden FOXE	Defender	Sebastian SCHEMMEL	Defender/Midfielder
Richard GARCIA	Midfielder	Trevor SINCLAIR	Midfielder
Shaka HISLOP	Goalkeeper	Ragnvald SOMA	Defender/Midfielder
Don HUTCHISON	Midfielder	Rigobert SONG	Defender
David JAMES	Goalkeeper	Svetoslav TODOROV	Forward
Frederic KANOUTE	Forward	Nigel WINTERBURN	Defender/Left back

WIGAN ATHLETIC

Season	League	League Position	P	W	D	L	F	A	Pts	3 Point Equivalent
1978–79	Division 4	6	46	21	13	12	63	48	55	1.652174

SQUAD 1978–79   6TH IN DIVISION 4

John BROWN	Goalkeeper	Joe HINNIGAN	Full back
Derek BROWNBILL	Forward	Peter HOUGHTON	Forward
Frank CORRIGAN	Midfielder	Mick MOORE	Forward
Alan CROMPTON	Midfielder	Ian PURDIE	Winger
John CURTIS	Full back	Ian SEDDON	Midfielder
Neil DAVIDS	Central defender	Kevin SMART	Right back
Dave FRETWELL	Central defender	Noel WARD	Central defender
Geoff GAY	Midfielder	John WILKIE	Forward
Ian GILLIBRAND	Defender	Micky WORSWICK	Winger
Tommy GORE	Midfielder	Jeff WRIGHT	Midfielder
Mark GREW	Goalkeeper		

Season	League	League Position	P	W	D	L	F	A	Pts	3 Point Equivalent
1981–82	Division 4	3	46	26	13	7	80	46	91	1.978261
1986–87	**Division 3**	**4**	**46**	**25**	**10**	**11**	**83**	**60**	**85**	**1.847826**
1985–86	Division 3	4	46	23	14	9	82	48	83	1.804348
1979–80	Division 4	6	46	21	13	12	76	61	55	1.652174
1987–88	Division 3	7	46	20	12	14	70	61	72	1.565217
1980–81	Division 4	11	46	18	11	17	51	55	47	1.413043
1983–84	Division 3	15	46	16	13	17	46	56	61	1.326087
1984–85	Division 3	16	46	15	14	17	60	64	59	1.282609
1988–89	Division 3	17	46	14	14	18	55	53	56	1.217391
1982–83	Division 3	18	46	15	9	22	60	72	54	1.173913

SQUAD 1986–87   4TH IN DIVISION 3

Nigel ADKINS	Goalkeeper	Andy HOLDEN	Central defender
Paul BEESLEY	Defender	Graham HOUSTON	Winger
John BUTLER	Midfielder	Paul JEWELL	Forward/Midfielder
Bobby CAMPBELL	Forward	Barry KNOWLES	Left back
Paul COOK	Midfielder	David LOWE	Forward
Alex CRIBLEY	Central defender	John LOWEY	Midfielder
Ian GRIFFITHS	Outside left	Chris THOMPSON	Midfielder
David HAMILTON	Midfielder	Roy TUNKS	Goalkeeper
Mark HILDITCH	Forward	Alan WHITEHEAD	Central defender

Season	League	League Position	P	W	D	L	F	A	Pts	3 Point Equivalent
1996–97	L3	1	46	26	11	9	84	51	87	1.934783
1998–99	**L2**	**6**	**46**	**22**	**14**	**10**	**75**	**48**	**76**	**1.739130**
1995–96	L3	10	46	20	16	10	62	56	70	1.652174
1990–91	Division 3	10	46	20	9	17	71	54	69	1.500000
1997–98	L2	11	46	17	18	11	64	66	62	1.500000
1994–95	L3	14	42	14	18	10	53	60	52	1.428571
1991–92	Division 3	15	46	15	14	17	58	64	59	1.282609
1993–94	L3	19	42	11	19	12	51	70	45	1.238095
1992–93	L2	23	46	10	25	11	43	72	41	1.195652
1989–90	Division 3	18	46	13	14	19	48	64	53	1.152174

SQUAD 1989–99   6TH IN SECOND DIVISION

Stuart BALMER	Defender/Centre back	David LEE	Forward
Stuart BARLOW	Forward	Andy LIDDELL	Forward
Carl BRADSHAW	Defender/Right back	David LOWE	Forward
Roy CARROLL	Goalkeeper	Roberto MARTINEZ	Midfielder
Neil FITZHENRY	Defender	Pat McGIBBON	Defender/Centre back
Scott GREEN	Defender/Right back	Eric NIXON	Goalkeeper
Colin GREENALL	Defender	Michael O'NEILL	Midfielder
Gareth GRIFFITHS	Defender/Centre back	Andy PORTER	Midfielder
Simon HAWORTH	Forward	Paul ROGERS	Midfielder
Leigh JENKINSON	Midfielder	Kevin SHARP	Defender/Left back
Graeme JONES	Forward	Jorg SMEETS	Midfielder
Ian KILFORD	Midfielder	Paul WARNE	Forward

Season	League	League Position	P	W	D	L	F	A	Pts	3 Point Equivalent
2002–03	L2	1	46	29	4	13	68	25	100	1.978261
2004–05	Championship	2	46	25	9	12	79	35	87	1.826087
1999–2000	L2	4	46	22	7	17	72	38	83	1.586957
2000–01	L2	6	46	19	9	18	53	42	75	1.434783
2003–04	L1	7	46	18	11	17	60	45	71	1.413043
2001–02	L2	10	46	16	14	16	66	51	64	1.347826
2005–06	**Premier League**	**10**	**38**	**15**	**6**	**17**	**45**	**52**	**51**	**1.342105**
2006–07	Premier League	17	38	10	8	20	37	59	38	1.000000

SQUAD 2005–06   10TH IN THE PREMIER LEAGUE

Leighton BAINES	Defender/Left back	Lee McCULLOCH	Forward
Jimmy BULLARD	Midfielder	Stephen McMILLAN	Defender
Henri CAMARA	Midfielder/Forward	Neil MELLOR	Forward
Pascal CHIMBONDA	Defender/Right back	Mike POLLITT	Goalkeeper
David CONNOLLY	Forward	Jason ROBERTS	Forward
Arjan DE ZEEUW	Defender/Centre back	Paul SCHARNER	Defender
John FILAN	Goalkeeper	Josip SKOKO	Midfielder
Damien FRANCIS	Midfielder	Ryan TAYLOR	Defender/Right back
Stephane HENCHOZ	Defender/Centre back	Gary TEALE	Forward
Matt JACKSON	Defender/Centre back	David THOMPSON	Midfielder
Andreas JOHANSSON	Midfielder	David WRIGHT	Defender/Right back
Graham KAVANAGH	Midfielder	Reto ZIEGLER	Defender/Midfielder
Alan MAHON	Midfielder		

WIMBLEDON

Season	League	League Position	P	W	D	L	F	A	Pts	3 Point Equivalent
1978–79	**Division 4**	**3**	**46**	**25**	**11**	**10**	**78**	**46**	**61**	**1.869565**
1977–78	Division 4	13	46	14	16	16	66	67	44	1.260870

SQUAD 1978–79   3RD IN DIVISION 4

Paul BOWGETT	Central defender	Steve GALLIERS	Midfielder
Les BRILEY	Midfielder	Dave GALVIN	Central defender
Jeff BRYANT	Defender	Ray GODDARD	Goalkeeper
Roger CONNELL	Forward	Lee HARWOOD	Central defender
Alan CORK	Forward	Paul HAVERSON	Defender
Francis COWLEY	Winger	Steve KETTERIDGE	Midfielder
Tommy CUNNINGHAM	Central defender	Ray KNOWLES	Forward
Paul DENNY	Midfielder	John LESLIE	Forward
Dave DONALDSON	Defender	Steve PARSONS	Midfielder
Wally DOWNES	Midfielder	Steve PERKINS	Full back
Phil DRIVER	Winger	Paul PRIDDY	Goalkeeper
Mark DZIADULEWICZ	Midfielder	Phil SUMMERILL	Forward
Terry EAMES	Full back		

Season	League	League Position	P	W	D	L	F	A	Pts	3 Point Equivalent
1982–83	Division 4	1	46	29	11	6	96	45	98	2.130435
1983–84	Division 3	2	46	26	9	11	97	76	87	1.891304
1985–86	Division 2	3	42	21	13	8	58	37	76	1.809524
1980–81	Division 4	4	46	23	9	14	64	46	55	1.695652
1986–87	**Division 1**	**6**	**42**	**19**	**9**	**14**	**57**	**50**	**66**	**1.571429**
1987–88	Division 1	7	40	14	15	11	58	47	57	1.425000
1984–85	Division 2	12	42	16	10	16	71	75	58	1.380952
1988–89	Division 1	12	38	14	9	15	50	46	51	1.342105
1981–82	Division 3	21	46	14	11	21	61	75	53	1.152174
1979–80	Division 3	24	46	10	14	22	52	81	34	0.956522

SQUAD 1986–87   6TH IN DIVISION 1

Dave BEASANT	Goalkeeper	Vinny JONES	Midfielder
Andy CLEMENT	Full back/Midfielder	Francis JOSEPH	Forward
Alan CORK	Forward	John KAY	Right back
Wally DOWNES	Midfielder	Mark MORRIS	Central defender
Carlton FAIRWEATHER	Winger	Vaughan RYAN	Midfielder
John FASHANU	Forward	Lawrie SANCHEZ	Midfielder
Kevin GAGE	Midfielder/Full back	Andy SAYER	Forward
Steve GALLIERS	Midfielder	Mick SMITH	Central defender
John GANNON	Midfielder	Andy THORN	Central defender
Brian GAYLE	Central defender	Nigel WINTERBURN	Defender/Left back
Colin GORDON	Forward	Dennis WISE	Midfielder
Glyn HODGES	Midfielder		

Season	League	League Position	P	W	D	L	F	A	Pts	3 Point Equivalent
1993–94	Premier League	6	42	18	11	13	56	53	65	1.547619
1990–91	Division 1	7	38	14	14	10	53	46	56	1.473684
1996–97	Premier League	8	38	15	11	12	49	46	56	1.473684
1989–90	Division 1	8	38	13	16	9	47	40	55	1.447368
1994–95	Premier League	9	42	15	11	16	48	65	56	1.333333
1992–93	Premier League	12	42	14	12	16	56	55	54	1.285714
1991–92	Division 1	18	42	13	14	15	53	53	53	1.261905
1997–98	Premier League	15	38	10	14	14	34	46	44	1.157895
1998–99	Premier League	16	38	10	12	16	40	63	42	1.105263
1995–96	Premier League	14	38	10	11	17	55	70	41	1.078947

SQUAD 1993–94 — 6TH IN THE PREMIER LEAGUE

Neal ARDLEY	Midfielder
Warren BARTON	Defender/Right back
Greg BERRY	Left Winger
Dean BLACKWELL	Defender/Centre back
Gary BLISSETT	Forward
Stewart CASTLEDINE	Midfielder
Andy CLARKE	Forward
Gerald DOBBS	Midfielder
Robbie EARLE	Midfielder
Gary ELKINS	Left back
John FASHANU	Forward
Peter FEAR	Midfielder
Scott B. FITZGERALD	Defender/Centre back
Marcus GAYLE	Defender/Forward
Dean HOLDSWORTH	Forward
Vinny JONES	Midfielder
Roger JOSEPH	Right back
Alan KIMBLE	Defender/Left back
Brian McALLISTER	Full back
Chris PERRY	Defender/Centre back
Lawrie SANCHEZ	Midfielder
John SCALES	Defender/Centre back
Hans SEGERS	Goalkeeper
Neil SULLIVAN	Goalkeeper
Steve TALBOYS	Winger

Season	League	League Position	P	W	D	L	F	A	Pts	3 Point Equivalent
2002–03	L1	10	46	18	17	11	76	73	65	1.543478
2001–02	L1	9	46	18	15	13	63	57	67	1.500000
2000–01	L1	8	46	17	11	18	71	50	69	1.347826
2003–04	L1	24	46	8	33	5	41	89	29	1.239130
1999–2000	Premier League	18	38	7	12	19	46	74	33	0.868421

SQUAD 2002–03 — 10TH IN FIRST DIVISION

Patrick AGYEMANG	Forward
Gareth AINSWORTH	Midfielder
Trond ANDERSEN	Midfielder
Ben CHORLEY	Defender/Centre back
David CONNOLLY	Forward
Jermaine DARLINGTON	Defender/Midfielder
Kelvin DAVIS	Goalkeeper
Damien FRANCIS	Midfielder
Rob GIER	Defender/Centre back
Michael GORDON	Midfielder
Wayne GRAY	Forward
Peter HAWKINS	Defender
Darren HOLLOWAY	Defender/Midfielder
Malvin KAMARA	Defender/Midfielder
Par KARLSSON	Midfielder
Mikele LEIGERTWOOD	Defender/Midfielder
Dean LEWINGTON	Defender
Jobi McANUFF	Midfielder
Lionel MORGAN	Forward
Adam NOWLAND	Midfielder/Forward
Nigel REO-COKER	Midfielder
Neil SHIPPERLEY	Forward
Alex TAPP	Midfielder
Moritz VOLZ	Defender/Right back
Mark WILLIAMS	Defender/Centre back
Chris WILLMOTT	Defender/Centre back

WIMBLEDON

WOLVERHAMPTON WANDERERS

Season	League	League Position	P	W	D	L	F	A	Pts	3 Point Equivalent
1957–58	**Division 1**	**1**	**42**	**28**	**8**	**6**	**103**	**47**	**64**	**2.190476**
1958–59	Division 1	1	42	28	5	9	110	49	61	2.119048
1953–54	Division 1	1	42	25	7	10	96	56	57	1.952381
1946–47	Division 1	3	42	25	6	11	98	56	56	1.928571
1949–50	Division 1	2	42	20	13	9	76	49	53	1.738095
1952–53	Division 1	3	42	19	13	10	86	63	51	1.666667
1955–56	Division 1	3	42	20	9	13	89	65	49	1.642857
1956–57	Division 1	6	42	20	8	14	94	70	48	1.619048
1954–55	Division 1	2	42	19	10	13	89	70	48	1.595238
1947–48	Division 1	5	42	19	9	14	83	70	47	1.571429
1948–49	Division 1	6	42	17	12	13	79	66	46	1.500000
1950–51	Division 1	14	42	15	8	19	74	61	38	1.261905
1951–52	Division 1	16	42	12	14	16	73	73	38	1.190476

1940s & 50s

SQUAD 1957–58 — CHAMPIONS OF DIVISION 1

Colin BOOTH	Inside forward	Gwyn JONES	Full back
Peter BROADBENT	Inside forward	Micky LILL	Outside left
Eddie CLAMP	Wing half	Bobby MASON	Inside forward
Norman DEELEY	Outside right	Jimmy MULLEN	Outside left
Noel DWYER	Goalkeeper	Jimmy MURRAY	Centre forward
Malcolm FINLAYSON	Goalkeeper	George SHOWELL	Defender
Ron FLOWERS	Wing half	Bill SLATER	Wing half
Gerry HARRIS	Full back	Eddie STUART	Defender
Jackie HENDERSON	Centre forward	Dennis WILSHAW	Inside forward
Ron HOWELLS	Wing half	Billy WRIGHT	Centre half
Alan JACKSON	Inside forward		

Season	League	League Position	P	W	D	L	F	A	Pts	3 Point Equivalent
1966–67	Division 2	2	42	25	8	9	88	48	58	1.976190
1960–61	**Division 1**	**3**	**42**	**25**	**7**	**10**	**103**	**75**	**57**	**1.952381**
1959–60	Division 1	2	42	24	6	12	106	67	54	1.857143
1962–63	Division 1	5	42	20	10	12	93	65	50	1.666667
1965–66	Division 2	6	42	20	10	12	87	61	50	1.666667
1963–64	Division 1	16	42	12	15	15	70	80	39	1.214286
1967–68	Division 1	17	42	14	8	20	66	75	36	1.190476
1961–62	Division 1	18	42	13	10	19	73	86	36	1.166667
1968–69	Division 1	16	42	10	15	17	41	58	35	1.071429
1964–65	Division 1	21	42	13	4	25	59	89	30	1.023810

1960s

SQUAD 1960–61 — 3RD IN DIVISION 1

Peter BROADBENT	Inside forward	Phil KELLY	Full back
Chic BRODIE	Goalkeeper	John KIRKHAM	Wing half
Eddie CLAMP	Wing half	Gerry MANNION	Outside right
Les COCKER	Wing half	Bobby MASON	Inside forward
Norman DEELEY	Outside right	Jimmy MURRAY	Centre forward
Cliff DURANDT	Outside left	George SHOWELL	Defender
Ted FARMER	Centre forward	Geoff SIDEBOTTOM	Goalkeeper
Malcolm FINLAYSON	Goalkeeper	Bill SLATER	Wing half
Ron FLOWERS	Wing half	Barry STOBART	Centre forward
Gerry HARRIS	Full back	Eddie STUART	Defender
Des HORNE	Outside left		

Season	League	League Position	P	W	D	L	F	A	Pts	3 Point Equivalent
1976–77	Division 2	1	42	22	13	7	84	45	57	1.880952
1970–71	**Division 1**	**4**	**42**	**22**	**8**	**12**	**64**	**54**	**52**	**1.761905**
1972–73	Division 1	5	42	18	11	13	66	54	47	1.547619
1971–72	Division 1	9	42	18	11	13	65	57	47	1.547619
1973–74	Division 1	12	42	13	15	14	49	49	41	1.285714
1974–75	Division 1	12	42	14	11	17	57	54	39	1.261905
1969–70	Division 1	13	42	12	16	14	55	57	40	1.238095
1977–78	Division 1	15	42	12	12	18	51	64	36	1.142857
1978–79	Division 1	18	42	13	8	21	44	68	34	1.119048
1975–76	Division 1	20	42	10	10	22	51	68	30	0.952381

SQUAD 1970–71 — 4TH IN DIVISION 1

Mike BAILEY	Midfielder	Mike O'GRADY	Outside left
Hugh CURRAN	Forward	John OLDFIELD	Goalkeeper
Derek DOUGAN	Centre forward	Phil PARKES	Goalkeeper
Bobby GOULD	Forward	Derek PARKIN	Right back
Danny HEGAN	Midfielder	John RICHARDS	Forward
Kenny HIBBITT	Midfielder	Bernard SHAW	Full back
John HOLSGROVE	Central defender	Gerry TAYLOR	Full back
Bert LUTTON	Winger	David WAGSTAFFE	Winger
John McALLE	Central defender	Paul WALKER	Midfielder
Jim McCALLIOG	Midfielder	Les WILSON	Right back
Frank MUNRO	Central defender		

Season	League	League Position	P	W	D	L	F	A	Pts	3 Point Equivalent
1988–89	Division 3	1	46	26	14	6	96	49	92	2.000000
1987–88	Division 4	1	46	27	9	10	82	43	90	1.956522
1982–83	Division 2	2	42	20	15	7	68	44	75	1.785714
1986–87	Division 4	4	46	24	7	15	69	50	79	1.717391
1979–80	**Division 1**	**6**	**42**	**19**	**9**	**14**	**58**	**47**	**47**	**1.571429**
1980–81	Division 1	18	42	13	9	20	43	55	35	1.142857
1981–82	Division 1	21	42	10	10	22	32	63	40	0.952381
1985–86	Division 3	23	46	11	10	25	57	98	43	0.934783
1984–85	Division 2	22	42	8	9	25	37	79	33	0.785714
1983–84	Division 1	22	42	6	11	25	27	80	29	0.690476

SQUAD 1979–80 — 6TH IN DIVISION 1

Hugh ATKINSON	Midfielder	Emlyn HUGHES	Defender/Midfielder
Norman BELL	Centre forward	John HUMPHREY	Right back
George BERRY	Central defender	Mick KEARNS	Goalkeeper
Paul BRADSHAW	Goalkeeper	John McALLE	Central defender
Colin BRAZIER	Central defender	Craig MOSS	Winger
Willie CARR	Midfielder	Geoff PALMER	Right back
Wayne CLARKE	Forward	Derek PARKIN	Right back
Peter DANIEL	Midfielder/Right back	Martin PATCHING	Midfielder
Mel EVES	Forward	Billy RAFFERTY	Forward
Andy GRAY	Forward	John RICHARDS	Forward
Kenny HIBBITT	Midfielder	Dave THOMAS	Winger

1990s

Season	League	League Position	P	W	D	L	F	A	Pts	3 Point Equivalent
1996–97	L1	3	46	22	14	10	68	51	76	1.739130
1994–95	L1	4	46	21	12	13	77	61	76	1.630435
1997–98	L1	9	46	18	17	11	57	53	65	1.543478
1998–99	L1	7	46	19	11	16	64	43	73	1.478261
1989–90	Division 2	10	46	18	13	15	67	60	67	1.456522
1992–93	L1	11	46	16	17	13	57	56	61	1.413043
1991–92	Division 2	11	46	18	10	18	61	54	64	1.391304
1993–94	L1	8	46	17	12	17	60	47	68	1.369565
1990–91	Division 2	12	46	13	19	14	63	63	58	1.260870
1995–96	L1	20	46	13	17	16	56	62	55	1.217391

SQUAD 1996–97 — 3RD IN FIRST DIVISION

Name	Position	Name	Position
Mark ATKINS	Midfielder	Simon OSBORN	Midfielder
Steve BULL	Forward	Dennis PEARCE	Defender/Left back
Steve CORICA	Midfielder	Dean RICHARDS	Defender/Centre back
Glen CROWE	Forward	Iwan ROBERTS	Forward
Keith CURLE	Defender/Centre back	Carl ROBINSON	Midfielder
Robbie DENNISON	Winger	Serge ROMANO	Right back
Jens DOWE	Midfielder	Jamie SMITH	Defender/Midfielder
Neil EMBLEN	Defender/Midfielder	Mike STOWELL	Goalkeeper
Darren FERGUSON	Midfielder	Geoff THOMAS	Midfielder
Dominic FOLEY	Forward	Andy THOMPSON	Defender/Full back
Steve FROGGATT	Midfielder	Robin VAN DER LAAN	Midfielder
Michael GILKES	Midfielder	Mark VENUS	Defender/Centre back
Don GOODMAN	Forward	Adrian WILLIAMS	Defender/Centre back
Brian LAW	Central defender	Jermaine WRIGHT	Defender/Midfielder
Richard LEADBEATER	Forward	Eric YOUNG	Central defender

2000s

Season	League	League Position	P	W	D	L	F	A	Pts	3 Point Equivalent
2001–02	L1	3	46	25	10	11	76	43	86	1.847826
1999–2000	L1	7	46	21	14	11	64	48	74	1.673913
2006–07	Championship	5	46	22	10	14	59	56	76	1.652174
2002–03	L1	5	46	20	10	16	81	44	76	1.521739
2005–06	Championship	7	46	16	19	11	50	42	67	1.456522
2000–01	L1	12	46	14	19	13	45	48	55	1.326087
2004–05	Championship	9	46	15	10	21	72	59	66	1.195652
2003–04	Premier League	20	38	7	12	19	38	77	33	0.868421

SQUAD 2001–02 — 3RD IN FIRST DIVISION

Name	Position	Name	Position
Keith ANDREWS	Midfielder	Kenny MILLER	Forward
Nathan BLAKE	Forward	Kevin MUSCAT	Defender/Right back
Michael BRANCH	Forward	Lee NAYLOR	Defender/Left back
Paul BUTLER	Defender/Centre back	George NDAH	Forward
Stephen BYWATER	Goalkeeper	Shaun NEWTON	Midfielder
Mo CAMARA	Defender/Left back	Michael OAKES	Goalkeeper
Colin CAMERON	Midfielder	Ludovic POLLET	Defender/Centre back
Sean CONNELLY	Defender/Right back	Adam PROUDLOCK	Forward
Kevin COOPER	Midfielder	Alex RAE	Midfielder
Tony DINNING	Midfielder	Carl ROBINSON	Midfielder
Gunnar HALLE	Full back	Cedric ROUSSEL	Forward
Mark KENNEDY	Midfielder/Forward	Andy SINTON	Midfielder
Temuri KETSBAIA	Midfielder	Dean STURRIDGE	Forward
Jolean LESCOTT	Defender/Centre back		

GREATEST EVER
ENGLISH CLUB TOP FLIGHT TEAMS OF THE DECADE

THE TEAMS WITH THE HIGHEST POINTS TOTAL IN A SEASON DURING EACH TEN-SEASON PERIOD

Decade	Teams
1940s & 1950s	Wolverhampton Wanderers (1957–58)
1960s	Leeds United (1968–69)
1970s	Everton (1969–70)
1980s	Liverpool (1987–88)
1990s	Manchester United (1993–94)
2000s	Chelsea (2004–05)

GREATEST EVER
ARSENAL XI OF ALL TIME

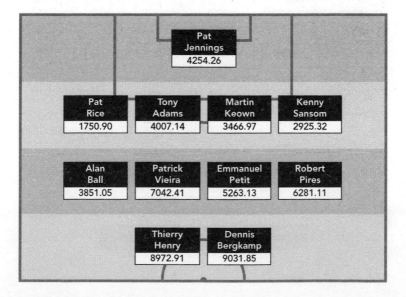

	Pat Jennings		
	4254.26		

Pat Rice	Tony Adams	Martin Keown	Kenny Sansom
1750.90	4007.14	3466.97	2925.32

Alan Ball	Patrick Vieira	Emmanuel Petit	Robert Pires
3851.05	7042.41	5263.13	6281.11

Thierry Henry	Dennis Bergkamp
8972.91	9031.85

GREATEST EVER
ASTON VILLA XI OF ALL TIME

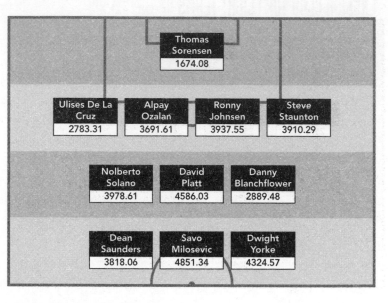

Thomas Sorensen
1674.08

Ulises De La Cruz
2783.31

Alpay Ozalan
3691.61

Ronny Johnsen
3937.55

Steve Staunton
3910.29

Nolberto Solano
3978.61

David Platt
4586.03

Danny Blanchflower
2889.48

Dean Saunders
3818.06

Savo Milosevic
4851.34

Dwight Yorke
4324.57

GREATEST EVER
BIRMINGHAM CITY XI OF ALL TIME

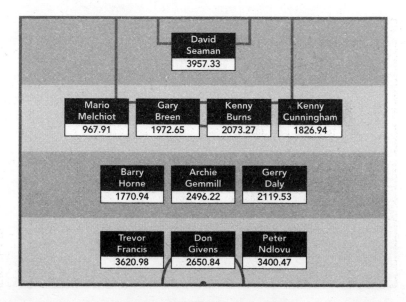

David Seaman
3957.33

Mario Melchiot
967.91

Gary Breen
1972.65

Kenny Burns
2073.27

Kenny Cunningham
1826.94

Barry Horne
1770.94

Archie Gemmill
2496.22

Gerry Daly
2119.53

Trevor Francis
3620.98

Don Givens
2650.84

Peter Ndlovu
3400.47

GREATEST EVER
BLACKBURN ROVERS XI OF ALL TIME

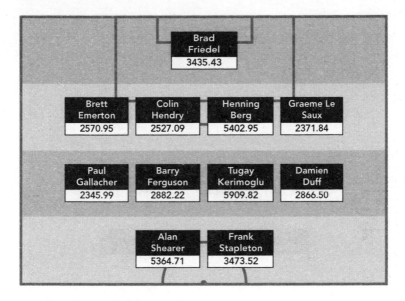

Brad Friedel		
3435.43		

Brett Emerton	Colin Hendry	Henning Berg	Graeme Le Saux
2570.95	2527.09	5402.95	2371.84

Paul Gallacher	Barry Ferguson	Tugay Kerimoglu	Damien Duff
2345.99	2882.22	5909.82	2866.50

Alan Shearer	Frank Stapleton
5364.71	3473.52

GREATEST EVER
BOLTON WANDERERS XI OF ALL TIME

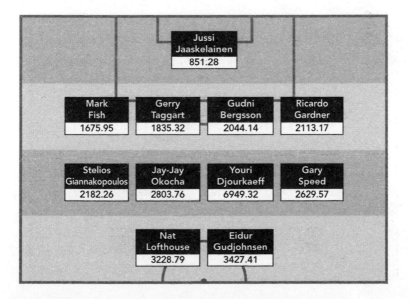

Jussi Jaaskelainen		
851.28		

Mark Fish	Gerry Taggart	Gudni Bergsson	Ricardo Gardner
1675.95	1835.32	2044.14	2113.17

Stelios Giannakopoulos	Jay-Jay Okocha	Youri Djourkaeff	Gary Speed
2182.26	2803.76	6949.32	2629.57

Nat Lofthouse	Eidur Gudjohnsen
3228.79	3427.41

GREATEST EVER
CHELSEA XI OF ALL TIME

GREATEST EVER
EVERTON XI OF ALL TIME

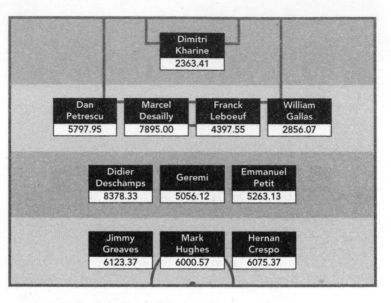

Dimitri Kharine 2363.41

Dan Petrescu 5797.95 | **Marcel Desailly** 7895.00 | **Franck Leboeuf** 4397.55 | **William Gallas** 2856.07

Didier Deschamps 8378.33 | **Geremi** 5056.12 | **Emmanuel Petit** 5263.13

Jimmy Greaves 6123.37 | **Mark Hughes** 6000.57 | **Hernan Crespo** 6075.37

GREATEST EVER
DERBY COUNTY XI OF ALL TIME

GREATEST EVER
FULHAM XI OF ALL TIME

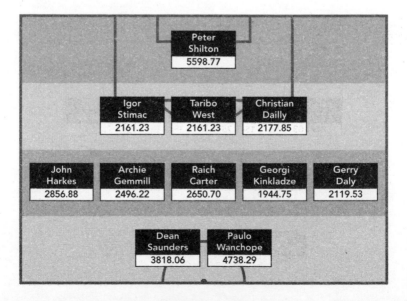

Peter Shilton 5598.77

Igor Stimac 2161.23 | **Taribo West** 2161.23 | **Christian Dailly** 2177.85

John Harkes 2856.88 | **Archie Gemmill** 2496.22 | **Raich Carter** 2650.70 | **Georgi Kinkladze** 1944.75 | **Gerry Daly** 2119.53

Dean Saunders 3818.06 | **Paulo Wanchope** 4738.29

GREATEST EVER
EVERTON XI OF ALL TIME

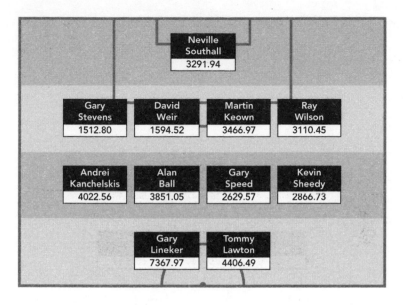

	Neville Southall 3291.94		
Gary Stevens 1512.80	David Weir 1594.52	Martin Keown 3466.97	Ray Wilson 3110.45
Andrei Kanchelskis 4022.56	Alan Ball 3851.05	Gary Speed 2629.57	Kevin Sheedy 2866.73
	Gary Lineker 7367.97	Tommy Lawton 4406.49	

GREATEST EVER
FULHAM XI OF ALL TIME

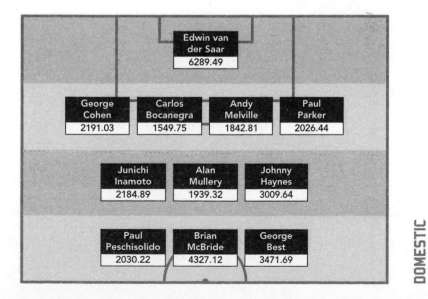

	Edwin van der Saar 6289.49		
George Cohen 2191.03	Carlos Bocanegra 1549.75	Andy Melville 1842.81	Paul Parker 2026.44
	Junichi Inamoto 2184.89	Alan Mullery 1939.32	Johnny Haynes 3009.64
	Paul Peschisolido 2030.22	Brian McBride 4327.12	George Best 3471.69

GREATEST EVER
LIVERPOOL XI OF ALL TIME

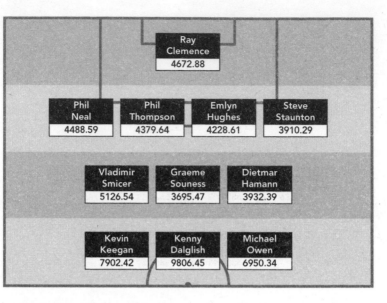

Ray Clemence
4672.88

Phil Neal	Phil Thompson	Emlyn Hughes	Steve Staunton
4488.59	4379.64	4228.61	3910.29

Vladimir Smicer	Graeme Souness	Dietmar Hamann
5126.54	3695.47	3932.39

Kevin Keegan	Kenny Dalglish	Michael Owen
7902.42	9806.45	6950.34

GREATEST EVER
MANCHESTER CITY XI OF ALL TIME

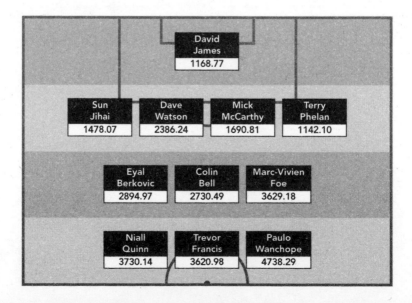

David James
1168.77

Sun Jihai	Dave Watson	Mick McCarthy	Terry Phelan
1478.07	2386.24	1690.81	1142.10

Eyal Berkovic	Colin Bell	Marc-Vivien Foe
2894.97	2730.49	3629.18

Niall Quinn	Trevor Francis	Paulo Wanchope
3730.14	3620.98	4738.29

GREATEST EVER
MANCHESTER UNITED XI OF ALL TIME

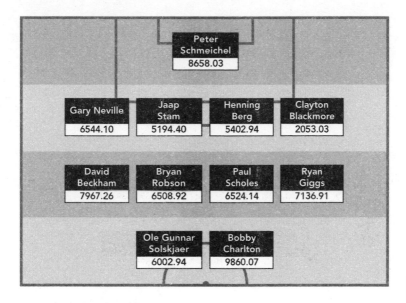

	Peter Schmeichel		
	8658.03		
Gary Neville	Jaap Stam	Henning Berg	Clayton Blackmore
6544.10	5194.40	5402.94	2053.03
David Beckham	Bryan Robson	Paul Scholes	Ryan Giggs
7967.26	6508.92	6524.14	7136.91
	Ole Gunnar Solskjaer	Bobby Charlton	
	6002.94	9860.07	

GREATEST EVER
MIDDLESBROUGH XI OF ALL TIME

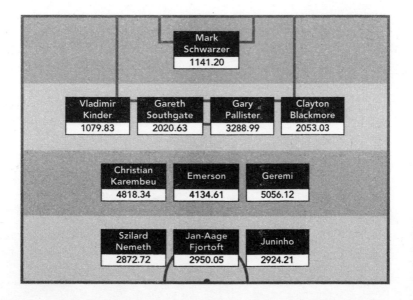

	Mark Schwarzer		
	1141.20		
Vladimir Kinder	Gareth Southgate	Gary Pallister	Clayton Blackmore
1079.83	2020.63	3288.99	2053.03
Christian Karembeu	Emerson	Geremi	
4818.34	4134.61	5056.12	
Szilard Nemeth	Jan-Aage Fjortoft	Juninho	
2872.72	2950.05	2924.21	

DOMESTIC

GREATEST EVER
NEWCASTLE UNITED XI OF ALL TIME

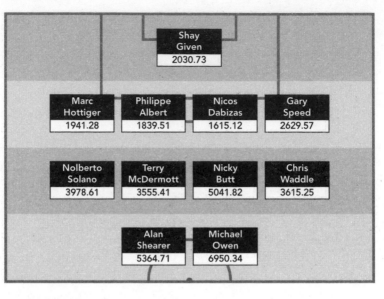

Shay Given — 2030.73

Marc Hottiger — 1941.28
Philippe Albert — 1839.51
Nicos Dabizas — 1615.12
Gary Speed — 2629.57

Nolberto Solano — 3978.61
Terry McDermott — 3555.41
Nicky Butt — 5041.82
Chris Waddle — 3615.25

Alan Shearer — 5364.71
Michael Owen — 6950.34

GREATEST EVER
PORTSMOUTH XI OF ALL TIME

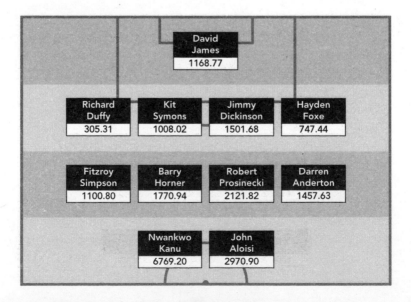

David James — 1168.77

Richard Duffy — 305.31
Kit Symons — 1008.02
Jimmy Dickinson — 1501.68
Hayden Foxe — 747.44

Fitzroy Simpson — 1100.80
Barry Horner — 1770.94
Robert Prosinecki — 2121.82
Darren Anderton — 1457.63

Nwankwo Kanu — 6769.20
John Aloisi — 2970.90

GREATEST EVER
READING XI OF ALL TIME

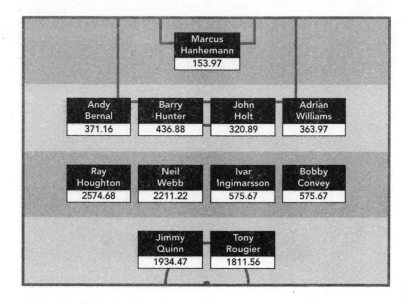

	Marcus Hanhemann 153.97		
Andy Bernal 371.16	Barry Hunter 436.88	John Holt 320.89	Adrian Williams 363.97
Ray Houghton 2574.68	Neil Webb 2211.22	Ivar Ingimarsson 575.67	Bobby Convey 575.67
	Jimmy Quinn 1934.47	Tony Rougier 1811.56	

GREATEST EVER
SUNDERLAND XI OF ALL TIME

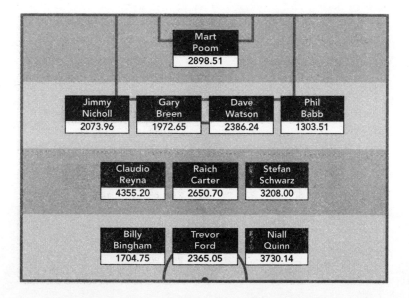

	Mart Poom 2898.51		
Jimmy Nicholl 2073.96	Gary Breen 1972.65	Dave Watson 2386.24	Phil Babb 1303.51
Claudio Reyna 4355.20	Raich Carter 2650.70	Stefan Schwarz 3208.00	
Billy Bingham 1704.75	Trevor Ford 2365.05	Niall Quinn 3730.14	

GREATEST EVER
TOTTENHAM HOTSPUR XI OF ALL TIME

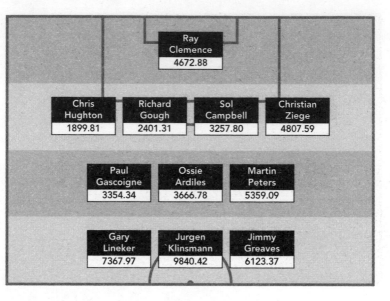

Ray Clemence
4672.88

Chris Hughton
1899.81

Richard Gough
2401.31

Sol Campbell
3257.80

Christian Ziege
4807.59

Paul Gascoigne
3354.34

Ossie Ardiles
3666.78

Martin Peters
5359.09

Gary Lineker
7367.97

Jurgen Klinsmann
9840.42

Jimmy Greaves
6123.37

GREATEST EVER
WEST HAM UNITED XI OF ALL TIME

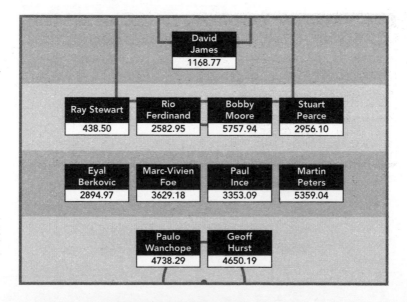

David James
1168.77

Ray Stewart
438.50

Rio Ferdinand
2582.95

Bobby Moore
5757.94

Stuart Pearce
2956.10

Eyal Berkovic
2894.97

Marc-Vivien Foe
3629.18

Paul Ince
3353.09

Martin Peters
5359.04

Paulo Wanchope
4738.29

Geoff Hurst
4650.19

GREATEST EVER
WIGAN ATHLETIC XI OF ALL TIME

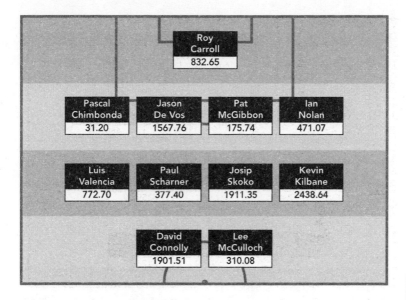

Roy
Carroll
832.65

Pascal
Chimbonda
31.20

Jason
De Vos
1567.76

Pat
McGibbon
175.74

Ian
Nolan
471.07

Luis
Valencia
772.70

Paul
Scharner
377.40

Josip
Skoko
1911.35

Kevin
Kilbane
2438.64

David
Connolly
1901.51

Lee
McCulloch
310.08

GREATEST EVER
ENGLISH TOP FLIGHT XI OF ALL TIME

Position	Player	Nationality	Points
Goalkeeper	Peter SCHMEICHEL	Danish	8658.03
Right back	Gary NEVILLE	English	6544.10
Centre back	Marcel DESAILLY	French	7895.00
Centre back	Laurent BLANC	French	7063.44
Left back	Steve STAUNTON	Irish	3910.29
Right midfield	David BECKHAM	English	7967.26
Centre half	Didier DESCHAMPS	French	8378.33
Centre half	Patrick VIEIRA	French	7082.41
Left midfield	Ryan GIGGS	Welsh	7136.91
Forward	Bobby CHARLTON	English	9860.07
Forward	Kenny DALGLISH	Scottish	9806.45

GREATEST EVER
TOP XI FROM ALL ENGLISH CLUBS BY DECADE

1940s & 1950s

Position	Player	Teams	Points
Goalkeeper	Gil MERRICK	Birmingham City	688.45
Right back	Alf RAMSEY	Tottenham Hotspur	1073.14
Left back	Roger BYRNE	Manchester United	1076.28
Right half	Danny BLANCHFLOWER	Tottenham Hotspur	1045.73
Centre half	Billy WRIGHT	Wolverhampton Wanderers	1572.65
Left half	Johnny HAYNES	Fulham	1837.63
Outside right	Stanley MATTHEWS	Blackpool	3820.65
Inside right	Ivor ALLCHURCH	Swansea City	1690.11
Centre forward	Nat LOFTHOUSE	Bolton Wanderers	3238.79
Inside left	Tommy TAYLOR	Manchester United	1658.36
Outside left	Tom FINNEY	Preston North End	5045.64

1960s

Position	Player	Teams	Points
Goalkeeper	Gordon BANKS	Leicester City/Stoke City	2690.73
Right back	Jimmy ARMFIELD	Blackpool	1281.49
Left back	Ray WILSON	Huddersfield Town/Everton	3110.45
Right midfield	Dave MACKAY	Tottenham Hotspur	1380.75
Centre half	Maurice NORMAN	Tottenham Hotspur	1317.08
Centre half	Bobby MOORE	West Ham United	4395.51
Left midfield	George BEST	Manchester United	2663.84
Forward	Jimmy GREAVES	Tottenham Hotspur	5967.17
Forward	Geoff HURST	West Ham United	3655.51
Forward	Denis LAW	Manchester United	2822.34
Centre midfield	Bobby CHARLTON	Manchester United	7943.04

1970s

Position	Player	Teams	Points
Goalkeeper	Ray CLEMENCE	Liverpool	3183.25
Right back	Phil NEAL	Liverpool	2186.19
Centre back	Phil THOMPSON	Liverpool	2343.72
Centre back	Emlyn HUGHES	Liverpool	4079.12
Left back	Mick MILLS	Ipswich Town	975.95
Right midfield	Billy BREMNER	Leeds United	1812.34
Central midfield	Colin BELL	Manchester City	2329.57
Central midfield	Trevor BROOKING	West Ham United	1215.19
Left midfield	Liam BRADY	Arsenal	692.37
Forward	Kevin KEEGAN	Liverpool	5654.65
Forward	Malcolm MACDONALD	Newcastle United	810.37

1980s

Position	Player	Teams	Points
Goalkeeper	Peter SHILTON	Forest/Southampton/Derby	3149.70
Right back	Mark LAWRENSON	Liverpool	1835.39
Centre back	Terry BUTCHER	Ipswich Town	2544.98
Centre back	Alan HANSEN	Liverpool	1878.52
Left back	Kenny SANSOM	Crystal Palace/Arsenal	2892.17
Right midfield	Glenn HODDLE	Tottenham Hotspur	2755.57
Central midfield	Bryan ROBSON	Manchester United	4494.19
Central midfield	Graeme SOUNESS	Liverpool	2615.05
Left midfield	John BARNES	Liverpool	2729.33
Forward	Kenny DALGLISH	Liverpool	4360.63
Forward	Ian RUSH	Liverpool	4018.06

1990s

Position	Player	Teams	Points
Goalkeeper	Peter SCHMEICHEL	Manchester United	5185.39
Right back	Denis IRWIN	Manchester United	1555.44
Centre back	Tony ADAMS	Arsenal	2314.47
Centre back	Gary PALLISTER	Manchester United	3223.19
Left back	Stuart PEARCE	Forest/Newcastle /West Ham	2350.71
Right midfield	David BECKHAM	Manchester United	1632.3
Central midfield	Roy KEANE	Manchester United	2767.83
Central midfield	Patrick VIEIRA	Arsenal	3441.35
Left midfield	Ryan GIGGS	Manchester United	3130.17
Forward	Dennis BERGKAMP	Arsenal	7156.62
Forward	Eric CANTONA	Leeds Utd/ Manchester Utd	5466.69

2000s

Position	Player	Teams	Points
Goalkeeper	Petr CECH	Chelsea	2236.46
Right back	Gary NEVILLE	Manchester United	2748.67
Centre back	Sami HYYPIA	Liverpool	2400.98
Centre back	John TERRY	Chelsea	2281.56
Left back	Ashley COLE	Arsenal/Chelsea	2775.02
Right midfield	Steven GERRARD	Liverpool	3212.86
Central midfield	Frank LAMPARD	West Ham United/Chelsea	3284.82
Central midfield	Gilberto SILVA	Arsenal	3414.61
Left midfield	Ryan GIGGS	Manchester United	2506.74
Forward	Thierry HENRY	Arsenal	7127.22
Forward	Ruud VAN NISTELROOY	Manchester United	5447.01

GREATEST EVER
PLAYERS FROM ENGLISH TOP FLIGHT CLUBS BY POSITION

GOALKEEPERS

Player	Points
Peter SCHMEICHEL	8658.03
Fabien BARTHEZ	6422.05
Edwin VAN DER SAR	6289.49
Ray CLEMENCE	6172.88
Peter SHILTON	5898.77
Jim LEIGHTON	5342.56
David SEAMAN	4257.33
Pat JENNINGS	4254.26
Gordon BANKS	3718.90
Brad FRIEDEL	3435.43

DEFENDERS

Player	Points
Marcel DESAILLY	7895.00
Laurent BLANC	7063.44
Gary NEVILLE	6544.10
Bobby MOORE	5757.94
Henning BERG	5402.95
Jaap STAM	5194.40
Alan HANSEN	4884.07
Phil NEAL	4488.59
Frank LEBOEUF	4397.55
Albert FERRER	4395.32

MIDFIELDERS

Player	Points
Ruud GULLIT	10306.85
Didier DESCHAMPS	8378.33
David BECKHAM	7967.26
Ryan GIGGS	7136.91
Patrick VIEIRA	7082.41
Youri DJORKAEFF	6949.32
Edgar DAVIDS	6538.15
Paul SCHOLES	6524.14
Bryan ROBSON	6508.92
Roy KEANE	6502.90

FORWARDS

Player	Points
Bobby CHARLTON	9860.07
Jurgen KLINSMANN	9840.02
Kenny DALGLISH	9806.45
Dennis BERGKAMP	9031.85
Thierry HENRY	8972.91
Hakan SUKUR	8118.29
Kevin KEEGAN	7902.42
Patrick KLUIVERT	7583.17
Jari LITMANEN	7538.97
Gary LINEKER	7367.97

GREATEST EVER
SCOTTISH CLUBS BEST SEASONS AND SQUADS

ABERDEEN

	Season	League	League Position	P	W	D	L	F	A	Pts	3 Point Equivalent
1940s & 50s	**1954–55**	**A**	**1**	**30**	**24**	**1**	**5**	**73**	**26**	**49**	**2.433333**
	1955–56	A	2	34	18	10	6	87	50	46	1.882353
	1946–47	A	3	30	16	7	7	58	41	39	1.833333
	1950–51	A	5	30	15	5	10	61	50	35	1.666667
	1956–57	1	6	34	18	2	14	79	59	38	1.647059
	1953–54	A	9	30	15	3	12	66	51	33	1.600000
	1957–58	1	12	34	14	2	18	68	76	30	1.294118
	1952–53	A	11	30	11	5	14	64	68	27	1.266667
	1947–48	A	10	30	10	7	13	45	45	27	1.233333
	1951–52	A	11	30	10	7	13	65	58	27	1.233333
	1949–50	A	8	30	11	4	15	48	56	26	1.233333
	1958–59	1	13	34	12	5	17	63	66	29	1.205882
	1948–49	A	13	30	7	11	12	39	48	25	1.066667

SQUAD 1954–55 — CHAMPIONS OF DIVISION A

John Grandison ALLISTER	Wing half	James S MITCHELL	Right back
James BROWN	Outside right	Reginald L MORRISON	Goalkeeper
Pat BUCKLEY	Centre forward	Joe O'NEIL	Right half
David CALDWELL	Left back	Robert B PATERSON	Right back
Archie GLEN	Inside forward	Billy SMITH	Inside right
George HAMILTON	Inside right	James R WALLACE	Centre half
John HATHER	Outside left	Bobby WISHART	Outside left
Graeme LEGGAT	Outside right	Harry YORSTON	Inside right
Fred G MARTIN	Centre forward	Alex YOUNG	Centre half

Season	League	League Position	P	W	D	L	F	A	Pts	3 Point Equivalent
1966–67	**1**	**4**	**34**	**17**	**8**	**9**	**72**	**38**	**42**	**1.735294**
1962–63	1	6	34	17	7	10	70	47	41	1.705882
1967–68	1	5	34	16	5	13	63	48	37	1.558824
1965–66	1	8	34	15	6	13	61	54	36	1.500000
1960–61	1	6	34	14	8	12	72	72	36	1.470588
1963–64	1	9	34	12	8	14	53	53	32	1.294118
1964–65	1	12	34	12	8	14	59	75	32	1.294118
1961–62	1	12	34	10	9	15	60	73	29	1.147059
1959–60	1	15	34	11	6	17	54	72	28	1.147059
1968–69	1	15	34	9	8	17	50	59	26	1.029412

SQUAD 1966–67 — 4TH IN DIVISION 1

Martin McLean BUCHAN	Left half
Robert B CLARK	Goalkeeper
Jim HERMISTON	Full back
David JOHNSTON	Centre forward
Billy LITTLE	Outside right
Bernard J McCABE	Full back
Tommy McMILLAN	Centre half
Harry W MELROSE	Outside left
David A MILLAR	Inside forward
Francis Michael MUNRO	Inside forward
Jens PEDERSEN	Wing half
David Thomson ROBB	Inside forward
Ally SHEWAN	Centre half
Jim SMITH	Inside right
Jim STORRIE	Inside forward
Ian Wishart TAYLOR	Centre forward
William Douglas WATT	Outside left
James Boslem WHYTE	Right back
Jimmy WILSON	Outside left
Pat WILSON	Outside right
Ernest T WINCHESTER	Centre half

Season	League	League Position	P	W	D	L	F	A	Pts	3 Point Equivalent
1970–71	1	2	34	24	6	4	68	18	54	2.294118
1971–72	1	2	34	21	8	5	80	26	50	2.088235
1977–78	**Premier Division**	**2**	**36**	**22**	**9**	**5**	**68**	**29**	**53**	**2.083333**
1972–73	1	4	34	16	11	7	61	34	43	1.735294
1974–75	1	5	34	16	9	9	66	43	41	1.676471
1976–77	Premier Division	3	36	16	11	9	56	42	43	1.638889
1973–74	1	4	34	13	16	5	46	26	42	1.617647
1978–79	Premier Division	4	36	13	14	9	59	36	40	1.472222
1969–70	1	8	34	14	7	13	55	45	35	1.441176
1975–76	Premier Division	7	36	11	10	15	49	50	32	1.194444

SQUAD 1977–78 — 2ND IN THE PREMIER DIVISION

Steven ARCHIBALD	Inside forward
George CAMPBELL	Centre forward
Robert B CLARK	Goalkeeper
Neil COOPER	Inside forward
Duncan DAVIDSON	Inside forward
John Hairs (Ian) FLEMING	Inside forward
William GARNER	Centre half
Ian GIBSON	Inside forward
Robert GLENNIE	Centre half
Alex GRANT	Wing half
Joseph Montgomery HARPER	Centre forward
Andrew JARVIE	Inside forward
R Stewart KENNEDY	Full back
Alexander McLEISH	Centre half
Charles McLELLAND	Inside right
John McMASTER	Outside left
William Ferguson MILLER	Centre forward
Steve Kilcar RITCHIE	Full back
David Thomson ROBB	Inside forward
Douglas ROUGVIE	Centre half
John (Ian) SCANLON	Inside forward
John Alexander SCOTT	Inside forward
James W SHIRRA	Inside forward
Joe SMITH	Inside forward
Gordon David STRACHAN	Inside forward
Dominic SULLIVAN	Outside right
Andrew WATSON	Wing half

Season	League	League Position	P	W	D	L	F	A	Pts	3 Point Equivalent
1984–85	**Premier Division**	**1**	**36**	**27**	**5**	**4**	**89**	**26**	**59**	**2.388889**
1983–84	Premier Division	1	36	25	7	4	78	21	57	2.277778
1982–83	Premier Division	3	36	25	5	6	76	24	55	2.222222
1981–82	Premier Division	2	36	23	7	6	71	29	53	2.111111
1988–89	Premier Division	2	36	18	14	4	51	25	50	1.888889
1980–81	Premier Division	2	36	19	11	6	61	26	49	1.888889
1979–80	Premier Division	1	36	19	10	7	68	36	48	1.861111
1987–88	Premier Division	4	44	21	17	6	56	25	59	1.818182
1986–87	Premier Division	4	44	21	16	7	63	29	58	1.795455
1985–86	Premier Division	4	36	16	12	8	62	31	44	1.666667

SQUAD 1984–85   CHAMPIONS OF THE PREMIER DIVISION

Ian Allan ANGUS	Midfielder	Alexander McLEISH	Centre half
Douglas BELL	Midfielder	John McMASTER	Midfielder
John Eric BLACK	Centre forward	Thomas Feeney McQUEEN	Full back
Neale James COOPER	Midfielder	Joseph MILLER	Centre forward
Steven J COWAN	Midfielder	William Ferguson MILLER	Centre half
William Henry FALCONER	Wing half	Charles Brian MITCHELL	Centre half
Bryan James GUNN	Goalkeeper	Ian PORTEOUS	Midfielder
John HEWITT	Centre forward	Neil SIMPSON	Midfielder
James LEIGHTON	Goalkeeper	William STARK	Midfielder
D Francis McDOUGALL	Centre forward	Peter Russell WEIR	Outside left
Stewart McKIMMIE	Full back		

Season	League	League Position	P	W	D	L	F	A	Pts	3 Point Equivalent
1990–91	**Premier Division**	**2**	**36**	**22**	**9**	**5**	**62**	**27**	**53**	**2.083333**
1992–93	Premier Division	2	44	27	10	7	87	36	64	2.068182
1989–90	Premier Division	2	36	17	10	9	56	33	44	1.694444
1993–94	Premier Division	2	44	17	21	6	58	36	55	1.636364
1995–96	Premier Division	3	36	16	7	13	52	45	55	1.527778
1991–92	Premier Division	6	44	17	14	13	55	42	48	1.477273
1996–97	Premier Division	6	36	10	14	12	45	54	44	1.222222
1994–95	Premier Division	9	36	10	11	15	43	46	41	1.138889
1997–98	Premier Division	6	36	9	12	15	39	53	39	1.083333
1998–99	SPL	8	36	10	7	19	43	71	37	1.027778

SQUAD 1990–91   2ND IN THE PREMIER DIVISION

James BETT	Midfielder	Alexander McLEISH	Centre half
Scott BOOTH	Centre forward	Craig Peter ROBERTSON	Midfielder
Ian CAMERON	Outside left	David Alexander ROBERTSON	Outside left
Robert CONNOR	Midfielder	Ian William ROBERTSON	Midfielder
Andrew DIBBLE	Goalkeeper	Theodorus G.A. SNELDERS	Goalkeeper
Hans GILHAUS	Centre forward	Peter VAN DE VEN	Midfielder
Brian Joseph GRANT	Midfielder	Willem VAN DER ARK	Centre forward
Brian Alexander IRVINE	Centre half	Gregg WATSON	Midfielder
Eoin JESS	Centre forward	Michael WATT	Goalkeeper
Paul David MASON	Midfielder	Stephen WRIGHT	Full back
Stewart McKIMMIE	Full back		

Season	League	League Position	P	W	D	L	F	A	Pts	3 Point Equivalent
2006–07	**SPL**	**3**	**38**	**19**	**8**	**11**	**55**	**38**	**65**	**1.710526**
2004–05	SPL	4	38	18	7	13	44	39	61	1.605263
2001–02	SPL	3	38	16	7	15	51	49	55	1.447368
2005–06	SPL	6	38	13	15	10	46	40	54	1.421053
2002–03	SPL	8	38	13	10	15	41	54	49	1.289474
2000–01	SPL	9	38	11	12	15	45	52	45	1.184211
1999–2000	SPL	10	36	9	6	21	44	83	33	0.916667
2003–04	SPL	10	38	9	7	22	39	63	34	0.894737

SQUAD 2006–07　　　　　　　　　　3RD IN THE SPL

Russell ANDERSON	Defender	James LANGFIELD	Goalkeeper
Craig BREWSTER	Forward	Steve LOVELL	Forward
Richie BYRNE	Defender	Darren MACKIE	Forward
Chris CLARK	Forward	Chris MAGUIRE	Forward
Andrew CONSIDINE	Defender	Lee MILLER	Forward
Stevie CRAWFORD	Forward	Barry NICHOLSON	Midfielder
Dyron DAAL	Forward	Scott SEVERIN	Midfielder
Gary DEMPSEY	Midfielder	Jamie SMITH	Forward
Zander DIAMOND	Defender	Dan SMITH	Defender
Richard FOSTER	Midfielder	John STEWART	Forward
Michael HART	Defender	Karim TOUZANI	Defender

CELTIC

Season	League	League Position	P	W	D	L	F	A	Pts	3 Point Equivalent
1954–55	**A**	**2**	**30**	**19**	**8**	**3**	**76**	**37**	**46**	**2.166667**
1953–54	A	1	30	20	3	7	72	29	43	2.100000
1957–58	1	3	34	19	8	7	84	47	46	1.911765
1955–56	A	5	34	16	9	9	55	39	41	1.676471
1949–50	A	5	30	14	7	9	51	50	35	1.633333
1956–57	1	5	34	15	8	11	58	43	38	1.558824
1946–47	A	7	30	13	6	11	53	55	32	1.500000
1958–59	1	6	34	14	8	12	70	53	36	1.470588
1948–49	A	6	30	12	7	11	48	40	31	1.433333
1950–51	A	7	30	12	5	13	48	46	29	1.366667
1952–53	A	8	30	11	7	12	51	54	29	1.333333
1951–52	A	9	30	10	8	12	52	55	28	1.266667
1947–48	A	12	30	10	5	15	41	56	25	1.166667

SQUAD 1954–55　　　　　　　　2ND IN DIVISION A

Andy BELL	Goalkeeper	John McPHAIL	Half back
Alexander BODEN	Centre half	Frank MEECHAN	Full back
John BONNAR	Goalkeeper	Neil MOCHAN	Centre forward
Bobby COLLINS	Inside forward	Bertie PEACOCK	Left half
Michael CONROY	Half back	(Ian) John Holt REID	Right half
Robert EVANS	Wing half	James ROWAN	Inside right
Sean FALLON	Right back	John Eric SMITH	Inside right
Willie FERNIE	Forward	Jock STEIN	Centre half
Mike HAUGHNEY	Right back	Charles TULLY	Inside forward
John HIGGINS	Outside right	Jimmy WALSH	Inside forward
Eamon McMAHON	Goalkeeper		

1960s

Season	League	League Position	P	W	D	L	F	A	Pts	3 Point Equivalent
1967–68	1	1	34	30	3	1	106	24	63	2.735294
1966–67	1	1	34	26	6	2	111	33	58	2.470588
1965–66	1	1	34	27	3	4	106	30	57	2.470588
1968–69	1	1	34	23	8	3	89	32	54	2.264706
1963–64	1	3	34	19	9	6	89	34	47	1.941176
1961–62	1	3	34	19	8	7	81	37	46	1.911765
1962–63	1	4	34	19	6	9	76	44	44	1.852941
1960–61	1	4	34	15	9	10	64	46	39	1.588235
1964–65	1	8	34	16	5	13	76	57	37	1.558824
1959–60	1	9	34	12	9	13	73	59	33	1.323529

SQUAD 1967–68　　　　CHAMPIONS OF DIVISION 1

Bertie AULD	Outside left	James Connolly JOHNSTONE	Outside right
James Andrew BROGAN	Left half	Bobby LENNOX	Inside forward
Dave CATTENACH	Full back	Joe McBRIDE	Centre forward
Thomas Steven CHALMERS	Inside forward	Pat McMAHON	Inside right
John CLARK	Wing half	Billy McNEILL	Centre half
James Philip CRAIG	Right back	Bobby MURDOCH	Midfielder
John FALLON	Goalkeeper	William O'NEILL	Full back
Charles GALLAGHER	Inside forward	Jimmy QUINN	Inside right
Tommy GEMMELL	Left back	Anthony C SHEVLANE	Right back
David HAY	Right half	Ronald Campbell SIMPSON	Goalkeeper
John HUGHES	Centre forward	William S B WALLACE	Centre forward

1970s

Season	League	League Position	P	W	D	L	F	A	Pts	3 Point Equivalent
1971–72	1	1	34	28	4	2	96	28	60	2.588235
1969–70	1	1	34	27	3	4	96	33	57	2.470588
1972–73	1	1	34	26	5	3	93	28	57	2.441176
1970–71	1	1	34	25	6	3	89	23	56	2.382353
1973–74	1	1	34	23	7	4	82	27	53	2.235294
1976–77	Premier Division	1	36	23	9	4	79	39	55	2.166667
1975–76	Premier Division	2	36	21	6	9	71	42	48	1.916667
1978–79	Premier Division	1	36	21	6	9	61	37	48	1.916667
1974–75	1	3	34	20	5	9	81	41	45	1.911765
1977–78	Premier Division	5	36	15	6	15	63	54	36	1.416667

SQUAD 1971–72　　　　CHAMPIONS OF DIVISION 1

James Andrew BROGAN	Left half	James Connolly JOHNSTONE	Outside right
Tommy CALLAGHAN	Inside forward	Bobby LENNOX	Inside forward
Denis CONNAGHAN	Goalkeeper	Luigi MACARI	Inside left
George CONNELLY	Inside forward	Patrick McCLUSKEY	Right half
James Philip CRAIG	Right back	Daniel Fergus McGRAIN	Right back
Kenneth M DALGLISH	Inside right	Billy McNEILL	Centre half
Victor DAVIDSON	Inside forward	Bobby MURDOCH	Midfielder
John Kelly (Dixie) DEANS	Centre forward	Jimmy QUINN	Centre forward
Tommy GEMMELL	Left back	William S B WALLACE	Centre forward
David HAY	Right half	Samuel Evan WILLIAMS	Goalkeeper
Harry HOOD	Inside forward	Paul WILSON	Inside forward
John HUGHES	Outside left		

Season	League	League Position	P	W	D	L	F	A	Pts	3 Point Equivalent
1987–88	**Premier Division**	**1**	**44**	**31**	**10**	**3**	**79**	**23**	**72**	**2.340909**
1980–81	Premier Division	1	36	26	4	6	84	37	56	2.277778
1982–83	Premier Division	2	36	25	5	6	90	36	55	2.222222
1981–82	Premier Division	1	36	24	7	5	79	33	55	2.194444
1984–85	Premier Division	2	36	22	8	6	77	30	52	2.055556
1986–87	Premier Division	2	44	27	9	8	90	41	63	2.045455
1983–84	Premier Division	2	36	21	8	7	80	41	50	1.972222
1985–86	Premier Division	1	36	20	10	6	67	38	50	1.944444
1988–89	Premier Division	3	36	21	4	11	66	44	46	1.861111
1979–80	Premier Division	2	36	18	11	7	61	38	47	1.805556

1980s

SQUAD 1987–88   CHAMPIONS OF THE PREMIER DIVISION

Robert Sime AITKEN	Centre half
Owen Duncan ARCHDEACON	Outside left
William Alexander (Lex) BAILLIE	Centre half
Patrick Joseph BONNER	Goalkeeper
Thomas BURNS	Outside right
Peter GRANT	Midfielder
Francis McAVENNIE	Centre forward
Dugald McCARRISON	Centre forward
Michael J McCARTHY	Centre half
Mark Edward McGHEE	Centre forward
Paul Joseph McGUGAN	Centre half

Douglas John McGUIRE	Centre forward
Allen Darrell McKNIGHT	Goalkeeper
Paul Michael Lyons McSTAY	Wing half
Joseph MILLER	Midfielder
Christopher Barry MORRIS	Full back
Anton Gerard Patrick ROGAN	Full back
Anthony SHEPHERD	Midfielder
William STARK	Midfielder
Andrew Francis WALKER	Centre forward
Derek WHYTE	Centre half

Season	League	League Position	P	W	D	L	F	A	Pts	3 Point Equivalent
1995–96	**Premier Division**	**2**	**36**	**24**	**11**	**1**	**74**	**25**	**83**	**2.305556**
1996–97	Premier Division	2	36	23	6	7	78	32	75	2.083333
1997–98	Premier Division	1	36	22	8	6	64	24	74	2.055556
1998–99	SPL	2	36	21	8	7	84	35	71	1.972222
1991–92	Premier Division	3	44	26	10	8	88	42	62	2.000000
1992–93	Premier Division	3	44	24	12	8	68	41	60	1.909091
1994–95	Premier Division	4	36	11	18	7	39	33	51	1.416667
1993–94	Premier Division	4	44	15	20	9	51	38	50	1.477273
1990–91	Premier Division	3	36	17	7	12	52	38	41	1.611111
1989–90	Premier Division	5	36	10	14	12	37	37	34	1.222222

1990s

SQUAD 1995–96   2ND IN THE PREMIER DIVISION

Thomas BOYD	Full back
Jorge Paolo CADETE (REIS)	Forward
John Angus Paul COLLINS	Midfielder
Simon Thomas DONNELLY	Centre forward
William Henry FALCONER	Midfielder
Peter GRANT	Midfielder
Stuart Edward GRAY	Midfielder
Christopher Drummond HAY	Centre forward
John HUGHES	Central half
Malcolm George MACKAY	Centre half
Gordon G B MARSHALL	Goalkeeper
Thomas Valley McKINLAY	Full back/Half back

Brian McLAUGHLIN	Outside right
Jackie McNAMARA	Defender
James Charles McQUILKEN	Full back
Paul Michael Lyons McSTAY	Wing half
Philip O'DONNELL	Midfielder
Brian O'NEIL	Midfielder
Andreas THOM	Forward
Pierre VAN HOOIJDONK	Forward
Rudi VATA	Full back
Andrew Francis WALKER	Centre forward
Morten WIEGHORST	Midfielder

CELTIC

Season	League	League Position	P	W	D	L	F	A	Pts	3 Point Equivalent
2001–02	SPL	1	38	33	4	1	94	18	103	2.710526
2003–04	SPL	1	38	31	5	2	105	25	98	2.578947
2000–01	SPL	1	38	31	4	3	90	29	97	2.552632
2002–03	SPL	2	38	31	4	3	98	26	97	2.552632
2004–05	SPL	2	38	30	2	6	85	35	92	2.421053
2005–06	SPL	1	38	28	7	3	93	37	91	2.394737
2006–07	SPL	1	38	26	6	6	65	34	84	2.210526
1999–2000	SPL	2	36	21	6	9	90	38	69	1.916667

2000s

SQUAD 2001–02 — CHAMPIONS OF THE SPL

Didier AGATHE	Full back/Winger	Simon George LYNCH	Forward
Dianbobo BALDE	Defender	Shaun Richard MALONEY	Forward
Thomas BOYD	Full back	Jackie McNAMARA	Defender
Stephen Daniel CRAINEY	Defender	Johan MJALLBY	Defender
Robert James DOUGLAS	Goalkeeper	Lubomir MORAVCIK	Midfielder
Jonathon GOULD	Goalkeeper	Stilian PETROV	Midfielder
Steve GUPPY	Midfielder	Bobby Alfred Manuel PETTA	Midfielder
John HARTSON	Centre forward	James SMITH	Midfielder
Colin HEALY	Midfielder	Christopher SUTTON	Forward
John KENNEDY	Defender	Mohammed SYLLA	Midfielder
Dmitri Victorvitch KHARINE	Goalkeeper	Olivier TEBILY	Defender
Paul LAMBERT	Midfielder	Alan THOMPSON	Midfielder
Henrik LARSSON	Forward	Joos VALGAERAN	Defender
Neil Francis LENNON	Midfielder	Morten WIEGHORST	Midfielder

294

DUNDEE

Season	League	League Position	P	W	D	L	F	A	Pts	3 Point Equivalent
1946–47	B	1	26	21	3	2	113	30	45	2.538462
1948–49	**A**	**2**	**30**	**20**	**5**	**5**	**71**	**48**	**45**	**2.166667**
1950–51	A	3	30	15	8	7	47	30	38	1.766667
1958–59	1	4	34	16	9	9	61	51	41	1.676471
1947–48	A	4	30	15	3	12	67	51	33	1.600000
1953–54	A	7	30	14	6	10	46	47	34	1.600000
1949–50	A	6	30	12	7	11	49	46	31	1.433333
1954–55	A	8	30	13	4	13	48	48	30	1.433333
1956–57	1	10	34	13	6	15	55	61	32	1.323529
1951–52	A	8	30	11	6	13	53	52	28	1.300000
1957–58	1	11	34	13	5	16	49	65	31	1.294118
1952–53	A	7	30	9	11	10	44	37	29	1.266667
1955–56	A	13	34	12	6	16	56	65	30	1.235294

1940s & 50s

SQUAD 1948–49 — 2ND IN DIVISION A

Robert F D ANCELL	Left back	Thomas D GRAY	Centre half
James Patrick ANDREWS	Outside left	Alistair Robert GUNN	Outside right
Reuben BENNETT	Goalkeeper	George R HILL	Outside left
Alfred BOYD	Midfielder	Andrew IRVINE	Centre half
John Bell BROWN	Goalkeeper	John LYNCH	Goalkeeper
John M BRUCE	Centre half	George S MACKAY	Outside left
Harold John (Jack) COURT	Forward	Jackie MALLOCH	Centre forward
Douglas COWIE	Half back	John Y PATTILLO	Inside forward
Ernest A EWEN	Inside right	Peter Kerr RATTRAY	Inside left
Gerald FOLLON	Full back	James C Reggie SMITH	Outside left
G Thomas GALLACHER	Inside right	George T S STEWART	Centre forward
Sydney GERRIE	Inside forward	Alex G STOTT	Inside right

Season	League	League Position	P	W	D	L	F	A	Pts	3 Point Equivalent
1961–62	**1**	**1**	**34**	**25**	**4**	**5**	**80**	**46**	**54**	**2.323529**
1963–64	1	6	34	20	5	9	94	50	45	1.911765
1959–60	1	4	34	16	10	8	70	49	42	1.705882
1966–67	1	6	34	16	9	9	74	51	41	1.676471
1964–65	1	6	34	15	10	9	86	63	40	1.617647
1965–66	1	9	34	14	6	14	61	61	34	1.411765
1967–68	1	9	34	13	7	14	62	59	33	1.352941
1962–63	1	9	34	12	9	13	60	49	33	1.323529
1960–61	1	10	34	13	6	15	61	53	32	1.323529
1968–69	1	9	34	10	12	12	47	48	32	1.235294

SQUAD 1961–62 — CHAMPIONS OF DIVISION 1

James Craig BROWN	Wing half	Hugh ROBERTSON	Outside left
Allan COUSIN	Centre forward	Bobby SEITH	Right half
Bobby COX	Left back	Gordon SMITH	Outside right
Alan John GILZEAN	Inside forward	Alec STUART	Left back
Alexander William HAMILTON	Right back	John Francombe (Ian) URE	Centre half
Pat LINEY	Goalkeeper	Bobby WADDELL	Centre forward
George McGEACHIE	Outside left	Bobby WISHART	Inside forward
Andy PENMAN	Inside right		

Season	League	League Position	P	W	D	L	F	A	Pts	3 Point Equivalent
1977–78	Division 1	3	39	25	7	7	91	44	57	2.102564
1978–79	Division 1	1	39	24	7	8	68	36	55	2.025641
1976–77	Division 1	3	39	21	9	9	90	55	51	1.846154
1972–73	**1**	**5**	**34**	**17**	**9**	**8**	**68**	**43**	**43**	**1.764706**
1971–72	1	5	34	14	13	7	59	38	41	1.617647
1973–74	1	5	34	16	7	11	67	48	39	1.617647
1974–75	1	6	34	16	6	12	48	42	38	1.588235
1970–71	1	5	34	14	10	10	53	45	38	1.529412
1969–70	1	6	34	15	6	13	49	44	36	1.500000
1975–76	Premier Division	9	36	11	10	15	49	62	32	1.194444

SQUAD 1972–73 — 5TH IN DIVISION 1

Thomson ALLAN	Goalkeeper	Alex PRINGLE	Wing half
Ian ANDERSON	Wing half	Robert Sharp ROBINSON	Wing half
John Pearson DUNCAN	Inside forward	Ian SCOTT	Centre forward
Robert Alan Cameron FORD	Wing half	John Alexander SCOTT	Inside forward
John GRAY	Inside right	Billy SEMPLE	Outside left
Michael A HEWITT	Goalkeeper	Ian Richard SMITH	Inside forward
Douglas A HOUSTON	Left back	George A STEWART	Centre half
Edwin David JOHNSTON	Left back	G Gordon WALLACE	Centre forward
Duncan LAMBIE	Inside left	Bobby A WILSON	Right back
Robert MATHIESON	Left back	Jimmy WILSON	Outside left
Iain Frederick PHILLIP	Centre half		

Season	League	League Position	P	W	D	L	F	A	Pts	3 Point Equivalent
1980–81	Division 1	2	39	22	8	9	64	40	52	1.897436
1986–87	Premier Division	6	44	18	12	14	74	57	48	1.500000
1984–85	**Premier Division**	**6**	**36**	**15**	**7**	**14**	**48**	**50**	**37**	**1.444444**
1985–86	Premier Division	6	36	14	7	15	45	51	35	1.361111
1987–88	Premier Division	7	44	17	7	20	70	64	41	1.318182
1982–83	Premier Division	6	36	9	11	16	42	53	29	1.055556
1983–84	Premier Division	8	36	11	5	20	50	74	27	1.055556
1988–89	Premier Division	8	36	9	10	17	34	48	28	1.027778
1981–82	Premier Division	8	36	11	4	21	46	72	26	1.027778
1979–80	Premier Division	9	36	10	6	20	47	73	26	1.000000

SQUAD 1984–85 — 6TH IN THE PREMIER DIVISION

John BROWN	Full back	C Walker McCALL	Centre forward
Thomas CARSON	Goalkeeper	John Duffy McCORMACK	Centre half
Robert CONNOR	Full back	George McGEACHIE	Wing half
Robert John DOCHERTY	Midfielder	Thomas Valley McKINLAY	Full back
Stewart FORSYTH	Full back	Derek McWILLIAMS	Outside left
Alexander Robert GEDDES	Goalkeeper	Stuart RAFFERTY	Midfielder
Robert GLENNIE	Centre half	Alexander S RICHARDSON	Midfielder
Colin HARRIS	Centre forward	Robert SHANNON	Defender
Graham HARVEY	Centre forward	James SMITH	Centre half
Edward Colin James HENDRY	Centre forward	Raymond Frank STEPHEN	Centre forward
Albert KIDD	Inside forward	John Robert WADDELL	Midfielder

295

DUNDEE

Season	League	League Position	P	W	D	L	F	A	Pts	3 Point Equivalent
1997–98	Division 1	1	36	20	10	6	52	24	70	1.944444
1990–91	Division 1	3	39	22	8	9	59	33	52	1.897436
1994–95	Division 1	3	36	20	8	8	65	36	68	1.888889
1991–92	Division 1	1	44	23	12	9	80	48	58	1.840909
1996–97	Division 1	3	36	15	13	8	47	33	58	1.611111
1995–96	Division 1	5	36	15	12	9	53	40	57	1.583333
1998–99	SPL	5	36	13	7	16	36	56	46	1.277778
1992–93	Premier Division	10	44	11	12	21	48	68	34	1.022727
1993–94	Premier Division	12	44	8	13	23	42	57	29	0.840909
1989–90	Premier Division	10	36	5	14	17	41	65	24	0.805556

SQUAD 1998–99   5TH IN THE SPL

Dariusz ADAMCZUK	Midfielder	Darren MAGEE	Midfielder
Iain ANDERSON	Forward	Stephen McCORMICK	Forward
Edward ANNAND	Forward	James Edward McINALLY	Midfielder
Graham BAYNE	Forward	Shaun Peter McSKIMMING	Midfielder
Steven BOYACK	Forward	William Nisbit MILLER	Defender
Thomas COYNE	Forward	Jerry William O'DRISCOLL	Forward
Robert James DOUGLAS	Goalkeeper	Stephane Z POUNEWATCHY	Centre half
William Henry FALCONER	Forward	Gavin RAE	Defender
Derek Adam FLEMING	Defender	Robert RAESIDE	Defender
Eric GARCIN	Midfielder	Hugh Scott ROBERTSON	Midfielder
James GRADY	Forward	David ROGERS	Defender
Brian Joseph GRANT	Midfielder	Lee SHARP	Defender
Gordon HUNTER	Defender	Barry Martin SMITH	Defender
Brian Alexander IRVINE	Defender	Gavin David STRACHAN	Midfielder
James LANGFIELD	Goalkeeper	Steven TWEED	Defender
Lee Robert MADDISON	Defender		

Season	League	League Position	P	W	D	L	F	A	Pts	3 Point Equivalent
2006–07	Division 1	3	36	16	5	15	48	42	53	1.472222
2000–01	SPL	6	38	13	8	17	51	49	47	1.236842
2003–04	SPL	9	38	12	10	16	48	57	46	1.210526
2005–06	Division 1	7	36	9	16	11	43	50	43	1.194444
2001–02	SPL	9	38	12	8	18	41	55	44	1.157895
2002–03	SPL	6	38	10	14	14	50	60	44	1.157895
1999–2000	SPL	7	36	12	5	19	45	64	41	1.138889
2004–05	SPL	12	38	8	9	21	37	71	33	0.868421

SQUAD 2002–03   6TH IN THE SPL

Gavin BEITH	Midfielder	Lee MAIR	Midfielder
Garry BRADY	Midfielder	Steven MILNE	Forward
Mark James BURCHILL	Forward	Georgi NEMSADZE	Midfielder
Fabian Orlando CABALLERO	Forward	Ignacio Javier Gomez NOVO	Forward
Luis Alberto CARRANZA	Midfielder	Gavin RAE	Defender
Barry FORBES	Midfielder	Steven ROBB	Midfielder
Jonay Miguel HERNANDEZ SANTOS	Full back	Mark William ROBERTSON	Midfielder
Thomas Peter HUTCHINSON	Defender	Juan Manuel SARA	Forward
Neil JABLONSKI	Midfielder	Barry Martin SMITH	Defender
Zurab KHIZANISHVILI	Defender	Julian SPERONI	Goalkeeper
Steve LOVELL	Forward	Lee WILKIE	Defender
David MACKAY	Defender		

DUNDEE UNITED

Season	League	League Position	P	W	D	L	F	A	Pts	3 Point Equivalent
1951–52	**B**	**4**	**30**	**16**	**5**	**9**	**75**	**60**	**37**	**1.766667**
1950–51	B	4	30	16	4	10	78	58	36	1.733333
1949–50	B	7	30	14	5	11	74	56	33	1.566667
1955–56	B	8	36	12	14	10	78	65	38	1.388889
1952–53	B	8	30	12	5	13	52	56	29	1.366667
1956–57	2	13	36	14	6	16	75	80	34	1.333333
1957–58	2	9	36	12	9	15	81	77	33	1.250000
1948–49	B	8	30	10	7	13	60	67	27	1.233333
1946–47	B	10	26	9	4	13	53	60	22	1.192308
1947–48	B	15	30	10	2	18	58	88	22	1.066667
1953–54	B	15	30	8	6	16	54	79	22	1.000000
1954–55	B	13	30	8	6	16	55	70	22	1.000000
1958–59	2	17	36	9	7	20	62	86	25	0.944444

1940s & 50s

SQUAD 1951–52 — 4TH IN DIVISION B

Douglas J BERRIE	Right back	George R McMILLAN	Left half
John C COYLE	Centre forward	George M MITCHELL	Inside forward
George J CRUICKSHANK	Outside left	George J MORRISON	Outside right
Earle DOWNIE	Right half	Hugh ORMOND	Right back
Tommy R DUNLOP	Centre half	Frank QUINN	Outside right
Andrew DUNSMORE	Inside forward	Robert Russell ROSS	Centre half
Alec R EDMISTON	Goalkeeper	Ian S SMART	Outside left
Cornelius FLECK	Inside forward	Richard (Dickie) SNEDDON	Right half
George D GRANT	Inside right	David G STRATTON	Left back
Jimmy KNIGHT	Outside right	Bobby SWAN	Right back
John McIVOR	Outside left	Robinson G N WYLIE	Goalkeeper
Peter Walker McKAY	Centre forward		

Season	League	League Position	P	W	D	L	F	A	Pts	3 Point Equivalent
1959–60	2	2	36	22	6	8	90	45	50	2.000000
1965–66	**1**	**5**	**34**	**19**	**5**	**10**	**79**	**51**	**43**	**1.823529**
1968–69	1	5	34	17	9	8	61	49	43	1.764706
1962–63	1	7	34	15	11	8	67	52	41	1.647059
1966–67	1	9	34	14	9	11	68	62	37	1.500000
1964–65	1	9	34	15	6	13	59	51	36	1.500000
1963–64	1	8	34	13	8	13	65	49	34	1.382353
1960–61	1	9	34	13	7	14	60	58	33	1.352941
1961–62	1	10	34	13	6	15	70	71	32	1.323529
1967–68	1	11	34	10	11	13	53	72	31	1.205882

1960s

SQUAD 1965–66 — 5TH IN DIVISION 1

Jimmy BRIGGS	Left back	Francis Michael MUNRO	Inside forward
Bobby CARROLL	Outside right	Tommy NEILSON	Right half
Alexander Grimmond DAVIE	Goalkeeper	Orjan PERSSON	Outside left
Finn DOSSING	Centre forward	Bernard ROONEY	Centre forward
Stewart FRASER	Wing half	Finn SEEMAN	Outside right
Denis GILLESPIE	Inside forward	Bobby SMITH	Wing half
Billy HAINEY	Centre forward	Douglas B SMITH	Centre half
Donald Scrimgeour McKAY	Goalkeeper	Ian J STEWART	Outside left
Thomas Thomson MILLAR	Inside forward	Lennart WING	Left half
Ian MITCHELL	Inside forward		

Season	League	League Position	P	W	D	L	F	A	Pts	3 Point Equivalent
1974–75	1	4	34	19	7	8	72	43	45	1.882353
1978–79	**Premier Division**	**3**	**36**	**18**	**8**	**10**	**56**	**37**	**44**	**1.722222**
1972–73	1	7	34	17	5	12	56	51	39	1.647059
1969–70	1	5	34	16	6	12	62	64	38	1.588235
1976–77	Premier Division	4	36	16	9	11	54	45	41	1.583333
1977–78	Premier Division	3	36	16	8	12	42	32	40	1.555556
1973–74	1	8	34	15	7	12	55	51	37	1.529412
1970–71	1	6	34	14	8	12	53	54	36	1.470588
1971–72	1	9	34	12	7	15	55	70	31	1.264706
1975–76	Premier Division	8	36	12	8	16	46	48	32	1.222222

SQUAD 1978–79 — 3RD IN THE PREMIER DIVISION

Derek ADDISON	Wing half	Hamish Robert McALPINE	Goalkeeper
David DODDS	Centre forward	David NAREY	Centre half
George FLEMING	Outside right	Graeme M PAYNE	Inside forward
James Derek F FRYE	Centre forward	Iain Frederick PHILLIP	
Paul Anthony HEGARTY	Centre forward	Robert Sharp ROBINSON	Wing half
John William HOLT	Full back	Walter SMITH	Wing half
Graham HONEYMAN	Inside forward	Derek STARK	Centre half
William J KIRKWOOD	Wing half	Raymond Straun M STEWART	Centre half
Frank KOPEL	Wing half	Paul Whitehead STURROCK	Centre forward

Season	League	League Position	P	W	D	L	F	A	Pts	3 Point Equivalent
1982–83	**Premier Division**	**1**	**36**	**24**	**8**	**4**	**90**	**35**	**56**	**2.222222**
1986–87	Premier Division	3	44	24	12	8	66	36	60	1.909091
1984–85	Premier Division	3	36	20	7	9	67	33	47	1.861111
1985–86	Premier Division	3	36	18	11	7	59	31	47	1.805556
1983–84	Premier Division	3	36	18	11	7	67	39	47	1.805556
1980–81	Premier Division	5	36	17	9	10	66	42	43	1.666667
1988–89	Premier Division	4	36	16	12	8	44	26	44	1.666667
1981–82	Premier Division	4	36	15	10	11	61	38	40	1.527778
1987–88	Premier Division	5	44	16	15	13	54	47	47	1.431818
1979–80	Premier Division	4	36	12	13	11	43	30	37	1.361111

SQUAD 1982–83 — CHAMPIONS OF THE PREMIER DIVISION

Eamonn John BANNON	Inside forward	John McNEILL	Inside forward
Ian BRITTON	Midfielder	Ralph MILNE	Wing half
John Brown CLARK	Centre forward	Derek R MURRAY	Full back
David DODDS	Centre forward	David NAREY	Centre half
Charles Richard GOUGH	Centre half	Graeme M PAYNE	Inside forward
Paul Anthony HEGARTY	Centre forward	Iain Frederick PHILLIP	Wing half
John William HOLT	Full back	John Paul REILLY	Centre forward
William J KIRKWOOD	Wing half	Derek STARK	Centre half
Maurice D R MALPAS	Inside forward	Paul Whitehead STURROCK	Centre forward
Hamish Robert McALPINE	Goalkeeper	Alexander TAYLOR	Midfielder

Season	League	League Position	P	W	D	L	F	A	Pts	3 Point Equivalent
1995–96	Division 1	2	36	19	10	7	73	37	67	1.861111
1996–97	**Premier Division**	**3**	**36**	**17**	**9**	**10**	**46**	**33**	**60**	**1.666667**
1990–91	Premier Division	4	36	17	7	12	41	29	41	1.611111
1991–92	Premier Division	4	44	19	13	12	66	50	51	1.590909
1992–93	Premier Division	4	44	19	9	16	56	49	47	1.500000
1989–90	Premier Division	4	36	11	13	12	36	39	35	1.277778
1993–94	Premier Division	6	44	11	20	13	47	48	42	1.204545
1997–98	Premier Division	7	36	8	13	15	43	51	37	1.027778
1994–95	Premier Division	10	36	9	9	18	40	56	36	1.000000
1998–99	SPL	9	36	8	10	18	37	48	34	0.944444

SQUAD 1996–97 — 3RD IN THE PREMIER DIVISION

Armand BENNEKER	Defender	Andrew McLAREN	Outside right
Paul Alexander BLACK	Winger/Full back	James Charles McQUILKEN	Full back
David BOWMAN	Midfielder	Gary John McSWEGAN	Forward
Owen Columba COYLE	Forward	Kjell OLAFSSON	Forward
Sieb DIJKSTRA	Goalkeeper	Erik PEDERSEN	Defender
James DOLAN	Midfielder	Mark George PERRY	Centre half
Cornelius DUFFY	Defender	Steven John PRESSLEY	Defender
Craig EASTON	Midfielder	Alexander ROBERTSON	Midfielder
David HANNAH	Midfielder	Robert SHANNON	Full back
Ian Grant JOHNSON	Midfielder	David SINCLAIR	Defender
Lance KEY	Goalkeeper	Steven THOMPSON	Forward
Maurice D R MALPAS	Full back	Paul WALKER	Forward
Alastair Espie MAXWELL	Goalkeeper	Robert WINTERS	Forward
James Edward McINALLY	Midfielder	Jonas WIRMOLA	Defender
Stewart McKIMMIE	Defender	Lars ZETTERLUND	Midfielder
Raymond McKINNON	Midfielder		

Season	League	League Position	P	W	D	L	F	A	Pts	3 Point Equivalent
2003–04	**SPL**	**5**	**38**	**13**	**10**	**15**	**47**	**60**	**49**	**1.289474**
2001–02	SPL	8	38	12	10	16	38	59	46	1.210526
2006–07	SPL	9	38	10	12	16	40	59	42	1.105263
1999–2000	SPL	8	36	11	6	19	34	57	39	1.083333
2004–05	SPL	9	38	8	12	18	41	59	36	0.947368
2000–01	SPL	11	38	9	8	21	38	63	35	0.921053
2005–06	SPL	9	38	7	12	19	41	66	33	0.868421
2002–03	SPL	11	38	7	11	20	35	68	32	0.842105

SQUAD 2003–04 — 5TH IN THE SPL

Alan ARCHIBALD	Centre back	Mark KERR	Midfielder
Gary BOLLAN	Defender/Left back	David McCRACKEN	Defender/Centre back
Tony BULLOCK	Goalkeeper	Derek McINNES	Midfielder
Aaron CONWAY	Forward	Jim McINTYRE	Midfielder
Owen COYLE	Forward	Andy McLAREN	Midfielder
Billy DODDS	Forward	Charlie MILLER	Midfielder
Stuart DUFF	Midfielder	James PATERSON	Midfielder
Craig EASTON	Midfielder	Scott PATERSON	Defender/Centre back
Paul GALLACHER	Goalkeeper	Barry ROBSON	Midfielder
Danny GRIFFIN	Defender/Centre back	Collin SAMUEL	Forward
Graeme HOLMES	Midfielder	Jason SCOTLAND	Forward
Chris INNES	Defender	Mark WILSON	Defender

DUNFERMLINE ATHLETIC

Season	League	League Position	P	W	D	L	F	A	Pts	3 Point Equivalent
1957–58	2	2	36	24	5	7	120	42	53	2.138889
1954–55	**B**	**2**	**30**	**19**	**4**	**7**	**72**	**40**	**42**	**2.033333**
1948–49	B	4	30	16	9	5	80	58	41	1.900000
1949–50	B	3	30	16	4	10	71	57	36	1.733333
1951–52	B	6	30	15	2	13	74	65	32	1.566667
1947–48	B	7	30	13	3	14	72	71	29	1.400000
1953–54	B	8	30	11	9	10	48	57	31	1.400000
1950–51	B	10	30	12	4	14	58	73	28	1.333333
1946–47	B	8	26	10	3	13	50	72	23	1.269231
1952–53	B	11	30	9	9	12	51	58	27	1.200000
1958–59	1	16	34	10	8	16	68	87	28	1.117647
1955–56	A	16	34	10	6	18	42	82	26	1.058824
1956–57	1	17	34	9	6	19	54	74	24	0.970588

SQUAD 1954–55 — 2ND IN DIVISION B

Alex ANDERSON	Outside left	Alec Watson LAIRD	Full back
Eric Johnston BAIKIE	Left half	Sinclair D MACKIE	Left back
James W M BENSON	Goalkeeper	Joe MACKIN	Goalkeeper
William P S BROWN	Outside right	Colin McKINLAY	Inside forward
Jim S CHALMERS	Left half	Jimmy MILLER	Wing half
Andrew CRAWFORD	Centre half	Jimmy MUIR	Centre forward
Donald CUTHBERTSON	Outside right	George O'BRIEN	Inside forward
Charlie DICKSON	Centre forward	Felix McCairney REILLY	Inside forward
Martin DUFFY	Inside left	George SAMUEL	Wing half
George R DUTHIE	Centre half	Eddie TURNER	Centre half
Samuel M FORSYTH	Full back	Jim WILLIAMSON	Centre half

Season	League	League Position	P	W	D	L	F	A	Pts	3 Point Equivalent
1964–65	**1**	**3**	**34**	**22**	**5**	**7**	**83**	**36**	**49**	**2.088235**
1963–64	1	5	34	18	9	7	64	33	45	1.852941
1968–69	1	3	34	19	7	8	63	45	45	1.882353
1965–66	1	4	34	19	6	9	94	55	44	1.852941
1961–62	1	4	34	19	5	10	77	46	43	1.823529
1967–68	1	4	34	17	5	12	64	41	39	1.647059
1966–67	1	8	34	14	10	10	72	52	38	1.529412
1962–63	1	8	34	13	8	13	50	47	34	1.382353
1960–61	1	12	34	12	7	15	65	81	31	1.264706
1959–60	1	13	34	10	9	15	72	80	29	1.147059

SQUAD 1964–65 — 3RD IN DIVISION 1

Tommy CALLAGHAN	Outside left	John McLAUGHLAN	Centre forward
Willie T CALLAGHAN	Inside forward	Jim McLEAN	Centre half
Alec W EDWARDS	Outside right	Harry W MELROSE	Wing half
Alexander C FERGUSON	Inside forward	George MILLAR	Left half
James Paterson FLEMING	Outside left	Robert MURRAY	Inside forward
Jim FRASER	Outside left	Bert PATON	Inside forward
James HERRIOT	Goalkeeper	George PEEBLES	Outside right
Ian HUNTER	Centre forward	John E W (Jackie) SINCLAIR	Outside right
John KILGANNON	Inside right	Alex SMITH	Right half
John LUNN	Outside left	Jim THOMSON	Wing half
Eric MARTIN	Goalkeeper	Pat WILSON	Outside right

1970s

Season	League	League Position	P	W	D	L	F	A	Pts	3 Point Equivalent
1972–73	2	2	36	23	6	7	95	32	52	2.083333
1978–79	Division 2	2	39	19	14	6	66	40	52	1.820513
1976–77	Division 2	3	39	20	10	9	52	36	50	1.794872
1977–78	Division 2	3	39	18	12	9	64	41	48	1.692308
1969–70	**1**	**10**	**34**	**15**	**5**	**14**	**45**	**45**	**35**	**1.470588**
1973–74	1	16	34	8	8	18	43	65	24	0.941176
1970–71	1	16	34	6	11	17	44	56	23	0.852941
1971–72	1	18	34	7	9	18	31	50	23	0.882353
1974–75	1	15	34	7	9	18	46	66	23	0.882353
1975–76	Division 1	13	26	5	10	11	30	51	20	0.961538

SQUAD 1969–70 — 10TH IN DIVISION 1

John ARROL	Goalkeeper
Douglas BAILLIE	Centre half
Roy Alexander BARRY	Wing half
James A BROWN	right half
Willie T CALLAGHAN	Inside forward
Ian COWAN	Outside right
Willie DUFF	Goalkeeper
Alec W EDWARDS	Outside right
Jim FRASER	Outside left
Patrick J GARDNER	Centre forward
Jim GILLESPIE	Outside left
Ian T LISTER	Inside forward
John LUNN	Outside left
Bent MARTIN	Goalkeeper
John McGARTY	Wing half
George McKIMMIE	Inside forward
William R McLAREN	Outside right
George Tomlinson McLEAN	Inside left
David G McNICOL	Centre forward
Barry MITCHELL	Inside forward
Bert PATON	Inside forward
Willie RENTON	Left half
Hugh ROBERTSON	Outside left
Jim THOMSON	Wing half
Jim TRAYNOR	Inside left

1980s

Season	League	League Position	P	W	D	L	F	A	Pts	3 Point Equivalent
1985–86	Division 2	1	39	23	11	5	91	47	57	2.051282
1988–89	**Division 1**	**1**	**39**	**22**	**10**	**7**	**60**	**36**	**54**	**1.948718**
1986–87	Division 1	2	44	23	10	11	61	41	56	1.795455
1984–85	Division 2	3	39	17	15	7	61	36	49	1.692308
1983–84	Division 2	9	39	13	10	16	44	45	36	1.256410
1981–82	Division 1	10	39	11	14	14	46	56	36	1.205128
1979–80	Division 1	10	39	11	13	15	39	57	35	1.179487
1982–83	Division 1	13	39	7	17	15	39	69	31	0.974359
1980–81	Division 1	12	39	10	7	22	41	58	27	0.948718
1987–88	Premier Division	11	44	8	10	26	41	84	26	0.772727

SQUAD 1988–89 — CHAMPIONS OF FIRST DIVISION

Stuart BEEDIE	Midfielder
Hugh BURNS	Full back
William Thomas CALLAGHAN	Centre forward
Graeme DAVIDSON	Midfielder
Raymond Paul FARNINGHAM	Midfielder
Martin FEENIE	Midfielder
Edward Adam GALLAGHER	Centre forward
John William HOLT	Midfielder
David John IRONS	Midfielder
James Ross JACK	Centre forward
Norman McCATHIE	Inside forward
Stephen MORRISON	Midfielder
Gary E RIDDELL	Centre half
Craig Peter ROBERTSON	Midfielder
Graeme W T ROBERTSON	Midfielder
Raymond SHARP	Full back
Mark Alexander SMITH	Outside left
Paul McKinnon SMITH	Centre forward
Robert Nisbet SMITH	Full back
Trevor Alan SMITH	Centre forward
Walter Gardner SPEIRS	Outside left
Peter Grant TIERNEY	Centre half
John Martin WATSON	Centre forward
Ian WESTWATER	Goalkeeper
Andrew WILLIAMSON	Centre half

DUNFERMLINE ATHLETIC

1990s

Season	League	League Position	P	W	D	L	F	A	Pts	3 Point Equivalent
1993–94	Division 1	2	44	29	7	8	93	35	65	2.136364
1995–96	Division 1	1	36	21	8	7	73	41	71	1.972222
1994–95	Division 1	2	36	18	14	4	63	32	68	1.888889
1992–93	Division 1	3	44	22	8	14	64	47	52	1.681818
1996–97	**Premier Division**	**5**	**36**	**12**	**9**	**15**	**52**	**65**	**45**	**1.250000**
1989–90	Premier Division	8	36	11	8	17	37	50	30	1.138889
1997–98	Premier Division	8	36	8	13	15	43	68	37	1.027778
1990–91	Premier Division	8	36	8	11	17	38	61	27	0.972222
1998–99	SPL	10	36	4	16	16	28	59	28	0.777778
1991–92	Premier Division	12	44	4	10	30	22	80	18	0.500000

SQUAD 1996–97 — 5TH IN THE PREMIER DIVISION

David Thomas BINGHAM	Forward	Colin Fyfe MILLER	Defender
Gerard Joseph BRITTON	Forward	Allan MOORE	Forward
John Brown CLARK	Forward	Stewart James John PETRIE	Forward
Henry CURRAN	Midfielder	Brian RICE	Midfielder
Ivo Johannes DEN BIEMAN	Midfielder	Craig Peter ROBERTSON	Midfielder
Derek Adam FLEMING	Defender	Raymond SHARP	Defender
John FRASER	Midfielder	Gregory SHAW	Centre forward
Hamish Mackie FRENCH	Centre forward	Andrew Mark SMITH	Forward
Craig IRELAND	Defender	Andrew TOD	Defender
Zoran LEMAJIC	Goalkeeper	Steven George WELSH	Defender
Mark Ross McCULLOCH	Defender/Midfielder	Ian WESTWATER	Goalkeeper
Marc MILLAR	Midfielder	Scott Robertson YOUNG	Midfielder

302

2000s

Season	League	League Position	P	W	D	L	F	A	Pts	3 Point Equivalent
1999–2000	Division 1	2	36	20	11	5	66	33	71	1.972222
2003–04	**SPL**	**4**	**38**	**14**	**11**	**13**	**45**	**52**	**53**	**1.394737**
2002–03	SPL	5	38	13	7	18	54	71	46	1.210526
2001–02	SPL	6	38	12	9	17	41	64	45	1.184211
2000–01	SPL	9	38	11	9	18	34	54	42	1.105263
2004–05	SPL	11	38	8	10	20	34	60	34	0.894737
2005–06	SPL	11	38	8	9	21	33	68	33	0.868421
2006–07	SPL	12	38	8	8	22	26	55	32	0.842105

SQUAD 2003–04 — 4TH IN THE SPL

Craig BREWSTER	Forward	Chris McGROARTY	Midfielder
Lee BULLEN	Defender	Keiran McGUIRE	Forward
Richie BYRNE	Defender	Billy MEHMET	Forward
Patrick CLARKE	Forward	Barry NICHOLSON	Midfielder
Stevie CRAWFORD	Forward	Marco RUITENBEEK	Goalkeeper
Jason DAIR	Defender	Greg SHIELDS	Defender
Gary DEMPSEY	Midfielder	Andrius SKERLA	Defender
Gary GREENHILL	Midfielder	Derek STILLIE	Goalkeeper
David GRONDIN	Defender	Scott M THOMSON	Defender
Noel HUNT	Forward	Andy TOD	Defender
Sean KILGANNON	Midfielder	Scott WILSON	Defender
Aaron LABONTE	Defender	Craig WILSON	Forward
Gary MASON	Midfielder	Darren YOUNG	Midfielder
Andrew McDERMOTT	Defender	Derek YOUNG	Forward
Mark McGARTY	Midfielder		

FALKIRK

Season	League	League Position	P	W	D	L	F	A	Pts	3 Point Equivalent
1948–49	**A**	**5**	**30**	**12**	**8**	**10**	**70**	**54**	**32**	**1.466667**
1947–48	A	7	30	10	10	10	55	48	30	1.333333
1957–58	1	10	34	11	9	14	64	82	31	1.235294
1952–53	A	13	30	11	4	15	53	63	26	1.233333
1955–56	A	14	34	11	6	17	58	75	28	1.147059
1946–47	A	11	30	8	10	12	62	61	26	1.133333
1953–54	A	13	30	9	7	14	47	61	25	1.133333
1956–57	1	14	34	10	8	16	51	70	28	1.117647
1958–59	1	17	34	10	7	17	58	79	27	1.088235
1954–55	A	12	30	8	8	14	42	54	24	1.066667
1949–50	A	14	30	7	10	13	48	72	24	1.033333
1950–51	A	16	30	7	4	19	35	81	18	0.833333

SQUAD 1948–49 — 5TH IN DIVISION A

Archibald W AIKMAN	Centre forward		Robert HENDERSON	Half back
James ALISON	forward		James McDougal INGLIS	Centre forward
Oliver ANDERSON	Inside right		William JAPP	Outside right
Allan BURNETT	Right half		Alexander R LOGAN	Full back
Robert CARRIE	Goalkeeper		James C McLAUGHLAN	Outside left
James (Jerry) DAWSON	Goalkeeper		James McPHIE	Full back
Ken DAWSON	Forward		George NICOL	Goalkeeper
Ernest DOIG	Wing half		James PEDEN	Left half
Tommy FARRELL	Centre half		David PERRIE	Centre forward
James FIDDES	Half back		James SILCOCK	Inside forward
Cornelius FLECK	Inside left		William TELFER	Half back
Jimmy GALLACHER	Half back		John WHITELAW	Right half
John GARDNER	Outside left		John Nimmo WHYTE	Full back
John S P HENDERSON	Forward			

303

Season	League	League Position	P	W	D	L	F	A	Pts	3 Point Equivalent
1960–61	2	2	36	24	6	6	100	40	54	2.166667
1959–60	2	8	36	15	9	12	77	43	39	1.500000
1965–66	**1**	**10**	**34**	**15**	**1**	**18**	**48**	**72**	**31**	**1.352941**
1963–64	1	14	34	11	6	17	54	84	28	1.147059
1962–63	1	13	34	12	3	19	54	69	27	1.147059
1966–67	1	14	34	11	4	19	33	70	26	1.088235
1961–62	1	14	34	11	4	19	45	68	26	1.088235
1967–68	1	15	34	7	12	15	36	50	26	0.970588
1964–65	1	16	34	7	7	20	43	85	21	0.823529
1968–69	1	17	34	5	8	21	33	69	18	0.676471

SQUAD 1965–66 — 10TH IN DIVISION 1

Douglas BAILLIE	Centre half		John MARKIE	Centre half
James Craig BROWN	Wing half		Robert McDONALD	Goalkeeper
Billy FULTON	Centre forward		Victor McKINNEY	Outside left
Billy GOURLAY	Outside left		Jim McMANUS	Outside right
John GRAHAM	Outside right		Douglas Walter MORAN	Inside forward
Andrew E R HADDOCK	Inside forward		Ian Johnstone RAE	Left back
Jim HALLIDAY	Outside left		James ROWAN	Wing half
John HUNTER	Full back		Kenny D SCOTT	Wing half
Harry Joseph KIRK	Outside left		Charles SMITH	Wing half
John LAMBIE	Inside forward		William M M WHIGHAM	Goalkeeper
Thomas S LOWRY	Centre half		Sammy WILSON	Centre forward

FALKIRK

Season	League	League Position	P	W	D	L	F	A	Pts	3 Point Equivalent
1969–70	2	1	36	25	6	5	94	34	56	2.250000
1974–75	2	1	38	26	2	10	76	29	54	2.105263
1978–79	Division 2	3	39	19	12	8	66	37	50	1.769231
1977–78	Division 2	5	39	15	14	10	51	46	44	1.512821
1970–71	**1**	**7**	**34**	**13**	**9**	**12**	**46**	**53**	**35**	**1.411765**
1975–76	Division 1	8	26	10	5	11	38	35	25	1.346154
1971–72	1	14	34	10	7	17	44	60	27	1.088235
1972–73	1	14	34	7	12	15	38	56	26	0.970588
1973–74	1	18	34	4	14	16	33	58	22	0.764706
1976–77	Division 1	14	39	6	8	25	36	85	20	0.666667

SQUAD 1970–71   7TH IN DIVISION 1

Gregor ABEL	Inside forward
Denis DEVLIN	Goalkeeper
Alexander C FERGUSON	Centre forward
Robert Alan Cameron FORD	Wing half
George GIBSON	Right half
Henry HOGGAN	Outside right
Billy LITTLE	Inside forward
John MARKIE	Centre half
George McCULLOCH	Forward
John Ian McLAUGHLIN	Left back
Thomas McLEOD	Centre forward
George MILLAR	Wing half
Stuart RENNIE	Goalkeeper
Robert Sharp ROBINSON	Inside forward
Andy ROXBURGH	Centre forward
Alexander Silcock SCOTT	Outside right
Denis G SETTERINGTON	Inside forward
James W SHIRRA	Inside forward
Billy SIMPSON	Centre half
Alex TOTTEN	Full back
Stuart WHEATLEY	Wing half
Thomas McIlwaine YOUNG	Inside left

Season	League	League Position	P	W	D	L	F	A	Pts	3 Point Equivalent
1988–89	Division 1	2	39	22	8	9	71	37	52	1.897436
1979–80	Division 2	1	39	19	12	8	65	35	50	1.769231
1984–85	Division 1	3	39	19	7	13	65	54	45	1.641026
1985–86	**Division 1**	**2**	**39**	**17**	**11**	**11**	**57**	**39**	**45**	**1.589744**
1983–84	Division 1	7	39	16	6	17	46	54	38	1.384615
1982–83	Division 1	8	39	15	6	18	45	55	36	1.307692
1981–82	Division 1	9	39	11	14	14	49	52	36	1.205128
1980–81	Division 1	9	39	13	8	18	39	52	34	1.205128
1987–88	Premier Division	10	44	10	11	23	41	75	31	0.931818
1986–87	Premier Division	10	44	8	10	26	31	70	26	0.772727

SQUAD 1985–86   2ND IN FIRST DIVISION

Crawford Bowie BAPTIE	Midfielder
Gary CLARK	Centre forward
George CLARK	Centre half
James DEMPSEY	Centre half
James GILMOUR	Midfielder
Peter HETHERSTON	Outside right
Peter HOUSTON	Midfielder
Jim HUGHES	Midfielder
Alan James IRVINE	Centre forward
Willie IRVINE	Centre forward
Brian KEMP	Full back
Charles LYTWYN	Centre forward
Roderick MANLEY	Centre half
Brian MARTIN	Full back
John Thomas McCORMACK	Right back
William M McGUIRE	Midfielder
John S MYLES	Midfielder
Andrew NICOL	Full back
Ian A PATERSON	Centre forward
Bryan PURDIE	Midfielder
Stuart ROBERTSON	Midfielder
Robert G STEWART	Centre forward
George WATSON	Goalkeeper

Season	League	League Position	P	W	D	L	F	A	Pts	3 Point Equivalent
1993–94	Division 1	1	44	26	14	4	81	32	66	2.090909
1998–99	Division 1	2	36	20	6	10	60	38	66	1.833333
1997–98	Division 1	2	36	19	8	9	56	41	65	1.805556
1990–91	Division 1	1	39	21	12	6	70	35	54	1.923077
1996–97	Division 1	5	36	15	9	12	42	39	54	1.500000
1994–95	**Premier Division**	**5**	**36**	**12**	**12**	**12**	**48**	**47**	**48**	**1.333333**
1989–90	Division 1	4	39	14	15	10	59	46	43	1.461538
1991–92	Premier Division	9	44	12	11	21	54	73	35	1.068182
1992–93	Premier Division	11	44	11	7	26	60	86	29	0.909091
1995–96	Premier Division	10	36	6	6	24	31	60	24	0.666667

SQUAD 1994–95   5TH IN THE PREMIER DIVISION

John BURRIDGE	Goalkeeper	Francis McAVENNIE	Centre forward
Richard Ray CADETTE	Centre forward	Ian Holland McCALL	Midfielder
John Brown CLARK	Forward	Colin McDONALD	Outside right
Colin CRAMB	Outside left	Jamie McGOWAN	Midfielder
Stephen FULTON	Midfielder	Paul Alexander McGRILLEN	Outside left
Graeme John HAMILTON	Midfielder	Joe McLAUGHLAN	Centre half
Nicholas S HENDERSON	Inside forward	Thomas Feeney McQUEEN	Full back
John HUGHES	Centre half	John McSTAY	Defender
Kevin Francis JAMES	Defender	Neil OLIVER	Full back
Forbes Duthie S JOHNSTON	Full back	Anthony PARKS	Goalkeeper
Maurice Thomas JOHNSTON	Forward	Jamie Ryan PATERSON	Outside left
Stephen David KIRK	Midfielder	Brian RICE	Midfielder
William Fleming LAMONT	Goalkeeper	Gregory SHAW	Centre forward
Scott MacKENZIE	Inside forward	David Gillespie WEIR	Centre half
Edward Skillion MAY	Midfielder		

Season	League	League Position	P	W	D	L	F	A	Pts	3 Point Equivalent
2002–03	Division 1	1	36	25	6	5	80	32	81	2.250000
2004–05	Division 1	1	36	22	9	5	66	30	75	2.083333
1999–2000	Division 1	3	36	20	8	8	67	40	68	1.888889
2000–01	Division 1	3	36	16	8	12	57	59	56	1.555556
2003–04	Division 1	4	36	15	10	11	43	37	55	1.527778
2006–07	**SPL**	**7**	**38**	**15**	**5**	**18**	**49**	**47**	**50**	**1.315789**
2001–02	Division 1	9	36	10	9	17	49	73	39	1.083333
2005–06	SPL	10	38	8	9	21	35	64	33	0.868421

SQUAD 2006–07   7TH IN THE SPL

Brian ALLISON	Defender	Ryan McSTAY	Midfielder
Darren BARR	Midfielder	Kenny MILNE	Midfielder
Liam CRAIG	Midfielder	Pedro MOUTINHO	Forward
Patrick CREGG	Midfielder	Stephen O'DONNELL	Midfielder
Karl DODD	Defender	Dayne ROBERTSON	Forward
Carl FINNIGAN	Forward	Jack ROSS	Midfielder
Alan GOW	Midfielder	Kasper SCHMEICHEL	Goalkeeper
Scott HIGGINS	Goalkeeper	Thomas SCOBBIE	Defender
Dean HOLDEN	Defender	John STEWART	Forward
Jeroen LAMBERS	Goalkeeper	Anthony STOKES	Forward
Russell LATAPY	Midfielder	Steven THOMSON	Midfielder
Vitor LIMA	Midfielder	Marc TWADDLE	Midfielder
Tam McMANUS	Forward	Cedric URAS	Defender

FALKIRK

GRETNA

Season	League	League Position	P	W	D	L	F	A	Pts	3 Point Equivalent
2004–05	Division 3	1	36	32	2	2	130	29	98	2.722222
2005–06	Division 2	1	36	28	4	4	97	30	88	2.444444
2003–04	Division 3	3	36	20	8	8	59	39	68	1.888889
2006–07	**Division 1**	**1**	**36**	**19**	**9**	**8**	**70**	**40**	**66**	**1.833333**
2002–03*	Division 3	6	36	11	12	13	50	50	45	1.250000

* 2002–03 was Gretna's first season in the Scottish Football League

SQUAD 2006–07 — CHAMPIONS OF DIVISION 1

Ryan BALDACCHINO	Midfielder
Craig BARR	Defender
Xavier BARRAU	Forward
Matthew BERKELEY	Forward
David BINGHAM	Forward
Mark BIRCH	Defender
Martin CANNING	Defender
David COWAN	Defender
Kenny DEUCHAR	Forward
Nicky DEVERDICS	Forward
Greg FLEMING	Goalkeeper
James GRADY	Forward
David GRAHAM	Forward
Danny GRAINGER	Defender
Steven HOGG	Midfielder
Chris INNES	Defender
Allan JENKINS	Midfielder
Neil MacFARLANE	Midfielder
Alan MAIN	Goalkeeper
Zibi MALKOWSKI	Goalkeeper
Brendan McGILL	Midfielder
Ryan McGUFFIE	Midfielder
Colin McMENAMIN	Forward
Jamie McQUILKEN	Defender
David NICHOLLS	Midfielder
John O'NEIL	Midfielder
Eric PAARTALU	Midfielder
Dene SHIELDS	Forward
Gavin SKELTON	Midfielder
Steven TOSH	Midfielder
Derek TOWNSLEY	Defender

HEART OF MIDLOTHIAN

Season	League	League Position	P	W	D	L	F	A	Pts	3 Point Equivalent
1957–58	**1**	**1**	**34**	**29**	**4**	**1**	**132**	**29**	**62**	**2.676471**
1956–57	1	2	34	24	5	5	81	48	53	2.264706
1949–50	A	3	30	20	3	7	86	40	43	2.100000
1958–59	1	2	34	21	6	7	92	51	48	2.029412
1955–56	A	3	34	19	7	8	99	47	45	1.882353
1954–55	A	4	30	16	7	7	74	45	39	1.833333
1946–47	A	4	30	16	6	8	52	43	38	1.800000
1953–54	A	2	30	16	6	8	70	45	38	1.800000
1950–51	A	4	30	16	5	9	72	45	37	1.766667
1951–52	A	4	30	14	7	9	69	53	35	1.633333
1948–49	A	8	30	12	6	12	64	54	30	1.400000
1952–53	A	4	30	12	6	12	59	50	30	1.400000
1947–48	A	9	30	10	8	12	37	42	28	1.266667

SQUAD 1957–58 — CHAMPIONS OF DIVISION 1

William Russell Logan BAULD	Centre forward
Robert Rankin BLACKWOOD	Outside left
Andrew BOWMAN	Wing half
Thomas Wilson BROWN	Goalkeeper
Alfie CONN	Inside forward
John (Ian) CRAWFORD	Outside left
John CUMMING	Inside left
Frederick GLIDDEN	Centre half
John HAMILTON	Outside right
William HIGGINS	Wing half
Bobby KIRK	Right back
William R H LINDORES	Full back
David Craig MACKAY	Half back
Thomas F MACKENZIE	Full back
Gordon MARSHALL	Goalkeeper
James MILNE	Centre half
James MURRAY	Centre forward
Bobby PARKER	Centre half
Robert (Danny) S R PATON	Inside forward
George THOMSON	Wing half
Jimmy WARDHAUGH	Inside left
Alec YOUNG	Inside forward

Season	League	League Position	P	W	D	L	F	A	Pts	3 Point Equivalent
1959–60	**1**	**1**	**34**	**23**	**8**	**3**	**102**	**51**	**54**	**2.264706**
1964–65	1	2	34	22	6	6	90	49	50	2.117647
1963–64	1	4	34	19	9	6	74	40	47	1.941176
1962–63	1	5	34	17	9	8	85	59	43	1.764706
1961–62	1	6	34	16	6	12	54	49	38	1.588235
1965–66	1	7	34	13	12	9	56	48	38	1.500000
1968–69	1	8	34	14	8	12	52	54	36	1.470588
1960–61	1	7	34	13	8	13	51	53	34	1.382353
1966–67	1	11	34	11	8	15	39	48	30	1.205882
1967–68	1	12	34	13	4	17	56	61	30	1.264706

(Left margin label: **1960s**)

SQUAD 1959–60 — CHAMPIONS OF DIVISION 1

William Russell Logan BAULD	Centre forward	Bobby KIRK	Right back
Robert Rankin BLACKWOOD	Outside left	Gordon MARSHALL	Goalkeeper
Andrew BOWMAN	Wing half	Jim McFADZEAN	Inside forward
Thomas Wilson BROWN	Goalkeeper	James MILNE	Centre half
John (Ian) CRAWFORD	Outside left	James MURRAY	Centre forward
John CUMMING	Inside left	Gordon SMITH	Outside right
John HAMILTON	Outside right	George THOMSON	Wing half
William HIGGINS	Wing half	Alec YOUNG	Inside forward

Season	League	League Position	P	W	D	L	F	A	Pts	3 Point Equivalent
1977–78	Division 1	2	39	24	10	5	77	42	58	2.102564
1971–72	1	6	34	13	13	8	53	49	39	1.529412
1973–74	1	6	34	14	10	10	54	43	38	1.529412
1969–70	**1**	**4**	**34**	**13**	**12**	**9**	**50**	**36**	**38**	**1.500000**
1974–75	1	8	34	11	13	10	47	52	35	1.352941
1970–71	1	11	34	13	7	14	41	40	33	1.352941
1975–76	Premier Division	5	36	13	9	14	39	45	35	1.333333
1972–73	1	10	34	12	6	16	39	50	30	1.235294
1976–77	Premier Division	9	36	7	13	16	49	66	27	0.944444
1978–79	Premier Division	9	36	8	7	21	39	71	23	0.861111

(Left margin label: **1970s**)

SQUAD 1969–70 — 4TH IN DIVISION 1

Arthur A D ANDERSON	Wing half	Billy McALPINE	Full back
James BROWN	Wing half	Alan McDONALD	Inside forward
Eric CARRUTHERS	Inside forward	Rene MOLLER	Centre forward
Dave CLUNIE	Wing half	Neil M MURRAY	Outside right
James F CRUIKSHANK	Goalkeeper	Peter Francis Raeside OLIVER	Right half
George FLEMING	Outside left	Ian SNEDDON	Right half
Donald FORD	Outside right	Eddie THOMSON	Centre half
Kenny GARLAND	Goalkeeper	James Clabby TOWNSEND	Wing half
Jim IRVINE	Inside forward	Tommy TRAYNOR	Outside left
Roald JENSEN	Outside right	Tommy VEITCH	Right half
Andy LYNCH	Outside left	Ernest T WINCHESTER	Centre forward

1980s

Season	League	League Position	P	W	D	L	F	A	Pts	3 Point Equivalent
1982–83	Division 1	2	39	22	10	7	79	38	54	1.948718
1985–86	**Premier Division**	**2**	**36**	**20**	**10**	**6**	**59**	**33**	**50**	**1.944444**
1987–88	Premier Division	2	44	23	16	5	74	32	62	1.931818
1979–80	Division 1	1	39	20	13	6	58	39	53	1.871795
1981–82	Division 1	3	39	21	8	10	65	37	50	1.820513
1986–87	Premier Division	5	44	21	14	9	64	43	56	1.750000
1983–84	Premier Division	5	36	10	16	10	38	47	36	1.277778
1984–85	Premier Division	7	36	13	5	18	47	64	31	1.222222
1988–89	Premier Division	6	36	9	13	14	35	42	31	1.111111
1980–81	Premier Division	10	36	6	6	24	27	71	18	0.666667

SQUAD 1985–86   2ND IN THE PREMIER DIVISION

Iain J JARDINE	Midfielder	Roderick D W MacDONALD	Centre half
Kenneth George BLACK	Full back	Billy MacKAY	Outside right
Paul Robert CHERRY	Centre half	Gary MACKAY	Wing half
Alexander CLARK	Centre forward	Colin C McADAM	Centre forward
John Mark COLQUHOUN	Outside right	Brian McNAUGHTON	Centre forward
Alexander George COWIE	Full back	John Grant ROBERTSON	Centre forward
Neil BERRY	Centre half	James William SANDISON	Midfielder
William (Sandy) JARDINE	Full back	Henry George SMITH	Goalkeeper
Walter Joseph KIDD	Full back	Andrew WATSON	Midfielder
Craig William LEVEIN	Centre half	Brian J WHITTAKER	Full back
Alex MacDONALD	Wing half		

1990s

Season	League	League Position	P	W	D	L	F	A	Pts	3 Point Equivalent
1991–92	**Premier Division**	**2**	**44**	**27**	**9**	**8**	**60**	**37**	**63**	**2.045455**
1997–98	Premier Division	3	36	19	10	7	70	46	67	1.861111
1989–90	Premier Division	3	36	16	12	8	54	35	44	1.666667
1995–96	Premier Division	4	36	16	7	13	55	53	55	1.527778
1996–97	Premier Division	4	36	14	10	12	46	43	52	1.444444
1992–93	Premier Division	5	44	15	14	15	46	51	44	1.340909
1993–94	Premier Division	7	44	11	20	13	37	43	42	1.204545
1994–95	Premier Division	6	36	12	7	17	44	51	43	1.194444
1998–99	SPL	6	36	11	9	16	44	50	42	1.166667
1990–91	Premier Division	5	36	14	7	15	48	55	35	1.361111

SQUAD 1991–92   2ND IN THE PREMIER DIVISION

Ian James BAIRD	Centre forward	Thomas Valley McKINLAY	Full back
Eamonn John BANNON	Midfielder	Alan James McLAREN	Centre half
Scott CRABBE	Midfielder	David McPHERSON	Centre half
Derek FERGUSON	Midfielder	John MILLAR	Midfielder
Ian FERGUSON	Centre forward	Steven Alexander PENNEY	Midfielder
Wayne Paul FOSTER	Centre forward	John Grant ROBERTSON	Centre forward
Thomas Edward HARRISON	Midfielder	Henry George SMITH	Goalkeeper
Graeme James HOGG	Centre half	Glynn SNODIN	Midfielder
Craig William LEVEIN	Centre half	George WRIGHT	Full back
Gary MACKAY	Wing half		

	Season	League	League Position	P	W	D	L	F	A	Pts	3 Point Equivalent
2000s	2005–06	SPL	2	38	22	8	8	71	31	74	1.947368
	2003–04	SPL	3	38	19	11	8	56	40	68	1.789474
	2002–03	SPL	3	38	18	9	11	57	51	63	1.657895
	2006–07	SPL	4	38	17	10	11	47	35	61	1.605263
	1999–2000	SPL	3	36	15	9	12	47	40	54	1.500000
	2000–01	SPL	5	38	14	10	14	56	50	52	1.368421
	2004–05	SPL	5	38	13	11	14	43	41	50	1.315789
	2001–02	SPL	5	38	14	6	18	52	57	48	1.263158

SQUAD 2005–06   2ND IN THE SPL

Bruno AGUIAR	Midfielder	Juho MAKELA	Forward
Steve BANKS	Goalkeeper	Jamie McALLISTER	Defender
Nerijus BARASA	Defender	Neil McCANN	Midfielder
Roman BEDNAR	Forward	Saulius MIKOLIUNAS	Forward
Christophe BERRA	Defender	Robbie NEILSON	Defender
Mirsad BESLIJA	Defender	Fyssas PANAGIOTIS	Defender
Julien BRELLIER	Midfielder	Martin PETRAS	Defender
Samuel CAMAZZOLA	Midfielder	Hjalmar PORARINSSON	Forward
Deividas CESNAUSKIS	Midfielder	Michal POSPISIL	Forward
Calum ELLIOT	Forward	Steven PRESSLEY	Defender
Jose GONCALVES	Defender	Stephen SIMMONS	Midfielder
Craig GORDON	Goalkeeper	Rudolf SKACEL	Defender
Chris HACKETT	Midfielder	Ludek STRACENY	Midfielder
Paul HARTLEY	Midfielder	Ibrahim TALL	Defender
Edgaras JANKAUSKAS	Forward	Lee WALLACE	Midfielder
Lee JOHNSON	Midfielder	Andy WEBSTER	Defender
Neil MacFARLANE	Midfielder		

HIBERNIAN

	Season	League	League Position	P	W	D	L	F	A	Pts	3 Point Equivalent
1940s & 50s	1949–50	A	2	30	22	5	3	86	34	49	2.366667
	1947–48	A	1	30	22	4	4	86	27	48	2.333333
	1950–51	**A**	**1**	**30**	**22**	**4**	**4**	**78**	**26**	**48**	**2.333333**
	1951–52	A	1	30	20	5	5	92	36	45	2.166667
	1946–47	A	2	30	19	6	5	69	33	44	2.100000
	1952–53	A	2	30	19	5	6	93	51	43	2.066667
	1955–56	A	4	34	19	7	8	86	50	45	1.882353
	1948–49	A	3	30	17	5	8	75	52	39	1.866667
	1953–54	A	5	30	15	4	11	72	51	34	1.633333
	1954–55	A	5	30	15	4	11	64	54	34	1.633333
	1956–57	1	9	34	12	9	13	69	56	33	1.323529
	1958–59	1	10	34	13	6	15	68	70	32	1.323529
	1957–58	1	9	34	13	5	16	59	60	31	1.294118

SQUAD 1950–51   CHAMPIONS OF DIVISION A

William M ALLAN	Outside left	John MUNRO	Outside right
William H BRUCE	Goalkeeper	John Forest OGILVIE	Left half
Archibald BUCHANAN	Left half	William Esplin ORMOND	Outside left
James CAIRNS	Left back	John Smith PATERSON	Centre half
James Robert COMBE	Inside forward	Lawrie REILLY	Forward
Michael GALLACHER	Right half	Gordon SMITH	Outside right
Jock GOVAN	Right back	James M SOUNESS	Outside right
James Michael GUNNING	Outside right	Edward Hunter TURNBULL	Inside left
Hugh HOWIE	Centre half	Pat WARD	Left half
Bobby JOHNSTONE	Inside right	Robert WOOD	Inside left
Jimmy MULKERRIN	Centre forward	Tommy YOUNGER	Goalkeeper

1960s

Season	League	League Position	P	W	D	L	F	A	Pts	3 Point Equivalent
1964–65	1	4	34	21	4	9	75	47	46	1.970588
1967–68	**1**	**3**	**34**	**20**	**5**	**9**	**67**	**49**	**45**	**1.911765**
1966–67	1	5	34	19	4	11	72	49	42	1.794118
1965–66	1	6	34	16	6	12	81	55	38	1.588235
1959–60	1	7	34	14	7	13	106	85	35	1.441176
1960–61	1	8	34	15	4	15	66	69	34	1.441176
1961–62	1	8	34	14	5	15	58	72	33	1.382353
1968–69	1	12	34	12	7	15	60	59	31	1.264706
1963–64	1	10	34	12	6	16	59	66	30	1.235294
1962–63	1	16	34	8	9	17	47	67	25	0.970588

SQUAD 1967–68 — 3RD IN DIVISION 1

Thomson ALLAN	Goalkeeper	John MURPHY	Wing half
John Henderson BLACKLEY	Centre half	Jimmy O'ROURKE	Inside forward
Peter Barr CORMACK	Inside right	Pat QUINN	Inside right
Allan COUSIN	Centre forward	Alexander Silcock SCOTT	Outside right
Joe DAVIS	Left half	Billy SIMPSON	Centre half
Bobby DUNCAN	Inside forward	Patrick Gordon STANTON	Inside forward
Colin GRANT	Inside forward	Colin STEIN	Centre forward
John MADSEN	Centre half	Eric STEVENSON	Inside forward
Peter MARINELLO	Outside right	Willie WILSON	Goalkeeper
Allan McGRAW	Inside forward		

1970s

Season	League	League Position	P	W	D	L	F	A	Pts	3 Point Equivalent
1973–74	**1**	**2**	**34**	**20**	**9**	**5**	**75**	**42**	**49**	**2.029412**
1974–75	1	2	34	20	9	5	69	37	49	2.029412
1972–73	1	3	34	19	7	8	74	33	45	1.882353
1969–70	1	3	34	19	6	9	65	40	44	1.852941
1971–72	1	4	34	19	6	9	62	34	44	1.852941
1975–76	Premier Division	3	36	18	7	11	55	43	43	1.694444
1977–78	Premier Division	4	36	15	7	14	51	43	37	1.444444
1978–79	Premier Division	5	36	12	13	11	44	48	37	1.361111
1976–77	Premier Division	6	36	8	18	10	34	35	34	1.166667
1970–71	1	12	34	10	10	14	47	53	30	1.176471

SQUAD 1973–74 — 2ND IN DIVISION 1

Gerry ADAIR	Centre half	Tony HIGGINS	Centre forward
Jim BLACK	Centre half	James J McARTHUR	Goalkeeper
John Henderson BLACKLEY	Wing half	Roddy McKENZIE	Goalkeeper
Desmond George BREMNER	Full back	Alexander I F MUNRO	Outside left
John Jack BROWNLIE	Inside forward	Willie MURRAY	Outside right
Alexander James CROPLEY	Outside right	Jimmy O'ROURKE	Inside forward
Arthur M DUNCAN	Outside left	Erich Peter SCHAEDLER	Full back
Alec W EDWARDS	Outside right	Robert Nisbet SMITH	Wing half
Alan GORDON	Inside forward	Derek SPALDING	Inside forward
Joseph Montgomery HARPER	Centre forward	Patrick Gordon STANTON	Wing half
John HAZEL	Left half		

	Season	League	League Position	P	W	D	L	F	A	Pts	3 Point Equivalent
	1980–81	Division 1	1	39	24	9	6	67	24	57	2.076923
	1988–89	**Premier Division**	**5**	**36**	**13**	**9**	**14**	**37**	**36**	**35**	**1.333333**
	1981–82	Premier Division	6	36	11	14	11	38	40	36	1.305556
	1987–88	Premier Division	6	44	12	19	13	41	42	43	1.250000
1980s	1983–84	Premier Division	7	36	12	7	17	45	55	31	1.194444
	1985–86	Premier Division	8	36	11	6	19	49	63	28	1.083333
	1984–85	Premier Division	8	36	10	7	19	38	61	27	1.027778
	1982–83	Premier Division	7	36	7	15	14	35	51	29	1.000000
	1986–87	Premier Division	9	44	10	13	21	44	70	33	0.977273
	1979–80	Premier Division	10	36	6	6	24	29	67	18	0.666667

SQUAD 1988–89 — 5TH IN THE PREMIER DIVISION

Steven ARCHIBALD	Centre forward	George M C J McCLUSKEY	Centre forward
John Angus Paul COLLINS	Midfielder	Patrick David McGINLAY	Midfielder
Gareth John EVANS	Centre forward	Thomas McINTYRE	Full back
David FELLINGER	Midfielder	Callum MILNE	Full back
William McCall FINDLAY	Midfielder	Graham MITCHELL	Centre half
Andrew Lewis GORAM	Goalkeeper	Neil Ian ORR	Midfielder
Keith M HOUCHEN	Centre forward	Gordon RAE	Centre half
Gordon HUNTER	Centre forward	Alan SNEDDON	Full back
Paul James KANE	Midfielder	Joseph TORTOLANO	Midfielder
Daniel Joseph LENNON	Midfielder	Andrew WATSON	Midfielder
Edward Skillion MAY	Outside right	Michael Graham WEIR	Midfielder
Joseph McBRIDE	Outside left		

311

	Season	League	League Position	P	W	D	L	F	A	Pts	3 Point Equivalent
	1998–99	Division 1	1	36	28	5	3	84	33	89	2.472222
	1991–92	Premier Division	5	44	16	17	11	53	45	49	1.477273
	1994–95	**Premier Division**	**3**	**36**	**12**	**17**	**7**	**49**	**37**	**53**	**1.472222**
1990s	1993–94	Premier Division	5	44	16	15	13	53	48	47	1.431818
	1989–90	Premier Division	7	36	12	10	14	34	41	34	1.277778
	1995–96	Premier Division	5	36	11	10	15	43	57	43	1.194444
	1992–93	Premier Division	7	44	12	13	19	54	64	37	1.113636
	1996–97	Premier Division	9	36	9	11	16	38	55	38	1.055556
	1990–91	Premier Division	9	36	6	13	17	24	51	25	0.861111
	1997–98	Premier Division	10	36	6	12	18	38	59	30	0.833333

SQUAD 1994–95 — 3RD IN THE PREMIER DIVISION

David Alan BEAUMONT	Centre half	Patrick David McGINLAY	Midfielder
Darren DODS	Centre half	Mark Robertson McGRAW	Centre forward
Gareth John EVANS	Centre forward	Andrew Frank MILLEN	Defender
David John FARRELL	Midfielder	William Nisbit MILLER	Centre half
William McCall FINDLAY	Midfielder	Graham MITCHELL	Centre half
Brian HAMILTON	Midfielder	Michael Andrew M O'NEILL	Midfielder
Kevin Patrick HARPER	Centre forward	Michael RENWICK	Defender
Gordon HUNTER	Centre half	Joseph TORTOLANO	Midfielder
Darren JACKSON	Centre forward	Steven TWEED	Centre half
James LEIGHTON	Goalkeeper	Michael Graham WEIR	Midfielder
Graeme James LOVE	Midfielder	Keith Arthur WRIGHT	Centre forward
Kevin McALLISTER	Outside right		

HIBERNIAN

Season	League	League Position	P	W	D	L	F	A	Pts	3 Point Equivalent
2000–01	**SPL**	**3**	**38**	**18**	**12**	**8**	**57**	**35**	**66**	**1.736842**
2004–05	SPL	3	38	18	7	13	64	57	61	1.605263
2005–06	SPL	4	38	17	5	16	61	56	56	1.473684
2002–03	SPL	7	38	15	6	17	56	64	51	1.342105
2006–07	SPL	6	38	13	10	15	56	46	49	1.289474
2003–04	SPL	8	38	11	11	16	41	60	44	1.157895
1999–2000	SPL	6	36	10	11	15	49	61	41	1.138889
2001–02	SPL	10	38	10	11	17	51	56	41	1.078947

SQUAD 2000–01   3RD IN THE SPL

Didier AGATHE	Forward	Marc LIBBRA	Forward
Lyndon ANDREWS	Midfielder	Stuart Andrew LOVELL	Forward
Frederic ARPINON	Midfielder	Martin Wylie McINTOSH	Defender
Scott John BANNERMAN	Forward	Thomas Kelly McMANUS	Forward
Grant Ian BREBNER	Midfielder	Ian William MURRAY	Midfielder
Nick COLGAN	Goalkeeper	Garry Lawrence O'CONNOR	Forward
Mark William DEMPSIE	Midfielder	John Thomas O'NEIL	Midfielder
Paul Joseph FENWICK	Defender	Mika-Matti P PAATELAINEN	Forward
James FRANKS	Goalkeeper	Hakim SAR-TEMSOURY	Midfielder
Matthias JACK	Defender	Franck Gaston Henri SAUZEE	Midfielder
Russell Nigel LATAPY	Forward	Gary SMITH	Defender
Ulrich Rosenloev LAURSEN	Defender	Thomas William SMITH	Midfielder
Dirk LEHMANN	Forward	David ZITELLI	Forward

INVERNESS CALEDONIAN THISTLE

Season	League	League Position	P	W	D	L	F	A	Pts	3 Point Equivalent
1996–97	Division 3	1	36	23	7	6	70	37	76	2.111111
1998–99	**Division 2**	**2**	**36**	**21**	**9**	**6**	**80**	**48**	**72**	**2.000000**
1995–96	Division 3	3	36	15	12	9	64	38	57	1.583333
1997–98	Division 2	5	36	13	10	13	65	52	49	1.361111
1994–95*	Division 3	6	36	12	9	15	48	61	45	1.250000

* 1994–95 was Inverness Caledonian Thistle's first season in the Scottish League

SQUAD 1998–99   2ND IN SECOND DIVISION

Wayne ADDICOAT	Midfielder	Robert MANN	Defender
Andrew ALLAN	Defender	Mark McCULLOCH	Defender
Martin BAVIDGE	Forward	Scott McLEAN	Forward
Jim CALDER	Goalkeeper	Gary NICOL	Forward
Paul CHERRY	Midfielder	Hugh ROBERTSON	Defender
Charlie CHRISTIE	Midfielder	Barry ROBSON	Midfielder
David CRAIG	Forward	Duncan SHEARER	Forward
Gary FARQUHAR	Midfielder	Paul SHEERIN	Midfielder
Les FRIDGE	Goalkeeper	Iain STEWART	Forward
Martin GLANCY	Forward	Michael TEASDALE	Defender
Richard HASTINGS	Defender	Ross TOKELY	Defender
Iain MacARTHUR	Defender	Barry WILSON	Forward

Season	League	League Position	P	W	D	L	F	A	Pts	3 Point Equivalent
2003–04	**Division 1**	**1**	**36**	**21**	**7**	**8**	**67**	**33**	**70**	**1.944444**
2002–03	Division 1	4	36	20	5	11	74	45	65	1.805556
2005–06	SPL	7	38	15	13	10	51	38	58	1.526316
2000–01	Division 1	4	36	14	12	10	71	54	54	1.500000
1999–2000	Division 1	6	36	13	10	13	60	55	49	1.361111
2001–02	Division 1	6	36	13	9	14	60	51	48	1.333333
2006–07	SPL	8	38	11	13	14	42	48	46	1.210526
2004–05	SPL	8	38	11	11	16	41	47	44	1.157895

SQUAD 2003–04

David BINGHAM	Forward	Craig MacMILLAN	Forward
Mark BROWN	Goalkeeper	David MacRAE	Midfielder
Charlie CHRISTIE	Midfielder	Robert MANN	Defender
Russell DUNCAN	Midfielder	Roy McBAIN	Midfielder
Stuart GOLABEK	Defender	Stuart McCAFFREY	Defender
Richard HART	Midfielder	Grant MUNRO	Defender
Steven HISLOP	Forward	David PROCTOR	Defender
Liam KEOGH	Forward	Paul RITCHIE	Forward
Anthony LOW	Midfielder	Darran THOMSON	Midfielder
Darren MACKIE	Forward	Ross TOKELY	Defender
Lewis MacKINNON	Forward	Barry WILSON	Forward

CHAMPIONS OF FIRST DIVISION

KILMARNOCK

Season	League	League Position	P	W	D	L	F	A	Pts	3 Point Equivalent
1953–54	B	2	30	19	4	7	71	39	42	2.033333
1952–53	B	4	30	17	2	11	74	48	36	1.766667
1956–57	**1**	**3**	**34**	**16**	**10**	**8**	**57**	**39**	**42**	**1.705882**
1951–52	B	5	30	16	2	12	62	48	34	1.666667
1949–50	B	8	30	14	5	11	50	43	33	1.566667
1957–58	1	5	34	14	9	11	60	55	37	1.500000
1947–48	B	6	30	13	4	13	72	62	30	1.433333
1958–59	1	8	34	13	8	13	58	51	34	1.382353
1955–56	A	8	34	12	10	12	52	45	34	1.352941
1954–55	A	10	30	10	6	14	46	58	26	1.200000
1948–49	B	11	30	9	7	14	58	61	25	1.133333
1950–51	B	12	30	8	8	14	44	49	24	1.066667
1946–47	A	15	30	6	9	15	44	66	21	0.900000

SQUAD 1956–57

Francis Whitfield BEATTIE	Inside left	John Boscoe LAWLOR	Inside left
Bertie BLACK	Outside right	Alistair MACKAY	Left half
James Robertson BROWN	Goalkeeper	John MALLOY	Goalkeeper
David McCathie BURNS	Outside left	Gerald Joseph MAYES	Centre forward
Tommy CAMPBELL	Inside forward	Gordon Archibald McBAIN	Outside right
John CAVEN	Centre forward	Willie MILLOY	Left back
Ralph COLLINS	Right back	William McKie MUIR	Outside right
David White CURLETT	Inside forward	David Knox (Billy) NEIL	Goalkeeper
Robert DOUGAN	Centre half	James STEWART	Left back
Bob FALLS	Wing half	Robert R T STEWART	Right half
Christopher C FLETCHER	Inside forward	George McGrory TAGGART	Wing half
William J HARVEY	Inside right	William TONER	Centre half
George D HILL	Centre half	Matthew McLuskie WATSON	Full back

3RD IN DIVISION 1

1960s

Season	League	League Position	P	W	D	L	F	A	Pts	3 Point Equivalent
1959–60	1	2	34	24	2	8	67	45	50	2.176471
1960–61	1	2	34	21	8	5	77	45	50	2.088235
1964–65	**1**	**1**	**34**	**22**	**6**	**6**	**62**	**33**	**50**	**2.117647**
1963–64	1	2	34	22	5	7	77	40	49	2.088235
1962–63	1	2	34	20	8	6	92	40	48	2.000000
1965–66	1	3	34	20	5	9	73	46	45	1.911765
1968–69	1	4	34	15	14	5	50	32	44	1.735294
1961–62	1	5	34	16	10	8	74	58	42	1.705882
1966–67	1	7	34	16	8	10	59	46	40	1.647059
1967–68	1	7	34	13	8	13	59	57	34	1.382353

SQUAD 1964–65 — CHAMPIONS OF FIRST DIVISION

Francis Whitfield BEATTIE	Inside left	Jim McFADZEAN	Inside forward
Bertie BLACK	Outside right	Jacky McGRORY	Left half
Hugh Murdoch BROWN	Inside forward	Brian McILROY	Outside left
Billy DICKSON	Centre half	John W M McINALLY	Inside forward
Bobby FERGUSON	Goalkeeper	Tommy McLEAN	Outside right
Robert Campbell FORSYTH	Goalkeeper	Eric McIntyre MURRAY	Centre forward
Ronald Douglas HAMILTON	Centre forward	Pat O'CONNOR	Wing half
Andy KING	Full back	David SNEDDON	Inside forward
Frank MALONE	Inside forward	Matthew McLuskie WATSON	Full back
Joseph Paul Smith MASON	Inside forward		

314

1970s

Season	League	League Position	P	W	D	L	F	A	Pts	3 Point Equivalent
1973–74	2	2	36	26	6	4	96	44	58	2.333333
1975–76	Division 1	2	26	16	3	7	44	29	35	1.961538
1978–79	Division 1	2	39	22	10	7	72	35	54	1.948718
1969–70	**1**	**7**	**34**	**13**	**10**	**11**	**62**	**57**	**36**	**1.441176**
1977–78	Division 1	6	39	14	12	13	52	46	40	1.384615
1974–75	1	12	34	8	15	11	52	68	31	1.147059
1971–72	1	11	34	11	6	17	49	64	28	1.147059
1970–71	1	13	34	10	8	16	43	67	28	1.117647
1972–73	1	17	34	7	8	19	40	71	22	0.852941
1976–77	Premier Division	10	36	4	9	23	32	71	17	0.583333

SQUAD 1969–70 — 7TH IN FIRST DIVISION

Robin ARTHUR	Centre half	Jacky McGRORY	Left half
Francis Whitfield BEATTIE	Inside left	Alexander D McLAUGHLAN	Goalkeeper
Jimmy COOK	Outside right	James Yuille McLEAN	Inside forward
Billy DICKSON	Centre half	Tommy McLEAN	Outside right
John M GILMOUR	Inside forward	Edward M MORRISON	Centre forward
Andy KING	Full back	Brian RODMAN	Centre half
Ross C MATHIE	Centre forward	Ronald McLean SHEED	Outside left
Samuel George MAXWELL	Inside left	Hugh Mair STRACHAN	Wing half
Alan McDONALD	Right half	Willie WADDELL	Inside forward

Season	League	League Position	P	W	D	L	F	A	Pts	3 Point Equivalent
1981–82	Division 1	2	39	17	17	5	60	29	51	1.743590
1985–86	Division 1	3	39	18	8	13	62	49	44	1.589744
1986–87	Division 1	6	44	17	11	16	62	53	45	1.409091
1983–84	Division 1	6	39	16	6	17	57	53	38	1.384615
1979–80	Premier Division	8	36	11	11	14	36	52	33	1.222222
1984–85	Division 1	12	39	12	10	17	42	61	34	1.179487
1987–88	Division 1	10	44	13	11	20	55	60	37	1.136364
1988–89	Division 1	13	39	10	14	15	47	60	34	1.128205
1980–81	Premier Division	9	36	5	9	22	23	65	19	0.666667
1982–83	Premier Division	10	36	3	11	22	28	91	17	0.555556

SQUAD 1981–82   2ND IN FIRST DIVISION

Kenneth C ARMSTRONG	Centre half	Alister Henry MAUCHLEN	Inside forward
John Francis BOURKE	Centre forward	James McBRIDE	Centre forward
Thomas Charles BRYCE	Outside left	Gordon McCREADY	Inside forward
James Ian Cook BRYSON	Inside forward	Alan William McCULLOCH	Goalkeeper
James Morrison CLARK	Wing half	Derrick Schendal McDICKEN	Centre half
Paul CLARKE	Centre half	Samuel Walker McGIVERN	Inside forward
James Hammond COCKBURN	Wing half	Stuart Donald McLEAN	Inside forward
Kenneth William EADIE	Centre forward	Alan David ROBERTSON	Half back
Brian GALLACHER	Centre forward	Keith ROBIN	Wing half
Alastair F MacLEOD	Full back	Gordon WILSON	Inside forward

Season	League	League Position	P	W	D	L	F	A	Pts	3 Point Equivalent
1989–90	Division 2	2	39	22	4	13	67	39	48	1.794872
1991–92	Division 1	4	44	21	12	11	59	37	54	1.704545
1992–93	Division 1	2	44	21	12	11	67	40	54	1.704545
1998–99	SPL	4	36	14	14	8	47	29	56	1.555556
1990–91	Division 1	5	39	15	13	11	58	48	43	1.487179
1997–98	Premier Division	4	36	13	11	12	40	52	50	1.388889
1994–95	Premier Division	7	36	11	10	15	40	48	43	1.194444
1993–94	Premier Division	8	44	12	16	16	36	45	40	1.181818
1995–96	Premier Division	7	36	11	8	17	39	54	41	1.138889
1996–97	Premier Division	7	36	11	6	19	41	61	39	1.083333

SQUAD 1998–99   4TH IN THE SPL

David BAGAN	Forward	Gordon G B MARSHALL	Goalkeeper
Martin BAKER	Defender	Alistair Murdoch McCOIST	Forward
Alexander BURKE	Forward	Gary Kyle McCUTCHEON	Forward
Iain DURRANT	Midfielder	Kevin McGOWNE	Defender
Steven James HAMILTON	Defender	Alistair Robert MITCHELL	Outside left
John HENRY	Midfielder	Samuel R MONTGOMERIE	Defender
Gary James HOLT	Midfielder	Patrick Kevin Francis NEVIN	Forward
Christopher INNES	Defender	Mark Francis REILLY	Midfielder
Dylan KERR	Defender	Mark Kingsley ROBERTS	Midfielder
James Harley LAUCHLAN	Defender	Jerome VAREILLE	Forward
Angus Ian MacPHERSON	Defender	Paul Hamilton WRIGHT	Forward
Alan Scott MAHOOD	Midfielder		

	Season	League	League Position	P	W	D	L	F	A	Pts	3 Point Equivalent
2000s	2002–03	**SPL**	**4**	**38**	**16**	**9**	**13**	**47**	**56**	**57**	**1.500000**
	2005–06	SPL	6	38	15	10	13	63	64	55	1.447368
	2006–07	SPL	5	38	16	7	15	47	54	55	1.447368
	2000–01	SPL	4	38	15	9	14	44	53	54	1.421053
	2001–02	SPL	7	38	13	10	15	44	54	49	1.289474
	2004–05	SPL	7	38	15	4	19	49	55	49	1.289474
	2003–04	SPL	10	38	12	6	20	51	74	42	1.105263
	1999–2000	SPL	9	36	8	13	15	38	52	37	1.027778

SQUAD 2002–03 · 4TH IN THE SPL

Samuel BOUTAL	Forward	Alan Scott MAHOOD	Midfielder
Kris BOYD	Forward	Gordon G B MARSHALL	Goalkeeper
Peter CANERO	Defender	Gary Matthew McDONALD	Forward
Mark CANNING	Defender/Midfielder	Andrew McLAREN	Midfielder
Craig Peter DARGO	Forward	Barry John McLAUGHLIN	Defender
Paul DI GIACOMO	Forward	Gary John McSWEGAN	Forward
Shaun DILLON	Defender	Colin George MELDRUM	Goalkeeper
Frederic DINDELEUX	Defender	Alistair Robert MITCHELL	Outside left
James FOWLER	Defender	Stephen MURRAY	Midfielder/Forward
Stephen FULTON	Midfielder	Jose Manuel QUITONGO	Forward
Garry HAY	Defender	Jesus Garcia SANJUAN	Midfielder
Sean HESSEY	Defender	Greg SHIELDS	Defender
Christopher INNES	Defender	Colin STEWART	Goalkeeper
Gary LOCKE	Midfielder		

LIVINGSTON

	Season	League	League Position	P	W	D	L	F	A	Pts	3 Point Equivalent
1990s	1998–99	**Division 2**	**1**	**36**	**22**	**11**	**3**	**66**	**35**	**77**	**2.138889**
	1995–96*	Division 3	1	36	21	9	6	51	24	72	2.000000
	1996–97	Division 2	3	36	18	10	8	56	38	64	1.777778
	1997–98	Division 2	3	36	16	11	9	56	40	59	1.638889

* 1995–96 was Livingston's first season in the Scottish Football League

SQUAD 1998–99 · CHAMPIONS OF SECOND DIVISION

Neil ALEXANDER	Goalkeeper	Ian James LITTLE	Midfielder
John Neil BENNETT	Midfielder	William James MACDONALD	Midfielder
David Thomas BINGHAM	Forward	Kevin MAGEE	Midfielder
James Thomson BOYLE	Defender	Ian McCALDON	Goalkeeper
Francis Joseph CONWAY	Defender	Mark Thomas McCORMICK	Forward
Graham COUGHLAN	Forward	Allan William McMANUS	Defender
Thomas COURTS	Defender	Grant Thomas McMARTIN	Forward
Paul Andrew DEAS	Defender	Brian McPHEE	Forward
Ian FERGUSON	Forward	John MILLAR	Midfielder
Craig FEROZ	Forward	Kai Marko Kalervo RAJAMAKI	Midfielder
Derek Adam FLEMING	Defender	John Grant ROBERTSON	Forward
Gordon Iain FORREST	Defender	James Cunningham SHERRY	Midfielder
Paul Edward HARVEY	Midfielder	Sean Brian SWEENEY	Defender
Charles Alexander KING	Forward	Gregg WATSON	Defender

Season	League	League Position	P	W	D	L	F	A	Pts	3 Point Equivalent
2000–01	**Division 1**	**1**	**36**	**23**	**7**	**6**	**72**	**31**	**76**	**2.111111**
1999–2000	Division 1	4	36	19	7	10	60	45	64	1.777778
2001–02	SPL	4	38	16	10	12	50	47	58	1.526316
2006–07	Division 1	6	36	11	12	13	41	46	45	1.250000
2003–04	SPL	9	38	10	13	15	48	57	43	1.131579
2002–03	SPL	9	38	9	8	21	48	62	35	0.921053
2004–05	SPL	10	38	9	8	21	34	61	35	0.921053
2005–06	SPL	12	38	4	6	28	25	79	18	0.473684

SQUAD 2000–01 — 3RD IN THE SPL

John Patton ANDERSON	Defender	Nocko JOKOVIC	Forward
Marvin Anthony ANDREWS	Defender	Marino KEITH	Forward
Carlos Dario AURELIO	Forward	Stuart Andrew LOVELL	Midfielder
David Thomas BINGHAM	Forward	Nathan Peter LOWNDES	Forward
Gary BOLLAN	Defender	Lee Robert MAKEL	Midfielder
Phillipe BRINQUIN	Defender	Mark Ross McCULLOCH	Midfielder
Richard BRITTAIN	Forward	David McEWAN	Goalkeeper
Francisco Javier Sanchez BROTO	Goalkeeper	Morten PETERSEN	Defender
Massimiliano CAPUTO	Forward	Oscar M (Rubio) RAMOS	Defender
Nick CULKIN	Goalkeeper	Didier SANTINI	Defender
Paul Andrew DEAS	Defender	Steven William TOSH	Midfielder
Simone DEL NERO	Forward	Cherif TOURE-MAMAN	Midfielder
Davide FERNANDEZ	Forward	Barry John WILSON	Forward
Francisco C (Quino) GUINOVART	Midfielder	Davide Antonio XAUSA	Forward
Michael HART	Forward		

MOTHERWELL

Season	League	League Position	P	W	D	L	F	A	Pts	3 Point Equivalent
1953–54	B	1	30	21	3	6	109	43	45	2.200000
1958–59	**1**	**3**	**34**	**18**	**8**	**8**	**83**	**50**	**44**	**1.823529**
1956–57	1	7	34	16	5	13	72	66	37	1.558824
1951–52	A	7	30	12	7	11	51	57	31	1.433333
1947–48	A	8	30	13	3	14	45	47	29	1.400000
1946–47	A	8	30	12	5	13	58	54	29	1.366667
1950–51	A	9	30	11	6	13	58	65	28	1.300000
1955–56	A	10	34	11	11	12	53	59	33	1.294118
1957–58	1	8	34	12	8	14	68	67	32	1.294118
1948–49	A	12	30	10	5	15	44	49	25	1.166667
1949–50	A	10	30	10	5	15	53	58	25	1.166667
1952–53	A	15	30	10	5	15	57	80	25	1.166667
1954–55	A	15	30	9	4	17	42	62	22	1.033333

SQUAD 1958–59 — 3RD IN DIVISION 1

Charles AITKEN	Inside right	William McSEVENEY	Full back
Gerard Austin BAKER	Outside right	Pat QUINN	Inside right
Stewart BROWN	Inside left	Billy REID	Inside forward
William COWIE	Centre half	Sammy REID	Inside forward
Jim FORREST	Outside right	Bobby ROBERTS	Right back
James Ian GARDINER	Centre forward	Ian ST JOHN	Inside forward
Patrick Carr HOLTON	Left back	Alan S STENHOUSE	Inside forward
William HUNTER	Outside right	John STEWART	Left back
John MARTIS	Centre half	Hugh Mair STRACHAN	Centre forward
Bobby McCALLUM	Left back	Andrew Best WEIR	Outside left
Robert Johnston McCANN	Inside right	S Hastie WEIR	Goalkeeper
John McPHEE	Inside left	Alan WYLIE	Goalkeeper

1960s

Season	League	League Position	P	W	D	L	F	A	Pts	3 Point Equivalent
1968–69	2	1	36	30	4	2	112	23	64	2.611111
1959–60	**1**	**5**	**34**	**16**	**8**	**10**	**71**	**61**	**40**	**1.647059**
1960–61	1	5	34	15	8	11	70	57	38	1.558824
1961–62	1	9	34	13	6	15	65	62	32	1.323529
1962–63	1	10	34	10	11	13	60	63	31	1.205882
1966–67	1	10	34	10	11	13	59	60	31	1.205882
1965–66	1	13	34	12	4	18	52	69	28	1.176471
1963–64	1	11	34	9	11	14	51	62	29	1.117647
1964–65	1	14	34	10	8	16	45	54	28	1.117647
1967–68	1	17	34	6	7	21	40	66	19	0.735294

SQUAD 1959–60   5TH IN DIVISION 1

Charles AITKEN	Inside right	Pat QUINN	Inside right
Pat DELANEY	Centre forward	Billy REID	Inside forward
Jim FORREST	Outside right	Sammy REID	Inside forward
William HUNTER	Outside right	Bobby ROBERTS	Right back
Joe MACKIN	Goalkeeper	Ian ST JOHN	Inside forward
John MARTIS	Centre half	Alan S STENHOUSE	Inside forward
Bobby McCALLUM	Left back	Hugh Mair STRACHAN	Centre forward
Robert Johnston McCANN	Inside right	Andrew Best WEIR	Outside left
John McPHEE	Inside left	S Hastie WEIR	Goalkeeper
William McSEVENEY	Full back	Alan WYLIE	Goalkeeper
Robert PATERSON	Right back	Bobby YOUNG	Centre forward

1970s

Season	League	League Position	P	W	D	L	F	A	Pts	3 Point Equivalent
1975–76	**Premier Division**	**4**	**36**	**16**	**8**	**12**	**57**	**49**	**40**	**1.555556**
1973–74	1	9	34	14	7	13	45	40	35	1.441176
1970–71	1	9	34	13	8	13	43	47	34	1.382353
1974–75	1	10	34	14	5	15	52	57	33	1.382353
1977–78	Premier Division	6	36	13	7	16	45	52	33	1.277778
1969–70	1	11	34	11	10	13	49	51	32	1.264706
1972–73	1	8	34	11	9	14	38	48	31	1.235294
1971–72	1	10	34	11	7	16	49	69	29	1.176471
1976–77	Premier Division	7	36	10	12	14	57	60	32	1.166667
1978–79	Premier Division	10	36	5	7	24	33	86	17	0.611111

SQUAD 1975–76   4TH IN THE PREMIER DIVISION

Victor DAVIDSON	Inside forward	Willie McVIE	Centre half
Patrick J GARDNER	Wing half	Peter MILLAR	Centre forward
John GOLDTHORPE	Inside left	William H PETTIGREW	Centre forward
Bobby GRAHAM	Centre forward	Stuart RENNIE	Goalkeeper
Ian KENNEDY	Outside left	Gregor McK STEVENS	Centre half
Peter MARINELLO	Outside right	Ian Wishart TAYLOR	Inside forward
Colin C McADAM	Wing half	Joe WARK	Left back
Jim McILWRAITH	Centre forward	Bobby WATSON	Wing half
Stewart Clarkston McLAREN	Full back	Willie WATSON	Full back
Michael Q McMANUS	Outside right		

Season	League	League Position	P	W	D	L	F	A	Pts	3 Point Equivalent
1981–82	Division 1	1	39	26	9	4	92	36	61	2.230769
1984–85	Division 1	1	39	21	8	10	62	36	50	1.820513
1980–81	Division 1	5	39	19	11	9	65	51	49	1.743590
1979–80	Division 1	6	39	16	11	12	59	48	43	1.512821
1987–88	Premier Division	8	44	13	10	21	37	56	36	1.113636
1982–83	Premier Division	8	36	11	5	20	39	73	27	1.055556
1986–87	Premier Division	8	44	11	12	21	43	64	34	1.022727
1988–89	Premier Division	9	36	7	13	16	35	44	27	0.944444
1985–86	Premier Division	9	36	7	6	23	33	66	20	0.750000
1983–84	Premier Division	10	36	4	7	25	31	75	15	0.527778

1980s

SQUAD 1981–82 — CHAMPIONS OF FIRST DIVISION

Joe CARSON	Centre half	Brian John McCLAIR	Centre forward
Bruce CLELLAND	Centre forward	John McKEEVER	Centre forward
Ian CLINGING	Outside right	Brian McLAUGHLIN	Inside forward
Alfie J CONN	Inside forward	Stephen J McLELLAND	Centre forward
Brian COYNE	Inside forward	Paul MILLS	Wing half
Graeme S A FORBES	Inside forward	Tommy O'HARA	Full back
John GAHAGAN	Outside left	Stuart RAFFERTY	Inside forward
Willie IRVINE	Inside forward	Howard SAMMEROFF	Goalkeeper
John MACKAY	Centre half	Gordon SOUTAR	Inside forward
Ian Murdo MacLEOD	Wing half	Hugh SPROAT	Goalkeeper
Gary McALLISTER	Inside forward	Joe WARK	Left back

Season	League	League Position	P	W	D	L	F	A	Pts	3 Point Equivalent
1993–94	Premier Division	3	44	20	14	10	58	43	54	1.681818
1994–95	Premier Division	2	36	14	12	10	50	50	54	1.500000
1998–99	SPL	7	36	10	11	15	35	54	41	1.138889
1995–96	Premier Division	8	36	9	12	15	28	39	39	1.083333
1996–97	Premier Division	8	36	9	11	16	44	55	38	1.055556
1992–93	Premier Division	9	44	11	13	20	46	62	35	1.045455
1990–91	Premier Division	6	36	12	9	15	51	50	33	1.250000
1989–90	Premier Division	6	36	11	12	13	43	47	34	1.250000
1991–92	Premier Division	10	44	10	14	20	43	61	34	1.000000
1997–98	Premier Division	9	36	9	7	20	46	64	34	0.944444

1990s

SQUAD 1993–94 — 3RD IN THE PREMIER DIVISION

Ian Allan ANGUS	Midfielder	Stephen David KIRK	Midfielder
Douglas ARNOTT	Centre forward	Miodrag KRIVOKAPIC	Centre half
George Elder BURLEY	Full back	Paul LAMBERT	Midfielder
Alexander BURNS	Midfielder	Brian MARTIN	Midfielder
Davie COOPER	Outside left	Christopher McCART	Midfielder
Thomas COYNE	Centre forward	Paul Alexander McGRILLEN	Outside left
William McIntosh DAVIES	Midfielder	Robert McKINNON	Full back
Sieb DIJKSTRA	Goalkeeper	Stephen McMILLAN	Defender
James DOLAN	Full back	Philip O'DONNELL	Midfielder
Iain John H FERGUSON	Centre forward	John PHILLIBEN	Centre half
Alastair Slowey GRAHAM	Forward	Robert SHANNON	Full back
James W GRIFFIN	Full back		

Season	League	League Position	P	W	D	L	F	A	Pts	3 Point Equivalent
1999–2000	SPL	4	36	14	10	12	49	63	52	1.444444
2005–06	SPL	8	38	13	10	15	55	61	49	1.289474
2004–05	SPL	6	38	13	9	16	46	49	48	1.263158
2003–04	SPL	6	38	12	10	16	42	49	46	1.210526
2000–01	SPL	8	38	12	7	19	42	56	43	1.131579
2001–02	SPL	11	38	11	7	20	49	69	40	1.052632
2006–07	SPL	10	38	10	8	20	41	61	38	1.000000
2002–03	SPL	12	38	7	7	24	45	71	28	0.736842

SQUAD 2000–01   4TH IN THE SPL

Derek Watt ADAMS	Forward	Lee Henry McCULLOCH	Forward
Gerard Daniel BRANNAN	Midfielder	Jamie McGOWAN	Defender
Martyn Alexander CORRIGAN	Defender	Stephen McMILLAN	Defender
Stephen James CRAIGAN	Defender	Patrick Kevin Francis NEVIN	Forward
Sasa CURCIC	Midfielder	Steven Arthur NICHOLAS	Forward
John DAVIES	Midfielder	Douglas RAMSAY	Midfielder
Greig Paterson DENHAM	Defender	John SPENCER	Forward
Michel Johannes DOESBURG	Defender	Greg STRONG	Defender
Donald Ralph GOODMAN	Forward	Shaun TEALE	Defender
Andrew Lewis GORAM	Goalkeeper	Tony THOMAS	Defender
Stephen HALLIDAY	Forward	Derek TOWNSLEY	Midfielder
Steven HAMMELL	Defender	Kevin TWADDLE	Midfielder
Paul Edward HARVEY	Midfielder	Simo Johannes VALAKARI	Midfielder
Benito KEMBLE	Defender	Stephen Gerard WOODS	Goalkeeper
Rob MATTHEI	Midfielder		

PARTICK THISTLE

Season	League	League Position	P	W	D	L	F	A	Pts	3 Point Equivalent
1947–48	A	3	30	16	4	10	61	42	36	1.733333
1953–54	A	3	30	17	1	12	76	54	35	1.733333
1946–47	A	5	30	16	3	11	74	59	35	1.700000
1957–58	1	6	34	17	3	14	69	71	37	1.588235
1950–51	A	6	30	13	7	10	57	48	33	1.533333
1951–52	A	6	30	12	7	11	48	51	31	1.433333
1958–59	1	9	34	14	6	14	59	66	34	1.411765
1949–50	A	7	30	13	3	14	55	45	29	1.400000
1956–57	1	8	34	13	8	13	53	51	34	1.382353
1955–56	A	9	34	13	7	14	62	60	33	1.352941
1954–55	A	9	30	11	7	12	49	61	29	1.333333
1952–53	A	9	30	10	9	11	55	63	29	1.300000
1948–49	A	11	30	9	9	12	50	63	27	1.200000

SQUAD 1953–54   3RD IN DIVISION A

Alexander Stewart BELL	Goalkeeper	Jimmy McGOWAN	Right back
William CRAWFORD	Inside right	Joseph Clarke McINNES	Outside left
James A DAVIDSON	Centre half	John (Ian) M McINTOSH	Inside forward
Robert GIBB	Left back	Tom McNAB	Left half
John HARVEY	Inside right	David McPARLAND	Inside forward
Jack James HENDERSON	Forward	William SHARP	Centre forward
Robert Gibb HOWITT	Inside forward	George SMITH	Outside right
Andy KERR	Centre half	William R SMITH	Goalkeeper
Thomas LEDGERWOOD	Goalkeeper	Bobby THOMSON	Right half
John Archibald MACKENZIE	Outside right	James WALKER	Forward
David Cochrane MATHERS	Left half	Alex WRIGHT	Inside right
Norman James McCREADIE	Full back		

Season	League	League Position	P	W	D	L	F	A	Pts	3 Point Equivalent
1962–63	1	3	34	20	6	8	66	44	46	1.941176
1961–62	1	7	34	16	3	15	60	55	35	1.500000
1963–64	1	7	34	15	5	14	55	54	35	1.470588
1959–60	1	10	34	14	4	16	54	78	32	1.352941
1960–61	1	11	34	13	6	15	59	69	32	1.323529
1964–65	1	11	34	11	10	13	57	58	32	1.264706
1967–68	1	10	34	12	7	15	51	67	31	1.264706
1965–66	1	12	34	10	10	14	55	64	30	1.176471
1966–67	1	12	34	9	12	13	49	68	30	1.147059
1968–69	1	14	34	9	10	15	39	53	28	1.088235

1960s

SQUAD 1962–63 — 7TH IN DIVISION 1

Alexander Dewar BROWN	Full back
David CLOSS	Inside forward
Ian COWAN	Inside right
Billy CUNNINGHAM	Inside forward
Neil DUFFY	Inside forward
Martin Murphy FERGUSON	Wing half
James Paterson FLEMING	Outside left
Billy GOURLAY	Inside forward
Billy HAINEY	Centre forward
John HARVEY	Inside right
Joe HOGAN	Centre forward
Joe McBRIDE	Centre forward
Donnie McKINNON	Centre half
David McPARLAND	Inside forward
George MUIR	Right back
George NIVEN	Goalkeeper
George SMITH	Outside right
Richard J STAITE	Centre half
Gordon WHITELAW	Inside forward
Dickie WILLIAMSON	Outside right

Season	League	League Position	P	W	D	L	F	A	Pts	3 Point Equivalent
1975–76	Division 1	1	26	17	7	2	47	19	41	2.230769
1970–71	2	1	36	23	10	3	78	26	56	2.194444
1971–72	1	7	34	12	10	12	53	54	34	1.352941
1978–79	Premier Division	8	36	13	8	15	42	39	34	1.305556
1977–78	Premier Division	7	36	14	5	17	52	64	33	1.305556
1976–77	Premier Division	5	36	11	13	12	40	44	35	1.277778
1974–75	1	13	34	10	10	14	48	62	30	1.176471
1972–73	1	13	34	10	8	16	40	53	28	1.117647
1973–74	1	11	34	9	10	15	33	46	28	1.088235
1969–70	1	18	34	5	7	22	41	82	17	0.647059

1970s

SQUAD 1976–77 — 5TH IN THE PREMIER DIVISION

Andy ANDERSON	Centre half
Jack CAMPBELL	Right back
Joe CRAIG	Inside left
John V CRAIG	Wing half
John Kelly (Dixie) DEANS	Centre forward
Sandy FRAME	Centre forward
Ian GIBSON	Inside forward
Alan David HANSEN	Centre half
John A McDonald HANSEN	Centre half
Robert Joseph HOUSTON	Wing half
Harry G F JOHNSTON	Inside forward
Jim KELLY	Outside left
Alastair James LOVE	Wing half
George Shearer MACKIE	Inside forward
John Gerard MARR	Wing half
Ian McDONALD	Inside forward
Denis McQUADE	Outside left
James Millsopp MELROSE	Inside forward
Alan Roderick ROUGH	Goalkeeper
Douglas M SOMNER	Centre forward
Brian J WHITTAKER	Wing half

Season	League	League Position	P	W	D	L	F	A	Pts	3 Point Equivalent
1982–83	Division 1	4	39	20	9	10	66	45	49	1.769231
1983–84	Division 1	3	39	19	8	12	67	50	46	1.666667
1979–80	**Premier Division**	7	36	11	14	11	43	47	36	1.305556
1987–88	Division 1	8	44	16	9	19	60	64	41	1.295455
1988–89	Division 1	8	39	13	11	15	57	58	37	1.282051
1984–85	Division 1	11	39	13	9	17	50	55	35	1.230769
1985–86	Division 1	8	39	10	16	13	53	64	36	1.179487
1988–87	Division 1	8	44	12	15	17	49	54	39	1.159091
1980–81	Premier Division	6	36	10	10	16	32	48	30	1.111111
1981–82	Premier Division	9	36	6	10	20	35	59	22	0.777778

SQUAD 1979–80   7TH IN THE PREMIER DIVISION

Andy ANDERSON	Centre half	Colin C McADAM	Centre half
Jack CAMPBELL	Right back	Ian McDONALD	Inside forward
James DOYLE	Right back	James Gordon McGREGOR	Centre forward
Ian GIBSON	Inside forward	Douglas G McNAB	Goalkeeper
Tony HIGGINS	Inside forward	James Millsopp MELROSE	Inside forward
Robert Joseph HOUSTON	Wing half	John MURRAY	Inside forward
Iain J JARDINE	Wing half	Alexander C O'HARA	Inside forward
John LAPSLEY	Full back	Donald J PARK	Inside forward
Alastair James LOVE	Wing half	Alan Roderick ROUGH	Goalkeeper
George Shearer MACKIE	Inside forward	Ronald McLean SHEED	Inside forward
David D MacKINNON	Full back	Brian J WHITTAKER	Wing half
John Gerard MARR	Wing half	Paul WILSON	Inside forward

Season	League	League Position	P	W	D	L	F	A	Pts	3 Point Equivalent
1991–92	**Division 1**	2	44	23	11	10	62	36	57	1.818182
1990–91	Division 1	4	39	16	13	10	56	53	45	1.564103
1996–97	Division 1	6	36	12	12	12	49	48	48	1.333333
1989–90	Division 1	8	39	12	14	13	62	53	38	1.282051
1998–99	Division 2	8	36	12	7	17	36	45	43	1.194444
1994–95	Premier Division	8	36	10	13	13	40	50	43	1.194444
1993–94	Premier Division	9	44	12	16	16	46	57	40	1.181818
1992–93	Premier Division	8	44	12	12	20	50	71	36	1.090909
1997–98	Division 1	9	36	8	12	16	45	55	36	1.000000
1995–96	Premier Division	9	36	8	6	22	29	62	30	0.833333

SQUAD 1991–92   2ND IN FIRST DIVISION

Edward ANNAND	Centre forward	Colin James McGLASHAN	Centre forward
Douglas BELL	Midfielder	Paul McGOVERN	Centre forward
James MacL DUFFY	Centre half	Paul Gerald McLAUGHLIN	Full back
Isaac ENGLISH	Outside left	Donald Frederick McVICAR	Full back
Raymond Paul FARNINGHAM	Midfielder	Mark Nicoll McWALTER	Centre forward
John Gerard FLOOD	Outside right	Andrew Gerard MURDOCH	Goalkeeper
John Paul FRIAR	Midfielder	Malcolm MURRAY	Full back
Scott Smith HARVIE	Full back	Craig Robert NELSON	Goalkeeper
David John IRONS	Midfielder	Gary James PEEBLES	Midfielder
Samuel JOHNSTON	Midfielder	Gordon RAE	Centre half
Alexander KENNEDY	Centre half	Graeme W T ROBERTSON	Full back
Paul KINNAIRD	Outside left	Declan F ROCHE	Midfielder
Robert Shearer LAW	Midfielder	George SHAW	Outside right
Ronald LOWRIE	Goalkeeper	Peter Grant TIERNEY	Centre half
Kevin MAGEE	Outside right		

Season	League	League Position	P	W	D	L	F	A	Pts	3 Point Equivalent
2000–01	Division 2	1	36	22	9	5	66	32	75	2.083333
2001–02	**Division 1**	**1**	**36**	**19**	**9**	**8**	**61**	**38**	**66**	**1.833333**
2005–06	Division 2	4	36	16	9	11	57	56	57	1.583333
1999–2000	Division 2	5	36	12	10	14	42	44	46	1.277778
2006–07	Division 1	7	36	12	9	15	47	63	45	1.250000
2004–05	Division 1	9	36	10	9	17	38	52	39	1.083333
2002–03	SPL	10	38	8	11	19	37	58	35	0.921053
2003–04	SPL	12	38	6	8	24	39	67	26	0.684211

SQUAD 2001–02 — CHAMPIONS OF FIRST DIVISION

Alan Maxwell ARCHIBALD	Defender		Richard John HUXFORD	Defender
Kenneth ARTHUR	Goalkeeper		Jean Philipe JAVARY	Midfielder
Gerard Joseph BRITTON	Forward		Patrick KELLY	Defender
Kevin BUDINAUCKAS	Goalkeeper		David KLEIN	Goalkeeper
Alexander BURNS	Forward		Daniel Joseph LENNON	Midfielder
Martin George W CAMERON	Forward		Derek LYLE	Forward
Denis CONNAGHAN	Defender		Stephen McANESPIE	Full back
Leon CONSTANTINE	Forward		Mark Ross McCULLOCH	Defender
Stephen James CRAIGAN	Defender		Murray J L McDOWELL	Forward
Paul Andrew DEAS	Defender		James Anthony McKINSTREY	Midfielder
James DOLAN	Midfielder		Scott James McLEAN	Forward
Barry Robert ELLIOT	Forward		Mark NICHOLLS	Forward
Derek Adam FLEMING	Midfielder		Scott Thomas PATERSON	Defender
Andrew Stewart GIBSON	Midfielder		Andrew Robert RODDIE	Midfielder
Garry Paul GOW	Goalkeeper		James SMITH	Defender
Martin HARDIE	Midfielder		Paul WALKER	Forward
William HOWIE	Midfielder		Stephen WATSON	Midfielder

RANGERS

Season	League	League Position	P	W	D	L	F	A	Pts	3 Point Equivalent
1949–50	**A**	**1**	**30**	**22**	**6**	**2**	**58**	**26**	**50**	**2.400000**
1956–57	1	1	34	26	3	5	96	48	55	2.382353
1946–47	A	1	30	21	4	5	76	26	46	2.233333
1947–48	A	2	30	21	4	5	64	28	46	2.233333
1948–49	A	1	30	20	6	4	63	32	46	2.200000
1955–56	A	1	34	22	8	4	85	27	52	2.176471
1958–59	1	1	34	21	8	5	92	51	50	2.088235
1957–58	1	2	34	22	5	7	89	49	49	2.088235
1952–53	A	1	30	18	7	5	80	39	43	2.033333
1954–55	A	3	30	19	3	8	67	33	41	2.000000
1951–52	A	2	30	16	9	5	61	31	41	1.900000
1950–51	A	2	30	17	4	9	64	37	38	1.833333
1953–54	A	4	30	13	8	9	56	35	34	1.566667

SQUAD 1949–50 — CHAMPIONS OF DIVISION A

Robert BROWN	Goalkeeper		John (Ian) McINTYRE	Outside right
Samuel Richmond COX	Right back		Willie PATON	Inside right
Jimmy DUNCANSON	Forward		William W RAE	Left half
William FINDLAY	Inside right		Eddie RUTHERFORD	Outside right
Terrance GILLICK	Inside right		Jock SHAW	Left back
Johnny HUBBARD	Outside left		William THORNTON	Centre forward
Joseph Robert JOHNSON	Inside right		Willie WADDELL	Outside right
John Smith LINDSAY	Full back		William WILLIAMSON	Forward
David MARSHALL	Inside right		William A WOODBURN	Centre half
John Miller (Ian) McCOLL	Half back		George Lewis YOUNG	Centre half
William McCULLOCH	Outside right			

Season	League	League Position	P	W	D	L	F	A	Pts	3 Point Equivalent
1967–68	1	2	34	28	5	1	93	34	61	2.617647
1962–63	1	1	34	25	7	2	94	28	57	2.411765
1963–64	1	1	34	25	5	4	85	31	55	2.352941
1965–66	1	2	34	25	5	4	91	29	55	2.352941
1966–67	1	2	34	24	7	3	92	31	55	2.323529
1960–61	1	1	34	23	5	6	88	46	51	2.176471
1961–62	1	2	34	22	7	5	84	31	51	2.147059
1968–69	1	2	34	21	7	6	81	32	49	2.058824
1964–65	1	5	34	18	8	8	78	35	44	1.823529
1959–60	1	3	34	17	8	9	72	38	42	1.735294

SQUAD 1967–68   2ND IN DIVISION 1

Alexander C FERGUSON	Inside forward	Andy PENMAN	Inside forward
John GREIG	Inside forward	Orjan PERSSON	Outside left
Willie HENDERSON	Outside left	Dave PROVAN	Centre half
John Roger Shankly HYND	Right back	Billy SEMPLE	Inside left
William (Sandy) JARDINE	Inside forward	Alex SMITH	Inside forward
Kaj JOHANSEN	Right back	David Bruce SMITH	Left half
William McClure JOHNSTON	Inside forward	Erik SORENSEN	Goalkeeper
Norrie MARTIN	Goalkeeper	Bobby WATSON	Wing half
Willie MATHIESON	Left back	Alex WILLOUGHBY	Inside forward
Ron McKINNON	Left half		

324

Season	League	League Position	P	W	D	L	F	A	Pts	3 Point Equivalent
1972–73	1	2	34	26	4	4	74	30	56	2.411765
1974–75	1	1	34	25	6	3	86	33	56	2.382353
1977–78	Premier Division	1	36	24	7	5	76	39	55	2.194444
1975–76	Premier Division	1	36	23	8	5	60	24	54	2.138889
1973–74	1	3	34	21	6	7	67	34	48	2.029412
1971–72	1	3	34	21	2	11	71	38	44	1.911765
1969–70	1	2	34	19	7	8	67	40	45	1.882353
1976–77	Premier Division	2	36	18	10	8	62	37	46	1.777778
1978–79	Premier Division	2	36	18	9	9	52	35	45	1.750000
1970–71	1	4	34	16	9	9	58	34	41	1.676471

SQUAD 1972–73   2ND IN FIRST DIVISION

Alfie J CONN	Inside forward	Joseph Paul Smith MASON	Wing half
Jim DENNY	Inside forward	Willie MATHIESON	Left back
George DONALDSON	Wing half	Peter McCLOY	Goalkeeper
Tom FORSYTH	Inside forward	Tommy McLEAN	Outside right
Graham FYFE	Inside forward	Alexander MILLER	Inside forward
John GREIG	Wing half	Gerhardt NEEF	Goalkeeper
Colin Macdonald JACKSON	Centre half	Derek James PARLANE	Inside forward
William (Sandy) JARDINE	Right back	David Bruce SMITH	Left half
William McClure JOHNSTON	Outside left	Colin STEIN	Centre forward
Derek Joseph JOHNSTONE	Centre forward	Quinton YOUNG	Outside right
Alex MacDONALD	Inside forward		

	Season	League	League Position	P	W	D	L	F	A	Pts	3 Point Equivalent
1980s	**1988–89**	**Premier Division**	**1**	**36**	**26**	**4**	**6**	**62**	**26**	**56**	**2.277778**
	1986–87	Premier Division	1	44	31	7	6	85	23	69	2.272727
	1987–88	Premier Division	3	44	26	8	10	85	34	60	1.954545
	1980–81	Premier Division	3	36	16	12	8	60	32	44	1.666667
	1981–82	Premier Division	3	36	16	11	9	57	45	43	1.638889
	1983–84	Premier Division	4	36	15	12	9	53	41	42	1.583333
	1979–80	Premier Division	5	36	15	7	14	50	46	37	1.444444
	1982–83	Premier Division	4	36	13	12	11	52	41	38	1.416667
	1984–85	Premier Division	4	36	13	12	11	47	38	38	1.416667
	1985–86	Premier Division	5	36	13	9	14	53	45	35	1.333333

SQUAD 1988–89   CHAMPIONS OF THE PREMIER DIVISION

John BROWN	Midfielder	Alistair Murdoch McCOIST	Centre forward
Terence Ian BUTCHER	Centre half	Gary John McSWEGAN	Centre forward
Davie COOPER	Outside left	Stuart David MUNRO	Outside left
Neale James COOPER	Midfielder	James Michael NICHOLL	Full back
Thomas COWAN	Full back	Scott NISBET	Centre half
Kevin Smith DRINKELL	Centre forward	Alexander ROBERTSON	Midfielder
Iain DURRANT	Midfielder	Graeme SOUNESS	Midfielder
Derek FERGUSON	Midfielder	Melvyn STERLAND	Full back
Ian FERGUSON	Midfielder	Michael Gary STEVENS	Full back
Charles Richard GOUGH	Centre half	Joseph Nicol WALKER	Goalkeeper
Andrew Mullen GRAY	Centre forward	Mark Everton WALTERS	Outside left
David Stewart KIRKWOOD	Midfielder	Raymond Colin WILKINS	Midfielder
Kevin Duncan MacDONALD	Midfielder	Chris WOODS	Goalkeeper
Ian Holland McCALL	Midfielder		

	Season	League	League Position	P	W	D	L	F	A	Pts	3 Point Equivalent
1990s	**1995–96**	**Premier Division**	**1**	**36**	**27**	**6**	**3**	**85**	**25**	**87**	**2.416667**
	1992–93	Premier Division	1	44	33	7	4	97	35	73	2.409091
	1991–92	Premier Division	1	44	33	6	5	101	31	72	2.386364
	1996–97	Premier Division	1	36	25	5	6	85	33	80	2.222222
	1990–91	Premier Division	1	36	24	7	5	62	23	55	2.194444
	1998–99	SPL	1	36	23	8	5	78	31	77	2.138889
	1997–98	Premier Division	2	36	21	9	6	76	38	72	2.000000
	1989–90	Premier Division	1	36	20	11	5	48	19	51	1.972222
	1994–95	Premier Division	1	36	20	9	7	60	35	69	1.916667
	1993–94	Premier Division	1	44	22	14	8	74	41	58	1.818182

SQUAD 1995–96   CHAMPIONS OF THE PREMIER DIVISION

Erik Bo ANDERSEN	Forward	Alan James McLAREN	Defender
Gary BOLLAN	Defender	Alexei MIKHAILITCHENKO	Midfielder
John BROWN	Midfielder	Charles David MILLER	Midfielder
Alexander CLELAND	Defender	Craig Andrew MOORE	Centre half
Gordon Scott DURIE	Centre forward	Neil Andrew MURRAY	Midfielder
Iain DURRANT	Midfielder	Gordan PETRIC	Defender
Ian FERGUSON	Midfielder	David A ROBERTSON	Full back
Paul GASCOIGNE	Midfielder	Oleg SALENKO	Forward
Andrew Lewis GORAM	Goalkeeper	Colin George SCOTT	Goalkeeper
Charles Richard GOUGH	Centre half	Greg SHIELDS	Full back
Brian LAUDRUP	Midfielder	Theodorus G.A. SNELDERS	Goalkeeper
Stuart Murray McCALL	Midfielder	Trevor McGregor STEVEN	Midfielder
Alistair Murdoch McCOIST	Centre forward	William Marshall THOMSON	Goalkeeper
Brian McGINTY	Midfielder	Peter Jacobus VAN VOSSEN	Forward
Derek John McINNES	Midfielder	Stephen WRIGHT	Full back

RANGERS

Season	League	League Position	P	W	D	L	F	A	Pts	3 Point Equivalent
2002–03	SPL	1	38	31	4	3	101	28	97	2.552632
1999–2000	SPL	1	36	28	6	2	96	26	90	2.500000
2004–05	SPL	1	38	29	6	3	78	22	93	2.447368
2001–02	SPL	2	38	25	10	3	82	27	85	2.236842
2000–01	SPL	2	38	26	4	8	76	36	82	2.157895
2003–04	SPL	2	38	25	6	7	76	33	81	2.131579
2005–06	SPL	3	38	21	10	7	67	37	73	1.921053
2006–07	SPL	2	38	21	9	8	61	32	72	1.894737

(2000s)

SQUAD 2003–04   CHAMPIONS OF THE SPL

Lorenzo AMORUSO	Defender	Russell Nigel LATAPY	Midfielder
Mikel AMATRIAIN ARTETA	Midfielder	Peter LOVENKRANDS	Forward
Shota ARVELADZE	Forward	Robert MALCOLM	Defender
Jerome BONNISSEL	Defender	Neil Docherty McCANN	Forward
Claudio CANIGGIA	Forward	Steven McLEAN	Forward
Ronald DE BOER	Midfielder	Michael MOLS	Forward
William DODDS	Forward	Craig Andrew MOORE	Defender
Barry FERGUSON	Midfielder	Kevin Vincent MUSCAT	Defender/Midfielder
Tore Andre FLO	Centre forward	Christian NERLINGER	Midfielder
Stephen HUGHES	Midfielder	Arthur NUMAN	Defender
Alan HUTTON	Midfielder	Fernando RICKSEN	Defender
Stefan KLOS	Goalkeeper	Maurice ROSS	Defender
Bert KONTERMAN	Defender	Steven THOMPSON	Forward

ST JOHNSTONE

Season	League	League Position	P	W	D	L	F	A	Pts	3 Point Equivalent
1955–56	B	3	36	21	7	8	86	45	49	1.944444
1949–50	B	4	30	15	6	9	64	56	36	1.700000
1950–51	B	5	30	14	5	11	68	53	33	1.566667
1954–55	B	7	30	15	2	13	60	51	32	1.566667
1948–49	B	6	30	14	4	12	58	51	32	1.533333
1958–59	2	6	36	15	10	11	54	44	40	1.527778
1953–54	B	6	30	14	3	13	80	71	31	1.500000
1956–57	2	12	36	14	6	16	79	80	34	1.333333
1947–48	B	9	30	11	5	14	69	63	27	1.266667
1957–58	2	11	36	12	9	15	67	85	33	1.250000
1946–47	B	9	26	9	4	13	45	47	22	1.192308
1951–52	B	11	30	9	7	14	62	68	25	1.133333
1952–53	B	14	30	8	6	16	41	63	22	1.000000

(1940s & 50s)

SQUAD 1955–56   3RD IN DIVISION B

Archibald N BAIRD	Inside forward	Alec S MENZIES	Centre half
Joe CARR	Outside left	William MONTGOMERY	Left back
Doug COPLAND	Goalkeeper	Peter Kerr RATTRAY	Inside forward
Ernest A EWEN	Wing half	Stewart ROBERTSON	Right half
Gerald FOLLON	Right back	Ian RODGER	Centre forward
Gordon FRASER	Outside right	Jimmy P RUSSELL	Inside forward
David HANSON	Goalkeeper	Billy STEEL	Inside forward
Billy HODGSON	Inside left	George WHITELAW	Inside right
Charlie McFADYEN	Right back	James WOODCOCK	Centre half
John James Roy McLAREN	Goalkeeper		

	Season	League	League Position	P	W	D	L	F	A	Pts	3 Point Equivalent
1960s	1962–63	2	1	36	25	5	6	83	37	55	2.222222
	1959–60	2	1	36	24	5	7	87	47	53	2.138889
	1968–69	**1**	**6**	**34**	**16**	**5**	**13**	**66**	**59**	**37**	**1.558824**
	1960–61	1	15	34	10	9	15	47	63	29	1.147059
	1963–64	1	13	34	11	6	17	54	70	28	1.147059
	1964–65	1	13	34	9	11	14	57	62	29	1.117647
	1967–68	1	14	34	10	7	17	43	52	27	1.088235
	1965–66	1	14	34	9	8	17	58	81	26	1.029412
	1966–67	1	15	34	10	5	19	53	73	25	1.029412
	1961–62	1	17	34	9	7	18	35	61	25	1.000000

SQUAD 1968–69　　　　　　　　　　　　　　6TH IN DIVISION 1

Kenneth AIRD	Inside forward	Ian McPHEE	Inside forward
Fred AITKEN	Outside left	George MILLAR	Left half
Jim ARGUE	Left back	Alex RENNIE	Right half
Willie S COBURN	Left back	Derek ROBERTSON	Goalkeeper
John CONNOLLY	Inside right	Bernard ROONEY	Centre forward
Jim DONALDSON	Goalkeeper	George RYDEN	Centre half
Henry Alexander GORDON	Wing half	N A (Eddie) SMITH	Centre half
Henry HALL	Outside left	Gordon WHITELAW	Inside forward
Alex MacDONALD	Inside forward	Kenneth Malcolm WILSON	Centre forward
Bill McCARRY	Left half	Tom WILSON	Inside forward
Finlay McGILLIVRAY	Right back		

	Season	League	League Position	P	W	D	L	F	A	Pts	3 Point Equivalent
1970s	**1970–71**	**1**	**3**	**34**	**19**	**6**	**9**	**59**	**44**	**44**	**1.852941**
	1974–75	1	9	34	11	12	11	41	44	34	1.323529
	1977–78	Division 1	8	39	15	6	18	52	64	36	1.307692
	1971–72	1	8	34	12	8	14	52	58	32	1.294118
	1969–70	1	13	34	11	9	14	50	62	31	1.235294
	1972–73	1	11	34	10	9	15	52	67	29	1.147059
	1973–74	1	12	34	9	10	15	41	60	28	1.088235
	1978–79	Division 1	12	39	10	11	18	57	66	31	1.051282
	1976–77	Division 1	11	39	8	13	18	42	64	29	0.948718
	1975–76	Premier Division	10	36	3	5	28	29	79	11	0.388889

SQUAD 1970–71　　　　　　　　　　　　　　3RD IN DIVISION 1

Kenneth AIRD	Inside forward	John LESLIE	Outside left
Fred AITKEN	Outside left	Bill McCARRY	Left half
Jim ARGUE	Left back	William McMANUS	Full back
Willie S COBURN	Left back	Ian McPHEE	Inside forward
John CONNOLLY	Inside right	John R MUIR	Centre forward
Jim DONALDSON	Goalkeeper	James Findlay PEARSON	Inside forward
Henry Alexander GORDON	Wing half	Alex RENNIE	Right half
Henry HALL	Outside left	Bernard ROONEY	Centre forward
John LAMBIE	Full back	Gordon WHITELAW	Inside forward

1980s

Season	League	League Position	P	W	D	L	F	A	Pts	3 Point Equivalent
1987–88	Division 2	2	39	25	9	5	74	24	59	2.153846
1982–83	**Division 1**	**1**	**39**	**25**	**5**	**9**	**59**	**37**	**55**	**2.051282**
1980–81	Division 1	3	39	20	11	8	64	45	51	1.820513
1986–87	Division 2	5	39	16	13	10	59	49	45	1.564103
1985–86	Division 2	6	39	18	6	15	63	55	42	1.538462
1981–82	Division 1	5	39	17	8	14	69	60	42	1.512821
1988–89	Division 1	6	39	14	12	13	51	42	40	1.384615
1979–80	Division 1	11	39	12	10	17	57	74	34	1.179487
1983–84	Premier Division	9	36	10	3	23	36	81	23	0.916667
1984–85	Division 1	14	39	10	5	24	51	78	25	0.897436

SQUAD 1982–83　　　　CHAMPIONS OF FIRST DIVISION

Derek ADDISON	Inside forward	Kenneth S MacDONALD	Centre forward
Douglas BARRON	Wing half	John MACKAY	Full back
Stuart BEEDIE	Inside forward	Thomas McCAFFERTY	Wing half
Raymond BLAIR	Outside right	Michael Flynn McDONALD	Goalkeeper
Andrew BRANNIGAN	Inside forward	Tom McNEILL	Full back
John Gerald BROGAN	Centre forward	Donald Frederick McVICAR	Inside forward
Alex CALDWELL	Full back	James M MORTON	Inside forward
Raymond DAY	Inside forward	Paul O'BRIEN	Inside forward
Gordon DRUMMOND	Goalkeeper	John PELOSI	Outside right
George FLEMING	Inside forward	Joseph REID	Centre forward
Ian GIBSON	Inside forward	Andrew T RUTHERFORD	Wing half
John KENNEDY	Centre half	George O TULLOCH	Goalkeeper
Rab KILGOUR	Full back		

1990s

Season	League	League Position	P	W	D	L	F	A	Pts	3 Point Equivalent
1996–97	Division 1	1	36	24	8	4	74	23	80	2.222222
1989–90	Division 1	1	39	25	8	6	81	39	58	2.128205
1995–96	Division 1	4	36	19	8	9	60	36	65	1.805556
1998–99	**SPL**	**3**	**36**	**15**	**12**	**9**	**39**	**38**	**57**	**1.583333**
1994–95	Division 1	5	36	14	14	8	59	39	56	1.555556
1997–98	Premier Division	5	36	13	9	14	38	42	48	1.333333
1990–91	Premier Division	7	36	11	9	16	41	54	31	1.166667
1992–93	Premier Division	6	44	10	20	14	52	66	40	1.136364
1993–94	Premier Division	10	44	10	20	14	35	47	40	1.136364
1991–92	Premier Division	8	44	13	10	21	52	73	36	1.113636

SQUAD 1998–99　　　　3RD IN THE SPL

Gary BOLLAN	Defender	Stuart Campbell McCLUSKEY	Defender
Patrick Martin CONNOLLY	Forward	Gerard Joseph McMAHON	Midfielder
Nick Robert DASOVIC	Midfielder	John McQUILLAN	Defender
Darren DODS	Defender	George O'BOYLE	Forward
Allan Thomas FERGUSON	Goalkeeper	Keith James O'HALLORAN	Midfielder
Roderick John GRANT	Forward	John Thomas O'NEIL	Midfielder
Daniel Joseph GRIFFIN	Defender	Keigan PARKER	Forward
Paul James KANE	Midfielder	Allan PRESTON	Defender
Alan Nigel KERNAGHAN	Defender	Philip Campbell SCOTT	Midfielder
Nathan Peter LOWNDES	Forward	Miguel A Da Cruz SIMAO	Midfielder
Alan David MAIN	Goalkeeper	James McIntosh WEIR	Defender
Kieran Liam McANESPIE	Forward	Andrew WHITEFORD	Defender
John Paul McBRIDE	Midfielder		

Season	League	League Position	P	W	D	L	F	A	Pts	3 Point Equivalent
2002–03	Division 1	3	36	20	7	9	49	29	67	1.861111
2005–06	Division 1	2	36	18	12	6	59	34	66	1.833333
2006–07	Division 1	2	36	19	8	9	65	42	65	1.805556
2003–04	Division 1	3	36	15	12	9	59	45	57	1.583333
2004–05	Division 1	8	36	12	10	14	38	39	46	1.277778
1999–2000	**SPL**	**5**	**36**	**10**	**12**	**14**	**36**	**44**	**42**	**1.166667**
2000–01	SPL	10	38	9	13	16	40	56	40	1.052632
2001–02	SPL	12	38	5	6	27	24	62	21	0.552632

SQUAD 1999–2000 — 5TH IN THE SPL

Gary BOLLAN	Defender
Patrick Martin CONNOLLY	Forward
Christopher T CONWAY	Defender
Nick Robert DASOVIC	Midfielder
Darren DODS	Defender
Allan Thomas FERGUSON	Goalkeeper
Stephen Charles FRAIL	Defender
Roderick John GRANT	Forward
Daniel Joseph GRIFFIN	Defender
Graeme JONES	Forward
Paul James KANE	Midfielder
Martin Thomas LAUCHLAN	Forward
Nathan Peter LOWNDES	Forward
Alan David MAIN	Goalkeeper
Kieran Liam McANESPIE	Forward
John Paul McBRIDE	Midfielder
Stuart Campbell McCLUSKEY	Defender
Gerard Joseph McMAHON	Midfielder
John McQUILLAN	Defender
Marc MILLAR	Midfielder
George O'BOYLE	Forward
Keith James O'HALLORAN	Midfielder
John Thomas O'NEIL	Midfielder
Keigan PARKER	Forward
Stephen ROBERTSON	Goalkeeper
Craig Stewart RUSSELL	Forward
Miguel A Da Cruz SIMAO	Midfielder
Kevin Roderick THOMAS	Forward
James McIntosh WEIR	Defender

ST MIRREN

Season	League	League Position	P	W	D	L	F	A	Pts	3 Point Equivalent
1947–48	**A**	**5**	**30**	**13**	**5**	**12**	**54**	**58**	**31**	**1.466667**
1954–55	A	6	30	12	8	10	55	54	32	1.466667
1958–59	1	7	34	14	7	13	71	74	35	1.441176
1948–49	A	9	30	13	4	13	51	47	30	1.433333
1952–53	A	6	30	11	8	11	52	58	30	1.366667
1953–54	A	11	30	12	4	14	44	54	28	1.333333
1956–57	1	12	34	12	6	16	58	72	30	1.235294
1957–58	1	13	34	11	8	15	59	66	30	1.205882
1951–52	A	14	30	10	5	15	43	58	25	1.166667
1950–51	A	11	30	9	7	14	35	51	25	1.133333
1949–50	A	11	30	8	9	13	42	49	25	1.100000
1955–56	A	15	34	10	7	17	57	70	27	1.088235
1946–47	A	14	30	9	4	17	47	65	22	1.033333

SQUAD 1947–48 — 5TH IN DIVISION A

Gerald BURRELL	Outside right
Alexander Allan CROWE	Inside forward
David CUNNINGHAM	Half back
William Clark DAVIE	Forward
John DEAKIN	Outside left
James Arthur DRINKWATER	Full back
John F GUTHRIE	Forward
George HUNTER	Outside right
Willie JACK	Centre forward
James KIRK	Goalkeeper
David LAPSLEY	Right back
Alfons LESZ	Inside left
David LINDSAY	Centre half
Oliver LUCAS	Centre half
Joseph D MARTIN	Full back
James McLEAN	Outside left
Arthur H MILNE	Centre forward
Malcolm NEWLANDS	Goalkeeper
Walter REID	Half back
William REID	Right half
Gordon RENNIE	Goalkeeper
Samuel SMITH	Inside left
Jimmy STENHOUSE	Inside right
William Douglas TELFER	Centre half
John TELFORD	Inside left

Season	League	League Position	P	W	D	L	F	A	Pts	3 Point Equivalent
1967–68	2	1	36	27	8	1	100	23	62	2.472222
1968–69	**1**	**11**	**34**	**11**	**10**	**13**	**40**	**54**	**32**	**1.264706**
1963–64	1	12	34	12	5	17	44	74	29	1.205882
1960–61	1	14	34	11	7	16	53	58	29	1.176471
1959–60	1	14	34	11	6	17	78	86	28	1.147059
1962–63	1	12	34	10	8	16	52	72	28	1.117647
1961–62	1	16	34	10	5	19	52	80	25	1.029412
1964–65	1	15	34	9	6	19	38	70	24	0.970588
1965–66	1	16	34	9	4	21	44	82	22	0.911765
1966–67	1	17	34	4	7	23	25	81	15	0.558824

1960s

SQUAD 1968–69   11TH IN DIVISION 1

Bobby ADAMSON	Outside right	Andrew McFADDEN	Centre half
James BLAIR	Inside right	Hugh McLAUGHLIN	Centre forward
Denis CONNAGHAN	Goalkeeper	Cameron MURRAY	Centre half
Tony CONNELL	Right back	Eric McIntyre MURRAY	Wing half
Bobby C DUFFY	Full back	Bobby PINKERTON	Wing half
Billy FULTON	Wing half	James H F THORBURN	Goalkeeper
Hugh GILSHAN	Outside right	George URQUHART	Inside forward
Billy HAINEY	Centre forward	Ian YOUNG	Right back
Peter KANE	Centre forward		

330

Season	League	League Position	P	W	D	L	F	A	Pts	3 Point Equivalent
1976–77	Division 1	1	39	25	12	2	91	38	62	2.230769
1971–72	Division 2	4	36	24	2	10	84	47	50	2.055556
1972–73	Division 2	5	36	19	7	10	79	50	45	1.777778
1974–75	Division 2	6	38	19	8	11	74	52	46	1.710526
1978–79	**Premier Division**	**6**	**36**	**15**	**6**	**15**	**45**	**41**	**36**	**1.416667**
1975–76	Division 1	6	26	9	8	9	37	37	26	1.346154
1973–74	Division 2	11	36	12	10	14	62	66	34	1.277778
1977–78	Premier Division	8	36	11	8	17	52	63	30	1.138889
1969–70	Division 1	15	34	8	9	17	39	54	25	0.970588
1970–71	Division 1	17	34	7	9	18	38	56	23	0.882353

1970s

SQUAD 1978–79   6TH IN THE PREMIER DIVISION

Billy ABERCROMBY	Inside forward	John MOWAT	Inside right
Alexander BECKETT	Full back	Alexander I F MUNRO	Inside forward
James BONE	Centre forward	Alexander S RICHARDSON	Wing half
Jackie COPLAND	Wing half	Richard Cameron SHARP	Centre forward
Brian DOCHERTY	Inside forward	William STARK	Inside forward
Andrew DUNLOP	Left half	William Marshall THOMSON	Goalkeeper
Anthony Charles FITZPATRICK	Inside forward	Robert F TORRANCE	Inside forward
Derek HYSLOP	Inside forward	Peter Russell WEIR	Inside forward
Francis Peter McGARVEY	Outside right	John YOUNG	Centre half
Alistair McLEAN	Goalkeeper		

	Season	League	League Position	P	W	D	L	F	A	Pts	3 Point Equivalent
	1980–81	Premier Division	4	36	18	8	10	56	47	44	1.722222
	1979–80	**Premier Division**	**3**	**36**	**15**	**12**	**9**	**56**	**49**	**42**	**1.583333**
1980s	1984–85	Premier Division	5	36	17	4	15	51	56	38	1.527778
	1981–82	Premier Division	5	36	14	9	13	49	52	37	1.416667
	1982–83	Premier Division	5	36	11	12	13	47	51	34	1.250000
	1985–86	Premier Division	7	36	13	5	18	42	63	31	1.222222
	1983–84	Premier Division	6	36	9	14	13	55	59	32	1.138889
	1988–89	Premier Division	7	36	11	7	18	39	55	29	1.111111
	1986–87	Premier Division	7	44	12	12	20	36	51	36	1.090909
	1987–88	Premier Division	9	44	10	15	19	41	64	35	1.022727

SQUAD 1979–80   3RD IN THE PREMIER DIVISION

Billy ABERCROMBY	Inside forward	D Francis McDOUGALL	Centre forward
Alexander BECKETT	Full back	Alexander I F MUNRO	Inside forward
James BONE	Centre forward	Robert REID	Centre half
Jackie COPLAND	Wing half	Alexander S RICHARDSON	Wing half
Geoffrey F CURRAN	Full back	Douglas M SOMNER	Centre forward
John H DEMPSTER	Outside right	William STARK	Inside forward
Brian DOCHERTY	Inside forward	William Marshall THOMSON	Goalkeeper
Andrew DUNLOP	Left half	Robert F TORRANCE	Inside forward
Mark A J FULTON	Centre half	Peter Russell WEIR	Inside forward
Alan LOGAN	Centre forward	John YOUNG	Centre half
Phil McAVEETY	Centre half		

	Season	League	League Position	P	W	D	L	F	A	Pts	3 Point Equivalent
	1992–93	**Division 1**	**4**	**44**	**21**	**9**	**14**	**62**	**52**	**51**	**1.636364**
	1993–94	Division 1	6	44	21	8	15	61	55	50	1.613636
1990s	1996–97	Division 1	4	36	17	7	12	48	41	58	1.611111
	1998–99	Division 1	5	36	14	10	12	42	43	52	1.444444
	1995–96	Division 1	6	36	13	8	15	46	51	47	1.305556
	1997–98	Division 1	6	36	11	8	17	41	53	41	1.138889
	1989–90	Premier Division	9	36	10	10	16	28	48	30	1.111111
	1994–95	Division 1	7	36	8	12	16	34	50	36	1.000000
	1991–92	Premier Division	11	44	6	12	26	33	73	24	0.681818
	1990–91	Premier Division	10	36	5	9	22	28	59	19	0.666667

SQUAD 1992–93   4TH IN FIRST DIVISION

William Alexander (Lex) BAILLIE	Centre half	Paul LAMBERT	Midfielder
Martin BAKER	Defender	Barry LAVETY	Centre forward
James BEATTIE	Centre half	Roderick MANLEY	Centre half
Alexander Syme Frew BONE	Forward	Kenneth McDOWALL	Centre forward
Julian Raymond BRODDLE	Full back	Daniel McGILL	Midfielder
James Callaghan CHARNLEY	Midfielder	Gary McGROTTY	Forward
Paul Robert CUMMINGS	Midfielder	Paul McINTYRE	Midfielder
Robert McQuillan DAWSON	Full back	Barry John McLAUGHLIN	Midfielder
David ELLIOT	Outside left	Gary McVIE	Full back
Roland FABIANI	Full back	Norman McWHIRTER	Full back
Stephen Edward FARRELL	Midfielder	Israel Campbell MONEY	Goalkeeper
Leslie Francis FRIDGE	Goalkeeper	Andrew PATERSON	Defender
James FULLARTON	Full back	John Scott PEACOCK	Midfielder
Edward Adam GALLAGHER	Centre forward	Mark REID	Full back
Kenneth GILLIES	Midfielder	Stuart TAYLOR	Midfielder
Richard Charles GILLIES	Forward	Gudmundor TORFASON	Centre forward
Brian HETHERSTON	Midfielder	Derek WATSON	Goalkeeper
John HEWITT	Forward		

ST MIRREN

	Season	League	League Position	P	W	D	L	F	A	Pts	3 Point Equivalent
	2005–06	Division 1	1	36	23	7	6	52	28	76	2.111111
	1999–2000	**Division 1**	**1**	**36**	**23**	**7**	**6**	**75**	**39**	**76**	**2.111111**
	2004–05	Division 1	2	36	15	15	6	41	23	60	1.666667
2000s	2001–02	Division 1	8	36	11	12	13	43	53	45	1.250000
	2003–04	Division 1	7	36	9	14	13	39	46	41	1.138889
	2002–03	Division 1	7	36	9	10	17	42	71	37	1.027778
	2006–07	SPL	11	38	8	12	18	31	51	36	0.947368
	2000–01	SPL	12	38	8	6	24	32	72	30	0.789474

SQUAD 1999–2000 — CHAMPIONS OF FIRST DIVISION

Sergei Sergeivich BALTACHA	Defender	Junior Albert MENDES	Forward
Gary BOWMAN	Midfielder	Hugh MURRAY	Midfielder
Thomas Heron BROWN	Forward	Iain NICOLSON	Midfielder
Stephen DONNACHIE	Forward	Jens PAESLACK	Forward
Colin DREW	Defender	Ryan R K ROBINSON	Defender
Richard Charles GILLIES	Forward	Ian ROSS	Midfielder
Christopher KERR	Defender	Ludovic ROY	Goalkeeper
Barry LAVETY		Paul RUDDEN	Defender
Steven Thomas McGARRY	Forward	Derek SCRIMGOUR	Goalkeeper
Paul Ronald McKNIGHT	Forward	Thomas Gibson TURNER	Midfielder
Joe McLAUGHLAN	Defender	Scott Edward WALKER	Defender
Barry John McLAUGHLIN	Defender	Mark YARDLEY	Forward

GREATEST EVER
SCOTTISH CLUB TOP FLIGHT TEAMS OF THE DECADE

THE TEAMS WITH THE HIGHEST POINTS TOTAL IN A SEASON DURING EACH TEN-SEASON PERIOD

Decade	Teams
1940s & 50s	Heart of Midlothian (1957–58)
1960s	Celtic (1967–68)
1970s	Celtic (1971–72)
1980s	Aberdeen (1984–85)
1990s	Rangers (1995–96)
2000s	Celtic (2001–02)

GREATEST EVER
CELTIC XI OF ALL TIME

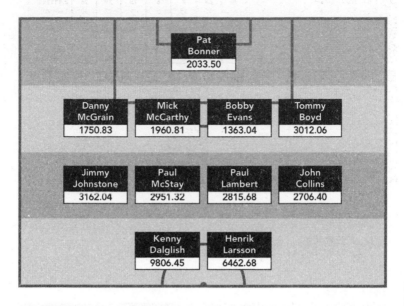

Pat Bonner	2033.50

Danny McGrain 1750.83	**Mick McCarthy** 1960.81	**Bobby Evans** 1363.04	**Tommy Boyd** 3012.06

Jimmy Johnstone 3162.04	**Paul McStay** 2951.32	**Paul Lambert** 2815.68	**John Collins** 2706.40

Kenny Dalglish 9806.45	**Henrik Larsson** 6462.68

GREATEST EVER
RANGERS XI OF ALL TIME

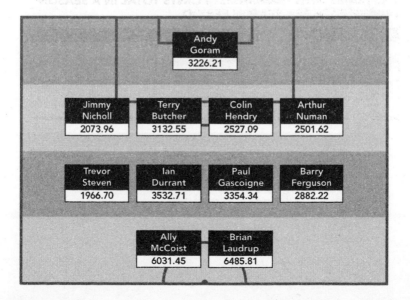

Andy Goram	3226.21

Jimmy Nicholl 2073.96	**Terry Butcher** 3132.55	**Colin Hendry** 2527.09	**Arthur Numan** 2501.62

Trevor Steven 1966.70	**Ian Durrant** 3532.71	**Paul Gascoigne** 3354.34	**Barry Ferguson** 2882.22

Ally McCoist 6031.45	**Brian Laudrup** 6485.81

GREATEST EVER
SCOTTISH TOP FLIGHT XI OF ALL TIME

Position	Player	Nationality	Points
Goalkeeper	Jim LEIGHTON	Scottish	5342.56
Right back	Jimmy NICHOLL	Northern Irish	2073.96
Left back	Tom BOYD	Scottish	3012.06
Right half	Colin HENDRY	Scottish	2527.09
Centre half	Terry BUTCHER	English	3132.55
Left half	Craig BURLEY	Scottish	2163.90
Outside right	Ian DURRANT	Scottish	3532.71
Inside right	Paul GASCOIGNE	English	3354.34
Centre forward	Henrik LARSSON	Swedish	6462.68
Inside left	Kenny DALGLISH	Scottish	9806.45
Outside left	Ally McCOIST	Scottish	6031.45

GREATEST EVER
TOP XI FROM ALL SCOTTISH CLUBS BY DECADE

1940s & 1950s

Position	Player	Teams	Points
Goalkeeper	Tommy YOUNGER	Hibernian	679.84
Right back	George CUMMINGS	Partick Thistle	300.87
Left back	Bobby EVANS	Celtic	1199.63
Right half	Alex FORBES	Dundee North End	485.22
Centre Half	Frank BRENNAN	Airdrieonians	550.13
Left half	Allan BROWN	East Fife	901.73
Outside right	Graham LEGGAT	Aberdeen	657.83
Inside right	Tommy WALKER	Hearts	1658.42
Centre forward	Bobby JOHNSTONE	Celtic	1199.63
Inside left	Billy STEEL	Dundee	1602.17
Outside left	Willie FERNIE	Celtic	397.56

1960s

Position	Player	Teams	Points
Goalkeeper	Ronnie SIMPSON	Celtic	588.00
Right back	Jim CRAIG	Celtic	468.07
Left back	Eddie McCREADIE	East Stirling	3110.45
Right midfield	Jimmy JOHNSTONE	Celtic	1381.56
Centre half	Billy McNEIL	Celtic	749.78
Centre half	Ian URE	Dundee	273.81
Left midfield	John CLARK	Celtic	552.11
Central midfield	Bertie AULD	Celtic	826.32
Forward	Alan GILZEAN	Dundee	1251.86
Forward	Stevie CHALMERS	Celtic	864.97
Forward	Colin STEIN	Hibernian/Rangers	664.98

1970s

Position	Player	Teams	Points
Goalkeeper	George WOOD	East Stirling	82.48
Right back	John BROWNLIE	Hibernian	194.21
Centre back	Martin BUCHAN	Aberdeen	1050.22
Centre back	Gordon McQUEEN	St Mirren	1045.76
Left back	Alex FORSYTH	Partick Thistle	374.32
Right midfield	Jimmy JOHNSTONE	Celtic	1780.48
Central midfield	Bobby MURDOCH	Celtic	1029.98
Central midfield	John CONNOLLY	St Johnstone	27.50
Left midfield	Arthur GRAHAM	Aberdeen	357.13
Forward	Kenny DALGLISH	Celtic	4845.82
Forward	Lou MACARI	Celtic	1070.94

1980s

Position	Player	Teams	Points
Goalkeeper	Jim LEIGHTON	Aberdeen	2743.37
Right back	Jimmy NICHOLL	Rangers	1384.17
Centre back	Willie MILLER	Aberdeen	1798.42
Centre back	Terry BUTCHER	Rangers	2544.98
Left back	Maurice MALPAS	Dundee United	1135.06
Right midfield	Gordon STRACHAN	Aberdeen	1733.68
Central midfield	Graeme SOUNESS	Rangers	2615.05
Central midfield	Ray WILKINS	Rangers	2220.92
Left midfield	Roy AITKEN	Celtic	1394.93
Forward	Steve ARCHIBALD	Aberdeen/Hibernian	1527.11
Forward	Andy GRAY	Rangers	1793.57

1990s

Position	Player	Teams	Points
Goalkeeper	Andy GORAM	Rangers	4409.84
Right back	Tom BOYD	Celtic	2209.58
Centre back	Richard GOUGH	Rangers	1522.27
Centre back	David WEIR	Hearts	359.40
Left back	Arthur NUMAN	Rangers	1379.89
Right midfield	Paul GASCOIGNE	Rangers	3132.93
Central midfield	Ian DURRANT	Rangers/Kilmarnock	2613.93
Central midfield	Brian McCLAIR	Motherwell	2920.56
Left midfield	Brian LAUDRUP	Rangers	6047.16
Forward	Ally McCOIST	Rangers	4586.65
Forward	Gordon DURIE	Rangers	2665.21

2000s

Position	Player	Teams	Points
Goalkeeper	Craig GORDON	Hearts	621.16
Right back	Jackie McNAMARA	Celtic/Aberdeen	1270.66
Centre back	Ronald DE BOER	Rangers	852.27
Centre back	Steven PRESSLEY	Hearts/Celtic	883.49
Left back	Giovanni Van BRONCKHORST	Rangers	2551.48
Right midfield	Neil McCANN	Hearts	1436.94
Central midfield	Paul LAMBERT	Celtic/Livingstone	1219.25
Central midfield	James McFADDEN	Motherwell	1359.16
Left midfield	Barry FERGUSON	Rangers	1754.44
Forward	Henrik LARSSON	Celtic	3672.19
Forward	JUNINHO	Celtic	2128.01

GREATEST EVER
PLAYERS FROM SCOTTISH TOP FLIGHT CLUBS BY POSITION

GOALKEEPERS

Player	Points
Jim LEIGHTON	5342.56
Andy GORAM	4926.21
Dimitri KHARINE	2363.41
Antti NIEMI	2248.76
Thomas MYHRE	1918.56
Magnus HEDMAN	1604.28
Chris WOODS	1439.95
Ronald WATERREUS	1433.64
Nick COLGAN	921.00
Artur BORUC	911.05

DEFENDERS

Player	Points
Frank DE BOER	6924.14
Alan HANSEN	4884.07
Terry BUTCHER	3132.55
Craig MOORE	3247.02
Tom BOYD	3012.06
Tony VIDMAR	2841.41
Marvin ANDREWS	2704.07
Colin HENDRY	2527.09
Stephane HENCHOZ	2516.85
Arthur NUMAN	2501.62

MIDFIELDERS

Player	Points
Roy KEANE	6502.90
Tugay KERIMOGLU	5909.82
Claudio REYNA	4355.20
Theo WHITMORE	4032.21
Andrei KANCHELSKIS	4022.56
Russell LATAPY	3929.48
Graeme SOUNESS	3695.47
Chris WADDLE	3615.25
Ian DURRANT	3532.71
Brian McCLAIR	3455.46

FORWARDS

Player	Points
Kenny DALGLISH	9806.45
Brian LAUDRUP	6485.81
Henrik LARSSON	6462.68
Ally McCOIST	6031.45
Shota ARVELADZE	4575.23
Tore Andre FLO	4416.52
Trevor FRANCIS	3620.98
Tony CASCARINO	3487.99
George BEST	3471.69
Gordon DURIE	3298.15